INSIDERS' GUIDE® TO
GLACIER NATIONAL PARK

HELP US KEEP THIS GUIDE UP TO DATE

We would love to hear from you concerning your experiences with this guide and how you feel it could be improved and kept up to date. Please send your comments and suggestions to:

editorial@GlobePequot.com

Thanks for your input, and happy travels!

INSIDERS' GUIDE® TO

GLACIER NATIONAL PARK

Including the Flathead Valley & Waterton Lakes National Park

SIXTH EDITION

MICHAEL McCoy

INSIDERS' GUIDE

GUILFORD, CONNECTICUT
AN IMPRINT OF GLOBE PEQUOT PRESS

All the information in this guidebook is subject to change. We recommend that you call ahead to obtain current information before traveling.

INSIDERS' GUIDE ®

Editor: Amy Lyons
Project Editor: Heather Santiago
Layout Artist: Kevin Mak
Text Design: Sheryl Kober
Maps: XNR Productions Inc. © Morris Book Publishing, LLC

ISSN 1544-4023
ISBN 978-0-7627-5672-8

Printed in the United States of America
10 9 8 7 6 5 4 3 2 1

CONTENTS

CONTENTS

Directory of Maps

ABOUT THE AUTHOR

Michael McCoy's articles on travel, history, and the outdoors have appeared in many national and regional publications. A former 18-year resident of western Montana, he now lives in Teton Valley, Idaho, where he edits *Jackson Hole Magazine* and *Teton Valley Magazine*, and serves as field editor for *Adventure Cyclist* magazine. McCoy is also the author of *Montana Off the Beaten Path* and *Wyoming Off the Beaten Path* (both by Globe Pequot Press) and the compilation editor of *Classic Cowboy Stories* (The Lyons Press).

ACKNOWLEDGMENTS

I would like to acknowledge and thank the authors of the previous editions of this book: Eileen Gallagher, Frank Miele, Jim Mann, Mary Pat Murphy, Rima Nickell, and Susan Olin. Their hard work laid the foundation for the current edition; in fact, it would not exist were it not for them. Also important are the many Glacier Country residents, including business owners, who helped when I was conducting research for the guide (as well as the many friends I made when living in western Montana for 18 years, from the mid-1970s to 1995). The enthusiasm of locals for their lives in Northwestern Montana is truly contagious. I would also like to acknowledge Amy Lyons of Globe Pequot Press, who sought me out for this project.

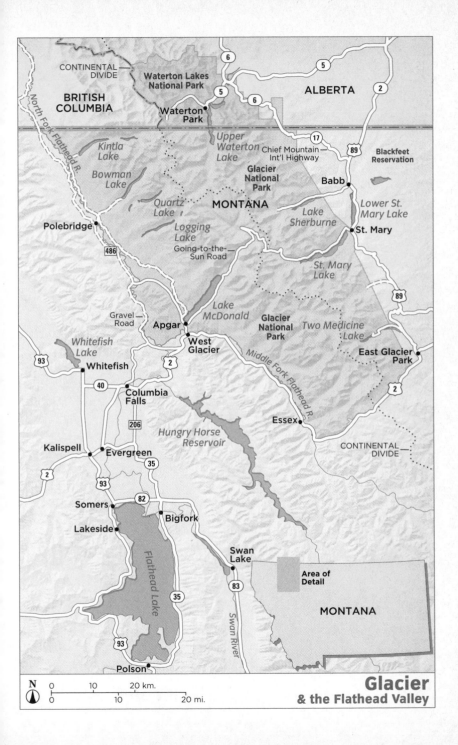

CONTINENTAL DIVIDE

BRITISH COLUMBIA

North Fork Flathead R.

Waterton Lakes National Park

ALBERTA

Waterton Park

Kintla Lake

Upper Waterton Lake

Chief Mountain Int'l Highway

Blackfeet Reservation

Bowman Lake

Glacier National Park

MONTANA

Babb

Lower St. Mary Lake

Quartz Lake

Lake Sherburne

St. Mary

Polebridge

Logging Lake

Going-to-the-Sun Road

St. Mary Lake

Gravel Road

Lake McDonald

Glacier National Park

Two Medicine Lake

Whitefish Lake

Apgar

West Glacier

East Glacier Park

Whitefish

Middle Fork Flathead R.

Columbia Falls

Hungry Horse Reservoir

Essex

Kalispell

Evergreen

CONTINENTAL DIVIDE

Somers

Bigfork

Lakeside

Flathead Lake

Swan Lake

Area of Detail

MONTANA

Swan River

Polson

N

0   10   20 km.

0   10   20 mi.

Glacier
& the Flathead Valley

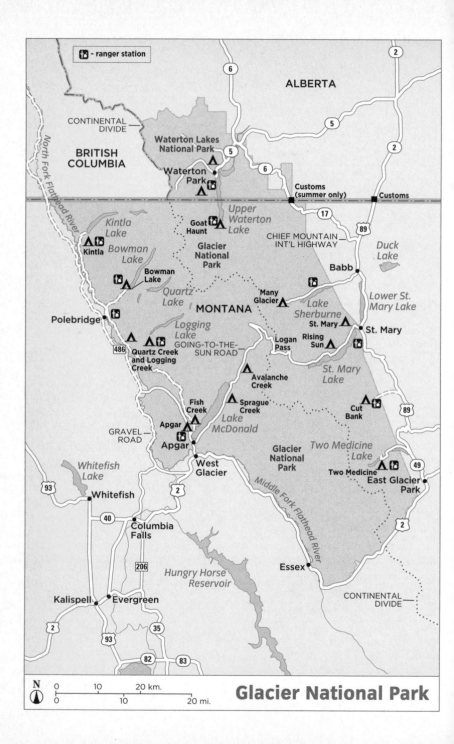

Glacier National Park

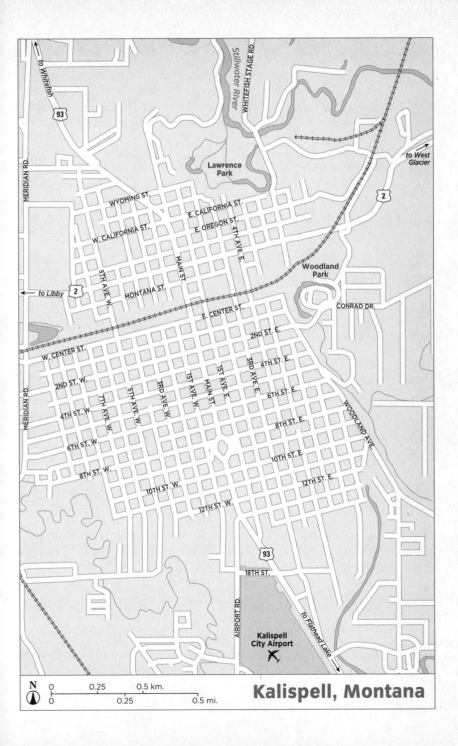

Kalispell, Montana

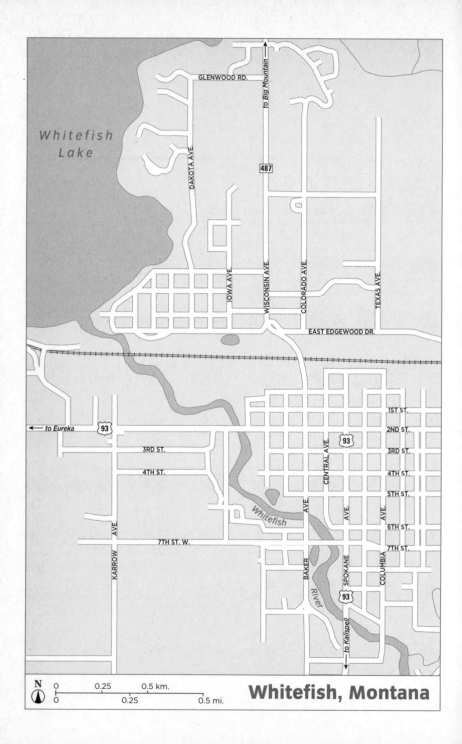

Whitefish, Montana

INTRODUCTION

Northwestern Montana is a summer paradise and winter lover's wonderland. On warm sunny days the river canyons echo with the sounds of canoeists, kayakers, and whitewater rafters; hours before, the quiet whip of the fly-fisherman's line and the call of a long-billed curlew may have been the only sounds to be heard. Hikers, horseback riders, and mountain bikers seek solitude on the nearby trails climbing above the rivers. Birding and wildlife-watching opportunities abound throughout it all.

When the winds begin to chill and the needles of the larch trees turn gold, the elk begin to bugle and hunters know the season is near. Then, before you know it, a hushing white blanket covers the landscape. Alpine skiers and snowboarders anticipate their first downhill runs through powder-filled glades, while Nordic skiers are eager to glide cross-country through a quiet forest.

Glacier National Park, with its knife-edged peaks and its alpine fields filled with the wondrous colors of summer wildflowers, is the reason many visitors first explore northwest Montana. A drive along Going-to-the-Sun Road introduces those in cars, vans, and RVs to the many natural spectacles the park offers, and entices a large share of them to get out of the car for a closer look from trailside. For some, that first trip through the park marks the beginning of a love affair with the entire region, and they'll soon be compelled to explore beyond the boundaries of Glacier: Kalispell, the Flathead Valley, the Swan Valley, and the grand expanses on the eastern slopes of the Rocky Mountains.

One of the special things about Glacier is that it is not only a national park, but also the United States contribution to the world's first international peace park, which extends into Alberta, Canada. A visit to the Alberta Visitor Centre in WestGlacier, Montana, is a wonderful introduction to the treasures found across the border—but a visit to the Prince of Wales Hotel by shimmering Waterton Lake in the Canadian portion of the Waterton-Glacier International Peace Park is even better.

To the south of Glacier, the Swan Valley and the Flathead Lake area are in themselves major recreation destinations. Kalispell and the several other charming towns that serve as gateways to Glacier National Park, are home to a wide variety of people who share a deep affection for the things that make the region so special. This area is renowned for its arts festivals, while a tour of any of the sometimes quirky but always interesting museums and well-known area attractions—such as the Stumptown Historical Society Museum in Whitefish and the House of Mystery near Columbia Falls—will add depth and insight to your western mountain adventures.

Even a brief summary of the area's wonders would be incomplete, however, without a mention of the major summer and winter playground known as the Whitefish Mountain Resort, one of Montana's premier all-season getaways. When it comes to culture, at the foot of

INTRODUCTION

Flathead Lake is the Flathead Indian Reservation, home to the Confederated Salish/Kootenai tribes. A visit to Polson and the smaller towns on the reservation serves as a great introduction to the history and lifeways of these Native peoples.

Over on the eastern side of the park, the Blackfeet Indian Reservation holds a number of small towns that serve as jumping-off points for explorations in Glacier and beyond, and offer great opportunities for long-range views of that part of Montana responsible for the state's best-known moniker, Big Sky Country. A trip to any of the area's museums, or a day spent at the North American Indian Days powwow in Browning, will serve as a fascinating introduction to the Blackfeet culture and reservation life.

The rugged look of the mountainous terrain falling away from both sides of the Continental Divide belies the fragility of the ecosystems it supports. Not only have mining, logging, and grazing had their effects on the pristine nature of some of these mountain settings, but recreational use has affected it as well. Those who venture out in their hiking boots or on their skis or in their snow machines must take responsibility for their actions and practice "zero impact" recreation if the attractions that draw us into this still-wild place are to remain for future generations. After all, it is the singular beauty of the mountains and rivers, and the quieting solitude they provide, that keeps our souls nourished.

If a mere *visit* to Glacier Country just isn't enough—and more and more people have found that it's not—then the real estate and other relocation information included in this book will be just what you're looking for. From rustic log cabins in remote settings to elegant Victorian homes blocks from downtown, this area offers something for just about any taste. Helpful insights for retirees seeking their own brand of northern exposure are also included, as is information about child care and education for the younger family.

The goal of this book is to provide something for everyone, from Glacier National Park newcomers to Flathead Valley veterans, with information about the best and brightest offerings of this very special place full of beautiful people and places. Let *Insiders' Guide to Glacier National Park,* with its details on restaurants, accommodations, and recreation, be your guide and companion as you explore this incredible region. Whether you're staying for a weekend or a lifetime, the tips, facts, and insights gleaned from Montana insiders included here will put all the information you need for your Glacier adventures within easy reach.

I wish you luck during your wanderings, and hope that you will wind up with a long list of your own Glacier Country favorites.

HOW TO USE THIS BOOK

From the fertile Swan and Flathead Valleys to the inspiring open expanses east of Glacier National Park, this guide to northwestern Montana's Glacier Country is designed to help you find what you're looking for, as well as to introduce you to things you might never have dreamed would exist in such an out-of-the-way place.

Of course, it's because of Glacier Country's off-the-beaten-path location that many of the people who do so choose to vacation or relocate here. The wildness, the closeness to nature, of this place is a major part of its appeal. Because this is so, you may be surprised to find out how relatively easy it is to get here, and how much the area has to offer not only in the way of great skiing, fishing, hiking, and other winter and summer recreation opportunities, but in the realm of the finer things in life—dining establishments, luxurious accommodations, and so on. And this is good, because you may be amazed at what a hike through a Douglas-fir forest to an alpine lake can do for your appetite; you'll definitely have a hankering for a hearty meal when you leave the woods. And if carrying a tent and all of the other necessary gear to a backcountry campsite isn't exactly your idea of how to spend a relaxing vacation, hints on great bed-and-breakfasts, cozy inns, downtown hotels, and even the more luxurious campgrounds (with showers and other amenities) may be more to your taste.

This book will help you get to Glacier and the Flathead Valley (see the Getting Here, Getting Around chapter) and also help you make the most of your visit once you arrive. The Area Overview, History, Attractions, The Arts, Kidstuff, and Annual Events chapters are designed to give you some general information about Glacier and the Flathead Valley that will encourage and inform your visit (if the legendary great outdoor recreation and spectacular scenery you've heard so much about weren't enough encouragement). Each of these chapters and the Outdoor Recreation chapter give general information about what can be found throughout the region. They provide details on the highlights and point you to additional sources of information.

Once you've exhausted yourself with a full day of horseback riding, rock climbing, or rafting, you'll want something to eat and a place to rest and rejuvenate your weary body. Or, prior to putting your head to a pillow, you may want to sample some of Montana's many microbrews in a chic pub or an old-fashioned saloon. If souvenirs or outdoor gear are on your wish list, you may also want to visit the local retail hot spots for a hand-carved wooden grizzly bear or some high-tech hiking boots. In the market for antiques? You'll find dozens of venues to explore in this arena, as well.

The sections of this book containing information about accommodations, nightlife, restaurants, and shopping are grouped geographically. If you're basing your adventures out of Bigfork, for instance, all of the best-and-brightest options for an overnight stay, a fine meal, a hearty ale, or a sturdy pair of cowboy boots in town or in the immediate area can be found within a few pages. You'll find recommendations for a range of options and opportunities, from bed-and-breakfasts to RV parks and from kid-friendly hamburger joints to elegant dining rooms.

Moving to Northwestern Montana or already live here? Be sure to check out the blue-tabbed pages at the back of the book, where you will find the **Living Here** appendix that offers sections on relocation, child care, education, health care, retirement, and media.

Within all chapters, you will find frequent cross-references and even, for the sake of convenience, some cross-listings.

Throughout this book you'll find **Insider's Tips** (indicated by an **i**), which offer quick insights, and **Close-ups,** which provide in-depth information on topics that are particularly interesting, unusual, or distinct. You'll also find listings accompanied by the ✳ symbol—these are our top picks for attractions, restaurants, accommodations, and everything in between that you shouldn't miss while you're in the area. You want the best this region has to offer? Go with our **Insiders' Choice.**

When your vacation is behind you but your mind is still on Montana, the handy relocation guide in this book offers information about real estate, health care, education and child care, and more. Then, finally, after you've settled into your dream cabin on the shore of Swan Lake, you'll no doubt continue to use this book to become even better acquainted with all the magic Northwestern Montana can make.

AREA OVERVIEW

In Glacier National Park and its surroundings, the seasons are dramatic, wildlife is abundant, and nature is your constant companion. Rocky peaks scratch the big sky, standing sentinel over mirror-surfaced lakes; streams gurgle through lovely valleys, nurturing the land as they go; and clear rivers run fast through agrarian farmscapes. The forces of nature are alive, and they influence the dynamic nature of the people who call this region home.

Winter, summer, fall, or spring, Glacier Country is a marvelous place to visit. In fact, many residents will quickly tell you that living here has a vacationlike quality of its own. But nature's beautiful bounty is not the region's only draw—the arts, annual festivals, and myriad attractions such as golf courses, museums, and excellent dining, lodging, and shopping all draw visitors and residents alike. From the area's smallest villages to its largest mini-cities, you'll never know what delightful surprises you might find under the restaurant sign or behind the bed-and-breakfast door—until you probe deeper, that is.

THE LAY OF THE LAND

Glacier National Park, carved by Pleistocene glaciers and still dotted with remnant ice fields, is at the center of one of the largest intact ecosystems in the United States. Its relative isolation from settlement, and the many thousands of acres both inside and outside the park that are under federal protection, have helped the region retain a rich biological diversity, even though more than two million visitors cross the park borders every year. The surrounding communities act as gateways to Glacier and its sister to the north in Canada, Waterton Lakes National Park. Together, the two parks are designated as the Waterton-Glacier International Peace Park—so named in 1932 as the first such park in the world.

With these two magnificent parks at the center of it all, it's natural to conclude that tourism is the mainstay of the surrounding communities. Learning that Flathead Lake, the largest natural freshwater lake west of Minnesota, is Glacier National Park's neighbor to the south will only strengthen that perception. Kalispell's population swells every summer to accommodate visitors, as do the populations of Bigfork at the north end of Flathead Lake, Polson at the lakes's south end, Columbia Falls on the way into Glacier National Park, and Whitefish, a vacationer's playground summer *and* winter, with the Whitefish Mountain Resort ski area. The Swan Valley, found by following Highway 83, is a less-visited, but equally beautiful vacation getaway. Tourism benefits the Blackfeet Indian Reservation, too, with its stunning views of the Rocky Mountain Front, and the Flathead Reservation, as well.

Don't be lulled into the belief that these communities exist only for the sake of the

Sources for Information on Glacier National Park

Website: www.nps.gov/glac/index.htm

Social Networking Info: www.nps.gov/glac/parknews/socialnetworking.htm

Information: (406) 888-7800

Glacier National Park Visitor Centers:

Apgar: Located at the foot of Lake McDonald, 2 miles from the West Glacier entrance. Open 8 a.m. to 4:30 p.m. during shoulder season, 8 a.m. to 8 p.m. during peak season, weekends only during the winter. Weekdays during winter, stop by the information desk at park headquarters, located just outside the entrance station in West Glacier.

Logan Pass: Opens with Going-to-the-Sun Road, usually mid-June. Peak season hours are 8 a.m. to 4:30 p.m. Usually closes for the season in late September.

St. Mary: Located at the foot of St. Mary Lake. Open 8 a.m. to 5 p.m. during shoulder season, 8 a.m. to 9 p.m. during peak season. Usually opens Memorial Day weekend and closes the third weekend in October.

Information is also available at Two Medicine, Polebridge, Many Glacier, and Goat Haunt Ranger Stations.

Entrance Fees: Inquire at entrance station or park headquarters about Golden Age and Golden Access passes. Special fees are charged for commercial vehicles. (Waivers may be available for educational groups.) These fees may be changed at any time.

Single vehicle pass: $25 May 1 through November 30; $15 December 1 through April 30. Valid for 7 days.

Single person entry (foot, bicycle, motorcycle): $12 ($10 in winter). Valid for 7 days.

Glacier National Park Annual Pass: $35. Valid for one year from month of purchase.

America the Beautiful Federal Lands Pass: $80. Valid for one year from month of purchase.

Weather: For historic weather averages, check Glacier National Park's website at www.nps.gov/glac/planyourvisit/weather.htm. This page has a detailed table of average highs and lows as well as precipitation averages for the entire year. As you'll observe, June, December, and January are the wettest months of the year; June often feels cooler than the average high listed of 71 degrees Fahrenheit, and it certainly won't be spring in the high peaks for a while! But it can be a beautiful time of year at the lower elevations, including in the verdant Flathead Valley. July and August have average highs of 79 and 78 (note, however, the maximum temperature of 99 recorded in both months), with average lows of 47 and 46 degrees Fahrenheit. Beautiful weather often lasts into September, though it's likely you'll start seeing frost in the mornings at high elevation. Indeed, if you're planning to camp or hike, be sure to bring warm clothes, because it can snow at virtually any time of the year (though the snow may not last long in summer). Be aware that the weather data found at this site reflects conditions in the park proper; the Flathead Valley and Swan Valley can be considerably warmer in both summer and winter. Summer will see some days over 100 degrees Fahrenheit; sometimes in winter it rains in the valleys when it's snowing in the mountains. Winter driving can occasionally be treacherous, especially when "black ice" forms on the roads as the temperature drops and rain freezes on the pavement.

Backcountry Permits: Permits for the park's more than five dozen backcountry campsites are required for backpackers. There is a $5 per person over the age of 17 ($3 for children 6 and older) per night charge. Permits may be obtained at the Apgar Backcountry Permit Center, St. Mary Visitor Center, and Many Glacier, Polebridge, and Two Medicine Ranger Stations. Permit desk hours are somewhat limited; be sure to check the current issue of the Waterton-Glacier Guide for details. A percentage of permits may also be reserved by mail in advance for a $30 fee. The entire backcountry camping guide can be found online at www.nps.gov /glac/planyourvisit/backcountry.htm.

Distance from West Glacier to:
Bigfork: 42 miles
Browning: 69 miles
Columbia Falls: 16 miles
East Glacier: 57 miles
Great Falls: 195 miles
Kalispell: 31 miles
Polebridge: 25 miles
St. Mary (via Going-to-the-Sun Road): 53 miles
Whitefish: 25 miles

While distances are useful, it's good to know that they don't always translate directly into time on the road. The 50-plus miles of Going-to-the-Sun Road between West Glacier and St. Mary take about 1½ hours to drive because the road is narrow and winding (and that's just drive time; you'll also want to stop to admire the views). It's about 25 miles from West Glacier to Polebridge; it might take 40 minutes via the Outside North Fork Road, but more like 2 hours if you follow the rough-and-tumble Inside North Fork Road.

Local Chambers of Commerce:
Bigfork: 8155 Montana Hwy. 35, P.O. Box 237, Bigfork, MT 59911; (406) 837-5888; www.big fork.org
Browning: 124 Second Ave. Northwest, P.O. Box 990, Browning, MT 59417; (406) 338-4015; www.browningchamber.com
Columbia Falls: 233 Thirteenth St. East, P.O. Box 312, Columbia Falls, MT 59912; (406) 892-2072; www.columbiafallschamber.com
Glacier Country: 1121 East Broadway, Suite 113, Missoula, MT 59802; (406) 532-3234; www .glaciermt.com
Kalispell: 15 Depot Park, Kalispell, MT 59901; (406) 758-2800; www.kalispellchamber.com
Polson: 418 Main St., Polson, MT 59860; (406) 883-5969; www.polsonchamber.com
Waterton Lakes: P.O. Box 55, Waterton Lakes National Park, Alberta T0K 2M0, Canada; (403) 859-2224; www.mywaterton.ca
West Shore (Somers, Lakeside): P.O. Box 177, Lakeside, MT 59922; (406) 844-3715; www .lakesidesomers.org
Whitefish: 520 East Second St., Whitefish, MT 59937; (406) 862-3501; www.whitefishchamber .org

tourist, however. They are vibrant, exciting towns with active arts communities, thriving businesses, and stunning mountain surroundings. It's no wonder that more and more people make the Flathead Valley home every year. Festivals and events abound, from North American Indian Days in Browning to the colorful arts festivals held in communities from Whitefish to Polson. Families who have lived here for generations and newcomers alike fill the seats at these gatherings. This is a place where community still means something; where neighbors share a cup of sugar now and then, and where everyone talks about how to keep deer out of the garden—though most would willingly let the deer feed on their flower beds if the alternative was losing the wildlife that is such an important component of the area's natural beauty and diversity.

QUIRKS, FOIBLES & OTHER IMPORTANT INFORMATION

As you wander through Glacier National Park and the Flathead and Swan valleys seeking adventure, there are some things you should be aware of that may affect your journey, your recreation, and your safety. Many of these topics are covered in Closeups and Tips throughout the book, but another reminder of things to keep in mind can't hurt, as you hit the highways and head off for the park's peaks or out on the water.

1. **This is a really large area**—We don't call it Big Sky Country for nothing! And though residents of the region may think nothing of hopping in the car and driving a couple of hours to get to a favorite restaurant or particular trailhead, this book is arranged so that if you're in Whitefish, all of the restaurants, accommodations, and other amenities in the area are listed in the same section of the book. If you want to head off from Whitefish to a restaurant in, say, Polson, calculate the mileage before you hit the road, and be sure to fill up on gas. Twenty-four-hour convenience stores do exist out here, but you can't count on finding one at every intersection.

2. **The weather can change very quickly**— Even during a warm summer day, storm clouds can build up, delivering thunder, lightning, and rain, and the temperature can drop dramatically. Be sure if you're heading out on the water or the trail to bring the appropriate gear to get you through such a storm. Watch for signs of hypothermia when you're out recreating, and think about carrying emergency gear. And, whether it's hot or cold outside, always stay hydrated by drinking plenty of fluids.

3. **Heed road information**—Going-to-the-Sun Road in Glacier National Park is generally closed from early to mid-October until early June because of snow, and other roads can become dangerous in winter driving conditions. Exercise caution, and call the state highway information number, (800) 226-ROAD (7623), or visit www.mdt.mt.gov/travinfo for details on road conditions.

4. **Make your reservations early**—Though thousands of visitors are expected in the summer, the quantity of accommodations in the park and surrounding communities is not unlimited. Call ahead to reserve rooms (especially for those inside the park) and arrive early at campgrounds to secure a site. Some campgrounds accept

reservations, as well, and that reservation may save you from hunting around in the dark to find a spot to pull into and set up the tent.

5. **Potentially dangerous animals, including bears, moose, and mountain lions live here**—If you're lucky, you'll see these wild creatures from a safe distance. Always remember that bears, especially, can be dangerous, and follow the precautions outlined in this book's "Bear Aware" Close-up on page 186. We also have an abundance of other wild creatures that are wonderful to watch. Just remember you are the visitor in their home, so treat wildlife with respect and always give them a wide berth. If your behavior changes that of the animal you're watching, you're too close.

TREAD LIGHTLY

Throughout this guide, especially in the Outdoor Recreation chapter, you'll find tips for being a responsible visitor to this area's sometimes fragile ecosystems. Part of what makes this area so special is its abundance of natural beauty, its biodiversity, and the people who care about both. The remoteness of Glacier Country, including the national forest lands flanking the park and the valleys, has helped sustain that diversity for the hundred-plus years that settlement has been taking place here. Still, with more than two million visitors coming into the park every year, there is definitely strain on the natural surroundings . . . it's unavoidable. Please keep your personal impact to a minimum, and encourage others to do so as well.

Some Basic Facts About Glacier National Park:

- Established in 1910
- Approximately 1 million acres
- More than 1,100 species of plants
- There are 62 species of mammals, ranging in size from the pygmy shrew to the grizzly bear
- Annual visitation is approximately 2.2 million
- Busiest months to visit are July and August
- Trails total approximately 700 miles, including more than 100 miles of the Continental Divide National Scenic Trail
- Triple Divide Peak: Rivers drain to Hudson Bay, the Gulf of Mexico, and the Pacific
- Highest peak: Mount Cleveland, 10,466 feet above sea level
- Geology: Primarily sedimentary rocks of the Belt Supergroup, 800 million to 1.6 billion years old
- Glaciers: The park is named for the late Pleistocene glaciers that scoured out U-shaped valleys, glacial cirques, and other dramatic landscape features. Currently there are about two dozen small active glaciers persisting from the recent "Little Ice Age," a cooling trend that ended approximately 160 years ago

GETTING HERE, GETTING AROUND

Montana is remote, large, and mountainous, three things that can make getting here and getting around a challenge for visitors and locals alike (though it seems to be getting easier every day). It's not getting faster, though. Let's dispel that notion right off the bat. Yes, it is true that for nearly four years in the recent past, Montana had no posted daytime speed limit. Instead, highways operated under the "Basic Rule," which stated that drivers had to drive in a reasonable and prudent manner based on road conditions and traffic. However, even during that time, tickets were still distributed by our diligent, reasonable, and prudent highway patrol. The state has since gone back to standard daytime speed limits. This brief chapter is designed to help you get here by plane, car, train, or bus, and to help you navigate the state once you arrive. A reasonable and prudent attitude is still recommended as you travel here—weather conditions, mountainous terrain, and long distances between services (such as gas stations) should always be kept in mind.

BY AIR

Montana boasts four reasonably large international airports—in Billings, Great Falls, Missoula, and, lucky for the visitor to Glacier Country, Kalispell. If you fly into one of the other locations, you'll need to arrange to get to the Flathead by car or by bus. From Billings it's a lengthy 420 miles to Kalispell; from Great Falls, 226 miles; and from Missoula, 115 miles. Additional regional airports are located in Bozeman, Butte, and Helena.

i Consider flying into Spokane, Washington, or Calgary, Alberta, Canada, for your visit to Glacier Country. Airfares are sometimes less expensive, as are car rentals.

GLACIER PARK INTERNATIONAL AIRPORT
4170 US 2 East, Kalispell
(406) 755-5362
Most people who fly in to visit Glacier and the Flathead Valley will choose the Kalispell airport as their destination. It's serviced by Delta, Alaska/Horizon, United, and Allegiant Air. Direct flights can be made to and from several major cities, including Atlanta, Chicago, Seattle, and Denver. Car rentals are available at the airport, and some hotels and other accommodations will arrange to pick you up there.

MISSOULA INTERNATIONAL AIRPORT
5225 Hwy. 10 West, Missoula
(406) 728-4381

(Q) Close-up

Bus Tours in Glacier National Park

Bus tours provide an opportunity to take your eyes off the road and see Glacier National Park while someone else does the driving—and along winding, narrow Going-to-the-Sun Road, that can be a real luxury! There are at least two tour operators offering guided trips through Glacier and the surrounding area. Both make stops along the way for visitors to take photos, stretch their legs, and generally enjoy the scenery.

Glacier Park, Inc. (GPI) (406-892-2525; www.glacierparkinc.com) offers tours based out of their lodges, connecting the different areas of the park. Visitors traditionally have ridden in the historic red buses, built by the White Motor Company between 1936 and 1938. These vintage, 17-passenger motor coaches have roll-back canvas tops that can be opened on sunny days for a wind-in-your-hair ride with unobstructed views to the peaks above. Refurbished through a public—private partnership, the red buses gleam today as if they were brand-new. They are, in fact, certified as "new" vehicles, and they meet all current safety standards, while powered by efficient, low-emission propane/gas bi-fuel engines. All of their original charm remains, and drivers provide a narrative during the ride and answer questions for visitors just as always. The red bus schedule includes half-day and full-day tours to different parts of the park, including Logan Pass and Going-to-the-Sun Road, for prices ranging between $30 and $85. Reservations are required and should be made at least the day before you wish to tour.

Sun Tours (406-226-9220; www.glaciersuntours.com) operates out of the park's east side, picking up visitors at Browning, East Glacier, and St. Mary. These guided tours of Going-to-the-Sun Road—or Natos'i At'apoo—highlight Blackfeet history and culture, and all guides are members of the Blackfeet Nation. Sun Tours operates small modern buses with large windows and air-conditioning. Private tours and tours of the Blackfeet Reservation can also be arranged.

Flying to Missoula is the second-best option for getting close to Glacier Country by air. Car rentals are plentiful, and the airport is serviced by the same airlines as Glacier Park International. While you're in Missoula and at the airport, consider taking a guided tour of the nearby Aerial Fire Depot and Smoke-jumper Center, where you'll learn a lot about how forest fires are fought.

GREAT FALLS INTERNATIONAL AIRPORT
2800 Terminal Dr., Great Falls
(406) 727-3404

If you fly into Great Falls and rent a car to get to Glacier, be sure to visit the city's splendid Lewis and Clark Interpretive Center, located above the storied waters of the Missouri River. The airport is serviced by Delta, Alaska/Horizon, United, and Allegiant Air.

LOGAN INTERNATIONAL AIRPORT
1901 Terminal Circle, Billings
(406) 247-8609

Billings is Montana's largest city, and it has the state's largest airport. Car rentals are available at the airport, and you can fly in on

Close-up

A Montana Primer

Most people visit Montana during the summer—which means many of them are planning their trips during the winter months. If you have some long winter evenings to read by the fire, why not visit the local library and immerse yourself in Montana's remarkable history and literature before you come? The list of great books about Montana is long, and many of them were written by Montanans. With such an inspiring subject to draw from, it's really not surprising that so many great writers have come from this state. Here's a "short list" (in no particular order) to get you started.

- *The Last Best Place: A Montana Anthology* edited by William Kittredge and Annick Smith

- *This House of Sky* by Ivan Doig

- *Tough Trip through Paradise, 1878–79* by Andrew Garcia

- *The Big Sky* by A. B. Guthrie

- *Fools Crow* by James Welch

- *The Indian Lawyer* by James Welch

- *A River Runs Through It* by Norman Maclean

- *Young Men and Fire* by Norman Maclean

- *All but the Waltz: A Memoir of Five Generations in the Life of a Montana Family* by Mary Clearman Blew

- *True Grizz: Glimpses of Fernie, Stahr, Easy, Dakota, and Other Real Bears in the Modern World* by Doug Chadwick

- *Bear Attacks: Their Causes and Avoidance* by Stephen Herrero

- *A Beast the Color of Winter* by Doug Chadwick

- *Grizzly Years: In Search of American Wilderness* by Doug Peacock

- *Backcountry Ranger in Glacier National Park, 1910–1913: The Diaries & Photographs of Norton Pearl* by Norton Pearl

- *Making Certain It Goes On: The Collected Poems of Richard Hugo* by Richard Hugo

- *PermaRed* by Debra Magpie Earling

Glacier Association (www.glacierassociation.org) is also a great place to look for relevant titles. And all the towns in the Flathead have fine independent booksellers that showcase regional publications (see each chapter for specific listings).

Delta, Alaska/Horizon, United, Allegiant Air, and Great Lakes Airline.

BY CAR

Montana has 1,200 miles of interstate and some 5,400 miles of primary highways. But remember, this is Big Sky Country, so this just means the roads are long. It's not that difficult to find the ones you need to get where you're going. Three interstate highways meander across the state: I-15 runs north and south, just to the east of Glacier National Park and the Blackfeet Indian Reservation; I-90 runs from southeast to northwest across the western two-thirds of the state, before continuing west through the panhandle of Idaho and across Washington state; and I-94 connects Billings with far eastern Montana and North Dakota.

If you're coming in from the west, you'll take I-90; from the north or south, I-15; and from the east, I-90 or I-94. US 93 runs the length of the Flathead Valley from north to south, starting near Missoula at I-90 and winding its way north to the Canadian border at Port of Roosville Montana/British Columbia. This will likely be your primary travel corridor. Alternatively, Highway 83 takes you through the Seeley-Swan Valley, one of the most scenic drives in the state. US 2 follows the southern boundary of Glacier National Park and passes through the heart of the Blackfeet Indian Reservation. US 89 traverses the reservation north to south, offering access to the eastern reaches of Glacier National Park before dipping to the southeast to meet up with I-15 near Great Falls.

If you want to travel to Canada from Glacier and the Flathead, you'll find border crossings at Roosville (on US 93, north of Eureka), open 24 hours a day; Chief Mountain (on Highway 17, northeast of Glacier), open 7 a.m. to 10 p.m. from June 1 to Oct 31;

and Piegan (16 miles north of Babb on US 89), open 7 a.m. to 11 p.m. year-round.

Montana travel information is available by contacting **Travel Montana** (800-847-4868 or 406-841-2870; http://visitmt.com).

For information on **road conditions statewide,** call (800) 226-ROAD (7623) or visit www.mdt.mt.gov/travinfo.

BY BUS

EAGLE TRANSIT
(406) 758-5728
http://flathead.mt.gov/eagle
Eagle Transit is Flathead County's public transportation system, with city routes in Kalispell, Whitefish, and Columbia Falls. Call or go online for schedules and route information.

RIMROCK TRAILWAYS
(800) 255-7655, (406) 245-5392
www.rimrocktrailways.com
Rimrock serves more than 60 Montana communities, including Kalispell, Whitefish, Great Falls, and Missoula. It also connects to points served by Greyhound Lines along I-90, including Missoula, Bozeman, and Billings.

BY TRAIN

Amtrak's _Empire Builder_ (800-872-7245; www.amtrak.com) provides east and west passenger service across northern Montana, making stops in Libby, Whitefish, West Glacier, Essex, East Glacier Park, Browning, Cut Bank, Shelby, Havre, Malta, Glasgow, and Wolf Point. The terminuses are Chicago on the east and Portland and Seattle to the west. The railroad follows Montana's Hi-Line (as the area bisected by US 2 is known), and a trip on the _Empire Builder_ is a romantic way to see this part of the state.

HISTORY

Just the thought of trying to get to this isolated part of the Northwest was enough to discourage many early-day settlers. Pioneers arrived on horseback or by horse and wagon, negotiating rough wagon trails that knifed through dense stands of virgin timber and crawled up and down steep mountainsides. Fur trappers and traders preceded settlers in the early 1800s. Before them, of course, were American Indians, the first human inhabitants of the region. In relatively recent times, three main Indian tribes—the Kootenai; the Upper Pend d'Oreille, or Kalispell; and the Salish, known as the Flatheads—coexisted in the area. They hunted and fished in the area's many rivers and lakes and vied for territory with the warring Blackfeet Indians from the eastern side of the Rocky Mountains and to the north in Canada.

This country remains home today to the Confederated Salish and Kootenai tribes (Flathead, Pend d'Oreille, and Kootenai). The Treaty of 1855 sliced Flathead Lake into two halves, with the southern half designated as part of the Flathead Indian Reservation. The reservation, which comprises 1.2 million acres, extends south to the Arlee area. The tribal headquarters is housed in the Confederated Salish and Kootenai Tribal Complex in Pablo.

Beginning about 1810 and continuing into the 1820s, traders and fur trappers sought adventure and wealth in the Flathead Valley, and their explorations would set the stage for profound changes in the lives of the Native peoples. Canadian trappers and traders were among the first to traverse the region; Joseph Howse, one of the first white men to winter in the Flathead, was sent by the Hudson's Bay Company to establish the company's original fur-trading post in 1810–11. This post at the north end of Flathead Lake was called Howse House (or Howse's House).

ARRIVAL OF THE HOMESTEADERS

Following the footsteps of the trappers came the homesteaders, hungry for land and a new start. A heavy influx of homesteaders populated the region throughout the 1870s and 1880s; many were European immigrants who brought their agricultural heritage with them. Many claimed land on the shores of Flathead Lake, regardless that some of it was reservation land.

The arrival of the Northern Pacific Railroad at Missoula in 1883 was one of the major contributors to the region's growth. By around 1890 public transportation was available from Missoula via a spur line north to Ravalli, located southwest of St. Ignatius. From Ravalli, passengers and goods were loaded onto overland wagons or stages and transported to Polson on Flathead Lake's southern shore.

From Polson, steamboats offered passenger service to the north end of the approximately 28-mile-long lake, connecting with Somers and Demersville, two early settlements. The first steamer to begin criss-crossing Flathead Lake was the US *Grant*, and by 1916 at least 16 steamers regularly traversed the waters of Flathead, the largest freshwater lake west of the Mississippi. Besides containing roomy freight decks with booms, many steamboats featured upper decks with private cabins for travelers, and dining salons. The largest of the lot, the *State of Montana*, was launched in 1889. It measured 150 feet long by 26 feet wide and was built for an estimated cost of $25,000.

In the 1880s agriculture boomed in the rich, fertile Flathead Valley, and steamboats hauled grain crops and potatoes to market. The temperate climate around Flathead Lake enabled even the successful cultivation of fruit orchards. Many tons of apples were produced and shipped to out-of-state markets. In the early 1900s, the Bear Dance Ranch reportedly harvested 3,000 fruit trees and boasted more than 40 varieties of apples. Later, sweet cherries were introduced to the Flathead and became a major crop, which they remain today.

Steamboat transportation on Flathead Lake thrived from about 1885 until 1917, when the Northern Pacific Railroad built a branch line north to Polson. The ease and speed of rail transportation hastened the end of the steamboat era, and the Northern Pacific was not the only railroad to help shape the region's history. It was empire builder James J. Hill's dream to build a railroad from St. Paul, Minnesota, to the West Coast. Some 6,000 men bent their backs

surveying, grading, and pounding rails to the upper Flathead Valley to bring Hill's transcontinental railroad, the Great Northern Railway, west from the eastern Montana prairies and over 5,280-foot Marias Pass, which is located along the Continental Divide at the southern edge of Glacier National Park. Hill's idea was to fill his cars with passengers going west, and he heavily advertised the agricultural opportunities of the Flathead Valley, offering cheap fares for homesteaders. As such, the railway played a prominent role in providing homesteaders access to the hinterlands of northwestern Montana.

By 1891, the train carried passengers to Columbia Falls and Kalispell, and late that same decade the Flathead Valley was home to more than 700 farms.

TWO EARLY TOWNS HAVE THEIR DAY

Historians consider Ashley the Flathead Valley's first "real town." Established at the crossing of Indian trails near the Ashley Creek Bridge, it sat about 1 mile west of Kalispell's present-day business district, and some of Ashley's streets were incorporated into Kalispell as that city developed. The town was named for Joe Ashley, a trader who arrived in 1857, one of the valley's first settlers. It died shortly after Demersville and Kalispell blossomed, almost overnight.

Demersville, situated a few miles south of Kalispell on the Flathead River, was founded by merchant T. J. Demers. The location came to be considered the head of navigation on the Flathead River. Demers set up his general store first in a large tent, and later in a log structure. With his death in 1889, the store was sold and became the Missoula Mercantile Co. Demersville boomed from 1888 to 1891, as steamboat traffic on Flathead Lake ferried the migration of settlers, equipment, and supplies up the lake.

Demersville was a hell-bent town, with an abundance of saloons and gambling. Townsfolk hoped the Great Northern Railway would lay tracks to Demersville, so that it would gain the double advantage of claiming both rail and water transportation. But when the Great Northern Railway extended its main line to Kalispell instead, most of the town folded up and moved there.

BIGFORK

The first wagon trails through this part of Montana followed the west shore of Flathead Lake. Thus the Bigfork area on the east shore was slower to be populated than its west-shore neighbors. The town perches on a bay where the Swan River spills into the northeast end of the nearly 200-square-mile Flathead Lake. The town was founded in 1901 or 1902, when E. L. Sliter filed a townsite plat. He divided a portion of his 160-acre homestead into 11 blocks and about 95 lots. Sliter built the town's first hotel and general store and served as its first postmaster. Some other early businesses were the Bigfork Mercantile, the Flathead Commercial Company, and the E. J. O'Brien Hotel. The first restaurant built was Cheinies. (A 1912 fire in Bigfork demolished many of the pioneer businesses.) The Bigfork Light and Power Company constructed the first hydroelectric power plant at Bigfork in 1901. Located at the mouth of the Swan River, the plant harnessed energy derived from the turbulent waters and sent power and light to neighboring Kalispell. The University of Montana originally operated its biological research station in Bigfork, until relocating it to Yellow Bay in 1912.

Bigfork and the surrounding area has been known historically for producing exceptional fruit, thanks to the lakeshore's relatively mild climate. The first orchard is thought to have been planted by homesteader George Lakin in about 1885. City founder E. L. Sliter soon followed suit, clearing timber and brush and eventually accumulating more than 500 acres of farmland. When his orchards were at peak production, he had upwards of 5,000 apple, pear, plum, and cherry trees. The area is perhaps most famous for its cherries; the industry as we know it today originated at nearby Wood's Bay in the 1890s.

Exactly how the town acquired the name Bigfork is not known for sure. However, Henry Elwood reported in his book *Kalispell, Montana and The Upper Flathead Valley* that local Indians told Sliter the site was the "Big Fork" of the Flathead Valley's rivers, hence the name. Later, the US Postal Service shortened the name to one word.

More than a century has passed since this little town was founded. As you will see if you visit, Bigfork is a thriving place today. Primarily a tourist town—the summer population swells to approximately 10,000—it is a draw in itself. Among other highlights, Bigfork is home to the renowned Bigfork Summer Playhouse and performing arts center. You'll also find fine-art galleries, gift shops, superb restaurants, and, nearby, a world-class golf course. (If you travel to Bigfork in mid- to late summer, don't miss sampling the region's sweet Flathead cherries!)

SOMERS

The old company houses of this former lumber town on US 93 are still lived in, and timeworn dock pilings stretch out into

Somers Bay. Both are mute reminders that the quiet community of Somers at one time enjoyed status as the second-largest town in the Flathead Valley.

In the early decades of the 20th century, Somers was abuzz as a shipping and logging hub and passenger port. Built on the northwest end of Flathead Lake, the town grew up fast. The Great Northern Railway needed to acquire ties to continue its railway expansion, and the abundant lumber in the area was responsible for an economic boom. About 1900, Great Northern Railway founder Hill contracted with John O'Brien of Stillwater, Minnesota, to build a sawmill capable of producing at least 600,000 railroad ties annually for 20 years. Some 40 million board feet of lumber were contracted for each year. In turn, the Great Northern was to build a 10-mile spur track from its main line through Kalispell to the O'Brien mill in Somers.

O'Brien purchased 350 acres of the Tom McGovern ranch and built the sawmill. The railroad recruited loggers from back in Minnesota, offering them fare to Montana for only $12.50. Besides the Minnesotans, mill workers composing the labor force hailed from Sweden, Germany, Norway, and Italy. Somers was known for the friendliness of these hard-working immigrants.

Operations at the mill began in August 1901, and a boomtown was born. The boom lasted more than two decades, until the 1920s, when virgin timber resources became less plentiful. Logging was done in winter because it was easier to haul timber over snow than over dry land. Logs were cut, loaded onto horse-drawn sleighs, and sledded to riverbanks or lakeshores, where they were stockpiled. In spring, when the water was high, logs going to the Somers mill were driven down the Flathead, Whitefish, Stillwater, and Swan rivers to the head of Flathead Lake, from which point they were towed by tugboat to a large pond in Somers Bay for processing. The sawmill operated a planing mill for lumber, a sash and door division, and, for a time, a box factory. The Great Northern built their tie-treatment facility and operated a power plant on the grounds to provide steam for all the operations.

Great Northern representative George O. Somers was in town, keeping track of the railroad's interests in 1901, the same year the post office was built. Both the new post office and the new town needed a name, and the well-liked and respected railroad official was chosen as the namesake.

The Great Northern acquired the sawmill from O'Brien in 1906 when he left Somers. Eventually, its name was changed to the Somers Lumber Company. Operating day and night, the mill could produce 225,000 board feet of lumber in 24 hours.

The company employed most of Somers' 500 inhabitants, and provided them with places to live. According to authors Lou Bain and Frank Grubb, in their book *Flathead Valley Yesteryear*, workers paid from $5 to $9 per month for rent, and the lumber company furnished water and electricity. Workers were also charged $1 per month for medical services from the company doctor.

In 1900, George Wilson constructed the first general store in Somers. The Flathead Commercial Company later purchased it and did business as the Normann and Smith Company. In 1933, Everit Sliter of Bigfork fame purchased the interest of one of the store's original owners, and renamed it the People's Mercantile. Sliter became sole owner in 1937.

⊙ Close-up

Flathead Valley & Glacier National Park Time Line

1810—Joseph Howse of the Hudson's Bay Company spends the winter of 1810–11 in Flathead Valley, establishing company's first local trading post—Howse House—at north end of Flathead Lake.

1857—Trader Joe Ashley first to settle in upper Flathead Valley on Ashley Creek. (In 1883 community of Ashley founded, 1 mile west of present-day Kalispell.)

1862—Major gold strikes in Montana bring prospectors swarming to the northern Rocky Mountains in search of mineral riches.

1885—First steamboat hauls freight and passengers up Flathead Lake, as the Swan sailboat is transformed into the US *Grant* steamboat.

1887—Town of Demersville founded several miles south of Kalispell on Flathead River by Frenchtown, Montana, merchant T. J. Demers.

1891—Great Northern Railway brings transcontinental rail service to the valley. Great Northern establishes Kalispell Townsite Company and names Kalispell new railway division point. Kalispell now valley's major town.

1893—Montana Legislature creates Flathead County from part of Missoula County.

1901—John O'Brien Lumber Company Mill built at Somers to manufacture ties for Great Northern Railway's westward expansion. Somers becomes the second-largest town in the valley.

1902—Townsite of Bigfork platted and filed by E. L. Sliter.

1902—Whitefish Townsite Company established. Land surveyed and divided into lots.

1904—Main line of Great Northern moves from Kalispell to Whitefish for better routing by James J. Hill. Whitefish becomes new division point (which it remains today).

1905—Citizens vote to incorporate Whitefish.

1910—On May 11, President William Howard Taft signs bill establishing Glacier National Park as nation's 10th national park.

1910—Severe forest fires burn 3 million acres in Idaho and western Montana, including parts of newly established Glacier National Park.

1910—Flathead Indian Reservation opened for homesteading; Flathead Valley sees influx of pioneers.

1913—First of Glacier Park's Great Lodges built by the Great Northern Railway at East Glacier.

1927—Great Northern depot is built in Whitefish and soon becomes Whitefish icon.

1929—Half Moon Fire burns 100,000 acres, racing across Teakettle Mountain near Columbia Falls and into Glacier Park.

1929—First Great Northern passenger train, the soon-to-be-famous *Empire Builder*, passes westbound through Whitefish.

1932—Waterton and Glacier are designated as world's first International Peace Park.

1933—Dedication ceremony atop Logan Pass kicks off official opening of Glacier Park's scenic Going-to-the-Sun Road.

1935—Big Mountain's Hellroaring Ski Club founded.

1937—First golf club organizes in Whitefish.

1939—Izaak Walton Inn at Essex, just outside southern edge of Glacier Park, is built to serve Great Northern locomotives and rail-work crews. (Filled with railroad memorabilia, the inn today caters to cross-country skiers and tourists.)

1947—Big Mountain ski area incorporates and is run by Winter Sports, Inc.

1950—A day's ski pass on Big Mountain costs $1.50.

1953—Hungry Horse Dam built. Structure is 564 feet high (and still today is the tenth-tallest dam in the United States).

1955—Columbia Falls Aluminum Company built north of Columbia Falls.

1960—Whitefish Winter Carnival is formed. (It remains an important part of today's Whitefish winter scene.)

1964—Huge flood hits north Flathead Valley and floods community of Evergreen. Sections of highway and rail lines wash away at Marias Pass.

1967—In apparently unrelated incidents, grizzlies in Glacier Park kill two campers on same night, which becomes known as the Night of the Grizzlies.

1976—Glacier National Park designated a World Biosphere Reserve.

1988—Red Bench Fire burns 37,500 acres on west side of Glacier Park.

1990—Whitefish Stumptown Historical Society saves run-down railroad depot, restoring it to much like it was when built in 1927.

1998—Blacktail Mountain Ski Area opens near Lakeside.

2001—Moose Fire burns more than 70,000 acres, mostly in Flathead National Forest and Glacier National Park.

2002—Ford Motor Company, in partnership with the National Park Service, refurbishes Glacier's famous fleet of historic red buses.

2003—Wedge Canyon, Robert, Trapper, and Middle Fork Complex fires burn approximately 150,000 acres in Glacier National Park; with numerous other fires around the region, western Montana becomes the top priority for firefighting in the nation. Hottest summer on record for the area.

2006—Blackfeet Nation opens Glacier Peaks Casino in Browning.

2006—Late season rains on top of snow create massive flooding in much of Glacier National Park. The November storm sweeps away backcountry bridges and trails as well as two portions of Going-to-the-Sun Road.

2007—Big Mountain Resort changes its name to Whitefish Mountain Resort (to prevent confusion with Big Sky, south of Bozeman), but the mountain itself is still called Big Mountain.

2007—Glacier National Park institutes a free shuttle system, which takes visitors over Going-to-the-Sun Road.

2008—Logan Pass and St. Mary visitor centers added to National Register of Historic Places.

2010—Rededication ceremony held in May to commemorate Glacier National Park's centennial.

2010—Owing to the unique variety of sensitive species found there, the Montana Native Plant Society designates Glacier National Park's Logan Pass area as the first Important Plant Area (IPA) in the state of Montana.

The town's first hotel and eating house, established around 1900, were under the roof of the McGovern ranch house. The Somers Hotel and boardinghouse was constructed in 1901; also that year a company general store was opened by the Great Northern.

Another historic Somers building is a popular restaurant today. Tiebuckers Pub and Eatery, featuring fine dining, is housed in the former office building of the Somers Lumber Company. Constructed in 1929, it shared space with the Great Northern, serving as its depot. The building has been put to many other uses over the decades; according to the folks at Tiebuckers, it's been a makeshift school, a mini-mall, a cafe, and more.

When growth was at its peak, the Great Northern offered not only freight service but also twice-daily passenger service from Kalispell to Somers. Passenger traffic reached an all-time high in about 1910, when the Flathead Indian Reservation was opened for homesteading. At that time, passengers from either east or west were routed via the Great Northern to Somers, ferried across Flathead Lake to Polson by steamboat, and then carried south by the Northern Pacific Railroad—or vice versa. But by the late 1920s traffic had dwindled considerably, with the decline of the steamboat era, the advent of the automobile, and the availability of public bus transportation. Consequently, the Great Northern abandoned its rail passenger service.

Similarly, as Somers was no longer a transportation hub, the old order was passing in the lumber business. Plentiful timber was no longer available, and in 1948 the Great Northern shut down its large mill.

Today, residents of the town and surrounding valley enjoy unlimited recreational activities on Flathead Lake and in the mountains above. You, too, can enjoy sunbathing or boating at the public park and boat launch at Somers Bay.

Nearby Lakeside, south of Somers, also makes available to travelers a public dock and park. The first settlers here consisted of a group of Methodist church Congregationalists, who in 1896 attempted to establish an educational camp. The Reverend W. W. Van Orsdel, known as "Brother Van," helped purchase some 240 acres of lakeshore property at Lakeside, according to historian R. C. "Chuck" Robbin. The hopeful settlers called the camp "Chautauqua," a namesake of the original Chautauqua site in New York state. But financial woes caused the mission to fail, and parts of the large tract were sold. John Stoner bought 25 acres here and built a boardinghouse; he also opened Lakeside's first post office in 1901.

Lakeside's residents and visitors alike enjoy spectacular lake and mountain panoramas. A growing village, it offers most services.

COLUMBIA FALLS

Columbia Falls, on US 2, sits near the west entrance to Glacier National Park; from there, travelers wind through Bad Rock Canyon to access the breathtaking and enchanting scenery of this world-renowned park.

Like many Flathead Valley towns, Columbia Falls grew up around the Great Northern Railway. Railroad tycoon James J. Hill decided in 1889 to extend the line from the eastern plains of Montana to Puget Sound, Washington, without the benefit of government land grants. His major problem wasn't funding, but finding a viable route over the Continental Divide through the Rocky Mountains. Although history tells tales of other white men using the pass decades earlier, John F. Stevens, a Great Northern railroad surveyor sent by Hill to locate a passable route, is generally credited with discovering Marias Pass. In 1891 the railroad line was completed through that pass to Columbia Falls, then on to Kalispell.

The town of Columbia Falls had been established several years earlier, as settlers were drawn to the area's good farmland and generous supply of timber. In addition, coal discovered up the North Fork of the Flathead River was mined in limited quantities and barged downstream through Demersville and on to Flathead Lake, then transported to points beyond by the Northern Pacific Railroad.

The group of pioneers who established the village named it Columbia, or Columbus. The original townsite was located on the flats next to the Flathead River, but early settlers decided their town stood a better chance of persevering up on dryer ground and closer to the coming rails. So, much of the town relocated to the present site before the railroad steamed into town.

Although it is not clear why residents named the town Columbia, speculation has it being named for nearby Columbia Mountain, a long, horizontal feature situated at the mouth of Bad Rock Canyon, a mile or so to the east. When first postmaster Jim Kennedy applied for a town name in 1891, he was declined the name Columbia, since there was a town in Montana already called Columbus, and it was feared that such a similar name would cause confusion. Kennedy's wife actually named the town by adding "Falls" after Columbia, although no falls existed there then.

With the railroad coming, a group of enterprising Butte, Montana, businessmen looked ahead to profit. Organizing the Northern International Improvement Company and betting that Columbia Falls would become the new division point for the railroad, and that land would be in high demand, they purchased property from Mrs. Nellie LaFrombois, an Indian woman, and platted it. Much of the land was located in what would become the town's business district. But even railroad magnate Hill thought the prices in Columbia Falls too steep, so he continued laying tracks to Kalispell, designating it the division point instead. (Not surprisingly, Kalispell citizens were sorely disappointed when Hill later moved the division point to Whitefish.)

Still, moderate growth continued in Columbia Falls. Beatrice Macomber reports in Columbia Falls Yester-Years that in 1891 the small community sported 18 saloons and a general store, men's store, barbershop, flour mill, sawmill and lumber company, and railroad depot. The year 1891 also marked the building of the town's first bank by James A. Talbott, a prominent businessman who some regard as the father of Columbia Falls. He and G. E. Gaylord, both members of the Northern International Improvement Company, built the sophisticated 31-room Gaylord Hotel (which burned down in 1929). Talbott donated land for the first Episcopal church and first school, erected in 1892. Here he also built his family home, a lavish mansion with 8 fireplaces and overlooking the Flathead River. (Unfortunately, it too was ravaged by fire in 1941.)

A windfall for Columbia Falls was its being chosen as the location for the state's "old soldiers' home" in 1895, when Talbott's and the Northern International Improvement

Company's offer to donate cash and equipment as well as acreage just outside Columbia Falls was accepted by the state board of review, from among proposals submitted by towns throughout the state. The governor approved the decision, and the 2-story structure was built for the sum of $9,985. By the end of 1908, the home provided care for 88 residents. The rules prohibited drinking and profanity, permitted smoking in rooms, and required a bath at least once a week. Residents were signaled to rise at reveille and had to be in their rooms when taps played each night.

In 1909, the citizens of Columbia Falls voted to incorporate. The following year, the modern amenities of electricity and telephone were installed in town, and a sewer line was laid along Nucleus Avenue.

In its early years, the survival of Columbia Falls hinged on the grain and lumber industries. Lumber still plays an important role in the well-being of the economy today, with Plum Creek operating a sawmill and couple of plants in town and Stoltze Lumber Company running a nearby mill. Construction of the Hungry Horse Dam near the little town of Hungry Horse gave a shot in the arm to the economy in the early 1950s, and some workers stayed to put down roots.

Another industry, vital to Columbia Falls' economy since 1955, has been the Columbia Falls Aluminum Company north of town. Sadly, the plant shut down late in 2009, eliminating nearly 100 jobs. A processing plant, the company originally manufactured aluminum ingots.

Today, Columbia Falls is changing. Long considered the blue-collar corner of the Flathead Valley, its profile and economy are shifting as the town gains recognition as the western gateway to Glacier National Park.

WHITEFISH

When trappers penetrated the virgin forests of the north Flathead Valley early in the 1800s, they shared the long lake that sprawls at the foot of the Whitefish Mountain Range with Native Americans living in the vicinity. Trappers and early settlers came to call it Whitefish Lake, named for the rich supply of whitefish that had long provided a food staple for the Indians. When a permanent town was founded in the present location, it too was called Whitefish.

By 1883, the first permanent settlers, John Morton and Charles Ramsey, had hewn homes out of the primitive countryside near the mouth of the Whitefish River. Ramsey also constructed a rooming house for hunters and anglers who came to pursue the area's abundant fish and wildlife. By the end of the decade, lumbermen were lured to the valley by its dense timber stands. Loggers put Whitefish Lake to good use; timber was cut on nearby slopes and floated on the lake to the Whitefish River; and, from there, downriver to lumber mills in and around Kalispell.

The first Whitefish sawmill was built by the Baker brothers, who played a prominent role in Whitefish's early history. For decades, logging and farming remained the primary livelihoods in Whitefish.

Originally located at the foot of Whitefish Lake, the town was moved to its present location so that commerce and other activity would be situated closer to the Great Northern railroad's tracks. The Whitefish Townsite Company was established in 1902 by a group of four individuals, and the land was surveyed and platted, but it wasn't until the following year that articles of incorporation were filed for the company. The Whitefish Townsite Company hired loggers to thin the dense timber stands that spread over the townsite, and tree felling began in earnest for the new railroad town. Although great progress was made, many stumps remained for a number of years after the trees were downed, earning Whitefish the nickname "Stumptown." In 1905, townspeople voted to incorporate the village of Whitefish, the town council met for the first time, and the first census was gathered—the population of the boomtown pegged at 950 hardy souls.

Five years later, citizens driving horse-drawn wagons down city streets were still compelled to negotiate their way around tree stumps, so in 1910 the town council decided that prying out the offending stumps would be a good way for jail offenders to pay their debts. Thus, jailbirds accomplished a major town beautification effort.

The Great Northern Railway main line had come to the Flathead in 1891. The railroad announced that Whitefish would be the new division point on the main line 10 years later, because it offered better routing options than Kalispell. In 1903, a spur line was added that linked Columbia Falls with Whitefish, and the Great Northern's Hill pulled division headquarters out of Kalispell. The steel ribbon was realigned to the north, reaching from Columbia Falls to Rexford via Whitefish, then connecting with Libby and points west. The "Columbia Falls Cutoff" was completed in 1904, eliminating the difficult previous route that crossed the Salish Mountains west of Kalispell.

Another reason Hill chose Whitefish as division headquarters was because of its proximity to Whitefish Lake. The big pond provided a water supply for the railroad's steam-powered equipment, and in winter crews of sawyers hauled out blocks of ice for the Great Northern's icehouses in Whitefish. A natural means of refrigeration, the ice was used to cool fruit in the express cars.

Mechanical refrigeration later replaced the need for ice storage, and in the late 1970s the giant icehouses were demolished.

ℹ️ **Locals refer to the Flathead Valley simply as "the Flathead," a name deriving from the Flathead Indians. No one knows for sure how the Flathead Indians came by their name, although several theories exist. A popular one is that when the explorers Lewis and Clark came across the Indians near the future site of Hamilton, Montana, they saw some of them visiting Chinook Indians from the West Coast. The Chinooks flattened their children's temples with headboards on their papooses (cradles strapped to the back to carry babies). The explorers mistakenly called them all Flatheads. Another theory has it that other Salish Indians (a grouping of Northwest Indians to whom the Flatheads belong) had wedge-shaped heads, while the Flatheads didn't; they had "flat" heads.**

Whitefish Lake and the Whitefish River also provided citizens with water. Frank Baker and a man named Rile hauled wagonloads laden with jostling barrels of water down bumpy city streets to provide residents with water; the cost was around 25 cents a barrel. The Baker brothers (there were five) reportedly owned much of the land adjoining Whitefish, and they gave liberally of their labor and money to help build a solid foundation for the fledgling town. Baker Avenue is named after them.

🔍 Close-up

Going-to-the-Sun Road

Going-to-the-Sun Road bisects the heart of Glacier National Park, providing most visitors their best access to the subalpine and alpine regions of the park. The road winds up from the dense forests of the west slope, and from the prairies of the east, to top out at **Logan Pass,** elevation 6,646 feet. Magnificent views are standard fare for the entire way along this winding mountain road. An engineering marvel, the road was completed in 1932 and opened to the public in 1933.

Many anecdotes illustrate the difficulties of building the road. Considering the amount of blasting that had to be done, the steep angles at which the rock was worked, the state of technology at the time, and the harsh environment, it is probably testimony to safety measures taken that only three men died during the road's construction. But more than one man quit his job to save his hide, even though the project took place during the Great Depression, when work was so hard to come by.

One story tells of how, during construction of the 408-foot-long east-side tunnel, workers had to shimmy down a hundred feet of rope over a cliff to get to the job site. Once there, the work involved removing the excavated rock from the tunnel by hand— it was impossible to get any power equipment down the steep slope. In another case, when preparing to blast one particularly large cliff just east of the **Loop** (the hairpin turn on the west side of the Continental Divide), workers wore wool socks over their boots to avoid generating sparks! In 1931 a Caterpillar tractor slipped off the road and rolled 200 feet down a mountainside, but its operator drove it back up with only minor damage.

The difficult environment continues to affect Going-to-the-Sun Road today. Opening the road over Logan Pass each spring is a major undertaking that starts with plowing efforts in early April. Regular snowplows, a rotary plow, and a front-end loader begin the task of clearing the **snow** at low elevations, gradually working their way higher. The speed at which the road can be plowed depends on the depth of the winter's snowpack and spring weather conditions. What falls as spring rain in the valleys can turn to snow higher up; sometimes certain stretches of road need to be cleared more than once. **Avalanches** are inevitable in the springtime, so avalanche spotters keep their eyes trained on the slopes above the road, watching for any sign of movement that could put the road crew and/or equipment in harm's way. Occasionally, **fog** sets in, making it impossible for avalanche spotters to assess the conditions and forcing a hiatus in the plowing efforts. Crews have even been known to plow their way home, after an avalanche stormed down the mountains below their work location.

As the plow crew works its way toward Logan Pass, the snow gets deeper and deeper. The last part of Going-to-the-Sun Road to be plowed is usually the **Big Drift,** which has

One of the first businesses in Whitefish was a tent saloon, out of which two entrepreneurs peddled whiskey to sawyers clearing trees downtown on Central Avenue and Second Street. The town experienced a building boom in 1903 and 1904, when an atmosphere of optimism prevailed. "By 1910, Whitefish had 1,479 people," Betty Schafer and Mable Engelter write in *Stump Town to Ski Town: The Story of Whitefish, Montana;*

measured as deep as 80 feet when plowing began. The Big Drift has to be surveyed each year so that the equipment operators are sure they're plowing the road and not something else! Going-to-the-Sun Road usually opens for through-travel sometime between the last week of May and the third week of June. When it first opens, the snowpack at the **Logan Pass Visitor Center** is typically about 12 feet deep. In the fall, the road is progressively closed down in sections from Logan Pass, beginning on the third Monday of October (unless weather conditions have forced an even earlier closure). The lower sections of the road, along **Lake McDonald** and **St. Mary Lake,** are kept open throughout the winter.

Maintaining the nearly 80-year-old road is a challenge, too. Going-to-the-Sun Road is on the **National Register of Historic Places,** and preserving its historic character is one of the National Park Service's mandates. In recent years, a major reconstruction of the road has begun and will continue for some time into the future. Although technology has advanced far beyond that which existed when the road was built, reconstruction is still difficult in such a challenging environment with such a short work season. In addition, visitation to the park—and the number of vehicles that drive Going-to-the-Sun Road—has increased well beyond anything that could have been imagined in the 1930s. Thus, rebuilding the road is no minor undertaking—the work has to take place during the peak season of the short alpine summer, when hordes of people are visiting, animals are up and around, and delicate plants are budding, flowering, and setting seed. You may encounter delays due to construction during your drive over the pass—ask at the gate as you enter; generally delays are short, and much of the major work is being done at night. Should you be stopped, however, why not take the opportunity to turn off your car's engine, enjoy the view, have a snack, and step outside for a moment?

Logan Pass is the literal and symbolic apex of Going-to-the-Sun Road. It can be difficult to find a parking spot here in the middle of the day; try arriving before 10:30 a.m. or visiting late in the afternoon or early evening—daylight is long in the northern summer. Or, consider taking the **free park shuttle** up and back from lower elevation—leave the driving to someone else and you'll enjoy the views that much more. However you get there, you'll admire the **Garden Wall,** the **Hanging Gardens,** and the 360-degree view from Logan Pass of both sides of the **Continental Divide.** At the pass, consider making the walk to **Hidden Lake Overlook**—look for ptarmigan nesting under the boardwalk and for shaggy white mountain goats—or perhaps strike off down the **Highline Trail** for as far as it captures your fancy. Alternatively, you can simply spend a few minutes with binoculars scoping the slopes for mountain goats, bighorn sheep, and grizzly bears, all of which frequent the Logan Pass area.

"a business district primarily along Central Avenue and Second Street, a water system, a light and power plant, telephones, some wooden sidewalks, and a couple of crosswalks, some graded streets, some filled gullies." The council was discussing sewers and parking. Civilization, indeed, had arrived.

A hundred years later many original downtown buildings remain in use, offering food, shopping, and services in this thriving resort town. The charm of yesteryear endures, and visitors are invited to take a historical downtown walking tour.

The heart of Whitefish has always been the Great Northern Railway (though later it became the Burlington Northern Railroad). The first official passenger train cruised by the train platform in October 1904 westbound for Seattle. The steam-powered train was on time, and the town's citizens were on hand to cheer. It was at this time that the city was formally proclaimed the new railroad division point.

Beginning around 1913, passenger trains going through Whitefish continued eastward to follow the southern boundary of Glacier National Park during daylight hours, so that summer travelers could enjoy the scenery while crossing the Continental Divide. The daytime schedule remains the same today, even since Amtrak took over passenger service in 1971. The storied *Empire Builder* passenger train rolled into Whitefish for the first time in 1929, and today it still carries both east- and westbound passengers past the park.

The first train depot built in 1906 was replaced in 1927 with a building that merged half-timbered English Tudor style with a Swiss-chalet look. The Swiss-chalet architectural vernacular was popular for the lodges being built at the time in Glacier National Park. By 1990, the aging depot needed refurbishing, and the Burlington Northern Railroad donated it to the Whitefish Stumptown Historical Society for restoration. (The Burlington Northern formed in 1970 with the merging of the Great Northern Railway, the Northern Pacific Railroad, and numerous other lines.) The renovation of the treasured landmark resurrected its 1927 appearance and character, while adding modern amenities. Be sure to stop by the historical society museum located there—it's on the walking tour—to learn more about the town's railroad history.

You can't help but notice the "Rocky the Goat" logo, which the Great Northern chose for its trademark symbol in 1923. Emblazoned on Great Northern freight cars, the mountain goat logo was a familiar sight for decades, until the merger that created the Burlington Northern ended Rocky's ride through the Flathead.

If the railroad was the heart of Whitefish, Big Mountain was—and is—its soul. Hiking and huckleberry picking have long been summertime pursuits on this massive mountain. Snow-encrusted trees, known as "snow ghosts," are a familiar winter sight on the mountain. Skiers using homemade wooden skis found a way to schuss down the mountain as early as 1935, without the benefit of a resort company to hack out and groom trails. The Hellroaring Ski Club had unofficially formed by 1935. A little more than a decade later—in 1947—two entrepreneurs from Great Falls, along with numerous interested Whitefish community members, financed a fledgling resort operation called Winter Sports, Inc. The company developed and operated Big Mountain, eventually expanding it to include year-round recreation as well as a substantial real estate operation. In 2007, to the consternation of many locals, the company renamed the complex "Whitefish Mountain Resort." (Truthfully, it was probably a good move, because it eliminates the name confusion surrounding Big Mountain and another mega-resort south of Bozeman known as Big Sky, originally developed by the late newsman Chet Huntley.)

But the mountain itself is still Big Mountain. It is annually buried in 330-plus inches of snow, and it offers a broad variety of terrain—some 3,000 skiable acres—for great downhill skiing. The resort, just a snowball's throw from Glacier National Park, continues to be a popular draw and an important source of revenue for the resort-and-retirement community cradled in the valley below.

KALISPELL

True, Kalispell was cut off from the Great Northern Railway's main line when the division point went north to Whitefish in 1904. But the town did not go bust, as had other early towns in the Flathead Valley that were bypassed by the railroad. In fact, Kalispell managed to remain the financial and commercial hub of the valley.

Back in 1891 when James J. Hill decided to relocate the division point from Columbia Falls to Kalispell, he sent Charles E. Conrad to find a site for the Great Northern's facilities and for the Kalispell Townsite Company. Conrad purchased part of a homestead on the west side of Kalispell, and had the land surveyed, platted, and recorded. The name Hill chose for the new town was "Kalispel," derived from the Pend d'Oreille Indian language. (The word is said to have at least two meanings: "camas" and "prairie above the lake.")

Land speculators had also bought up nearby ranches and homesteads and divided them into lots in anticipation of the railroad's arrival. In spring 1891, when newly divided pieces of land came on the market, an unheard of $100,000 worth of lots were snapped up overnight. Inside lots along Main Street were priced at $1,000, while corner lots cost as much as $1,250. It wasn't long before the first building was constructed along Main Street.

Everyone in Kalispell eagerly anticipated the coming of the railroad; and December 31, 1891, was a red-letter day for the town. According to historian Henry Elwood, a story in a special edition of the *Kalispell Graphic* newspaper went like this: "After eight months of waiting anxiety, the most devout and earnest wish of the people of Kalispell is consummated. The iron horse has at last snorted in the Garden of Eden of Montana. The locomotive pealed forth its welcome sound to the people of Kalispell." A silver spike was driven to hail the triumph amid a wildly cheering crowd, and the band played "Yankee Doodle." A parade, barbecue, and public ball were part of the festivities. And at last, the first passenger train steamed into Kalispell in summer 1892, complete with a dining car and sleeper, a combination smoker and day coach, and a baggage car.

Kalispell boomed throughout the final decade of the 19th century, with many residences and large brick buildings constructed.

Unfortunately, though, its status as the Great Northern division headquarters lasted only about a dozen years. As mentioned in the section on Whitefish's history, the Great Northern's Hill in 1904 relocated the division point north to Whitefish, due to the difficulty of the route west of Kalispell over the Salish Mountains. It was a sad day in town when the last train wailed a farewell salute to Kalispell. The railway did keep the branch-line train running between Kalispell and Columbia Falls; it was known as the "Gallopin' Goose." But in 1950 the railroad discontinued that train, as well, ending Kalispell's passenger train service.

Flathead County had been created out of part of Missoula County in 1893, and Kalispell was voted county seat over

Columbia Falls the following year. This factor helped Kalispell remain stable after the railroad pulled out. All county government business was conducted from here. By 1903, a permanent, 3-story brick courthouse had been completed; it still is used today. (US 93 splits around it on South Main Street.) The town claimed a solid foundation—it had incorporated in 1892, and the citizens had elected city officials. Water and electric light utilities were already there, as were a post office and fire department. By 1904, a new city hall was operating and additional progress had produced a library, hospital, and numerous churches.

On the commercial front, Kalispell counted at least three national banks, stores representing almost every trade—from meat markets to furniture, and from hardware to photographers—and several posh hotels, including The West and the Grand Central. The fertile farmlands and timber stands surrounding Kalispell also provided the town with solid anchors.

The earliest buildings were mostly one-story structures built of wood, but soon the building codes became stricter. "Because of fire codes, commercial-district buildings were later built of brick or other fireproof material," Kathryn McKay wrote in her book *Looking Back: A Pictorial History of the Flathead Valley, Montana*. "These brick buildings typically had corbeling or terra cotta decorations. Some earlier buildings had native rock pilasters, sills, and lintels. Cloth awnings shaded the shop windows, and most stores had recessed entries and glass block or leaded glass transoms." Several Kalispell-area brickyards furnished "common" brick to be used locally.

Many of the historic downtown buildings are still utilized today. Among the noteworthy is the Kalispell Hotel on Main Street, now the Kalispell Grand Hotel, built in 1911 to serve upscale travelers. In the early days, rooms cost $2 per night. After falling on hard times in the middle and later parts of the 20th century and becoming more or less a flophouse, the gracious landmark was finally remodeled, including the lobby, and it reopened in 1991.

Just across the street stands the McIntosh Opera House, erected in the late 1890s. Its expansive upper floor served as a stage for many kinds of entertainment—plays, recitals, music programs, dances, lodge meetings, wrestling matches, and more. The presentation of "Uncle Tom's Cabin" drew one of the biggest-ever audiences—1,132 people, according to one report. In 1905 it was pressed into service as a gymnasium, and spectators could watch basketball games on the top floor. Although the dance-hall-cum-basketball-court lies vacant today, the main floor contains a busy western store and soda fountain, while an antiques mall sprawls in the basement.

Another prominent old building housed the Kalispell Mercantile. The mercantile originated in 1888 in Demersville as part of the Missoula Mercantile, and was first operated out of a tent. The fine department store was reportedly known for its quality, variety, customer service, and staff product knowledge. In 1892 it was moved from Demersville to Kalispell, with its final location at First Avenue East and Second Street. Originally, the store was just 50 feet by 80 feet, but it eventually grew to eight times that size. Known as northwest Montana's largest store, the Missoula Mercantile offered groceries, hardware and paint, appliances, china, farm tools, plumbing, sporting goods, mill supplies, and even firewood. Eventually the name was changed to the Kalispell Mercantile, and over the decades many Kalispell residents vied for a chance to work at the popular store, which was forced by modern competition to close its doors in 1980. Various businesses have occupied the KM Building since. Recently the historic structure has been undergoing a restoration aimed at returning it to its turn-of-the-20th-century grandeur. Original stained-glass windows have been reinstalled as part of the exterior face-lift, while interior restoration provides retail and business space. On the first-floor arcade, early black-and-white photos are a link to the past. If you're in the mood for coffee, stop by Mel's Coffee Stand for a great cup of coffee and browse through Kalispell's early days.

Late in the 1990s, two other treasured downtown buildings were renovated. The old Central School, opened in 1895, was thoroughly overhauled, with pains taken to match original materials and retain the building's integrity. The major renovation was made possible by $2.5 million in funds from the city of Kalispell and the leadership of the Northwest Montana Historical Society. It served as the junior high school from 1929 to 1969, when the Flathead Valley Community College took over the building. The college moved to a new campus in 1990, and Central School's doors closed. In 1999, heralding in a new century, the building reopened as the Northwest Montana Heritage, Education, and Cultural Center. Visitors are encouraged to stop by for a glimpse of the valley's history.

Nearby, at 15 Depot Park, off Main Street, stands the original Great Northern Railway Depot. Respect for the newly refurbished depot's past was maintained during the remodel, while Montana-style casualness and comfort were incorporated.

These and other charming buildings can be seen as you make the Main Street District walking tour. A second walking tour on the east side routes visitors by beautiful old residences, many of them built between 1900 and 1920. Pick up a historical walking tour brochure at the chamber of commerce.

Not to be missed is the Conrad Mansion, built by Charles E. Conrad (see the Attractions chapter). As previously mentioned, James Hill had asked Conrad to take charge of the Great Northern's Kalispell Townsite Company, and Conrad is now widely considered to be the founding father of Kalispell. A prominent businessman, Charles, with his brother William, established one of the town's first banks, the Conrad National Bank. Charles purchased 72 acres overlooking the east side of the valley, where he built the Conrad Mansion. Designed in the early Norman style, the shingle-clad mansion contains 23 main rooms and 8 fireplaces. The opulent home belonged to the Conrad family until 1975, when it was given to the city. The house has been restored, and turn-of-the-20th-century antiques fill the rooms. Summer guided tours of the mansion are available.

Kalispell remains the economic hub of the Flathead Valley. The tourism trade continues to bring the town a steady flow of visitors and their dollars, while the traditional industries of lumber and agriculture are still going strong. Beginning sometime in the 1980s, most would say, out-of-state retirees "discovered" the valley, and this continuing influx of people has become a viable industry.

The Flathead experienced a building boom during the 1990s, but, as in so many places today, the job market is experiencing a low ebb.

Still, although job prospects are somewhat slim, people stay in the Flathead for the reasons they hold dear: beautiful scenery and fresh air, recreational opportunities, ties to family and friends, and not too much noise or overcrowding. Living in the Flathead Valley remains a treasured lifestyle, and nearby Glacier National Park is an enduring reason for visitors to flock in.

GLACIER NATIONAL PARK

Here, serrated ridges and horn-shaped peaks reign over a jumble of turquoise lakes, waterfalls, cascades, river valleys, hanging gardens, and alpine meadows. Born of geologic and glacial violence, this random landscape couldn't be more perfect had it been designed and executed by Michelangelo. Like the ocean, its sheer scope has a way of putting humanity in its place.

—GEORGE BIRD GRINNELL,
Grinnell's Glacier: George Bird Grinnell and Glacier National Park

Slow-moving "rivers" of ice carved the craggy pinnacles of Glacier National Park's mountains during a succession of ice ages occurring over the past 2 to 3 million years. About 10,000 years ago, during the most recent period of massive glaciation, an enormous ice cap several thousand feet thick and miles long covered Glacier's high country. As it melted, it heaved down the canyons, sculpting new shapes and gouging out glacial lakes. The melted remains of the last ice age have long since shriveled up. Today's much smaller, remnant glaciers formed long after the last ice age ended. They are puny compared to the ice mantle that smothered the park eons ago. And they

are shrinking—they're substantially smaller than when first mapped in the early 1900s. But Glacier Park remains an excellent outdoor classroom for studying the handiwork of glaciers.

Glacier National Park was first home to Native Americans, at least for parts of the year. The fierce Blackfeet Indians of the northern plains gained dominion over the other tribes after the 1750s. (The name Blackfeet came from an early group that, after walking through a burned-over prairie, encountered another tribe, who called them Blackfeet, according to C. W. Buchholtz in his history of Glacier Park, Man in Glacier. The name also may have resulted from the black color of the soles of their moccasins.) The aggressive Piegan branch of the Blackfeet tribe protected its bison-hunting grounds, located on the east side of the northern Rocky Mountains, against other intruding tribes, including the Kootenai, Flathead, and Kalispel Indians, all of whom lived on the west side of the Continental Divide. These Indians would cross through the mountain passes annually to hunt buffalo on the eastern plains. The much-feared Blackfeet would retaliate by crossing the mountains and raiding the others' camps, further establishing their supremacy.

It was mostly the Piegan that regularly used the trails of Glacier Park. The Blackfeet were a very spiritual people. They, and members of other tribes, revered these northern mountains, believing them to be home to the spirits. Many visited the high country to conduct vision quests. In Glacier's northeast corner looms Chief Mountain, a symbol of the powerful medicine that Indians still believe stirs in these mystical mountains.

Breaking the backbone of these denizens of the northern plains was one unlikely factor: fashion. Plentiful in nearby mountain streams, the beaver attracted white trappers because it brought them top dollar for top hats. White traders and trappers had established a permanent trading relationship with the Blackfeet by the 1780s, and the white man's foothold spelled the decline of the tribe. Captain Meriwether Lewis explored the headwaters of the Marias River on the return trip of the Lewis and Clark Expedition in 1806. His party viewed the front range of Glacier Park's mountains, but for various reasons did not explore further. On returning to St. Louis, the expedition stimulated great interest in the upper Missouri River and the northern Rocky Mountains, especially among the fur trade.

In 1810, Finian MacDonald, a Scotsman, and two other traders became the first white men known to enter the lands encompassing present-day Glacier Park, according to Buchholtz. Attacked by Blackfeet at Marias Pass, the party survived, but this episode convinced other fur traders to choose safer routes across the Rockies. Yet by the 1850s, more white men had ventured in. Their missions included government-sponsored surveys to mark the international boundary, bringing Christianity to the Indians, and identifying a potential transcontinental railroad route.

Major gold strikes in Montana in 1862 brought prospectors scouring Glacier's mountainsides in search of mineral wealth. And another rush to stake mining claims occurred soon after the Blackfeet sold the east side of the future national park to the federal government. Gold, copper, quartz—even oil and coal—attracted those hoping for a lucky strike. Despite the initial promise, nothing was discovered in sufficient quantities, and soon after the turn of the 20th century mining and drilling interest waned greatly.

The Blackfeet had managed to dominate the area until the 1870s. By then, a combination of factors—the US Army, smallpox epidemics, illegal hooch proffered by whiskey traders, the decimation of the great bison herds, and the general surge of white men into their territory—conspired to break the power of the tribe. Two proponents of the Blackfeet intervened in their welfare: James Willard Schultz, an American who lived among the Blackfeet, and George Bird Grinnell, the prominent editor of *Forest and Stream* magazine. After Schultz called the plight of the Blackfeet to Grinnell's attention, the latter visited the reservation in 1885, and then used his political clout to help increase government-subsidized food and supplies for the Indians.

Anticipating a flood of American homesteaders and hoping to attain peace among local Indian tribes, Isaac Stevens, governor of the Territory of Washington (which included the Flathead Valley and Glacier Park), talked the Kootenai, Flathead, and Kalispel Indians of the park's west side into settling on a reservation surrounding the southern half of Flathead Lake. Glacier's west side then became federally owned public lands.

In 1895 the Blackfeet sold the Ceded Strip—all of what is now Glacier Park east of the Continental Divide—to the federal government, though the terms of this transaction are contested to this day. The remaining Blackfeet land—today's Blackfeet Reservation—borders the east boundary of the park. Names of Indian legends and chiefs were given to many landscape features in the park by Schultz and Grinnell.

PROTECTION FOR A PRISTINE WILDERNESS

When George Bird Grinnell visited the starving Blackfeet, he was introduced to the St. Mary Lakes region. With James Schultz and an Indian as guides, he hunted and explored. Excited about the area, the editor returned east and wrote a number of essays about his experiences in *Forest and Stream* magazine. Grinnell returned to the Glacier country many times. His articles extolled the exceptional scenery and wild-game hunting out West, which appealed to wealthy hunters, many of whom visited the region in turn.

Despite their use of the resource, Grinnell, and a handful of other proponents, came to believe that this special place should be protected. By 1891, a national conservation movement prompted the US Congress to allow establishment of national forest "reserves" (later called national forests).

Present-day Glacier Park was first protected as a forest reserve. But Grinnell's intent was to see the area established as a national park, and he lobbied to that end for a decade. He was the most influential advocate in the founding of the park. Promoting his cause in a 1901 article in *Century* magazine, he bestowed the name "The Crown of the Continent" on the magnificent wilderness. His cause was furthered by the support of Great Northern Railway officials, who saw tourism in the park as a way to promote use of their transcontinental train service.

By 1910 the period of heavy exploitation of the park's natural resources had pretty much ended. That year President Taft signed the bill to create Glacier National Park, and 1,600 square miles of wilderness were preserved (today, that number has grown to more than 1 million acres protected within park boundaries). Glacier's first superintendent was Maj. William R. Logan. Waterton Lakes Forest Park, to the north of Glacier in Alberta, Canada, already had been established in 1895.

The act that created Glacier Park called for "preserving the park in a state of nature." But attempting to please everyone, the US Congress also mandated that the park provide a "pleasure ground for the benefit and enjoyment of the people." Indeed, early emphasis was mostly on the value of recreational opportunities, and the act also permitted mining, some private land ownership, railroad routes, and harvesting dead and downed timber inside the park.

THE GREAT LODGES

The Great Northern already carried passengers through the Glacier area before it was designated a national park. To serve railroad travelers, the first private accommodations were constructed at the foot of Lake McDonald. Built by Milo Apgar and Charlie Howe, these tourist cabins were the beginnings of the village of Apgar. Escorted tours were provided of the sparkling lake, marking the onset of pioneer tourism in the park.

In 1895 George Snyder built a 2-story hotel at the present site of Lake McDonald Lodge. Later, John and Olive Lewis acquired the property. (Legend has it John won it in a poker game.) The Lewises moved the first structure and commissioned a lodge to be built on the original site, which was to be in keeping with the grand style of the other lodges being built in the park, only on a smaller scale. The Swiss-style architecture was similar to Great Northern's lodges, which were constructed of stone and log. Opened in 1914 as the only private hotel in the park, the Lewis Glacier Hotel operated for several decades before being purchased by the

National Park Service and converted into the Lake McDonald Lodge.

Soon after the park was established, the Great Northern embarked on a flurry of building construction. Setting out to create a playground for the rich, Louis Hill, son of railroad tycoon James J. Hill, directed the building of several huge, rustic lodges within the park to attract tourists. A network of these lodges, along with eight backcountry chalets, were spaced a convenient day's horseback ride apart. (Horses and boats were the main modes of seeing the park's splendors at the time.)

The Great Northern launched an aggressive advertising campaign, featuring colorful railroad timetables depicting scenes of Glacier National Park. "See America First" became the slogan. First-class scenery required first-class accommodations, Louis Hill believed, and the great lodges of the park spared no luxury. In this way the Great Northern became Glacier Park's first concessionaire, managing and operating the concessions by way of a subsidiary, the Glacier Park Hotel Company.

First of the extraordinary hotels, the Glacier Park Lodge was erected in East Glacier in 1913. Almost immediately it proved inadequate to house the great number of visitors that arrived. (An annex soon doubled the original size.) The lodge served as the eastern gateway to the park for arriving Great Northern passenger trains. It was modeled after the Forestry Building constructed for the 1905 Portland, Oregon, Lewis and Clark Exposition. Sixty massive trees were used in construction of the mammoth lodge, trees the Great Northern hauled in from Washington and Oregon—only one or two per flatcar, since each weighed about 15 tons. Measuring 36 to 42 inches in diameter,

bark-covered Douglas firs gave structural support in the lobby, while cedar trees were incorporated into exterior verandas.

Equally as impressive was the Many Glacier Hotel, the park's largest chalet, built to serve as a rustic showplace amid breathtaking surroundings, at the edge of a crystalline lake rimmed by chiseled peaks. Hill also built the Prince of Wales Hotel in Waterton, up Canada way.

Two of the park's original eight backcountry chalets remained in operation through 1992, but then were closed by the National Park Service because of inadequate water and sewage disposal systems. However, Granite Park Chalet (built in 1914–15) and Sperry Chalet (built in 1913) were subsequently restored and upgraded and are again open for visitor use. A ninth chalet is located outside the park's west entrance; known as Belton Chalet, it too has been renovated recently, and is under private ownership. The main chalet, with a bar and restaurant, and the upper lodge with 25 rooms, are open May through Oct for guests. Two guest cabins (each with microwave and refrigerator) are available through the winter months.

The lodges and chalets enjoyed phenomenal popularity for several decades. When the automobile appeared on the scene, however, it precipitated long-term changes. Travel through this splendid wilderness was no longer the exclusive domain of the rich, but could be enjoyed by everyday people. Motoring became the popular way to see Glacier Park, and utilization of the backcountry chalets, accessible only by horseback or foot, declined. In response to a growing need, the Park Service opened public campgrounds, and business at the chalets and main lodges dropped off even more.

At the same time, railroad traffic decreased. All of this added up to capital losses for the Great Northern. Later, World War II would sharply curtail visitation to Glacier, and many of the park's facilities would be shut down. All but the two previously mentioned backcountry chalets deteriorated badly and never reopened.

GOING-TO-THE-SUN ROAD

A ribbon of pavement 52 miles long connecting the east and west sides of Glacier Park, Going-to-the-Sun Road has over the course of almost 80 years transported millions of adventurous travelers up Logan Pass, over the Continental Divide—the backbone of the Rocky Mountains—and down the other side. Viewed from a distance, the road appears to be an eyebrow of a trail chiseled out of limestone, hugging the mountainside.

In 1933 when Going-to-the-Sun Road opened, park visitation jumped a whopping 44 percent—mostly from automobile touring. Today, an average of more than 2 million visitors travel through Glacier National Park annually. The Park Service determined some time ago that the spectacular and venerable road needed to be reconstructed if it were to continue to accommodate the volume of traffic it sees every summer. Park officials report that continuing summer roadwork will focus for the next several years on structural repairs to historic stone retaining walls and guard walls in the high-alpine area between the west and east tunnels. The road will not close, and much of the work will be done at night. But you may experience delays all the same, park officials caution.

THE PARK TODAY

In 1932 Glacier National Park and Waterton Lakes National Park in Canada were named the world's first International Peace Park. Only a strip cut through dense timber delineates the international boundary line, and managers from both parks maintain a strong working relationship and spirit of cooperation.

During the 1960s, wilderness resource conservation gained renewed public awareness and favor. The Wilderness Act of 1964 provided for large natural areas of Glacier and other parks to be designated "wilderness," prohibiting both mechanical intrusions and additional development. Furthermore, because of its unique natural and cultural qualities, Glacier Park was designated a World Biosphere Reserve in 1976.

By the late 1990s, the national Leave No Trace program had gained strong momentum among many government agencies. Implemented in Glacier Park, the program promotes responsible outdoor-use ethics to the public to help us all preserve the pristine landscape of Glacier National Park. And now, as in the other national parks, you will encounter newly launched green efforts by the Park Service and park concessionaires aimed at increasing sustainability and decreasing carbon footprints.

And as always, park administrators continue to struggle with achieving a balance between protecting the resource and encouraging public use of it.

GLACIER NATIONAL PARK

S cenery is a hollow enjoyment if the tourist starts out after an indigestible breakfast and a fitful sleep on an impossible bed."

So complained one national park visitor to Secretary of the Interior Franklin Lane in 1914. Lane's reply? "If you don't like the way the national parks are being run, come on down to Washington and run them yourself."

Lane recognized his correspondent's name: Stephen T. Mather, philanthropist, mountain climber, and self-made millionaire. What Lane didn't know was that, at age 47, Mather was restless and ready for something new—and would eventually become the first director of the National Park Service in 1916. It was Mather's vision of what the parks should be that set the tone for the early years of the new agency.

OVERVIEW

In Glacier National Park (established in 1910) the work of development—opening up this remote part of the West to vacationing Easterners—was primarily accomplished by the Great Northern Railway. While Mather was still climbing mountains, rambling with the likes of John Muir, and making his own fortune, James J. Hill and his son Louis were the "empire builders" of the great northern plains. Once John F. Stevens located Marias Pass—the lowest route through the Rocky Mountains in the United States, and now also the US 2 corridor—in 1889, it took only 3 years for the Great Northern to complete its rail line from Chicago to Seattle, opening up vast territories for settlement. Louis Hill, in particular, had a vision: He wanted people to ride his train, and he was ready to build destinations for them. His slogan was "See America First," and he aimed it at wealthy Easterners who otherwise might vacation in Europe. He billed the Rockies as the "Alps of America," and developed the

Swiss-chalet-style design for his enormous mountain hotels. Waitresses wore dirndls and bellhops wore lederhosen. Visitors could spend their time luxuriating in the hotels, or head out on horseback to rough it—in groups of 50 or more. The Great Northern built trails and horse camps and the system of backcountry chalets. Mary Roberts Rinehart, a well-known novelist, gave the park further publicity in her account *Through Glacier Park* in 1915, with vivid descriptions of the "call of the mountains." This all dovetailed perfectly with Stephen Mather's view of how the western parks needed to be developed in order for visitors to enjoy them.

Most of the historic lodges and chalets that visitors still enjoy today were built between 1910 and 1920: Glacier Park Lodge, Many Glacier Hotel, Granite Park and Sperry Chalets, as well as the Prince of Wales Hotel in Canada (1927) and the privately built Lake McDonald Lodge on the west side of Glacier National Park. But the Great Depression and

World War II brought many changes. The Many Glacier Chalets (but not the hotel) burned in the Heaven's Peak Fire of 1936. The Gunsight Chalet was destroyed in an avalanche. Wooden structures—which included many of the original backcountry chalets, such as St. Mary, Going-to-the-Sun, and Cut Bank chalets—suffered neglect and were soon beyond repair. They never reopened after the war, and were razed in the late 1940s.

i In the summer of 2007, Glacier National Park launched a free shuttle service that takes visitors up and down Going-to-the-Sun Road, so leave the driving to them! The shuttles, which begin daily at 7 a.m. and run until 7 p.m. from July through early Sept, run frequently and make stops all along the road. They are convenient to use for hikes that start in one place and end at another, such as the Highline-Loop route. A new transit center is found in Apgar, 2 miles inside the park's west entrance. On the east side, the terminus is St. Mary Visitor Center. Schedules are available at visitor centers and ranger stations throughout the park.

Other things changed, too. After World War II, the family car became common, and, as previously mentioned, the majority of visitors began driving to Montana rather than taking the train. They hadn't the money of those who had patronized the *Empire Builder* passenger train, and they found the big hotels too expensive. Gradually, the park began to realize it had a new visitor—the middle-income family, arriving by car. And so the motor inns were built: first Swiftcurrent, built before the war but later expanded; then

Roes Creek Inn, now called Rising Sun Motor Inn; and, finally, the Village Inn at Apgar. In conjunction with the campgrounds, they add to a spectrum of accommodations that enables just about anyone to get a good night's sleep and a decent breakfast—and so also get to enjoy the unparalleled scenery and wildlife of the park.

There are as many ways to experience Glacier National Park as there are people who visit it. Be sure to stop at a visitor center or ranger station for information and a schedule of naturalist-guided activities. But whether you choose to drive Going-to-the-Sun Road in 2 hours or backpack for 2 weeks; whether you come to watch birds, count goats, or take a swim in an excruciatingly cold lake, do leave your worries behind. Let the place work its magic on you.

ACCOMMODATIONS

Price Code

Lodging code per night for two people:

$................. **Less than $85**
$$ .... **$85 to $115**
$$$ .... **$115 to $150**
$$$$ .... **More than $150**

The lodging at Glacier National Park encompasses a broad array of options: from historic lodges, to one-room cabins with a bath down the way, to high-mountain hostels. The recent history of what is now the park—the last 100 or so years—is reflected in its structures. You may, for instance, want to check out the Two Medicine Campstore building, knowing that it is the last standing of the Two Medicine Chalets, built about the same time as the extant Granite Park and Sperry chalets. You may want to trace the history of the Great Northern Railway by way of the lodges it built—until recently, Many

Glacier Hotel was the largest hotel in Montana. Or perhaps the subalpine landscape will draw you to the Granite Park Chalet, providing the "best sunset in the park" since before World War I.

i A word of warning: No food or drink is available along Going-to-the-Sun Road between Lake McDonald Lodge on the west side and Rising Sun Campground on the east side. The only pay phone in that distance is at Avalanche Campground. Logan Pass Visitor Center has wonderful exhibits, information, and book sales, but offers only public restrooms and a drinking fountain as services.

Overall, a wide scale of variously priced lodging can be found within the park. Make your reservations early—especially for the peak season of July and Aug, when most park facilities will be completely booked. That said, if you're in the area but don't have a reservation, it's still worth a phone call to check on space—cancellations do occur, and you may be able to find yourself a room with a view on very short notice. With the exceptions of Apgar Village Lodge, Granite Park Chalet, and Sperry Chalet, all lodging within Glacier National Park's boundaries is operated by Glacier Park, Inc. (GPI), a concession under contract with the National Park Service.

Most facilities have an information desk where a staff member will be happy to help you with schedules for naturalist-guided activities, bus tours, boat tours and small-boat rentals, the Going-to-the-Sun Road shuttle, the Many Glacier hikers' shuttle, and horseback trips. Each of the large hotels has a gift shop that sells film, postage stamps, huckleberry treats, books and maps, hiking snacks, outdoor clothing, and a variety of souvenirs. Campstores are located at Swiftcurrent Motor Inn, Rising Sun Motor Inn, and the Lake McDonald Lodge complex, and they carry a similar selection with the addition of limited food supplies, some camping equipment, and bundled firewood. The descriptions that follow highlight the unique character and attributes of each location.

Glacier Park Lodge, Lake McDonald Lodge, and Many Glacier Hotel all have ATMs; all GPI locations have pay phones. Wheelchair-accessible rooms are available at Glacier Park Lodge, Lake McDonald Lodge, the Village Inn, Swiftcurrent Motor Inn, Many Glacier Hotel, and Rising Sun Motor Inn. Be aware that the historic lodges do not have elevators servicing their upper floors; a bell-hop will carry your luggage to your room, but if climbing stairs is a health concern or limiting factor, be sure to mention this when you make your reservation.

Hotels & Motels

APGAR VILLAGE LODGE $$
Apgar Village, P.O. Box 410, West Glacier 59936
(406) 888-5484
www.westglacier.com
Located among old-growth cedar trees at the foot of Lake McDonald, Apgar Village Lodge offers a longer season than most accommodations inside the park boundaries (the other exception being the Lake McDonald Lodge and Cabins). It opens in late May, giving visitors an opportunity to see Glacier National Park in spring. Although the upper elevations of the park will still be buried in snow and inaccessible to all but backcountry skiers, at Lake McDonald you'll be delighted to see the bright green of new

Close-up

Geology of Glacier National Park

Glacier National Park is a geology-lover's dreamscape: Its rocks and formations offer vivid clues to the processes that fashioned them. The park's geology could be the basis for a study of many years (and no doubt has been), but here we'll offer a four-stage thumbnail, 101 class for starters:

Stage 1: Sedimentation. Glacier National Park's surface is mostly sedimentary rock, laid down, geologists say, approximately 2 billion years ago as silts and sands drifted to the bottom of the shallow ocean known as the Great Belt Sea. Over time, these muds began to compress under their own accumulating weight. We see the rocks today in the brightly colored strata of the park: toward the bottom, the greenish-gray Apikuni mudstone or argillite; next, the reddish Grinnell mudstone (formed when the presence of larger quantities of oxygen caused iron in the mudstone to oxidize); and, finally, the layers of more resistant limestone that make up most of the peaks. Sometime later, magma from the earth's core expanded up through a weak layer in the sediments and spread out to form the black stripe seen running through some mountains, called the diorite sill (also known as the Purcell sill). This intrusion of igneous rock is the hardest, yet most brittle rock in the park. In a few places it bubbled through the limestone layers and surfaced, still under water, to form pillow basalts (such as those found at **Granite Park**).

Stage 2: Faulting and uplift. A mere 150 million years ago, major changes began again. Large plates under the earth's crust began to shift, with the North American plate and the oceanic plate just to its west starting to move toward one another. (Movement of plates is ongoing—consider the active San Andreas Fault in California, or the fact that the Himalayas are being pushed higher as the plate beneath the Indian subcontinent continues to ram into the Asian plate.) Eventually, the pressure of the oceanic plate began to elevate the North American plate. Forces of compression became so great that a fold began to develop in the rock strata west of this area. Over tens of millions of years, pressure caused a huge slab of rock—at least 15,000 feet thick—to finally buckle, break, and slide eastward as a unit some 50 to 100 miles. These are the rocks of the **Lewis Overthrust Fault** that make up Glacier National Park today. Evidence of faulting can be seen throughout the park in both small ways—bent and angled rock strata—and on a large scale: at **Marias Pass**, for example, you can see where the rocks of the fault layer rode up and over the lower layers. And anywhere along the eastern front you'll be impressed by how suddenly the mountains end and the prairie begins. That line of demarcation is at the limit of where the faulting process pushed the upper layer of rocks.

Stage 3: Glaciation. At this point we had a huge slab of layered rock shoved out onto the plains, marked only by some gentle, relatively shallow drainages. Enter the

leaves coming out all along the shore. A walk in the woods will bring you the special pleasure of early season wildflowers: trillium, glacier lilies, or even lady's slipper orchids.

Like the GPI lodgings, Apgar Village Lodge is very busy during the summer months, but it stays open into and through Sept, when the crowds are thinner and the days

ice ages! About 2 million years ago, the most recent period of glaciation began. The entire planet became just a touch colder . . . more snow fell in the winter, and less melted in the summer. In the northern climes, snow began to accumulate. As the snow grew deeper and deeper, its nature began to change: Under the pressure of its own weight, crystals in the bottom of the snowpack began to deform and to turn into ice; further pressure then changed their molecular structure so that they became almost plastic. Where the ice had formed on a slope, gravity began to pull it downhill. The moving glaciers scoured away at the little valleys beneath them, over time turning them into the deep, U-shaped valleys we see today. Other glacial features include hanging valleys, arêtes, horns, passes, and cirques. These massive glaciers had all melted away by about 10,000 years ago.

Stage 4: The Little Ice Age, the present, and the future. The glaciers you see in the park today are leftovers of the Little Ice Age. Geologists debate about exactly when this period started, but they tend to agree that the glaciers reached their greatest extent probably in the 18th century. They are receding very quickly, so now is the time to see them! Global climate change has been evidenced from data collected at these glaciers, and it is certainly a factor in their shrinkage. Blackfoot-Jackson, Grinnell, and Sperry are the largest of the glaciers today. Other elements affecting modern park geology include the small but continual effects of wind and rain, and freezing and thawing—all processes that tend to smooth out the rugged mountains over time. Slowly, the peaks wear down and the valleys are filled with sediment. Occasionally, sudden events dramatically change the landscape, such as avalanches and rock slides. In recent years, for instance, an earthquake centered on the Blackfeet Reservation brought down a huge rock slide on Chief Mountain. Change is ongoing.

The **Continental Divide** runs through Glacier National Park—the line separating watersheds flowing to the east from those flowing to the west. Look for **Triple Divide Peak** on your map—it's southwest of St. Mary at the end of the Cut Bank Creek drainage. This mountain marks the meeting place of the Continental Divide and the **Hudson Bay Divide,** separating the park's waters into three: those that flow north and east to Hudson Bay and the Arctic Ocean; those flowing south and east into the Missouri, the Mississippi, and eventually the Gulf of Mexico; and those flowing west, via the Flathead and Columbia rivers to the Pacific Ocean. The high Continental Divide is also a significant factor in the weather: It stops moisture moving eastward from the Pacific with its wall of rock, so that more precipitation falls on the west side. The east side is drier and more subject to strong winds rushing off the divide. The effects of these climatic differences are keenly visible in the park landscape—the west side supports lush forests, including a bit of true rain forest, while the east side is typified by open meadows and wind-whipped aspen groves.

cooler and crisper. You'll enjoy the contrast of the Western larch trees, whose needles turn golden all along the slopes above Lake McDonald, with the deep blue of the sky and the shocking white of newly fallen snow frosting the high peaks.

Apgar Village itself includes the west-side visitor center, a backcountry permit office, a number of shops, a restaurant and other snack shops, and the amphitheater for evening programs at the nearby campground (note that some of these have shorter operating seasons than Apgar Village Lodge). A paved bike trail runs along Lower McDonald Creek back toward West Glacier, providing one of the few opportunities in Glacier National Park for biking off the roadways.

Apgar Village Lodge includes 48 rustic cabin and motel units, all with private baths. Some have views of Lake McDonald or Lower McDonald Creek, but all are within footsteps of spectacular mountain vistas. Most cabins have a kitchen, and several barbecues and picnic tables are available to guests. Regular season rates range from motel rooms for $105 per night for 2 people to a cabin that will accommodate 10 for $275 per night. Rates are discounted in spring and fall; call for availability during these times. You can also write to Apgar Village Lodge, c/o West Glacier Mercantile, at the address above for further information.

✳GLACIER PARK LODGE $$$–$$$$
East Glacier, P.O. Box 2025, Columbia Falls 59912
(406) 892-2525
www.glacierparkinc.com
The first of the lodges to be built by the Great Northern Railway, Glacier Park Lodge continues to serve as the eastern gateway to Glacier National Park. Located not far outside the borders of the park, high peaks rise behind the lodge, creating an unforgettable backdrop. Lovely, well-tended flower gardens line the way as you approach the historic building. Walking through the lodge doors, you'll be startled to see the huge logs that support the lobby ceiling: immense

Douglas firs, still bark-covered, imported from the Pacific Northwest to grace this hall. The neighboring Blackfeet Indians referred to the building as the "Big Tree Lodge." They seem to have a way of getting to the point.

In contrast with its historic past, Glacier Park Lodge also offers modern amenities in addition to its 161 rooms. The hotel features a heated swimming pool, a 9-hole golf course, a gift shop, the **Empire Bar,** the **Empire Cafe Espresso Stand,** the **Remedies Day Spa,** and the **Great Northern Dining Room** (see Restaurants). Those working the information desk will be happy to set you up with a bus tour or hayride.

Additionally, East Glacier is home to many small businesses, including shops and restaurants (see the Blackfeet Reservation chapter); you'll enjoy walking about the little town located where the mountains meet the prairie. And it's just a 12-mile drive to Browning, where you can visit the Museum of the Plains Indian (see the Attractions chapter). You might also want to take in a hike. The Two Medicine subdistrict of Glacier National Park is a short drive away to the northwest; its web of trails lead to such destinations as Dawson Pass, Cobalt Lake, Twin Falls, and Old Man Lake. Glacier Park Boat Company (406-257-2426) also offers boat tours and rental boats on Two Medicine Lake. The Lubec and Autumn Creek Trails, beginning along US 2 west of East Glacier, will lead you along the aspen-covered foothills. Be sure to check first with a ranger station for current trail conditions.

Glacier Park Lodge has a longer season than some other GPI facilities, generally opening Memorial Day weekend and closing for the winter in late Sept. Rooms range in price from $140 to $360 per night for 2 people.

i Glacier National Park has several sources of information readily available. At its website, www.nps.gov /glac/index.htm, you'll find answers to practically any question you can think of. Printed publications include the *Waterton-Glacier Guide,* a summer vacation planner, and a backcountry guide, as well as more specific brochures on concession operations, lodging, and so on. For printed materials, write Superintendent, Glacier National Park, P.O. Box 128, West Glacier, MT 59936, or phone (406) 888-7800. Most available publications can now be downloaded from the web, as well.

LAKE MCDONALD LODGE $$$–$$$$
Going-to-the-Sun Road, west side
P.O. Box 2025, Columbia Falls 59912
(406) 892-2525
www.glacierparkinc.com

Originally built as the Lewis Glacier Hotel by John Lewis in 1914, the Lake McDonald Lodge rests on the southeast shore of Lake McDonald, 12 miles from the West Glacier park entrance. You can take a comfy seat on the veranda and enjoy views across the water, or grab a chair in the lobby, surrounded by Lewis's hunting trophies. Rural legend has it that Charlie Russell, "America's Cowboy Artist," drew the pictographs on the massive stone fireplace. In the early years, guests arrived by water, and the lodge's original facade faced the lake. But now, of course, virtually all visitors arrive by car or bus, and in more recent years what was once the "back" of the lodge has been modified to present a proper welcome. As at the other historic hotels, you'll find Lake McDonald Lodge brilliant with hanging flower baskets and gardens in the summertime.

Although the lodge itself has a pleasantly relaxed atmosphere, you'll find plenty of sources of exertion not far away. The Glacier Park Boat Company's DeSmet, the flagship of its fleet of historic wooden boats, docks in front of the lodge; cruises are available at several times each day. The company also rents rowboats and 8-horsepower motorboats. Just across the Going-to-the-Sun Road are the corrals of Swan Mountain Outfitters, the park horse concession, which offers rides of varying lengths to several destinations. If you prefer traveling under your own steam, you might pick up the trail that leads to Avalanche Creek and Lake, or try hiking up to Mount Brown Lookout from the Sperry trailhead—it's one of the steepest trails in the park, but the lookout rewards with an astonishing view of the entire Lake McDonald Valley and beyond. After dinner, you can join a Park Service naturalist at the auditorium for an evening talk.

Lake McDonald Lodge includes 100 guest rooms, with lodge, motel, and duplex-style cabin accommodations. The complex also includes a general store, **Lucke's Lounge,** and a gift shop, as well as **Russell's Fireside Dining Room** and **Jammer Joe's Grill and Pizzeria** (see Restaurants). It operates for a longer season than some park facilities, opening in late May and closing in late Sept. A small cottage room for 2 people begins at $125 per night; while motel, cabin, and lodge rooms for 2 range up to $180 per night.

✳MANY GLACIER HOTEL $$$–$$$$
Many Glacier Valley, P.O. Box 2025,
Columbia Falls 59912
(406) 892-2525
www.glacierparkinc.com

Many Glacier Hotel is located in the northeast quadrant of Glacier National Park, just east of the Continental Divide in the Swiftcurrent Valley. Built by Louis Hill and the Great Northern Railway in 1914–1915, it is the largest hotel in the park, with 214 guest rooms. Lofty peaks—including Mount Gould, probably the most-photographed mountain in the park—surround the hotel, and its balcony overlooking Swiftcurrent Lake offers one of the finest mountain views anywhere. From there you may have the chance to spot grizzly and black bears, mountain goats, bighorn sheep, moose, and deer—or perhaps a double rainbow arcing across the sky in the wake of a summer storm.

The Many Glacier Hotel offers indoor comforts as well. The lobby's large, freestanding fireplace is a warm, cozy place to curl up with a book. Each evening a Park Service naturalist presents a slide program—on topics such as history, geology, wildflowers, and wildlife—in the Lucerne Room, and live evening music is another regular source of entertainment.

In addition to the **Ptarmigan Dining Room** (see Restaurants), the Many Glacier Hotel houses **Heidi's Snack Shop & Espresso Stand** downstairs in the St. Moritz Room, which offers a variety of foods. And down the hall from the lobby is the **Swiss Lounge,** a fully stocked bar that features huckleberry daiquiris and Montana microbrews. If you arrive for dinner at the Ptarmigan Dining Room on a busy evening, the **Interlaken Lounge** makes a pleasant place to wait for your table. Take a moment to walk around; to inspect the paintings on the lobby walls, or to savor the magnificent views of Mount Wilbur across Swiftcurrent Lake.

Many Glacier Hotel's season runs from early June to mid-Sept. Accommodations range from value rooms to suites, and rates vary correspondingly, from $145 to $290 per night.

Note: In 2011, half of the hotel is slated for an extensive interior renovation. During the construction, approximately 107 of its 214 rooms will be closed. There will be construction noise in the northern half of the building during daytime hours on weekdays only. Dining is available in the Swiss Interlaken Lounges, while construction takes place in the closed Ptarmigan Dining Room. The main kitchen will remain open with a full dining menu and bar offered.

RISING SUN MOTOR INN $$–$$$
Going-to-the-Sun Road, east side
P.O. Box 2025, Columbia Falls 59912
(406) 892-2525
www.glacierparkinc.com

Rising Sun Motor Inn, located on Going-to-the-Sun Road 6 miles west of St. Mary, catches the morning light across the biggest lake in Glacier National Park. It's nestled at the edge of open forest, where it meets Two Dog Flats, a series of meadows that are part-time home to elk, deer, coyotes, and other critters. Just across Going-to-the-Sun Road is the St. Mary Lake at Rising Sun location for the Glacier Park Boat Company, so it takes only a moment to access one of their guided tours or join in on a sunset cruise. Logan Pass, the high point of Going-to-the-Sun Road, is just 12 miles away, and both the park shuttle and Red Bus Tours stop at Rising Sun. In the evening, Park Service naturalists present talks and slideshows for the public at the Rising Sun Campfire Circle.

Rising Sun Motor Inn has 72 rooms, split among several motel buildings and 3 dozen cottages. In addition, you'll find public showers, a campstore, and the **Two Dog Flats Grill** (see Restaurants). Open from mid-June through mid-Sept, its rooms are simple and relatively economical, with rates ranging from $125 to $140 per night for 2 people.

SWIFTCURRENT MOTOR INN $–$$
Many Glacier Valley, P.O. Box 2025, Columbia Falls 59912
(406) 892-2525
www.glacierparkinc.com

The Many Glacier Valley attracts day hikers like few places in the National Park System. Here, five major drainages—and the trails traversing them—come together on the valley floor. The trail to Ptarmigan Lake leads through the unique Ptarmigan Tunnel, constructed for use by both equestrians and hikers. It's 183 feet long, 6 feet wide, and 9 feet tall, with an arched ceiling. If you look from below up the Iceberg drainage toward the Iceberg Notch, and then follow the jagged Pinnacle Wall a little farther to the east, you'll see what's locally known as the B-7 Pillar. Tradition has it that the pillar was named for the Swiftcurrent cabin B-7, in which the first people to climb that knob of rock stayed while at Many Glacier. Swiftcurrent Motor Inn has long been the budget mainstay for many such visitors. It includes not only the Pinetop Motel (featuring 1-bedroom cottages with bath, and 1- and 2-bedroom cottages without bath), but also a campstore, laundry, public showers, and the **Italian Gardens Ristorante** (see Restaurants). And the lengthy Motor Inn porch serves as a gathering place—whether for refreshments after a long day of hiking or as a sheltered place to hang out on a rainy afternoon. Several guided hikes meet and depart from this central location, and every evening a

Park Service naturalist presents a talk at the nearby Campfire Circle.

In short, Swiftcurrent Motor Inn is a hip hub of activity. Rooms are simple and affordable, ranging in price from $70 per night for 2 people in a 1-bedroom cottage with no bath to $140 per night for a cottage with bath or a motel room. The season runs from early June to late Sept.

THE VILLAGE INN
AT APGAR $$$–$$$$
Apgar Village, P.O. Box 2025, Columbia Falls 59912
(406) 892-2525
www.glacierparkinc.com

Scientists say that summer in Glacier is warmer than it used to be. What better way to cool off than take a jump in the lake? With their origins in snow and ice, the park's deep lakes rarely tempt more than wading. But the foot of Lake McDonald, where the water is shallow and receives a lot of sun, is a place where you might even enjoy (well, tolerate, perhaps) a *swim*. The pebbly beach is perfect for skipping stones, spreading out a picnic, or just admiring the mountain vistas. Built in 1956, the Village Inn sits directly on the southwest shore of Lake McDonald at Apgar. Each of its 36 rooms offers a view of the lake and the mountains at the head of the valley. Several rooms have kitchenettes; both 1- and 2-bedroom units are available. Easy access to the lakeshore—literally just out your door—is a prime draw, and you'll also find other services nearby, such as small-boat rentals just a short walk away. Apgar Village includes the west-side visitor center, a backcountry permit office, a number of shops, a restaurant and other snack shops, and the amphitheater for evening programs at the nearby campground. A paved bike trail runs along Lower McDonald Creek back toward West Glacier, providing one of the park's few opportunities for biking off the roadways.

The Village Inn is open from late May until late Sept. Accommodations vary—1 bedroom, 1 bedroom with kitchen, 2 bedrooms, and living-room suite—and prices range from $140 to $215 per night for 2 people.

The Chalets

✳GRANITE PARK CHALET $$
Just below Swiftcurrent Pass on the Highline Trail
(888) 345-2649
www.graniteparkchalet.com

Both Granite Park and Sperry chalets offer backcountry experiences with a difference: in the case of Granite Park Chalet, a room with an incomparable view. Built by the Great Northern Railway in 1914, Granite Park sits atop a knoll just below Swiftcurrent Pass on the Continental Divide. The historic stone building, residing just above tree line, offers magnificent views to the north, south, and west. With just a little hiking, you can stand on the Continental Divide and look east into the Swiftcurrent Valley; with a good bit of steep hiking, you can look down on Grinnell Glacier from above. The Highline Trail, one of the most popular trails in Glacier National Park, runs from Logan Pass to Canada by way of Granite Park. All in all, it's a place of unique subalpine beauty that will give you a sense for the dramatic sweep of the mountains.

Granite Park operates as a hikers' shelter. You must provide your own flashlight, sleeping bag, and water (there's a creek nearby, and the chalet does have a water filter for guest use, but it's a good idea to bring your own filter). The dining room and porch both have stunning views of Heaven's Peak, across the McDonald Creek drainage. A full kitchen is available for meal preparation. Granite Park has 12 sleeping rooms with bunk beds, accommodating 2 to 6 people per room. If you'd like to save some weight on your hike in, the chalet has an optional linen/bedding service as well as packaged meals, snacks, and soft drinks for sale. (A prepared meal must be ordered in advance.)

Most people choose to hike to Granite Park along the relatively flat 7.4-mile Highline Trail from Logan Pass, though others come up the Loop Trail or over Swiftcurrent Pass from Many Glacier. Finding a parking place at Logan Pass or the Loop can be challenging; consider parking at lower elevation and taking the shuttle up.

Granite Park Chalet is open, conditions permitting, from late July until early Sept. Overnight rates are $85 for the first person, and $73 for each additional person in the same room, per night plus 7 percent Montana accommodations tax. Linens and bedding are available for $16 per person for the duration of the stay (arrangements for this service must be made at reservation time). Be sure to read the policy on deposits, refunds, and cancellations, and before hitting the trail, check on current trail conditions by stopping at a visitor center or ranger station.

SPERRY CHALET $$$$
Just below Lincoln Peak on the Sperry Trail
(888) 345-2649
www.sperrychalet.com

Sperry Chalet, built by the Great Northern Railway in 1913, is the second of the 2 chalets remaining from a time when visitors arrived at East Glacier by train and toured the park on horseback. Even today it is accessible only by trail; you must hike or ride a horse to the chalet, perfectly perched on a rocky bench some 6.7 miles and 3,300 feet up from the trailhead at Lake McDonald Lodge. The hike to the chalet is strenuous, but well worth the effort. Once there, you will be awestruck by the surroundings of craggy rock walls and waterfalls, as well as by the view of Lake McDonald far below. The chalet is located at the junction of 2 trails, where day hikers choose between going to see Sperry Glacier, Lincoln Peak, Lake Ellen Wilson, or Gunsight Pass—or staying long enough to check them all out. Those equipped with the proper gear and skills will find mountain climbing options here, as well, along with mountain goats sharing the rugged habitat.

Sperry Chalet is actually two buildings made of native stone: a kitchen/dining hall and a 2-story hotel building. There is no electricity; in the evening the dining room and kitchen are lit with propane lanterns, and you are encouraged to bring your own flashlight for use at night. Other than that flashlight and what you need to hike in, just a "smile and a toothbrush" will be enough, as Sperry Chalet provides all bedding and 3 meals per day, along with the lodging.

Sperry Chalet is open, conditions permitting, from early July to early Sept. It offers overnight accommodations on the American plan; that is, dinner, breakfast, and lunch (or trail lunch) are included in the lodging price. Rates are $180 per night for the first person, plus $125 for each additional person in the same room. A 7 percent Montana accommodations tax is added to lodging charges. Sperry has 17 guest rooms, ranging from single occupancy to rooms for 4, with double and single beds

available. Reservations are required; be sure to check the policy on deposits, refunds, and cancellations.

Swan Mountain Outfitters, the park horse concession, offers horseback rides to Sperry Chalet. In addition, a la carte service is available in the dining room from 11:30 a.m. to 5 p.m., and some hikers visit Sperry as a day trip. The Sperry Trail runs from Lake McDonald Lodge past the chalet to Gunsight Pass and then down to trailheads on the east side; a visit to the chalet can be part of this longer outing.

Due to its remote location and high elevation (around 6,500 feet above sea level), Sperry offers a unique opportunity to explore the backcountry of Glacier without carrying a heavy backpack. This same remoteness requires that you be well informed, so be sure to check on current trail conditions at any visitor center or ranger station before setting out.

Campgrounds

Glacier National Park has 13 campgrounds, containing a total of more than 1,000 sites. They offer a variety of camping experiences: Some are accessible only by dirt road, have just a few sites, and are relatively primitive; others are large campgrounds with more amenities, located on the main routes through the park. Most are available on a first-come, first-served basis, and at the height of the summer many will fill by midday (and a few by 10 a.m.). Two campgrounds, St. Mary and Fish Creek, have individual sites that may be reserved in advance through the **National Park Service Reservation System** (877-444-6777; www.recreation.gov). **Apgar Campground** has group sites that may be reserved through the same reservation system. Operating dates vary from

🔍 Close-up

Granite Park & Sperry Chalets

We crossed many passes . . . There was a time when I had thought that a mountain pass was a depression. It is not. A mountain pass is a place where the impossible becomes barely possible.

—MARY ROBERTS RINEHART,
Through Glacier Park in 1915

Granite Park Chalet and **Sperry Chalet** might also be said to reside where "the impossible becomes barely possible." Located, respectively, on the **Highline Trail**, just south of Swiftcurrent Pass, and on the **Sperry Trail**, just west of Lincoln Pass, these stone buildings are reminders of an era of travel preceding the private automobile. Like Mary Roberts Rinehart, most people then came to Glacier on the train and traveled through the park on horseback. In addition to the great hotels—**Glacier Park Lodge, Many Glacier Hotel,** the **Prince of Wales Hotel,** and **Lake McDonald Lodge**—and horse camps at **Red Eagle Lake, Cosley Lake, Fifty Mountain,** and **Goat Haunt**— guests stayed overnight at a series of backcountry chalets. Many were elaborate wooden structures in the Swiss-chalet style used by the Great Northern for its other park chalets, Two Medicine, Cut Bank, St. Mary, Going-to-the-Sun, Many Glacier, Gunsight, and Belton. The two most remote were Granite Park and Sperry chalets, and these were constructed of native stone. As time took its toll on the wooden chalets in different ways (see the introduction to this chapter), the stone buildings proved their durability and, since undergoing renovations in the 1990s, they continue to offer lodging today.

These two remaining backcountry chalets each boast spectacular locations. Granite Park sits on a knoll just at tree line. At an elevation of about 6,600 feet, snow melts relatively late here; those hiking into the chalet along the Highline Trail will be treated to "spring" wildflowers even into late July. The meadows embracing the chalet are a mass of yellow glacier lilies in the early season; later they will burst into a kaleidoscope of colors as summer brings the high-country flowers into bloom: penstemon, asters, paintbrush, cinquefoil, beargrass, and many more. **Swiftcurrent Pass** straddles the Continental Divide about ¾-mile above the chalet. The hike to the pass is not difficult, and it offers a huge view east into the Swiftcurrent Valley and even out onto the plains. If you have energy to burn, try the **Grinnell Glacier Overlook Trail,** a spur

campground to campground; check for up-to-date information.

Most campgrounds have drinking water and restrooms with flush toilets and cold running water. Several campgrounds have a disposal station; there is a small fee to dump RV holding tanks. No utility hookups are provided. Some campgrounds cannot accommodate large RVs; others have a limited number of spaces available for larger vehicles (see individual descriptions). The park newspaper, the *Waterton-Glacier Guide,* and the park website, www.nps.gov/glac /index.htm, carry complete details.

In the descriptions that follow, "primitive" means a campground with a vault toilet (nonflusher, that is); water is available but may need to be filtered or boiled before drinking. Several primitive camp-

off the Highline Trail: It's only 1 kilometer (just over a half a mile) to the overlook, but it's known as the longest kilometer in the park! It's a steep climb to the divide here, but when you arrive you'll be rewarded with an astonishing view of **Grinnell Glacier** from above, as well as of the Grinnell Valley beyond. Like other glaciers in North America, Grinnell Glacier is shrinking rapidly, but it is still one of the largest glaciers in the park (see the Geology Close-up in the Glacier National Park chapter). And just a quick note on the chalet's name: Granite Park Chalet sits on a flow of igneous pillow basalt, a hard, dark-colored rock that was first taken for granite . . . but there is no granite in the area.

Sperry Chalet sits high in a hanging valley, just below **Comeau Pass** and **Lincoln Pass,** and with Gunsight and Edwards Mountains towering over it. Mountain goats frequent the rugged terrain around the chalet. You'll have a hard time deciding how to spend your time here: Trails lead in three different directions and to several destinations. Just over Comeau Pass is Sperry Glacier, about the same size as Grinnell Glacier. The hike to the glacier itself is remarkable: The trail winds its way up a series of benches, each dotted with pools and huge boulders left behind by the receding glaciers. No natural pass existed here, so a man-made one was created: You'll feel like you're in *Raiders of the Lost Ark* as you step up these stairs carved into the rock and steady yourself with the rope handrail! The basin offers a view not only of the glacier, but of peaks that you'll recognize as some of those seen from Logan Pass—but now you'll be seeing them from the south side. If you choose instead to hike east, toward **Gunsight Pass,** you'll want to stop at stunning **Lake Ellen Wilson,** which glitters in a high cirque known to produce lots of huckleberries in some years. And Gunsight Pass is a place where you're almost certain to encounter mountain goats.

As mentioned above, both Sperry and Granite Park chalets underwent extensive renovation in the mid- to late 1990s. As historic structures, the original integrity of the buildings had to be preserved, and you'll find it interesting to see how historic construction materials and methods were used in the work. The construction season is short at these lofty elevations, and, even in the summer, weather conditions sometimes precluded work. The amount of skill, time, and money that was required to renovate these remarkable buildings lends us a greater appreciation for those who built the original structures, in 1913 and 1914. The chalets do indeed exist "where the impossible becomes barely possible."

grounds are accessible only by dirt roads not recommended for large trailers or RVs.

The fee per site per night at the campgrounds is $10 to $23. Campsites are limited to 8 people and 2 vehicles. Apgar has 11 group sites and Many Glacier and Two Medicine Campgrounds each have 1 group site; these larger sites accommodate parties of 9 to 24 people. They are available on a first-come, first-served basis (Apgar's may be reserved in advance; see information above).

Several campgrounds also have hiker-biker sites for those traveling through the park under their own steam. These shared sites accommodate up to 8 people and cost $5 per person per night.

Most campsites have a fire grate or fire ring. Wood can be purchased at the campstores throughout the park. Collecting firewood is prohibited except along the Inside North Fork Road from 1 mile north of Fish Creek Campground to Kintla Lake, and along the Bowman Lake Road.

Be sure to inform yourself about current conditions in the park before you visit. Like all national parks, Glacier enforces rules designed to protect both visitors and the park's resources, including wildlife. In particular, the presence of grizzly bears requires that food be stored properly—in a hard-sided vehicle or bear-proof food locker (provided at some sites)—whenever it is not being prepared. Pet owners also should check park regulations carefully. For more information, or if you are interested in backcountry campgrounds, visit http://home.nps.gov /applications/glac/cgstatus/cgstatus.cfm, call **park headquarters** at (406) 888-7800, or write to Superintendent, Glacier National Park, P.O. Box 128, West Glacier, MT 59936.

Apgar

Apgar Campground is located at the foot of Lake McDonald. It is the largest campground in the park at 194 sites (25 of them can accommodate RVs up to 40 feet long). The campsites are in the trees, but a magnificent view of the lake and surrounding mountains is only a short walk away, and the shore of the lake is a very pleasant place to while away some time. Apgar Village, which includes the west-side visitor center, a backcountry permit office, small-boat rentals, a number of shops, and a restaurant and other snack shops, is close at hand. Evening programs are held at the campground amphitheater. A paved bike trail runs from Apgar along Lower McDonald Creek back toward West Glacier, providing one of the few opportunities in Glacier National Park for biking off the roadways.

Avalanche

Avalanche Campground fills early in the morning during the peak season for a number of reasons. Its 87 sites are tucked among the big trees of an old-growth cedar-hemlock forest, creating a magical atmosphere for campers. There are 50 sites that will fit RVs up to 26 feet long. The 1-mile, wheelchair-accessible Trail of the Cedars is nearby, with

---

Navigating Logan Pass

At the peak of the summer—from mid-July to Labor Day—parking at Logan Pass can be a test of anyone's patience. The busiest times are from 10 a.m. to 3:30 p.m. On a few occasions, gridlock has occurred as people try to move in and out of the lot. Park rangers do their best to control the situation, but sometimes it's best just to avoid it. If your goal for the day is to see Logan Pass, check out the visitor center, and maybe hike the Highline Trail or walk to Hidden Lake, consider riding the shuttle bus up and back down from either the east or west side. If you want to hike the Highline Trail out to Granite Park and down to the Loop, consider leaving your car at the Loop and picking up the morning shuttle to Logan Pass to start your hike. Alternatively, you can park at Avalanche and take the shuttle up and down. Pick up a schedule at any visitor center. A little creative planning will lower your stress level and help reduce congestion, as well!

🔍 Close-up

Grizzly Bear DNA Project

Grizzly bears and Glacier National Park are inextricably linked in the minds of everyone who visits this place. Indeed, the power of the bear in the human mind is amply demonstrated throughout Montana: From University of Montana sports teams to business names, the "grizzly" figures prominently in Montana life. And so it should. The wilderness area that stretches from Canada down through Glacier National Park and the adjoining Bob Marshall Wilderness is one of the last places in the lower 48 states where you have even a chance of seeing one of the great bears.

The grizzly was listed in 1975 as an **endangered species** under the Threatened and Endangered Species Act. One element of getting the grizzly population on the road to recovery is finding out just exactly how many bears there are. This is tougher than it might sound: Until just recently, radio-collaring bears was really the only reliable way to identify individual bears. Radio-collaring is very intrusive, expensive, and hard to apply to an entire population of animals, especially ones that frequent some of the least accessible parts of the country. But now scientists have developed DNA monitoring techniques that allow individual bears to be identified and tracked over long periods of time.

The **Greater Glacier Bear DNA Project,** which took place between 1997 and 2002, was just that. Bear "sign" includes hair and scat, two sources of DNA that can be collected without direct contact with the animal. Over several summers, field stations were set up in Glacier with scent lures (no food rewards) to draw bears into an area where their fur would rub up against barbed wire. Known rub trees were set with barbed wire, also to collect hair. Volunteers and project personnel documented their collection of scat from along Glacier's 700 miles of trails. Both the hair samples and scat were then analyzed for their DNA content, producing an ID for the bear in question. In this way individual bears could be identified for baseline purposes, eventually giving researchers the first statistically sound estimate of the Glacier area's grizzly population. In addition, DNA profiles can tell bear experts more about the degree of genetic variation within these populations, the relatedness of individuals, and the bear's gender—all critical to informed bear management.

This study evolved to look at grizzly populations on a larger, regional scope, as the **Northern Divide Bear Project** of 2003–2008. If you would like to learn more about both projects, visit www.nrmsc.usgs.gov/research/glac_beardna.htm on the Internet. Links will take you to maps of the study areas, information on techniques used, and photos (including some of bears).

its views along Avalanche Creek and into Avalanche Gorge. An undulating, 2-mile-long trail leads to Avalanche Lake, which sits at the base of a headwall below Sperry Glacier. Waterfalls cascade down the cliffs above the lake, bringing icy waters to feed this little gem of a subalpine cirque. And Upper McDonald Creek (and the Avalanche Picnic Area) is just across Going-to-the-Sun Road. Park Service naturalists present programs at the campground's outdoor amphitheater every night during the peak season.

Bowman Lake

Bowman Lake is another of those spots in Glacier that seems to keep cropping up in photo books, its tranquil surface reflecting Rainbow, Carter, and Chapman peaks, with Numa Ridge flanking it to the northwest. This primitive, 48-site campground sits at the end of the Bowman Lake Road (not recommended for RVs), which begins just north of the Polebridge Ranger Station. As at Quartz Creek and Logging Creek campgrounds, you are in wolf territory here, so be sure to keep your ears and eyes on the alert! Several good hikes leave from **Bowman Lake Campground;** you might visit the lookout at Numa Ridge, do all or part of the Quartz Lake Loop, or go to Akokala Lake. Here you'll also find the trailhead for Brown Pass and points farther north.

i Glacier Park's peak period for backcountry use is mid-July through Aug, and competition for coveted backcountry campsites is keen during this time. It helps to be flexible and have an alternative itinerary in mind in case your first choice is already booked. Fifty percent of campsites are allocated through an advance reservation system. The backcountry brochure and applications can be downloaded from the web at www.nps.gov/glac /planyourvisit/backcountry.htm and will be processed and confirmed for a $30 fee. Or call in advance (406-888-7800) and request the *Glacier Backcountry Guide* for complete details and application forms.

Cut Bank

If you're one of those who likes to escape the crowds, **Cut Bank Campground** is usually a good place to do so. Cut Bank is a primitive campground located 5 miles west of US 89 from a point about 12 miles south of St. Mary. Cut Bank has 14 sites and is not recommended for RVs. Hiking destinations include Morning Star Lake, Pitamakan Pass, Medicine Grizzly Lake, and Triple Divide Pass. Triple Divide Pass is just below Triple Divide Peak, which marks the three-way watershed sending water to the west through the Columbia River drainage, to the south and east through the Missouri-Mississippi system, and to the north and east via the St. Mary, Saskatchewan, and Nelson rivers to Hudson Bay and the Arctic Ocean.

Fish Creek

Fish Creek Campground is located just west of Apgar, also on the shore of Lake McDonald. This is one of two campgrounds where it's possible to reserve an individual site (877-444-6777). Of its 178 sites, 62 will accommodate RVs up to 26 feet long, and 18 will fit a 35-foot RV. Like the Apgar Campground, the sites at Fish Creek are nestled in the trees, but there's more space between sites here, and the campground tends to be a little quieter. A few sites are directly on the lakeshore. Park Service naturalists present an evening program each night during the height of the summer at the Fish Creek amphitheater.

Kintla

Kintla Lake Campground is the camping spot located farthest north on the west side of the park—almost in Canada. Its primitive status, difficulty of access, and the fact that no motorboats of any sort are permitted on Kintla Lake make for a remote experience that some will seek and others avoid. Kintla Lake Campground is 15 miles north of the

Close-up

Nevada Barr's *Blood Lure*

Blood Lure . . . now there's an intriguing title! Writer **Nevada Barr**, known for her mystery stories set in national parks, turned her attention to Glacier in 2001. The story revolves around her park-ranger heroine, Anna Pigeon, who's getting a break from her usual road-patrol duties while on a detail to Glacier National Park. Anna's headed out to collect samples for the Bear DNA Project with the park biologist, Joan Rand, and a young volunteer, Rory van Slyke. But on their first night out in Glacier's backcountry, a bear comes 'round their campsite, and things start shaking, including Anna's tent. She emerges with one 3-inch-long shallow laceration, but Rory has disappeared . . . and the tracks of the griz are disappearing with the dew as it evaporates from the meadows of Fifty Mountain.

Nevada Barr spent time working as a seasonal ranger for the National Park Service, and she does her homework for her fictional stories. She was along on a superintendent's hike in Glacier some years ago, which indeed passed through **Fifty Mountain** (which, despite its name, is a huge meadow, so named because you can see 50 peaks from it). Barr's books are fun reads, and they have a certain authenticity to them that makes all the local Park Service people want to read what she's written when she's "done" their park. What will the plot be? Often it's loosely based on real incidents. Who will turn up in the story? Occasionally, actual people crop up in her novels, more or less disguised: Kate Kendall, the director of the Grizzly Bear DNA Project, was the only real person mentioned in *Blood Lure,* although other renamed characters are identifiable by locals. But perhaps what's best is Barr's ability to portray how National Park Service rangers operate: what it's like to communicate with by radio; how long it may take for someone to hike into the scene of a backcountry crime; the local lingo for place names that aren't on the map. She stretches things a bit sometimes—be sure to get your information about the park from the park, not from fiction!—but she tells a good tale. Good enough that the **National Parks Conservation Association** has chosen Barr as the 2011 recipient of their **Robert Winks Award,** which goes to "an individual or organization that through the arts, media, or academia effectively and consistently communicates to the American public the values of the National Park System and the national park ideal." Barr will be presented with the award at the annual *Salute to the Parks* gala on April 6, 2011, at the Andrew Mellon Auditorium in Washington, D.C.

Blood Lure is just good enough, in fact, that if you're feeling even a bit "bearanoid" before you head to Glacier, you might want to save this story for after your visit. Reading it by flashlight in your tent at Fifty Mountain could be a bit too scary . . . keep it instead for an evening at home next winter, as you curl up by the fire with a warm drink. (Male readers beware: Barr's stories are told from a female's perspective, and could be likened to the literary equivalent of "chick flicks." That said, they're great!)

Polebridge Ranger Station on the Inside North Fork Road. This dirt road becomes narrower the farther north you go—it's a beautiful drive that passes through meadows and forest. Drive cautiously, for it's not always possible to see around the bends in the road (this drive is definitely not recommended for RVs). The campground has 13 sites and trailhead parking for the hike to Boulder Pass.

Many Glacier

Like Avalanche and Rising Sun campgrounds, **Many Glacier Campground** fills early in the morning during the peak season. The Many Glacier Valley attracts many day hikers for its web of trails threading up into the mountains, and from the campground it's an easy stroll to most of the major trailheads. The campground has 110 sites, 13 of which will fit RVs up to 35 feet long. The nearby Swiftcurrent Motor Inn includes a campstore, the Italian Gardens Ristorante, public showers, and a public laundry. Many Glacier Hotel is about a mile away. Each evening of the summer a Park Service naturalist presents a campfire talk at the Many Glacier Campfire Circle.

Quartz Creek & Logging Creek

Quartz Creek and **Logging Creek** campgrounds are located about 4.5 and 6 miles, respectively, south of Polebridge Ranger Station on the Inside North Fork Road. Both are primitive and tiny—each has 7 sites—campgrounds that offer peace and quiet, and the opportunity to ramble through some less-traveled parts of the park. The Inside North Fork Road is not recommended for RVs, and neither of these campgrounds has a site big enough to accommodate one. But the North Fork does have its own attractions—if you want to hear a wolf howl, your best chance anywhere in the park is probably between Logging Creek and Bowman Lake. If you set out to hike here—perhaps to Quartz or Logging Lakes, or to Hidden Meadow—keep your eyes open for wolf tracks. If you're lucky, you might even see the critters making tracks.

Rising Sun

Rising Sun Campground provides easy access to Going-to-the-Sun Road on the east side, and it tends to fill midmorning during the peak of the season. The immediate area provides huge views up and down St. Mary Lake, but the east-side wind in this valley can blow your hat off, so you'll appreciate that the campsites here are sheltered by trees. The neighboring Rising Sun Motor Inn complex includes the Two Dog Flats Grill, a campstore, and public showers. Each evening during the summer a Park Service naturalist presents a campfire talk at the Rising Sun Campfire Circle. Rising Sun Campground has 83 sites, 10 of them roomy enough to accommodate RVs up to 25 feet long. No towed units are permitted.

Sprague Creek

Sprague Creek is a candidate for the most crowded campground in the park: It fills up early and the sites are very close together. While these factors would seem to deter many campers, here that old truism of real estate is proven again: location, location, location! Sprague Creek is right on the banks of Lake McDonald and just off Going-to-the-Sun Road. Although the campground is crowded, the shoreline is very pleasant and offers views up and down the lake. Sprague Creek is also strategically placed for bicyclists who want to get an early start and ride to the top of Logan Pass (certain sections of the road on the west side are closed to cyclists between 11 a.m. and 4 p.m. during the summer). Its 25 sites are small, but a few will accommodate RVs up to 21 feet long. Because of its tight nature, Sprague Creek is closed to those with towed units.

St. Mary

St. Mary Campground is one of the largest in the park, with 148 sites, 25 of which will accommodate RVs up to 35 feet long. This is one of two campgrounds where it is possible to reserve an individual site (877-444-6777). It sits near the foot of St. Mary Lake and offers views south, north, and east. The campsites are in a lovely aspen grove—especially pretty in the fall, when the leaves turn golden—but the trees don't afford much protection from the oftentimes strong east-side winds. The campground lies along the St. Mary River, and the riparian habitat draws a wide variety of birds, including bald eagles. The St. Mary and Two Dog Flats are also home to a herd of elk that makes occasional appearances during the mornings and evenings throughout summer. The St. Mary Visitor Center is located just over a bridge across the river; Park Service naturalists give an evening program there each night of the summer. The town of St. Mary is less than a mile away.

Two Medicine

Two Medicine Campground is a little off the beaten track, about 12 miles northwest of US 2 at East Glacier. It was "rediscovered," however, in 2003, when west side campgrounds were closed due to fires—and now it's again a busy spot, as it was prior to the construction of Going-to-the-Sun Road. Two Medicine has 99 sites, 13 of which will fit RVs up to 32 feet long. The campsites are nicely spaced, and

many have a view of Two Medicine Lake, which is a short walk away. Like the Many Glacier Valley, Two Medicine Valley is formed by the convergence of a number of drainages—which translates into many wonderful trails for day hikers to explore. On some evenings a Park Service naturalist gives a talk at the Two Medicine Campfire Circle. The valley also has its own campstore, and Glacier Park Boat Company offers scenic boat tours.

RESTAURANTS

Price Code
Restaurant dinner price code, for two people exclusive of beverages, tips, and tax:

$	$10 to $20
$$	$20 to $28
$$$	$28 to $35
$$$$	More than $35

Although the lodge dining rooms are more formal than the smaller restaurants, casual dress is quite acceptable at all locations. All restaurants are designated nonsmoking. Reservations are not accepted. Generally prices are higher at the lodge dining rooms than at the other area restaurants. For more detail than what is outlined below, visit www .glacierparkinc.com/dining.php.

GREAT NORTHERN DINING ROOM $$
Glacier Park Lodge, East Glacier
(406) 892-2525
www.glacierparkinc.com
A Western theme dominates the Great Northern, and its menu features beef, barbecued ribs, chicken, and fish entrees. The restaurant offers a full buffet for breakfast, a luncheon carvery, and for dinner either a Western buffet or a la carte options. Breakfast runs from 6:30 to 10 a.m., lunch from 11:30 a.m. to 2 p.m., and dinner from 5 to 9:30 p.m.

ITALIAN GARDENS RISTORANTE $
Swiftcurrent Motor Inn, Many Glacier Valley
(406) 732-5531 (summer only)
www.glacierparkinc.com

The reincarnation of the Swiftcurrent Coffee Shop as the Italian Gardens Ristorante introduced a new era in the Many Glacier Valley: Not only can you design your own pizza or specialty pasta at the restaurant, but you can also get pizza to go—and it frequently goes to the campground with campers. Breakfast is served from 6:30 to 10 a.m., lunch from 11:30 a.m. to 2 p.m., and dinner from 5 to 9:30 p.m.

JAMMER JOE'S GRILL AND PIZZERIA $
Lake McDonald Lodge
Going-to-the-Sun Road, west side

A casual atmosphere and a la carte breakfast, lunch, and dinner make this an easy stop for a meal. The restaurant is from 11 a.m. to 9:30 p.m., but hours may vary in early and late seasons.

❇PTARMIGAN DINING ROOM $$
Many Glacier Hotel, Many Glacier Valley
(406) 732-4411 (summer only)

The Ptarmigan Dining Room echoes an "Alps of America" theme with its Swiss decor and windows opening to magnificent views of the mountains across Swiftcurrent Lake. The restaurant features a breakfast, lunch, and dinner buffet, all serving continental and American cuisine. Breakfast goes from 6:30 to 10 a.m., lunch from 11:30 a.m. to 2 p.m., and dinner from 5 to 9:30 p.m.

RUSSELL'S FIRESIDE DINING ROOM $$
Lake McDonald Lodge
Going-to-the-Sun Road, west side
(406) 892-2525
www.glacierparkinc.com

Russell's Fireside Dining Room preserves the historic character of Lake McDonald Lodge with its rough-hewn beams and big-game trophies hanging from the walls. A full buffet breakfast and a la carte lunch are served; dinner features a fine American menu with a taste of the outdoors (wild game, that is). Breakfast is from 6:30 to 10 a.m., lunch from 11:30 a.m. to 2 p.m., and dinner from 5 to 9:30 p.m.

> **i** Maps are vital for safe, enjoyable visits in Glacier National Park. A good source for maps is the Glacier Association, which offers a full selection of USGS topographic quadrangle maps and an excellent park-wide map by Trails Illustrated. The association's sales outlets are located at the Apgar, St. Mary, and Logan Pass Visitor Centers; the Many Glacier, Two Medicine, and Polebridge Ranger Stations; and the Apgar Backcountry Permit Center. To purchase products in advance of your visit, go to www.glacierassociation.org/store.

TWO DOG FLATS GRILL $
Rising Sun Motor Inn
Going-to-the-Sun Road, east side
(406) 732-5523 (summer only)

This family-style restaurant sits just across Going-to-the-Sun Road from St. Mary Lake. It features "American comfort food," including sandwiches, salads, steaks, and fish. Breakfast is served from 6:30 to 10 a.m., and lunch and dinner from 11 a.m. to 9:30 p.m.

WEST GLACIER RESTAURANT $
Apgar Village
(406) 888-5359

The West Glacier Restaurant is located in Apgar Village at the foot of Lake McDonald. It offers breakfast, lunch, and dinner but is perhaps best remembered for the ice-cream window just outside the door featuring huckleberry ice cream among many other flavors! The casual, family-friendly eatery is open from mid-May through late Sept.

NIGHTLIFE

"Nightlife" within the park is generally a quiet affair, but it has its charms. Park naturalists give evening slide programs and campfire talks at many locations each night (as detailed in the Campgrounds section). Members of the local Blackfeet and Salish-Kootenai tribes talk about their history and culture in the "Native America Speaks" weekly program. And some special events do occur during the summer—these might include performances by Blackfeet dancers or Montana singer-songwriter David Walburn. Check the park publication Glacier Explorer for current listings.

Evening is a wonderful time for certain outdoor activities, too. Stargazing is exceptional, especially on cloudless and moonless nights, and the northern lights occasionally reward nighthawks awake to see them. Glacier is not, however, a good place to go hiking at night, when bears may be both more active and less likely expecting to share the trail with *Homo sapiens*.

Quiet hours in the campgrounds are from 10 p.m. to 6 a.m. Fireworks may not be used within the park, but many communities around the park have fireworks displays for the Fourth of July.

SHOPPING

While few come to Glacier National Park with shopping as their chief goal, it's unlikely that you'll leave without buying something—a souvenir poster, perhaps, or a book or locally made hand-thrown pottery.

The Glacier Association runs an operation through the visitor centers, selling books, videos, tapes, maps, and posters specific to Glacier. Proceeds from this nonprofit organization support educational programs and publications in the park.

Concessionaire Glacier Park, Inc. operates gift shops in all of the major lodges. They carry Native American jewelry and crafts, film, postage stamps, huckleberry treats, books and maps, hiking snacks, outdoor clothing, and a variety of souvenirs. Campstores are located at Swiftcurrent Motor Inn, Rising Sun Motor Inn, and Two Medicine. At the Lake McDonald Lodge complex they carry a similar selection with the addition of limited food supplies, some camping equipment, and bundled firewood.

Apgar Village also has several gift shops, each with a unique selection. The Cedar Tree offers Montana-made gifts and souvenirs as well as huckleberry products, Pendleton woolens, and t-shirts. Other shops include the West Glacier Mercantile, the West Glacier Gift Shop, and the Shirt Company.

WATERTON-GLACIER INTERNATIONAL PEACE PARK

Wildlife and natural processes recognize no political boundaries, a fact easily recognized when traveling between the United States and Canada. Some elk that summer in Glacier National Park migrate to the grasslands of Waterton Lakes National Park for the winter. Eagles fitted with tiny radio transmitters in Glacier have been tracked far into the Canadian north. Glacier began to regain its wolf population when a female wolf moved south from British Columbia into the North Fork Valley and raised a litter of pups. Wind and water disperse seeds across the international border . . . all these are good examples of how the international boundary means little in the natural world.

OVERVIEW

The concept of the International Peace Park—an idea that has since been copied around the world—originated here in 1932. It was the brainchild of the Montana and Alberta chapters of the Rotarians, who recognized that the political line between the two parks sometimes interfered with managing the shared ecosystem. By designating the two parks as one International Peace Park, both parks and countries acknowledged the need to work together to maintain the unique and incredibly rich natural resources. While each park retains control over its portion of the Peace Park, staff from both parks work jointly on such projects as scientific research, resource management (including fire control), visitor services, and education. The Peace Park designation is also an opportunity to celebrate the beauties of this rugged landscape of mountains and lakes, on both sides of the border.

You can share in the International Peace Park experience in specific ways. The 200-passenger *M.V. International* runs cruises at least twice daily on Waterton Lake from early May through early Oct, going from the Waterton townsite to Goat Haunt in the United States. You'll mix with citizens from both countries (as well as visitors from around the world), and have a chance to gaze up and down the boundary as you cruise by. On Saturdays during the peak of the summer season, the International Peace Park hike departs in the morning from Waterton townsite. Guided by naturalists from each of the two countries, you'll hike the 8 miles from the townsite to Goat Haunt. Along the way, the naturalists will talk not only about the landscape but also about the differences and similarities in how the two parks are managed. The return trip is aboard the *M.V. International* in the late afternoon. And each summer a "Hands Across the Border" celebration takes place, usually at the Chief Mountain Customs crossing. Check with either park's information centers for specific information.

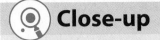

Close-up

The Wilderness Concept

If we are to have broad thinking men and women of high mentality, of good physique, and with a true perspective on life, we must allow our populace a communion with nature in areas of more or less wilderness condition.

—ARTHUR CARHART

There's no better place in North America to gain an understanding of the meaning and spirit of Arthur Carhart's words than the **northern Continental Divide ecosystem.** This region is home to huge tracts of protected wilderness sprawling along both east and west sides of the divide. Glacier National Park lies at the heart of this wildland complex.

Glacier's backcountry is managed in accordance with the **Wilderness Act of 1964.** This ensures that wilderness values will not be impaired before such time as the US Congress acts to include the park's wildlands in the more-protective wilderness preservation system. More than 95 percent of Glacier's million-plus acres are proposed for inclusion in this wilderness preservation system.

South of Glacier Park the **Bob Marshall, Great Bear,** and **Scapegoat Wilderness Areas** adjoin to form a massive, 1.5-million-acre wilderness complex. Additional wildlands in Alberta's Waterton Lakes National Park and British Columbia's Akamina-Kishinena Provincial Park adjoin Glacier's northern boundary, adding to the extensive wilderness acreage.

The Wilderness Act of 1964 was the culmination of a uniquely American ideal "to secure for the American people of present and future generations the benefits of an enduring resource of wilderness."

Wilderness is intended to provide visitors with outstanding opportunities for solitude (motorized access and activities are prohibited) and a primitive-type recreation. Wilderness areas are intended to retain their primeval character and appearance of having been created by the forces of nature. The wilderness is a place in which visitors can leave behind the pressures of modern society and experience risks, challenges, and rewards on nature's terms.

Maintaining wilderness as an enduring resource is the responsibility of all visitors. Ever-increasing use and cumulative resource impacts make it imperative for visitors to learn and practice Zero Impact outdoor skills and ethics.

The international park isn't of significance only to Canadians and Americans, either. In 1995, the Waterton-Glacier International Peace Park was recognized for its value to the world through the World Heritage Site designation. This status was awarded based on the park's scenic, geologic, and ecological values, as well as on its cultural importance as an example of two agencies working together, across an international boundary, in the name of shared stewardship and peace.

WATERTON LAKES NATIONAL PARK, ALBERTA

Waterton Lakes National Park, "where the mountains meet the prairie," sits just over the Canadian border in Alberta, Canada's Wild

Rose Country. For those from the United States, visiting Canada is a fascinating combination of familiarity and foreignness. They speak the same language, they'll accept US dollars (though it's usually smarter to use a credit card or exchange cash at a bank), and things seem to happen in pretty much the same ways . . . but still it's so different!

For one thing, there's a town in the park, something you generally will not see in American national parks. Waterton townsite is dominated by the spectacular ✳**Prince of Wales Hotel,** built by the Great Northern Railway in 1927, another part of the James J. Hill empire. The Prince of Wales is well worth a visit, even if you don't intend to stay overnight or dine there. Its lobby commands one of the most remarkable views in the Rockies: the vista down Waterton Lake, flanked by parades of mountains on both sides, including Mount Cleveland, the highest peak in Glacier National Park. And if you step outside to enjoy the view, chances are you'll experience the strong winds that buffet this building on a regular basis. During construction, the unfinished building was actually blown several inches off its foundation one night. Although moved back into place, parts of the building have never been quite plumb since. Rumor has it that the top floors sway several inches during a good blow. For more information on this historic hotel, visit www.glacierparkinc.com/lodging.php or phone (406) 892-2525.

Waterton boasts quite a few other accommodations as well, ranging from bed-and-breakfasts to a hostel to both modest and upscale motels. One of the most popular for years, the Kilmorey Inn, burned to the ground in January 2009 (a new Kilmorey Lodge is in the planning stages). Other local favorites include the **Waterton Lakes Lodge Resort** (www.watertonlakeslodge.com), the **Crandell Mountain Lodge** (www.crandellmountainlodge.com), and the **Aspen Village Inn** (www.aspenvillageinn.com).

Top-notch shopping, fun night spots, and numerous restaurants make for a lively little town. You'll definitely sense a European influence here, with Scottish woolens, Irish lace, and china featuring pictures of the British royal family all for sale. On a warm summer day, be sure to check out at least one of the town's ice-cream shops—delicious! Also drop in at the **Waterton Heritage Centre,** located at 117 Waterton Ave. It features historical displays and a fine collection of books, videos, maps, and souvenirs of the area.

When it comes to the great outdoors, Waterton offers a variety of activities. The cruise boat *M.V. International* plies the cold waters of Waterton Lake two or three times a day to Goat Haunt in the United States; you'll see the docks as you drive into town (403-859-2362; www.watertoncruise.com). The same company offers a water taxi across Waterton Lake to the trailhead at Crypt Landing; the hike to Crypt Lake is often rated one of the best in Canada. Plan for a full-day trip. In addition to hiking, some of Waterton's excellent trails are open to mountain biking; check at the visitor center for details. (This is another difference compared to Glacier, where mountain bikes are not permitted on single-track trails.)

For more information on Waterton Lakes National Park, visit www.pc.gc.ca/eng/pn-np/ab/waterton/index.aspx or www.watertoninfo.com, or write **Waterton Lakes National Park,** P.O. Box 200, Waterton Park, Alberta T0K 2M0, Canada. The park visitor center may be reached at (403) 859-2224. The *Waterton-Glacier Guide,* published jointly by the two parks, carries a full listing of services at Waterton and may be requested from either park.

ATTRACTIONS

"Give a month at least to this precious reserve. The time will not be taken from the sum of your life. Instead of shortening, it will indefinitely lengthen it and make you truly immortal."

So wrote John Muir of Glacier National Park, which he also called "the most care-killing scenery" on the continent. Even if you can't take a month to explore Glacier Country, you'll find that each day offers countless opportunities to discover new treasures in this magnificent place.

The waters and mountains of Northwestern Montana dominate the lives of all who have ever lived in or traveled through the region. The lakes and rivers have been travel routes for Native American canoes, 19th-century steamboats, and modern-day kayaks. Prehistoric trails have evolved into paved roads for commerce and travelers. The mountains are ancient sites of worship as well as places for unparalleled backcountry recreation. The number of places you could visit is essentially infinite, encompassing everything from theme parks and high peaks to art galleries and historic structures.

The "Attractions" represented here are chosen for one or more of several reasons. Some because of the views they offer—the gondola ride to the top of Big Mountain, for example. Others allow you to immerse yourself in the area's past, whether it's the history of the Plains Indians or a 19th-century logging town. Some "Attractions" are included because they are near and dear to the hearts of local residents—when you see the lines of folks in swimsuits waiting their turn on a hot summer's day at the top of the Big Sky Waterpark, you'll want to be there, too! The chapter closes with a pair of driving loops that will lead you through a stunning cross-section of Glacier Country. Though each can be done in a day, you may find—like John Muir might tell you—that even a few days is not enough.

The information here is as up-to-date and complete as possible, but things have a way of changing. It's always good to call ahead to confirm prices and schedules.

So, explore Glacier Country as outlined below, but don't hesitate to turn off the designated roads to make your own discoveries!

COLUMBIA FALLS TO BROWNING, US 2

✴ALBERTA VISITOR CENTRE
West Glacier
(406) 888-5743

If the greater Glacier Country is your grand tour of the northern Rockies, the Alberta Visitor Centre in West Glacier is a great place to start learning more about Wild Rose Country to the north. And even if you don't plan to cross the international boundary, the center is worth a stop in its own right.

Immediately you'll be greeted by a life-size dinosaur model, reminding you that Alberta is the home of the Royal Tyrrell Museum, which houses the world's largest display of dinosaur skeletons. Photos so large you'll feel like you're walking into the mountains introduce you to two jewels of the Parks Canada system, Banff and Jasper National Parks. The Calgary Stampede—which some have called a "Mardi Gras of the North"—comes to life in displays and pictures, and you'll discover historic sites such as Head-Smashed-In Buffalo Jump and the Frank Slide. If you've dreamed of becoming an Olympian, you can scream down the (simulated) bobsled course on an actual sled from the 1988 Calgary Games—it doesn't take long, but it's exhilarating and exhausting!

The copper-topped building houses a wealth of information about Alberta, including on its history and magnificent mountains. Although it is closed during the winter, in the summer its staff of friendly Albertans will answer questions for you. Even if you hadn't planned on going farther north, a visit here might persuade you to add Alberta to your itinerary!

∗BIG SKY WATERPARK
7211 US 2 East, P.O. Box 2311, Columbia Falls 59912
(406) 892-5026
www.bigskywp.com
Hot summer day under the Big Sky? For kids of all ages, there's no easier, more fun way to cool down than to spend the afternoon at the Big Sky Waterpark. You'll have trouble deciding which ride to try next—the Big Splash River Ride, the 7-story Geronimo Speed Slide, the Roller Coaster Bullet Speed Slide, or the four Twister Waterslides. And Water Wars—a catapulting water-balloon game—will get your inner little brother going! For the very young or for the mellower adult, minislides and a huge whirlpool may be just the ticket.

And, should you prefer to stay dry, the waterpark offers Miniature Greens Adventure Golf, a video arcade, beach volleyball, and a 1938 antique carousel that's a favorite. Bring your own picnic or pick up some snacks and drinks at the concession stand. Changing rooms have free lockers, and locks may be rented.

The Big Sky Waterpark is open from approximately Memorial Day to Labor Day, 7 days a week. For full-day admission, the adult fee (by height; 48 inches and over) is $23.95, kids (under 48 inches) pay $18.95; inquire about nonrider admissions. Twilight rates are lower, and a mini-golf day pass costs $4.95. Monthly passes and group rates are available; call to arrange group visits in advance. You'll find Big Sky Waterpark at the junction of US 2 and MT 206.

HUNGRY HORSE DAM
Just south of US 2, Hungry Horse
(406) 387-3800
The numbers are as impressive as a visit to the dam. At 564 feet high and with a crest length of 2,115 feet across, the Hungry Horse Dam dwarfs every other structure in Glacier Country. Water cascades over the spillway to drop as far as 490 feet into the South Fork of the Flathead River. The capacity of the spillway is 50,000 cubic feet per second, and the reservoir has a total capacity of 3,468,000 acre-feet. The principal power benefit comes from the dam's storage of water from the

spring runoff for later release when needed. On average, this water generates 4.6 billion kilowatt-hours of power as it passes through a series of 19 downstream power plants.

Guided tours of the dam, completed in 1953, begin daily every hour on the hour at the visitor center, from mid-June to early Sept. Parking is permitted only in designated areas and not on top of the dam roadway. Displays and photos show the stages in building this fascinating structure, and they discuss the costs and benefits of damming a large river. The visitor center is open from 8 a.m. to 3 p.m. during the summer months.

MARIAS PASS MEMORIAL SQUARE
Crossed by US 2, 12 miles west of East Glacier

Mile high Marias Pass is the lowest driveable pass through the Rocky Mountains in the United States. Nevertheless, it was one of the last to be discovered during westward expansion. Weather deterred some explorers, and the Blackfeet Indians, who controlled the region, refused to lead exploring parties through the area. Meriwether Lewis of the Lewis and Clark Expedition came within 25 miles of the pass before a fateful encounter with the Blackfeet hindered his further progress. Eventually, the pass was named after the Marias River, which Lewis had named for his cousin Maria Wood.

At the pass, Memorial Square commemorates the history of the immediate area. One statue is dedicated to John F. Stevens, chief surveying engineer for the Great Northern Railway, who located the pass in 1889; thanks to his discovery, the railroad was running trains over the pass just 3 years later.

The Theodore Roosevelt monument honors the president who made forest conservation a national policy; it also commemorates the 25th anniversary of the USDA Forest Service. Constructed in 1931, the monument is a 60-foot-tall obelisk sheathed in granite that was quarried near the state capital in Helena. Originally located in the center of the highway, it was moved to its present site in 1989.

William "Slippery Bill" Morrison, a trader and prospector who had squatters' rights to 160 acres of land at the Marias Pass summit, is also acknowledged. He donated a portion of his land for Memorial Square, and, according to his wishes, at his death in 1932 the balance of his property was also deeded to the federal government.

The Burlington Northern Stewardship Plaque, dedicated in 1991, recognizes the Burlington Northern Railroad's commitment to responsible stewardship of the environment. The railroad runs through important habitat for grizzly bears, mountain goats, elk, and other wildlife species. This route has been an important transportation corridor since the arrival of the Great Northern Railway in 1892.

Marias Pass is a great spot to take a break on your way across the mountains. You might enjoy your lunch with a view of Summit and Little Dog Mountains, the peaks that dominate Marias Pass from the north. The slopes below these peaks offer one of the best places in Glacier to view the Lewis Overthrust Fault (see the Geology Close-up in the Glacier National Park chapter). The rest area offers public outhouses, as well as a seasonal Forest Service campground (see the Campgrounds section of the Columbia Falls chapter).

Three Bears Lake, a level, 15-minute trail walk north of the tracks, was dammed by the Great Northern Railway and its water used to refill steam engines. This earthen dam from the 1890s was intentionally broached in the 1990s to prevent the possible consequences of its failure; now the little lake's water runs again to both sides of the Continental Divide, as it did before the arrival of the railroad.

BROWNING

✳MUSEUM OF THE PLAINS INDIAN
P.O. Box 400, Browning 59417
(406) 338-2230
www.browningmontana.com/museum.html

Browning is the social, economic, and administrative headquarters for those Blackfeet Indians living south of the international border. Here you'll find the Museum of the Plains Indian, home to a comprehensive collection of Blackfeet artifacts. The museum also showcases arts and crafts—not only the Blackfeet's, but also those of the Crow, Northern Cheyenne, Sioux, and other Plains tribes, all traditional enemies of the Blackfeet. A highlight in the permanent display area is an exhibit of traditional costumes, while "Winds of Change," a multi-media show narrated by the late Vincent Price and produced by Montana State University, illuminates the continuing evolution of Indian cultures.

In the changing-exhibits area the works of modern-day sculptors, carvers, painters, and other artists and craftspeople are highlighted. The sales shop, offering a wide variety of contemporary products, is operated by the Indian-owned Northern Plains Indian Crafts Association. It has an excellent selection of books and Native crafts for sale.

Founded in 1941, the museum is administered by the Indian Arts and Crafts Board, operating under the Department of the Interior. The Museum of the Plains Indian, located at the junction of US 2 and 89 just west of town, is open daily June through Sept from 9 a.m. to 4:30 p.m. and, during the rest of the year, Mon through Fri from 10 a.m. to 4:30 p.m. Admission is free in winter and $4 for adults and $1 for children 6 to 12 in summer.

North American Indian Days is held each July in Browning at the Blackfeet Tribal Fairgrounds, next to the Museum of the Plains Indian and near the new Glacier Peaks Casino. The 4-day celebration brings together Indians from throughout the United States and Canada, as well as non-Indian visitors, for dancing, games, sporting events, and more. For details call (406) 338-7406 or check out www.blackfeetcountry.com.

WHITEFISH

✳WHITEFISH MOUNTAIN RESORT
P.O. Box 1400, Whitefish 59937
(406) 862-2900
www.skiwhitefish.com

Rocky Mountain High? Probably the highest place around here that you can get to without hiking is the top of Big Mountain, at 6,817 feet above sea level. On a clear day you'll be able to see the Cabinet Mountains to the west, the Canadian Rockies off to the northeast, the peaks of Glacier National Park, and a magnificent view south to the Flathead Valley, including the Swan Range, the Mission Mountains, Blacktail Mountain, and Flathead and Whitefish Lakes. Summer or winter, it's magnificent.

The Big Mountain Express offers access to the summit of Big Mountain both summer and winter. The summer season typically runs from Memorial Day to late Sept, when the resort offers scenic chairlift rides (one-way, $5; round-trip, $10), trails for hiking and mountain biking, an alpine slide, a zip line, and the unique "Walk in the Treetops," a 2½-hour guided nature walk through sub-alpine forest taking place along an elevated boardwalk.

In the winter, nonskiers may access the mountaintop with a foot passenger ticket. They will be loaded on with skiers and snow-boarders. Sightseers are welcome to enjoy the winter view, as well as something hot to eat or drink, in the warmth of the **Summit House.** The lifts operate daily during ski season—early Dec to early Apr (call to confirm, as snow conditions may affect operation of the lifts during early and late season)—from 9:30 a.m. to 4 p.m.

You'll find more information on White-fish Mountain Resort in both the Whitefish and Outdoor Recreation chapters.

✳**GREAT NORTHERN BREWERY**
2 Central Ave.
(406) 863-1000
www.greatnorthernbrewing.com

Those who know their beer, as well as those who want to become acquainted with it, should take an afternoon to visit Whitefish's Great Northern Brewery. Built in 1994 by Minott Wessinger, the great-great-grandson of Oregon's Henry Weinhard, the brewery was located here to take advantage of the area's excellent water. The brewhouse is built in a gravity-flow arrangement and is mostly automated; for its size it is one of the most complexly designed operations in the country. A photo display describes the brewing process.

The Great Northern Brewery produces several beers, including Fred's Black Lager, Wild Huckleberry Wheat Lager (a local favorite), Wheatfish Hefeweizen, Going to the Sun IPA, and Hellroaring Amber Lager, as well as occasional seasonal brews such as Snow Ghost Winter Lager. The **Draught House,** which serves Great Northern beers exclusively, along with a variety of regional wines, is open from 11 a.m. to 10 p.m. in the summer; hours vary at other times of the year.

✳**LES MASON STATE PARK**
Montana Fish, Wildlife & Parks
(406) 444-3750

Until recently, this 7.5-acre park was a hidden gem managed by a local group, the Friends of Les Mason. But the state parks department assumed management in 2009. The agency intends to continue running it as a day-use area only, and as a quieter alternative to Whitefish City Beach and other high-use areas around the lake. To find it, from Whitefish Lake Road at a point 1 mile north of the Whitefish Mountain Resort junction, you'll see a left-hand turn onto a gravel road that leads down to the parking area for Les Mason Park. From the parking area, a short trail leads to a brush-embraced beach. In the past, this quiet lakeside spot could be all but deserted even when sunbathers were lying nose-to-toes at the ultra-popular City Beach.

STUMPTOWN HISTORICAL SOCIETY MUSEUM
Whitefish Railroad Depot
500 Depot St., Suite 101
(406) 862-0067
www.stumptownhistoricalsociety.org

Even if you don't arrive in Whitefish by train, you'll want to make a point of visiting the historic depot. Like the train stations at West Glacier and East Glacier, and the Izaak Walton Inn at Essex, it is built in the chalet style the Great Northern Railway developed for this area. Now owned by the Stumptown Historical Society, the building has been completely restored to its original 1927 appearance and is on the National Register of Historic Places.

Be sure to check out the restored 1950s Great Northern Railway Locomotive 181 on display outside the depot.

Inside you'll find the Stumptown Historical Society Museum, devoted to illuminating Whitefish's past. You'll see Native American beading, handmade quilts from the early 20th century, and photos and artifacts from the trapping, trading, and logging era that gave the region the name "Stumptown." Photos from the Great Northern Railway document its history—including wrecks and snowslides—and the railroad's tremendous influence. Train models, a telegrapher's desk, and dinner china with patterns exclusive to the *Empire Builder* service between Chicago and Seattle are a few of the objects that bring alive the railroad's impact on people across the northern plains. Posters, along with calendar art commissioned by the Great Northern—including Blackfeet portraits from the 1920s by the German painter Winold Reiss—offer a unique account of the past. Many other objects represent aspects of local history, as well.

The Stumptown Historical Society Museum is open from 10 a.m. to 4 p.m. Mon through Sat. Admission is free, but donations are greatly appreciated.

i Altitude sickness is a serious condition, marked by nausea, headache, loss of appetite, and vomiting. It is relatively uncommon in Glacier Country, as most peaks are below 10,000 feet in elevation. Still, if you experience symptoms, the best remedy is to return to a lower elevation as quickly as possible.

STUMPTOWN ICE DEN SKATING RINK
Whitefish Parks and Recreation
725 Wisconsin Ave., P.O. Box 158,
Whitefish 59937
(406) 863-2477
www.stumptowniceden.com

It's winter, it's cold, and you've been in the car for most of the day . . . it's time to stretch a leg! Come out to the Stumptown Ice Den and brush up on your triple axel, or, maybe, just try not to fall on the Zamboni-groomed ice. You can take a break to enjoy a cup of hot chocolate at the snack bar . . . let your legs relax for a moment, then back to the ice!

Located behind the Saddle Club in Mountain Trails City Park, 5 blocks north of the train tracks on Wisconsin Avenue, the rink operates from late Sept to late Mar. It offers open (public) skating sessions at specific hours morning, afternoon, or evening, every day of the week. Hockey leagues and skating classes also use the ice, so be sure to check on the schedule. General admission is $5 for everyone age 6 and older. Children 5 and younger skate for free when accompanied by a paying skater. Skate rentals are $2.50 for all ages.

WHITEFISH CITY BEACH
Whitefish Parks and Recreation
(406) 863-2470

Year-round this little jewel of a park is a treasured asset to the town of Whitefish. With its spectacular views, it offers a quiet retreat for walkers and joggers in the fall, winter, and spring. In the summer, it's a hopping hub of activity: two docks go in, the buoys go out, lifeguards arrive, and swimming happens every day, all day.

Whitefish Parks and Recreation runs a small concession that sells snacks, drinks, and ice cream, and bathrooms are right at hand. Several small pavilions are available to rent; call in advance to make arrangements. City Beach also has a boat-launching ramp and boat dock.

Located at the southeast end of Whitefish Lake; take Baker Avenue north over the viaduct, turn left at the light onto Edgewood, and follow signs to the lake.

KALISPELL

✳CONRAD MANSION
Woodland Avenue between Third and Fourth Streets, P.O. Box 1041, Kalispell 59901
(406) 755-2166
www.conradmansion.com
Step back in time—in the home of Charles and Alicia Conrad. Built in 1895, this Norman-style mansion reflects the wealth and elegance sometimes seen in the West in an era better known for its rough-and-tumble living. Charles Conrad, born and raised in Virginia, came west at the age of 18 and built a fortune in trade and freight on the Missouri River. Later he moved to the Flathead Valley and helped to found the city of Kalispell. His herd of buffalo sometimes pastured on what today is known as Buffalo Hill in Kalispell. Conrad and his wife, Alicia, established a reputation for hospitality and generosity in the new town; from the Great Hall, with its massive stone fireplace and oak woodwork, servants escorted notable guests upstairs to bedrooms boasting marble lavatories, sleigh beds, and canopied 4-posters. Alicia Conrad Campbell, the youngest Conrad child, donated the mansion to the city of Kalispell in 1975. Today, all 3 floors, interior and exterior, have been restored to their original grandeur. Inside you will see the Conrads' original furniture, clothing, and even toys; outside, exquisite gardens surround the building. The mansion offers a unique glimpse into the lives of privileged Montanans at the turn of the 20th century.

The Conrad Mansion, located 6 blocks off Main Street on Fourth Street East, is open to the public from May 15 to Oct 15. Hours are 10 a.m. to 5 p.m. Tues through Sun with the last tour starting at 4 p.m. Admission is $8 for adults, $7 for seniors, and $3 for children under 12. Call in advance for groups of 20 or more.

HOCKADAY MUSEUM OF ART
302 Second Ave. East
(406) 755-5268
www.hockadaymuseum.org
The Hockaday Museum of Art, located in downtown Kalispell, provides an intimate setting for displays by both local and nationally recognized artists. The permanent collection features works of Montana artists such as Russell Chatham, Ace Powell, Gary Schildt, and Bob Scriver. Exhibits change on a regular basis and may include everything from the work of local watercolorists or photographers to historic doll collections to sculpture in a variety of materials. The "Crown of the Continent" permanent exhibition captures the beauty of Glacier Country, and takes evocative looks back at the early days of the *Empire Builder* passenger train, the powerful Blackfeet Nation, and the region's first white settlers. The museum building itself, originally constructed as a Carnegie Library, is now on the National Register of Historic Places.

Hours are 10 a.m. to 5 p.m., Tues through Sat year around. Admission is $5 for adults, $4 for seniors, $2 for college students, and free for those 18 and under. Guided tours are available on request. The museum gift shop offers an array of fine works by

Montana artists (see The Arts chapter for more information).

✳ LAWRENCE PARK
North end of Main Street
(406) 758-7718

Looking for some quiet time away from big-town busy-ness? Take a few moments to enjoy the out-of-doors here at Lawrence Park, which offers outdoor play equipment for children and pavilions to rent. All in all, it feels a little more peaceful and "wilder" than Woodland Park (described below), where Kalispell Parks and Recreation runs the majority of its public programs. Lawrence Park's paved path runs close to the Stillwater River and are sought out by walkers and joggers as well as bicyclists. Birders will enjoy getting out early in the day here to look for feathered friends.

MUSEUM AT CENTRAL SCHOOL
Northwest Montana Historical Society
124 Second Ave. East, P.O. Box 2293,
Kalispell 59901
(406) 756-8381
www.yourmuseum.org

Built in 1894, Kalispell's Central School is on the National Register of Historic Places. It is a beautiful old building, renovated to high standards. Highlights of the Central School Museum include permanent and changing exhibits relating to the history of Central School itself; native nations of the area; the development of nonnative settlements; local industrial and technological development, including the histories of the logging, mining, and transportation industries in the area; Glacier National Park; and regional wildlands. The museum also has facilities for speakers, research, oral history, and genealogy, as well as public meeting rooms.

The Northwest Montana Historical Society operates the Central School Museum, which is open Mon through Fri from 10 a.m. to 5 p.m. Admission is $5 for adults, $4 for seniors, and children are free.

WOODLAND PARK
Second Street at Woodland, Park Drive
(406) 758-7718

For a delightful afternoon in town, take some time to explore expansive Woodland Park. In the summer you'll enjoy its formal gardens and rose beds for their beauty and fragrance. Both a swimming pool and wading pool are open to the public for a small fee; check with Kalispell Parks and Recreation for hours. To make a day of it—or for a bigger event—pavilions can be rented in advance. When the lagoon freezes over in the wintertime it is flooded and plowed for ice-skating, which is available to the public free of charge. Kalispell Parks and Recreation also offers day activities for children in the summer months; call for a current schedule.

DAYTON

✳ MISSION MOUNTAIN WINERY
82420 US 93, Box 100, Dayton 59914
(406) 849-5524
www.missionmountainwinery.com

Montana may not be the first state that comes to mind when wine aficionados consider their favorites reds or whites, but the Mission Mountain Winery has produced quite a few award-winning wines recognized at both national and international competitions. Primarily Pinot Noir and Pinot Gris grapes are grown at the winery's Dayton location, but Mission Mountain also maintains vineyards in the Rattlesnake Hills of Washington state. Grapes grown there are crushed, transported as juice, and then fermented and bottled here in Montana. This family-run operation offers Johannisberg Riesling, Sundown (Riesling blended with Cabernet Sauvignon), Muscat Canelli, Chardonnay, Cabernet Sauvignon, Pinot Noir, Huckleberry Mountain, and others.

The winery, located on the western shore of Flathead Lake, is open daily from 10 a.m. to 5 p.m. between May 1 and Oct 31. Stop by for a talk about the art and science of winemaking, as well as for complimentary tasting, which includes reserve wines available only at the winery. Special events are posted on the website, where you'll also find information about the winery's vacation cottage, available to rent on a weekly basis. When the season is right, visitors may also have a chance to watch harvesting of the grapes or bottling of new wines.

POLSON

POLSON-FLATHEAD HISTORICAL MUSEUM
708 Main St., P.O. Box 206, Polson 59860
(406) 883-3049
www.polsonflatheadmuseum.org
From buggies to boats, from the Kerr Dam to historic documents, the Polson-Flathead Historical Museum depicts regional history with great variety and depth. Homesteaders, steamboaters, cattle ranchers, city developers, and Native Americans past and present all make their appearance—up to and including Calamity Jane, whose saddle is here. Polson's first building, a trading post, is restored and stocked as it would have been in the 1880s. Local histories described and illustrated—of the Flathead Indian Reservation or the construction of the Kerr Dam, for example—provide insight into the broader history of the region and of the country at large. Local citizens, many of

them descendants of early Montana pioneers, have made generous donations of family artifacts, documents, photographs, and even vehicles to enhance the museum's collection. Here you can also learn about the legendary Flathead Lake Monster.

The Polson-Flathead Historical Museum is open between Memorial Day and Labor Day, from 10 a.m. to 5 p.m. Mon through Sat and 1 to 3 p.m. on Sun. Admission is $3 for adults, while kids under 12 are admitted free.

GLACIER NATIONAL PARK

GLACIER PARK SCENIC BOAT TOURS
Glacier Park Boat Company
P.O. Box 5262, Kalispell 59903
(406) 257-2426
www.glacierparkboats.com
Dance through the mountains on the waters of glacially carved and fed, blue-green lakes . . . watch for wildlife on the surrounding slopes . . . see vistas not visible from the roads . . . and learn more about Glacier National Park's history, geology, flora, and fauna. Glacier Park Boat Company invites you to cruise on Lake McDonald, St. Mary Lake, Two Medicine Lake, and Swiftcurrent and Josephine Lakes in the Many Glacier Valley. Each of the 4 locations offers several daily cruises that last from 45 minutes to 1½ hours. In conjunction with the boat ride, some cruises include National Park Service ranger-naturalist-guided walks to places such as Grinnell Glacier, St. Mary Falls, and Twin Falls. Boat trips can also be used as transportation to trailheads located some distance from the park roads. During peak season be sure to ask about sunset cruises on these spectacular mountain lakes.

Glacier Park Boat Company also offers small boat rentals. Call to check on cost per hour and availability of canoes, sea kayaks, rowboats, and low-horsepower motorboats at each location.

Adult fares for cruises run between $11 and $22, with children ages 4 through 12 riding for half price, and those younger than 4 for free. Each location has its own schedule, opening in late May or early June and closing sometime after Labor Day. Glacier Park Boat Company has phone service during the summer months at Lake McDonald, (406) 888-5727; Many Glacier, (406) 732-4480; Two Medicine, (406) 226-4467; and St. Mary, (406) 732-4430. Don't miss the boat! Allow yourself a good 10 minutes to park your car and walk to the boat dock.

✳GOING-TO-THE-SUN ROAD & US 2 LOOP DRIVING TOUR
Glacier National Park, West Glacier
(406) 888-7800

Going-to-the-Sun Road in Glacier National Park is widely regarded as one of the most beautiful drives in North America. This narrow, winding road leaves West Glacier heading east, skirts Lake McDonald, and climbs from the forest floor up along mountain cliffs to summit the Continental Divide at 6,646-foot-high Logan Pass. The roadway then descends to St. Mary Lake and into the windblown meadows and aspen groves of the east slope, ending at St. Mary. From there, you can turn south along US 89, which snakes along the edge of the eastern foothills and offers spectacular views of both mountains and prairie. At Kiowa Junction, turn right onto Highway 49 to head toward East Glacier, by way of Looking Glass Pass and its huge views of the Two Medicine Valley. In East Glacier you'll meet up with US 2 for the final 60 miles back to West Glacier, tracing the southern boundary of Glacier National Park the entire way. In its first 12 miles, US 2 rises gradually toward the Continental Divide at Marias Pass. At 5,280 feet above sea level, Marias is lower than Logan Pass, but Summit and Little Dog Mountains tower over this wind-scoured, wild stretch of country. Once you begin the descent from Marias Pass, you'll initially follow Bear Creek, then the Middle Fork of the Flathead River.

The mileage for this world-class tour is about 135 miles, and total driving time (in good weather conditions in the summer and minus any delays due to construction) is only about 3½ hours. Nevertheless, this is an excursion you should devote an entire day to, because you'll definitely want to stop again and again to take in views, watch for animals, and learn more about the park's natural history and architecture. Picnic areas are found at several scenic points along the way, if you opt to pack your own lunch; alternatively, restaurants and other facilities are of course located at various points along the route (see the chapter on Glacier National Park for more details).

To begin at the beginning: Parts of Going-to-the-Sun Road can be driven the year around, but as winter arrives, the higher portions are closed by heavy snows. The road typically reopens all the way over Logan Pass sometime in June, but occasionally in May—it all depends on the depth of the snowpack and the plowing conditions. The road usually closes to traffic over Logan Pass sometime in Oct, though Sept closures are not unheard of. This means that the window for driving the full loop tour is generally open only from sometime in June to sometime in Oct. Check at one of the low-elevation park visitor centers to inquire about current conditions at the time of your visit, because snow has been known to briefly shut down Logan Pass even in July and Aug.

You Are in Hypothermia Country!

Sometimes the combination of wind, moisture, and cold can cause hypothermia, or a subnormal body temperature, even when the air temperature is above freezing. Hypothermia is life threatening. The symptoms a victim exhibits are progressive shivering, slow reactions, stumbling and clumsiness, slurred speech, confusion, and loss of judgment. If hypothermia goes untreated, coma and death may result within a few hours. Treatment should be immediate and decisive. Move the victim out of the weather to a sheltered spot; remove wet clothing and cover with a dry blanket or sleeping bag; if necessary, warm the victim with the body heat of another person. If the victim is conscious, administer small amounts of warm drinks. Many avoidable backcountry tragedies have occurred because hikers used poor judgment, induced by hypothermia. You can help prevent this condition by dressing (and undressing) in layers of synthetic fabrics to regulate your body temperature, wearing good rain and wind gear when appropriate, drinking lots of fluids, and minimizing prolonged exposure to wind and rain.

Length restrictions are imposed for vehicles traveling over Logan Pass due to the narrowness of the road and increasing congestion. Vehicles exceeding 21 feet in length, or 8 feet in width (including mirrors), may not drive over Logan Pass; they are also prohibited from the stretch of Highway 49 between Kiowa Junction and East Glacier (for an alternate route, take US 89 from St. Mary all the way into Browning and pick up US 2 there for the trip back to West Glacier). If your vehicle, or vehicle and attached trailer, exceeds 21 feet in length or 8 feet in width, contact Glacier National Park for more information on restrictions. You might consider traveling the road with a Red Bus Tour or Sun Tour, or taking the shuttle. Another popular way to experience the road, by the fit and adventurous, is via bicycle. Note, however, that from June 15 through Labor Day bicycles are prohibited on certain stretches of the road between 11 a.m. and 4 p.m.

These things said, most visitors will drive over Going-to-the-Sun Road in their own car or truck when they want to, during the period that it's open to travel. So, sit back, roll down the windows, and enjoy! You'll be offered the park newspaper—tailored to answer frequently asked questions—in exchange for your entrance fee at the park gate. Apgar Visitor Center, just 2 miles ahead, is a good spot to stop for information and to get your bearings; you might ask here for the brochure *Points of Interest along Going-to-the-Sun Road*.

As you leave the Apgar area and head up Going-to-the-Sun Road, you'll immediately be treated to views of the peaks at the head of the **McDonald Valley.** Or, you might land there on a moody day, with fog lingering close to the lake and only occasional glimpses of what lies ahead.

Everyone has a different idea about where you "just have to stop" along the road. It might be **Lake McDonald Lodge,** or **Jackson Glacier Overlook,** or an unnamed pullout along the shore of **St. Mary Lake.** Some like to pull off to read the **roadside exhibits,** which point out and explain prominent features. Others will incorporate short **hikes** into their driving trip, perhaps the Trail of the Cedars, the Hidden Lake boardwalk, or the Sun Point Nature Trail. It's also possible to include one of the scenic boat cruises (see below) as part of your itinerary. Whatever you choose, you can't go wrong.

Logan Pass, which straddles the Continental Divide, is the high point of the trip, often figuratively as well as literally. Expansive views stretch north to Canada; tiny alpine wildflowers bloom in abundance amid ancient rock; ptarmigan have been known to nest under the Hidden Lake boardwalk; and bears are often enough seen in the meadows surrounding the visitor center. If stopping at Logan Pass is a "high" priority, consider arriving there before 10 a.m. or after 4 p.m.—you'll have an easier time parking and a less crowded subalpine experience! The **Logan Pass Visitor Center**'s huge glass windows allow you to comfortably enjoy the view even if it's nippy outside, and National Park Service naturalists staffing the center will happily answer any questions you may have. The Glacier Association also offers sales of park-related books and other items. Keep in mind that between Lake McDonald Lodge and Rising Sun Motor Inn, no food or drink service is available. There's a phone at Avalanche, but then none until Rising Sun. Logan Pass Visitor Center has public washrooms and drinking fountains only.

You will no doubt discover your own favorite places along Going-to-the-Sun Road. As you leave the park at St. Mary, you enter the **Blackfeet Reservation** and will be within its borders almost until you reach **Marias Pass** on US 2. Several opportunities

on the east side of the park will tempt you to leave the main route and take side trips: **Many Glacier** is about a 40-minute, 20-mile drive north of St. Mary; a winding dirt road leads into the Cut Bank Valley of the park, heading west from US 89 some 12 miles south of St. Mary; or you might explore the **Two Medicine Valley,** a 7-mile drive west from Highway 49. US 89 and Highway 49 are narrow, twisting roads that run along the foothills—take time to enjoy the scenery and drive carefully. You might also opt to stay on US 89 from Kiowa Junction and drive over the plains to **Browning** for a visit to the **Museum of the Plains Indian** and/or the **Glacier Peaks Casino,** returning to US 2 in that town.

Once you reach **East Glacier,** continue west along US 2, which is maintained year-round. Be prepared to battle the potentially vicious eastside winds! Train cars have been blown off the tracks in East Glacier—if the weather is like that, perhaps it's time to look for a hotel or motel room to hole up in. Most likely, though, you'll get a milder dose of what the breeze gods can dish up along the east front of the Rockies.

Soon, you'll top out at Marias Pass (see Marias Pass Memorial Square, earlier in this chapter), and once you drop down to the west side those winds will likely diminish.

For much of the way between Marias Pass and West Glacier, you'll parallel the **Middle Fork** of the **Flathead River.** The **Burlington Northern Railroad,** successor to the Great Northern Railway that opened this area in the 1890s, shares the narrow corridor. Chances are you'll see more than one train wending its way up or down the pass. Extra "helper" engines are added to each train as it leaves Spokane eastbound, or Havre, Montana, westbound to head into the mountains. As you drive along the Middle Fork, you'll notice snowsheds over the railroad tracks at certain places. These avalanche sheds slough away huge amounts of snow from the tracks so that trains can keep running in winter.

About 10 miles before West Glacier, you might keep your eyes out for **Loneman Mountain,** a double-topped peak just across the river to the north. On its second summit sits **Loneman Lookout,** built in 1930 as one of a network of fire lookouts in the park. These days most fire surveillance is done with small planes or helicopters, but these lookouts are still used when fire danger is high locally, and they make fascinating hike destinations.

The last few miles into West Glacier wind along a deep cleft cut by the Middle Fork. The **whitewater** here draws kayakers and rafters. Look for their brightly colored clothing and boats. They often "take out" at the West Glacier bridge—wet, but smiling!

With any luck you'll be smiling at the end of the day, too. And there's always more to explore!

✳ FLATHEAD LAKE SCENIC DRIVE

Flathead Lake is the largest natural freshwater lake west of Minnesota. Its immensity, paired with the mighty peaks surrounding it, make for scenery as striking as you'll find anywhere. Although the variations in landscape are not as dramatic as those you'll see on the Going-to-the-Sun Road/US 2 loop, the ongoing change of perspective as you round the lake will continually surprise and delight you. Sometimes the road runs close to the water's edge; at other times, high through deep cuts made in the lakeshore bluffs. Parts of the valley are verdant

and green, while others tend toward being open, windswept, and dry. The six units of Flathead Lake State Park—Wayfarers, Yellow Bay, Finley Point, Wild Horse Island (accessible by boat only), Big Arm, and West Shore (see the Outdoor Recreation chapter)—all offer opportunities to stop and do a little exploring. And the colorful communities around Flathead Lake provide a wide range of services and attractions.

The total distance around Flathead Lake is about 90 miles, and driving time (in good conditions in summer, minus time lost to any construction delays) is about 2½ hours. You'll want to plan on at least a half a day, though—and why not more? Bring a camera, as you'll no doubt make frequent stops to admire the views.

You can jump in just about anywhere, but we'll begin the trip in Bigfork, situated where the Swan River enters the lake. From here, Highway 35 heads south toward **Polson,** rising and falling gently as it meanders over the hills dropping down to meet the lake. Much of the way the road runs right along and just above **Flathead Lake.** You'll also drive through the famous **Flathead cherry orchards** and no doubt notice the many roadside stands along the way—if it's cherry season, it's yet another reason to stop!

As you enter Polson, Highway 35 joins US 93 at a T-intersection. Turning right will take you into the town, which is a good place to stretch your legs and take a break. Polson offers a full range of services (see the Polson chapter), as well as the captivating Polson-Flathead Historical Museum.

If you follow Seventh Avenue west out of town, signs will direct you to the concrete gravity-arch **Kerr Dam,** situated about 8 miles below Polson. Completed in 1939, the Kerr Dam holds 1.1 million acre-feet

> ## Cherry Season
>
> Each year in May, Bigfork holds its **Cherry Blossom Festival.** Expansive orchards of cherry trees burst into beautiful bloom, mostly along the east shore of Flathead Lake. So, it's not too hard to guess what comes about two months later—cherry-pickin' time! All along Highway 35, between Bigfork and Polson, cherry stands pop up along the road in mid- to late July. If that's when you're there, be sure to stop for a taste of these incredibly delicious cherries, most of them of the Lambert or Lapin varieties. Vendors from the local orchards will be delighted to have you sample their crop, and they'll sell directly to you—by the bag, the bucket, or the pound. You'll also find stands on the west side of the lake, and some even as far away as Hungry Horse. Local groceries stock local cherries, when just about everyone around is enjoying them fresh and turning out pies, jams, and desserts.

bathrooms, changing area, picnic tables, and drinking water. Definitely worth the side trip.

Back in Polson, head north on US 93. Immediately after crossing the Flathead River, you'll notice the high-and-dry hills southwest of Flathead Lake. As you climb the steep hill leaving town, this dry pocket will be left behind; but as you drive farther north, look off to the west from time to time and you'll see more open grasslands. Variations in rainfall, slope, aspect, and soil combine to create dramatic effects on the landscape within very short distances.

i Each season in the Northern Rockies offers its own remarkable attributes and attractions. Summer and autumn, of course, are the best times for hiking, after the heavy winter snowpack has finally melted and the spectacular high country is accessible by foot. Many locals prefer autumn over summer hiking. Crisp, clear days are common; aspen, birch, and larch display their golden hues; the summer crowds are nowhere to be found, and neither are the flies and mosquitoes often common during the warmer months.

of water at full pool; its construction converted Flathead Lake into a manipulated reservoir. Every year, Kerr churns out more than a billion kilowatts of power. The dam operates under a joint agreement between the Confederated Salish-Kootenai tribes and PPL Montana, LLC. You can see the dam and power plant, with a spectacular view of the Flathead River canyon, from the overlook and recreation area south of Polson. The recreation area includes a boat launch,

Soon you'll see two fairly large islands in Flathead Lake—**Wild Horse Island,** a component of Flathead Lake State Park, and, farther west, **Cromwell Island,** which is privately owned. Much romance surrounds Wild Horse Island, home not only of a handful of the namesake wild horses but also bighorn sheep, deer, bald eagles, and the occasional black bear. One local legend has it that Indians once used the island to hide their ponies from marauding tribes, but no one really knows if it's true. The imported horses inhabiting the island today are courtesy of the Bureau of Land Management's adopt-a-horse program. The bighorn sheep population is doing well, and animals from here are occasionally relocated to other places where sheep populations need some bolstering.

Soon the road will sweep around **Big Arm,** treating driver and passengers to an eastward view of the islands and across the lake to the **Mission Mountains.** During the summer months the **Mission Mountain Winery** in Dayton opens a tasting room where visitors can sample select vintages. The vineyards are quite picturesque, with their neat rows of well-tended vegetation.

Continuing north on US 93 toward Kalispell, the route passes through some huge road cuts in the bluffs lining the western shore of Flathead Lake. Watch for a scenic pullout that has a magnificent view—it's a good opportunity to stop for a few minutes and take photos. After you pass through the communities of Lakeside and Somers, look for the intersection of US 93 with Highway 82. Turn right—east toward Bigfork—here. This last stretch of road will take you through the sort of open farmlands that are becoming less and less common as the Flathead Valley develops. You'll pass once more over the Flathead River, this time at the point where it flows from the north into Flathead Lake. The slow-moving water here creates excellent habitat for many birds, from migrating swans to resident bald eagles. On reaching the junction with Highway 35, make a quick right turn and you'll return to Bigfork in short order.

THE ARTS

The arts scene is alive and well in Glacier Country. Not all that long ago, the Flathead Valley wouldn't have been on anybody's short list of art meccas, but now you could spend several days (and several thousand dollars) visiting the galleries in Kalispell, Bigfork, Whitefish, and Polson alone. And, while you might expect to find Western art dominating the studios and galleries around here, that's not necessarily the case. Today, many galleries in the area tend more toward the contemporary or even avant garde than the traditional, though you can readily find plenty of cowboy- and wildlife-themed art, too, if that's what you're looking for.

The same can be said about theater, dance, and music.

OVERVIEW

The scenic grandeur that lures tourists to the region also attracts permanent residents, and many recent settlers have brought with them a wide array of talents and interests that have fueled an artistic explosion over the past 25 years. Indeed, given the Flathead Valley's disbursed population base of around 100,000, it is hard to conceive of the breadth of opportunities and venues found here. But one look at the listings in this chapter will demonstrate that there is something for every interest, from foreign films to blues concerts to, yes, Western art.

Part of the reason for this is, of course, that most of the 2 million visitors a year to Glacier National Park pass through Kalispell and other Flathead communities, bringing an influx of dollars into the local economy. During the summer months especially, this adds up to a healthy contribution to the arts through ticket sales, art purchases, and more.

Another part of the explanation is that Kalispell, Bigfork, and Whitefish have

all developed their own arts communities, along with pride in them, so there's a hint of competition spurring each town to bigger and better things. An example of this can be found in the community-theater scene. The Whitefish Theatre Company (WTC) started in 1978, at about the same time the Flathead Valley Community College's drama department was closing its doors. The success of the WTC goaded Bigfork into tackling its own theater project, and the group known as the Bigfork Community Players (not to be confused with the Bigfork Summer Playhouse) was born. Then, in the early 1990s, when Kalispell actors grew weary of the commute north or south to perform, they founded the Flathead Valley Community Theater. This brought the story full circle, as the new group is affiliated with Flathead Valley Community College, which once again has a dynamic and energetic theater program.

And it's not all about competition among the various Flathead Valley communities.

They are also working together synergistically to create an art scene that is greater than the sum of its diverse parts; art that reflects the majesty of nature apparent everywhere around here. One example of many is the Glacier Symphony and Chorale, a 75-voice adult symphonic choir that draws members from throughout the Flathead Valley—from West Glacier to Polson—and sometimes beyond. Indeed, music director and conductor John Zoltek arrived from the Seattle area several years ago and immediately sensed something special about the orchestra and the environs. "I have a very strong connection to nature," he says, "and so I am delighted to have this opportunity to work and live in the Flathead. Because of the beautiful land that surrounds the area, it is a prime location for beautiful music making."

There is plenty to do for the arts-minded, that's for sure. What follows is a listing of some of the best the valley has to offer in dance, music, art, and more. This summary is by no means comprehensive, but includes a representative sampling from different communities and representing different styles. Do not expect to find every one of the valley's art galleries listed here. There are too many of them, with a constantly changing lineup of exhibits, to be entirely inclusive. But it's easy to find additional galleries by stopping at any of those listed and asking where to go next. The Flathead Valley and great Glacier Country is tourist-friendly, and you'll have little trouble finding a helpful resident who will be glad to point you in the right direction.

MUSEUMS & ART CENTERS

BIGFORK ART & CULTURAL CENTER
525 Electric Ave., Bigfork
(406) 837-6927

Founded 30 years ago, this community-run, nonprofit gallery exhibits artwork and crafts by local artists, with special showings in the summer. The museum seeks to inspire visitors and community members alike through exhibitions, programs, and collections in arts, sciences, and the humanities. The gallery is open Tues through Sat the year around; in summer from 10 a.m. 5 p.m., and with abbreviated hours the rest of the year.

✳THE HOCKADAY MUSEUM OF ART
302 Second Ave. East, Kalispell
(406) 755-5268
www.hockadaymuseum.org

This nonprofit gallery and museum is a longtime hub of the cultural scene in the Flathead. It has been instrumental in developing the community spirit that's led to a range of artistic activities in the Flathead going far beyond the Hockaday's offerings in the visual arts. Hugh Hockaday was an important figure in the area's arts community for more than 20 years; when he died in 1968, the Flathead Valley Art Association, a group of artists who had just begun leasing the 1903 Carnegie Library building, decided to honor Hockaday by naming the new art center after him. A number of his art works are included in the permanent collection, which also features works by many more of Montana's best-known artists, both living and deceased. Throughout the years, the Hockaday has brought high-quality exhibits to the Flathead, including Deena des Rioux and her robotic portraiture; Tim Holmes, a sculptor who showed at the world-famous Hermitage in St. Petersburg, Russia; Russell Chatham, whose delicate watercolors depict the great wide-open spaces of Montana; Dale Chihuly, an internationally renowned glass sculptor; and Gary Schildt, a noted Western artist and member of the Blackfeet tribe. Executive director Elizabeth Moss oversees a program that also sponsors workshops with nationally known local artists. Admission is $5 for adults, $4 for seniors, and $2 for college students. Hours of operation are 10 a.m. to 5 p.m., Tues through Sat year-round.

MUSEUM OF THE PLAINS INDIAN
Junction of US 2 and 89 Browning
(406) 338-2230
**www.browningmontana.com/museum
.html**

The splendid Museum of the Plains Indian offers a comprehensive collection of Blackfeet Indian tribal artifacts, and also has a collection of art by Native American artists and craftsmen, some of which is available for sale. The museum is open daily June through Sept from 9 a.m. to 4:30 p.m. and, during the rest of the year, Mon through Fri from 10 a.m. to 4:30 p.m. Admission is free in winter and $4 for adults and $1 for children 6 to 12 in summer.

THE PEOPLE'S CENTER
53253 US 93, Pablo
(406) 883-5344

This cultural center focuses on the history of the Salish, Pend d'Oreille, and Kootenai Indian tribes, but also has exhibitions of Native American art. The facility includes a learning center, exhibit gallery, and gift shop, and interpretive, guided tours of the Flathead Reservation are offered. It describes itself as "more than a museum; a vital, living encounter with Native American culture, as centuries-old wisdom for living harmoniously with the earth is practiced and taught." It's open the year-round Mon through Fri

from 9 a.m. to 5 p.m., and the same hours on Sat from early June through Labor Day.

STUMPTOWN ART STUDIO
145 Central Ave., Whitefish
(406) 862-5929
www.stumptownartstudio.org

Stumptown Art Studio is a grassroots, community-oriented, nonprofit visual arts center. It aims to provide a place where children and adults feel free and confident to express their inherent creative nature and learn about the world of art. In addition to workshops and lectures, there are exhibits by local artists and a variety of classes and camps offered year-round, including art treks up the Big Mountain in the summer. Painting, fiber arts, sketching, and sculpting all happen here—and don't forget to inquire about the Ceramics Annex. The hours vary throughout the year; call for details. You can also inquire about Whitefish First Thursday Gallery Nights, which take place from the spring into the fall, visiting some 18 galleries each evening.

GALLERIES

ABBRESCIA FINE ART AND POTTERY STUDIOS
12 First Ave. West, Kalispell
(406) 755-6639
www.abbresciafineart.com

A gallery that over the years has carried the works of a Southwestern potter, a landscape oil painter, and a chainsaw artist, along with sculpture and historic etchings, might be considered somewhat eclectic. But in the case of the Abbrescia Studios, it's just a matter of keeping it in the family. According to the late painter and sculptor Joe Abbrescia, the gallery opened in the early 1990s, when his family returned from an extended stay in Scottsdale, Arizona. Today, Joe Abbrescia Jr. specializes in art restoration and art conservation services of fine oil paintings. The gallery is open 11 a.m. to 5 p.m. Mon through Fri.

✳ARTFUSION
471 Electric Ave., Bigfork
(406) 837-3526
www.bigforkartfusion.com

ARTfusion owners Chad and Kathy Leslie say their gallery focuses on bright, colorful contemporary art in a wide variety of media, and of the highest quality. The gallery represents an array of painters and artists working in glass, photography, and ceramics, many of the latter having been residents at the heralded Archie Bray Foundation in Helena, Montana. Representing more than a dozen jewelry artists, ARTfusion also boasts one of the broadest selections of handmade jewelry in the region. The gallery's hours change throughout the year; call ahead for detailed information.

BJORGE GALLERY
603 Electric Ave., Bigfork
(406) 837-3839
www.bjorgegallery.com

When you coast down the hill into Bigfork Bay after turning off of Highway 35, one of the first structures that will catch your eye is the Bjorge Gallery. Sculptor Ken Bjorge converted an old-time service station into a comfortable gallery and studio space. Then, a few years ago, he and his wife built their home on top of the gallery, and the imposing 3-story log structure is a fitting introduction to Bigfork's special blend of artsiness and Western hospitality. "This place is just magical—it really is—and there's room for even more artists in Bigfork," says Bjorge,

who gave up a career as a lawyer and law professor to move to Bigfork and start his midlife adventure as a wildlife and Old West sculptor. Bjorge's work is exhibited in various states of completion in the studio, and new work can be seen taking shape under the hand and knife of the sculptor. Bjorge does many commission pieces, and often monumental-size work can be viewed here before it's shipped to its final destination. The gallery also displays the paintings of such artists as John Nieto, Joe Ferrara, Jack Koonce, Judith Syverson, and Margaret Graziano.

ERIC THORSEN'S FROG SHOP
570 Electric Ave., Bigfork
(406) 837-4366
www.wix.com/thorsen/frog-shop

Oftentimes, it seems as though artists intentionally adopt an imposing or even arrogant persona, perhaps to keep themselves isolated from the demands of celebrity. Eric Thorsen is just the opposite—a sculptor who is so affable and charming that it seems a miracle he gets any work done at all in his studio and gallery, when he'd rather obviously prefer to be chatting with customers. "Our focus is on people coming in and seeing the process of creating sculpture," he says. Though he has done all sorts of wildlife works, and human forms as well, Thorsen recently has been focusing on one of our favorite amphibians, as evidenced by the name of his gallery. The Frog Shop is open from 10 a.m. to 4:30 p.m. Mon through Sat.

GLACIER GALLERY
1498 Montana Hwy. 35 East, Kalispell
(406) 752-4742
www.glaciergallery.com

One of the most extensive collections of Western art in Montana can be found here

🔍 Close-up

James Welch, Montana Author

As you travel through the **Blackfeet Reservation,** you drive through an area that has been inhabited for thousands of years. The Blackfeet Indians traversed the Old North Trail, which can still be traced in a few places where once thousands of dog-drawn travois made their way along the eastern front of the Rockies. Later the Blackfeet acquired horses and became known as the "raiders of the plains" for their fierce defense of their buffalo-hunting grounds. French trappers, Hudson's Bay Company traders, and Jesuit missionaries began to make their appearance as European civilization pushed westward. Smallpox and alcohol followed soon after, and eventually even the buffalo were all but gone. After such profound changes, compounded by more change brought by the 20th century, today the Blackfeet Nation numbers about 14,000 enrolled members, most of whom live on the Blackfeet Reservation.

James Welch is well known for his novels about life among the Blackfeet and other northern plains tribes. Born in Montana of Blackfeet and Gros Ventre descent, he went to school on the Blackfeet and Fort Belknap Reservations. Later he studied creative writing and graduated from the University of Montana in Missoula. *Fools Crow* (1986), probably his best-known work, is set among the Blackfeet of the Two Medicine area in the 1870s, when white men are just beginning to influence the tribes significantly.

in the Glacier Gallery, with paintings and bronzes from the early 1900s to contemporary works. The gallery is owned by Dr. Van Kirke Nelson, a noted art collector, and opened in 1969. Today much of Nelson's extensive collection of Indian artifacts and Charles M. Russell memorabilia is on display periodically for their historical value. Old West paintings by such famed artists as Russell, Edgar S. Paxson, Frank Tenney Johnson, and Olaf Carl Seltzer hang on the walls. There's also Southwestern art from Alfred Jacob Miller; an extensive collection of bronzes by Earle E. Heikka featuring pack trains and other Old West scenes; contemporary sculpture by Sherri Salari Sander, Tom Sander, and Frank Di Vita; and modern paintings by Charles Fritz, Gary Schildt, and Sheryl Bodily. In addition, Glacier Gallery carries prints and a variety of hand-thrown pottery

by local potters. The gallery is open from 10 a.m. to 5 p.m. Mon through Sat.

GOING TO THE SUN GALLERY
137 Central Ave., Whitefish
(406) 862-2751
www.goingtothesungallery.com
Located in the heart of downtown Whitefish, Going to the Sun Gallery specializes in fine art, handmade jewelry, bronzes, and antique furnishings, with an emphasis on historic art. Currently, 17 Montana and regional artists are represented, including Rob Akey, Sheryl Bodily, Joe Kronenberg, Margot Lutz, Nick Oberling, Masako Setoguchi, and Linda Tippetts. The gallery is open daily during the summer to "enhance your civilized wilderness," as the owners, Rochelle Lombardi and Marlene Denny, like to say. Lombardi, a

It is arguably the best reconstruction of pre-European contact Blackfeet culture—or perhaps any precontact American Indian society—ever written. Its protagonist, the young warrior Fools Crow, is born into a traditional world that he will live to see greatly changed.

Other works by Welch are set in contemporary times: Two novels, *Winter in the Blood* (1974) and *The Death of Jim Loney* (1979), represent both hope and despair on the Hi-Line—the high plains of Montana traversed by US 2. More recently, *The Indian Lawyer* (1991) spins the tale of a successful "Indian lawyer" in Helena, Montana, who considers a bid for Congress. Welch's fiction speaks eloquently for those who find themselves still divided between two worlds.

Killing Custer: The Battle of the Little Bighorn and the Fate of the Plains Indians (1994) is a nonfiction account of that debacle that includes the Native American perspective. It originally grew out of work Welch did with director Paul Stekler for the PBS documentary *Last Stand at Little Bighorn,* part of the American Experience series. As with his novels, here Welch adds depth to our knowledge of the past in his recapturing of Native American history. All these works are thoughtfully crafted pieces that will increase your appreciation for what was once buffalo country and the wellspring of a very different way of life. James Welch died in the summer of 2003; his more recent titles are *Riding the Earthboy 40* (1998) and *The Heartsong of Charging Elk* (2000).

sculptor of bronzes, is another of the artists whose work is displayed in the gallery.

MARK OGLE STUDIO
101 East Center, Kalispell
(406) 752-4217
www.markogle.com

Mark Ogle is a native Montanan who has established himself in recent years as one of the premier painters of America's national parks. He has won most of the top artistic awards in the Pacific Northwest and Canada, and he has frequently been among the top finishers in the National Parks Academy of the Arts annual painting competition. Glacier Park is his special love. "As the lower areas of the park see more visitors every year, it's refreshing to hike up where the air is thinner and the bears are free to romp around undisturbed," Ogle says. "We only see the tip of Glacier from the roads, and it's exciting to discover and paint some of the park's more remote regions. You find a different world up there, and it's a painter's paradise." Ogle has also produced and sold oil paintings and prints of Yellowstone, Grand Teton, Yosemite, and Grand Canyon National Parks, as well as parks in Alaska and elsewhere. His work is for sale exclusively in his own gallery, and even then it's hard for him to keep it in stock, since nearly 40 percent of his work is done on a commission basis. You can visit the studio, where you'll frequently find Ogle at work on a new painting. He estimates that he's painted more than 5,000 pieces, but he always has time to share his insights with visitors, and he's a noted raconteur who's handy with a pool cue, and has a love not just of art, but also of the outdoors and the Western life.

✳NOICE STUDIO AND GALLERY
127 Main St., Kalispell
(406) 755-5321
www.marshallnoice.com

Marshall Noice is typical of artists who are also gallery owners in the Flathead. He is accessible, friendly, and prolific. You will find a wide selection of his work at his downtown Kalispell studio and gallery, ranging from naturalistic photography to abstract oils and pastels featuring bold, saturated colors and often an aspen-grove motif. But more importantly, you will usually find *him*. That's one of the aspects of the Flathead art scene that is particularly rewarding for both the dedicated art collector and the curious tourist.

Noice has been photographing Glacier Park for more than 30 years, and that is perhaps what he is best known for. "My fine art photography is black and white," he says. "That probably stems from the summer of 1977, when I was fortunate enough to spend the summer working with [pioneering landscape photographer] Ansel Adams in California. When I want color I want more of it than photography can give me, and that's why my paintings and pastels tend to be very bold. If I'm interested in a literal image, nothing does it better than a photograph, so painting in a literal fashion doesn't capture my imagination."

SAMARAH FINE ART
15 Central Ave., Whitefish
(406) 862-3339
www.samarahfineart.com

Founded in 2004 by artist Rob Stern, a native Montanan, Samarah Fine Art represents nearly 3 dozen artists from Montana and elsewhere in the West. You'll find both traditional and contemporary works

hanging in the gallery, by such artists as Russell Chatham, Kevin Red Star, Bye Bitney, Carol Hagen, and Chad Poppleton. Samarah—a portmanteau of Sam and Sarah, Stern's two children—also offers industry services like locating, brokering, and appraisals, as well as custom-framing services. The gallery's annual show season runs from May through Oct. And they're proud say, "We're a down-home, locally owned establishment, so leave your jeans and boots on and saunter on down for some good ol' Montana hospitality."

SANDPIPER GALLERY
306 Main St., Polson
(406) 883-5956
www.sandpiperartgallery.com

A fine-arts nonprofit corporation, the Sandpiper Gallery features many wonderful displays, which rotate once or twice a month. Space is devoted to well-known local artists, as well as to school-age artists, photographers, potters, woodworkers, and more. On display are exhibits showcasing a variety of 2- and 3-dimensional works, and the gallery hosts many receptions throughout the year that are open to the public free of charge. The Sandpiper also offers gallery talks, demonstrations, and art workshops by nationally and locally known artists. The gallery's annual outdoor Art Festival features a hundred juried artists and craftspeople in conjunction with community and regional events. The nonprofit also maintains a scholarship program for local students enrolled in an art curriculum at a college or accredited art school, as well as offering art programs for younger kids. The gallery is open Mon through Fri from 10 a.m. to 5 p.m. and Sat from 10 a.m. to 4 p.m.

DANCE

NORTHWEST BALLET COMPANY
1411 First Ave. West, Kalispell
(406) 755-0760
www.northwestballet.com
The Northwest Ballet Company is best known for its annual presentation of *The Nutcracker* each Christmas season, and for its Spring Concert, which has featured performances of *A Midsummer Night's Dream*, *Alice in Wonderland*, and other classics. The company was formed in 1980 by Carol Jakes, whose position as artistic director was assumed by Marisa Roth in 2007. The ballet school, which is affiliated with the Kalispell Dance Art Center, also conducts dance training in tap, jazz, modern, and hip hop.

MUSIC

FESTIVAL AMADEUS
P.O. Box 2491, Kalispell 59903
(406) 257-3241
www.glaciersymphonychorale.org
Organized by the Glacier Symphony and Chorale (see below), for a full week in early August Festival Amadeus features both resident and visiting musicians celebrating the soaring sounds of Mozart. Concerts take place at various venues, including the O'Shaughnessy Center in Whitefish and the Christian Center in Kalispell. There's also a big community picnic at Depot Park in Whitefish, as well as workshops, lectures, and student performances.

*FLATHEAD VALLEY BLUES SOCIETY
P.O. Box 219, Somers 59932
(406) 857-3119
www.flatheadblues.org
Steve Kelley, the founder and president of the Flathead Valley Blues Society, is better known 'round these parts as Big Daddy. And when Big Daddy plays, people listen. He's the leader of a band called Big Daddy and the Blue Notes, with artist Marshall Noice on drums, and is frequently heard as the opening act for major blues acts passing through Glacier Country. Most of the blues concerts these days are actually sponsored by the Blues Society, with as many as 7 concerts a year bringing top names in Chicago blues and other blues styles. "There's a dual purpose to the Blues Society," Kelley says. "To perpetuate and support blues music, which is a true American art form, and also to provide alternative live music entertainment." Some of the top names to appear in recent years have included blues harp player Mark Hummel and Chicago blues giant Jimmy Rogers, as well as Andrew "Junior Boy" Jones, Larry Garner, and Coco Montoya. And here's a special "note": the website listed above is streaming the blues right now.

FLATHEAD VALLEY CONCERTS ASSOCIATION
P.O. Box 894, Kalispell
(406) 257-2073
When it was started in 1939, and for many years thereafter, the Flathead Valley Concerts Association (formerly known as the Flathead Community Concerts Association) was bringing in pretty much the only top-name entertainment available to valley residents and visitors. Today there are many more options, but the organization's concert series continues to be popular because of its high standards. A membership drive is held in Apr for the entire series, with members receiving tickets for 4 concerts held between Oct and Apr (but none coinciding with the holiday season). Write to the address above for season ticket information, or call ahead to learn

if any tickets will be available at the door for particular shows. Performers in the 2010–11 series included the Afiara String Quartet, BrassWerks, and the Andy Stein Duo.

✳FLATHEAD VALLEY JAZZ SOCIETY
Glacier Jazz Stampede
P.O. Box 2627, Kalispell 59903
(406) 755-6088
www.glacierjazzstampede.com

The Flathead Valley Jazz Society sponsors concerts and jazz parties throughout the year, bringing regional and local entertainment to the fore. But since 1994 the society has been best known for the Glacier Jazz Stampede, which has grown into one of Glacier Country's most anticipated annual events. The Stampede, held over a 4-day period in early Oct, features some of the greatest musicians in traditional, swing, and Big Band jazz. Bands come from as far away as California, Washington, British Columbia, and Alberta; local favorites, including the Don Lawrence Orchestra, perform as well. Already the largest event of its kind in western Montana, the Jazz Stampede counts on local participation as well as the hundreds of jazz fans who travel from festival to festival in search of their favorite music. In addition to Dixieland and Big Band, the festival always features ragtime music and has also included different sounds, such as Latin jazz. The musicians perform on a rotating basis at 4 or 5 venues, usually including the Eagles Club and the Red Lion Hotel.

GLACIER SYMPHONY AND CHORALE
P.O. Box 2491, Kalispell 59903
(406) 257-3241
www.glaciersymphonychorale.org

The Glacier Symphony and Chorale (GSC) has grown from a core group of musicians who got together to perform at a wedding in 1981, to what it is today a gathering of nearly 300 volunteer and professional musicians who perform more than 30 concerts annually throughout northwest Montana. This group was one of 12 orchestras honored nationally in 1991 by the American Society of Composers, Authors and Publishers for excellence in programming of contemporary music. John Zoltek has been the music director and conductor since 1997, and his dynamic mastery of difficult music has helped turn the orchestra into a true showcase of fine talent. Guest performers are regularly featured as well, such as violin virtuoso Eugene Fodor and renowned composer and pianist (and Montana native) Philip Aaberg. The holiday concerts in Dec are usually sellouts, so plan to buy tickets early if you'll be in Glacier Country at that time.

NORDICFEST
P.O. Box 791, Libby 59923
(406) 293-2440
www.libbynordicfest.org

We may be stretching the limits of Glacier Country by talking about the town of Libby, but this event is worth the detour. On the second weekend of every Sept, this Lincoln County community rolls out the carpet and turns Scandinavian for Nordicfest, a celebration of local and international culture. J. Neils came to the area from Wisconsin at the turn of the 20th century to start a lumber mill, and his business attracted a lot of Scandinavian loggers and their families. So, both logging and Nordic roots are remembered during the festival, which features a variety of musical and theatrical events as well as crafts and ethnic foods. Special events include the ever-popular Fjord Horse Show, a fine-arts show, a quilt show, and the Kootenai Karacters Melodrama. Through the weekend there's also plenty of

Swedish pancakes, ham loaf, Swedish meatballs, and—for those with exceptionally strong Scandinavian stomachs—boiled fish.

RIVERBEND CONCERT SERIES
P.O. Box 237, Bigfork 59911
(406) 837-5888
www.bigforkevents.com
If you'd like to enjoy a musical experience in the great outdoors, you can do no better than the Riverbend Concert Series, held on Sun evenings in Bigfork's Everit Sliter Memorial Park from June through Aug. The music ranges from the big-band sounds of the Don Lawrence Orchestra to Celtic, folk, bluegrass, and rock/Americana. In other words, there's something for just about every musical taste.

THEATER

BIGFORK COMMUNITY PLAYERS
P.O. Box 23, Bigfork 59911
(406) 837-5888
www.bigforkcommunityplayers.com
The local amateur actors known as the Bigfork Community Players perform 3 or 4 plays every year, from the late fall to the spring. In addition to enthusiastic casts, the plays are produced in the Bigfork Center for the Performing Arts, where every one of the 435 seats is a good one. Recent productions have included *Don't Drink the Water*, *Blithe Spirit*, and *Drinking Habits*. The Players, who are in it strictly for the fun and camaraderie, have recently added a slate of children's theater workshops and productions, such as *Once on This Island Jr.*, to their calendar.

*BIGFORK SUMMER PLAYHOUSE
526 Electric Ave.
P.O. Box 456, Bigfork 59911
(406) 837-4886
www.bigforksummerplayhouse.com

Every summer, the Bigfork Center for the Performing Arts becomes the Bigfork Summer Playhouse, bringing in actors from across the United States to put on first-class musicals and comedies. The Bigfork Summer Playhouse was begun in 1960 and has provided a training ground for hundreds of aspiring theatrical performers, technicians, and musicians. It has been under the direction of owners Don and Jude Thomson since 1971. Recent productions at the playhouse have included *Dirty Rotten Scoundrels*, *Fiddler on the Roof*, *Tom Foolery*, *All Shook Up* (based on the music of Elvis Presley), *Sugar Babies*, and *Forbidden Broadway*. Each year, more than 3,000 people from throughout the United States apply to join the company. Note that tickets are less expensive for performances happening before July 4 (or if purchased at the beginning of the season). The box office opens around the middle of May; starting then, you can purchase tickets by telephone, mail, or in person. Discounts are available for groups. Mon through Sat, the performances begin at 8 p.m., and on Sun there's a 2 p.m. matinee.

FLATHEAD VALLEY COMMUNITY THEATER
777 Grandview Dr., Kalispell
(406) 756-3822
The local community college has also gotten into the act the past few years, theatrically speaking. Joe Legate, the head of the theater department, has been instrumental in reshaping a theater program that was quite active in the 1970s but eventually went on hiatus. Legate arrived in Kalispell in 1992 from North Dakota, where he had spent several years teaching at Dickinson State University. He has also worked in theater programs at Clemson University, the University of Southern

Mississippi, and the State University of New York. Though the theatrical program draws heavily from the students and faculty at the college, many of the shows use other members of the community, as well. Look for a broad variety of shows, from pure farce to high drama. Recent offerings have included *The Pillowman*, *Pygmalion*, *Much Ado About Nothing*, and *Evita*.

*THE PORT POLSON PLAYERS
P.O. Box 1152, Polson 59860
(406) 883-9212
www.portpolsonplayers.com

The Port Polson Players offer professional summer-stock theater, presenting classic comedies and musicals on Wed through Sat evenings and Sun afternoons during the summer. The company was begun in 1976 by Larry and Pat Barsness, who also started the Virginia City Players, in Virginia City, Montana, in 1948. The Polson group was purchased by Neal and Karen Lewing in 1983, and they have run it successfully ever since, adding a year-round community-theater schedule to what started as just a summer-stock company. The larger-scale community-theater offerings are now presented at the John Dowdall Theatre at the Polson golf course. Among the titles presented recently have been *Lover's Leap*, *That's the Poop*, and *The Dixie Swim Club*. The Lewings also write a children's show every year, including adaptations such as Sleeping Beauty and original titles such as Fortune's Fables.

WHITEFISH THEATRE COMPANY
1 Central Ave., Whitefish
(406) 862-5371
www.whitefishtheatreco.org

This is the oldest continuing community theater group in Glacier Country, performing since the mid-1970s. The company prides itself on diverse productions, including dramas, such as *The Diary of Anne Frank;* musicals, such as *Cinderella;* classics, like *A Midsummer Night's Dream;* family shows, such as *A Christmas Carol;* and comedies, like *Dividing the Estate*. Now installed at the new, 326-seat I. A. O'Shaughnessy Center, the Whitefish Theatre Company also sponsors performances of modern dance and music from around the world. Evening shows begin at 7:30 p.m.; Sun matinees at 2 or 4 p.m.

VENUES

BIGFORK CENTER FOR THE PERFORMING ARTS
526 Electric Ave., Bigfork
(406) 837-4885
www.bigforktheater.org

This 435-seat facility in Bigfork provides year-round entertainment. May through Aug the Bigfork Summer Playhouse offers musical repertory theater, while at other times throughout the year, it is home to productions by the Bigfork Community Players, and to fashion shows, ballet performances, and more. The playhouse is renowned for its comfort and for the great view from any of the seats.

I. A. O'SHAUGHNESSY CENTER
1 Central Ave., Whitefish
(406) 862-5371

The people of Whitefish are noted for giving generously to community projects, and during a several-year campaign, ample funds were raised to build a center for the performing arts as well as a nearby library building. The I. A. O'Shaughnessy Center, which includes a 326-seat theater facility, had its grand opening on July 4, 1998. The Whitefish Theatre Company holds a long-term lease on the building and is now focusing its schedule on the thrust stage, which has seating on three sides, plus a balcony. Concerts, dance, film, and other theatrical presentations are also booked into the facility year-round. The seating can be pushed back to accommodate other uses, such as public forums and chamber of commerce events.

LITERARY ARTS

AUTHORS OF THE FLATHEAD
Flathead River Writers Conference
P.O. Box 7711, Kalispell 59901
(406) 881-4066
www.authorsoftheflathead.org
"Writers helping writers" is the motto of the Authors of the Flathead, a group that boasts around 100 members. Authors of the Flathead conducts a craft-of-writing workshop or a speaker's meeting on most Thur nights. (A recording at the phone number listed above has details on times, locations, and each week's topic, as well as other upcoming activities.) Each year the group also holds its Flathead River Writers Conference in early Oct at Flathead Valley Community College (the 20th annual conference took place in 2010). "The conference is getting an excellent reputation in writing circles, from the Midwest to California and Canada," said a conference spokesman.

The gathering features a variety of writers, editors, and agents. Guests have included Jack Sowards, author of hundreds of television episodes and many movie screenplays, including *Star Trek II: The Wrath of Khan,* and Steve Chapple, a Livingston, Montana, author noted for his book *Confessions of an Eco-Redneck* as well as numerous magazine articles. The conference always includes editors or publishers who can help see new writers through the nuts and bolts of publishing. The conference is considered one of the most affordable of its kind in the Pacific Northwest, with a weekend filled with speakers, panel discussions, and one-on-one workshops.

ARTS & CRAFTS

ARTS IN THE PARK
P.O. Box 83, Kalispell 59903
(406) 755-5268
Ever consider doing your Christmas shopping in July? You can get it all out of the way at the popular Arts in the Park festival held the last weekend of July at Kalispell's Depot Park (located at the intersection of US 93 and Center Street). The festival is a fundraiser for the Hockaday Museum of Art and has been held ever since the museum was founded in 1968. It calls itself the oldest and best juried art fair in Montana. At the very least, it is a darn good time, regularly attracting as many as 10,000 people. More than 100 local and visiting artists and artisans exhibit works every year in numerous media, including painting, sculpture, pastel, photography, glass, jewelry, pottery, ceramics, weaving, wood carving, leather, metal, and more. A few artists will also be on hand to demonstrate how they go about making their creations, and you'll no doubt enjoy the usual generous helpings of musical entertainment and food that make these arts and crafts fairs so popular.

✳BIGFORK FESTIVAL OF THE ARTS
P.O. Box 237, Bigfork 59911
(406) 837-5888
www.bigforkfestivalofthearts.com
The Bigfork Festival of the Arts, held the first weekend in Aug every year, features more than 120 booths, with some artists coming from as far away as Oregon, Washington,

and California. Booths feature everything from paintings, prints, jewelry, stained glass, and pottery to wooden toys, wearable art, and baskets. There are also a variety of food booths, serving up such goodies as huckleberry milk shakes, German barbecue, and snow cones, as well as the usual hamburgers and hot dogs. Bigfork's main business street, Electric Avenue, is converted into a pedestrian mall for the festival, with opportunities for shopping both in the booths and in local shops, which sell everything from books to antiques to a wide variety of artworks. Musical performances throughout the day also provide entertainment, and activities for children take place at various locations. This is one festival you won't want to miss if you happen to be in the right place at the right time.

WHITEFISH ARTS FESTIVAL
P.O. Box 131, Whitefish 59937
(406) 862-5875
www.whitefishartsfestival.org

The Whitefish Arts Festival, held on the first weekend in July, turned 30 years old in 2010. And it has never disappointed. The event is a feast both for the eyes and for the palate, featuring nearly 100 artists from the Flathead Valley and beyond, as well as food vendors, local musicians and entertainers, and other fun. Up for sale is every variety imaginable of paintings, woodcraft, pottery, original clothing, and other handicrafts. The festival takes place in Parkside Credit Union Park, at the corner of Spokane Avenue and Railway Street. It serves as a fund-raiser for the Whitefish Christian Academy, which can be reached at the number listed above. Admission is free.

ANTIQUES

Postcard-worthy scenery, soul-nourishing outdoor activities, and world-class golf greens all draw visitors to Glacier Country. This corner of Montana, especially Flathead County, yields yet another, perhaps more unexpected, attraction: It is known as the antiquing mecca of western Montana. From Bigfork and Somers on Flathead Lake north to Whitefish and on to Hungry Horse, you can find dozens of antiques malls and shops—at last count they numbered more than 30, quite a respectable number for a county with a population of just 90,000. Most antiques stores keep the doors open year-round for those who search out the antiques experience no matter where they travel or what month of the year it is.

A logical way to antique the Flathead is to do a loop, beginning in Bigfork on Highway 35, then turning west onto Highway 82 (known locally as the Somers cutoff road). At its junction with US 93, turn south and proceed past Somers to visit the shops found there. Then do a short backtrack up US 93 and proceed north into Kalispell and then on to Columbia Falls. (If you begin in Somers, reverse the process.)

While Kalispell has the highest concentration of antiques stores, several new shops have opened in Columbia Falls over the past four years, thereby giving Kalispell a run for its antiquing money. You'll want to plan extra time to enjoy the pickings in both towns. Although space constraints limit this chapter to some top spots, be sure to visit other local antiques stores for more great finds as time allows. Many are interspersed along the way.

The listings here give a representative taste of what the Flathead Valley has to offer. They include contact information, days of business, and a general overview of what you might find. It's a good idea to call ahead to make sure the business you want to visit is open, although the beautiful drive to get to any of these locations can be worth a trip in itself. Generally, owners of the Flathead Valley's antiques stores are happy to open by appointment if you are looking for something special and cannot visit during regular business hours. The top antiques stores are not rated numerically as to which are the best, but are listed by location on the antiquing loop. Enjoy your antiques tour!

ARCHITECTURAL INNOVATIONS
7975 Montana Hwy. 35, Bigfork
(406) 837-2334

Looking for a place to retire, Margrit Matter chose Bigfork after a vacation visit in 1991. Instead of basking in retirement, however, she finds herself running the busy Swan River Inn in downtown Bigfork, as well as an affiliated antiques store and interior-design center that she calls Architectural Innovations. Established in summer 1998, the showroom contains Margrit's discerning

Old World Antiques furniture line, composed of European antiques dating from the late 1700s through the early 1900s. Her store is a little out of the ordinary for this corner of the country. From her West Coast ties to the construction and remodeling industry, in which she worked before relocating here, she is able to bring in fine imported pieces.

Besides being originals, furniture selected for her store must still function properly and be in excellent condition, she says. Here you might find a pine piece from the former Czechoslovakia, an oak armoire from England or Belgium, or a carved bed of French walnut or cherry. You'll discover other quality pieces—hutches, wardrobes, dressers, settees, tables, desks, and accessories. Look also for salvaged architectural details and original European and American art, as well as a selection of beautiful European crystal.

Margrit's home-design center houses several rooms featuring specialty items. The electrical room highlights antique light fixtures and lamps; the plumbing room features an unusual variety of sinks—including handpainted, granite, hand-blown glass, and copper. The kitchen showcases cabinets, sinks, faucets, knobs, and other hardware. In the tile room, you'll find a variety of floor tiles, from Mexican Saltillo to slate. Upstairs you can find wallpapers, fabrics, and carpet. Margrit's goal is for one-stop shoppers to find everything they need at her operation. If a customer wants to mix new furniture with old, she offers new locally handcrafted pieces in a variety of woods.

The store is open 7 days a week during summer. Off-season, it's open Mon through Sat, and closed Sun.

i Several of the antiques dealers in the region maintain sites on the Internet. One such site belongs to Columbia Falls-based Funtastic Finds, where owner Sally Petersen offers turn-of-the-20th-century antiques, along with vintage jewelry, purses, shoes, and clothing. You can make a virtual visit by tapping in to http://funtasticfinds.webs.com/index.htm.

SOMERS ANTIQUES
210 Hwy. 82, Kalispell
(406) 857-3234

At the intersection of US 93 and Highway 82, look for the large signs advertising the Somers Antiques store. Go east of US 93 on Highway 82. As you enter the yard, you pass by weathered furniture and bicycles. Miscellaneous old tables, chairs, cupboards, and iron headboards line the long porch. As you venture inside, you are greeted by 6,000 square feet of antiques and collectibles displayed in a mercantile-type atmosphere. Crammed with items from a bygone era, this store will yield up everything from blanket chests to cupboards, pine tables to primitive wood benches, and ice-cream-parlor chairs to Coca-Cola soda-pop machines.

Owners Larry and Carol Ask, collectors themselves for nearly three decades, offer several specialties at Somers Antiques. If you are looking for oak or pine, they provide a large selection of refinished furniture. The store is full of hundreds of old toys (some from Larry's personal collection), pedal cars, old bicycles, tools, and tins. Sporting paraphernalia, such as old fishing rods and golf clubs, mingles with other collectibles. You can find advertising signs, a piece of Western memorabilia, and lodge and cabin decor items. You might spot a handmade twig shelf, an old canoe converted into a bookshelf, or a reclining chair upholstered in cowhide.

"We usually have a good selection of old carpenter's tool chests, which work well for coffee tables," Larry says. Something you may not expect is a variety of Victorian-style lamps. Some of the floor lamps are old, while the table lamps are reproductions. Fringed and beaded shades, despite being new, impart a vintage look.

Somers Antiques is open 7 days a week in summer, from June to Labor Day. During winter, the store opens at noon 5 or 6 days a week, but the schedule is flexible, so be sure to call before you set out to visit.

✳SOUTHSIDE CONSIGNMENT CENTER AND ANTIQUES STORE
2699 US 93 South, Kalispell
(406) 756-8526

More than a dozen antiques dealers and hundreds of consigners keep this 6,000-square-foot store south of Kalispell stocked with collectibles and antiques. Owned by Donna Kouns, the rambling store offers a wide assortment of items. A stroll through here might turn up an old baker's table, a drop-leaf table, or a variety of hutches and dressers. You'll see lots of kitchen kettles, crockery, and old utensils. If you collect teacups, you may find a new favorite. Sterling-silver pieces, flatware, and rhinestone and antique jewelry add their sparkle to the mix. Old toys and books are interspersed among furniture and accessories. You might also run across Western memorabilia, such as a branding iron or lariat. Among Donna's favorite past pieces was a cast-iron wood cookstove with blue enamel, manufactured by Windsor.

At Southside Consignment goods can be viewed—and carted home with you—year-round Tues through Sat. The store is closed Sun and Mon.

TIMELESS TREASURES ANTIQUES & COLLECTIBLES MALL
124 Main St., Kalispell
(406) 752-4659

An attractive window display will charm you into entering Timeless Treasures, easy to locate on Main Street (US 93). Old music from the 1950s, '60s, and '70s played on an old-fashioned record player greets you. Take a trip down music's memory lane with such greats as Frank Sinatra, Lena Horn, Billie Holiday, Johnny Mathis, and even Simon and Garfunkel.

Diversity is the key to this 2,000-square-foot shop, says Linda Heim, who owns the business with husband Jim. The store is host for some three dozen dealers to showcase their wares. Many of them focus on specialty items and either own their own antiques stores or have booths in other local antiques malls, as well. A good collection of estate jewelry and costume jewelry, along with hard-to-find books, are just some of the items you can expect to find at Timeless Treasures. Glassware, including Fenton and Depression glass and American-made pottery and dinnerware, is available here. Collectible cars and John Deere toys mingle with reproduction pedal cars. Old dolls and Victorian-style lamps with beaded and fringed shades add a unique touch of yesteryear.

Besides the specialty goods of the dealers, you are likely to find primitive kitchen items and furniture, Linda says. Or, you might spot that rare Vaseline glass pickle jar with castor, or beautiful black Victorian purse with a mauve bird-and-flower design. A trip to the downstairs might net you a medicine cabinet made from an old church window or a charming table with barley-twist legs.

Timeless Treasures is a pleasant stop and stays open year-round 7 days a week.

i Karen Monaghan is the founder of Big Sky Country Antique Fair, held usually in June at the O'Shaughnessy Center in Whitefish. The show attracts dealers from across the country and specializes in Americana furniture and folk art. Definitely worth planning your antiquing trip around! Visit www.visitmt .com for dates and contact information.

KALISPELL ANTIQUES MARKET
48 Main St., Kalispell
(406) 257-2800

Up the street on the corner of First and Main is a must-stop antiques mall at Opera House Square. Located in the historic opera-house building, the mall is downstairs, tucked under a spacious Western clothing store. The market sprawls across 10,000 square feet, making it the Flathead Valley's largest antiques mall, where three dozen dealers display their merchandise. Proprietors are brother and sister Lee and JoAnn Eslick.

Since every square inch bursts with interesting items to look at, give yourself plenty of time to wend your way through 3 long rooms with aisles of booths. The store features a wide selection of antiques and collectibles reference books, in case you're looking for antiques guides.

Roseville pottery has long been a specialty at the Kalispell Antiques Market, with quite a bit of Fenton glassware also for sale, and the market boasts one of the best selections of vintage rhinestone jewelry in the valley. Look here for handmade primitive

furniture and decorator items, which might include a pie safe with punched tin doors.

A large section of Western Americana books can be perused as well; you might run across volumes by noted Montana authors A. B. Guthrie, J. W. Schultz, and Frank Linderman. Or, you might spot an old Hileman Glacier Park photo. Western memorabilia and lodge decor items come in but go back out quickly, since they remain ever popular in the Flathead, as do old hunting and fishing gear.

Adding to the mix are original oak pieces, many from the late 1800s to early 1900s. Antique oak furniture might include sideboards, buffets, dining tables with chairs, or glass-fronted bookcases. Other interesting collectibles spotted here range from linens to vintage paper goods, an extensive collection of old and new Hummel figurines, and an apartment-size oak icebox, manufactured by Garland. "We have [had] quite an increase in Art Deco collectibles," JoAnn says, "whether lighting or textiles."

The market welcomes visitors year-round 7 days a week.

ANGEL CONSIGNMENT
1420 Hwy. 35, No. 103, Kalispell
(406) 752-1342

From the intersection of Idaho (US 2) and Main (US 93), go east on US 2/Highway 35. Just past the Snappy Sport Senter, take a right at the Square One shopping center and you'll see Angel Consignment. Here, owner Von Hines has filled her 2,700-square-foot space with old and not-so-old pieces. Von takes pride in the fact that she carries only solid-wood furniture, and no pressed wood. The selection includes cherry, mahogany, oak, maple, walnut, cottonwood, and ash. She carries some solid-wood reproduction pieces, too. Spicing up the mix are a few rustic pieces, such as an old barnwood cabinet with mirror.

Canaries and cockatiels talk to you from their birdcages as you shop. Von likes to have them around, she says, because they are great for "conversation and they keep the little kids busy."

At Angel Consignment you might find an antique English gossip bench, or an old oak rocker sporting its original springs and wheels. The store has a good selection of library tables and secretaries, too, or you might discover a 1920s Haywood Wakefield dining table with four chairs, a sheet music cabinet, or an old Hoosier cabinet with metal countertop and green glass knobs. Most of the floor lamps are antiques, and Von also carries some Roseville pottery. Artwork is either original oils or watercolors or good quality prints, she notes. One of Von's favorite pieces is an oak buffet from the 1920s with ornately carved square feet. Its arched mirror reflects beveled glass, and the pulls are original. "Most of the old stuff all had the beveled glass," she says.

Stop by and visit year-round Mon through Sat, or Sun afternoon.

✳STAGELINE ANTIQUES
2510 Whitefish Stage Rd., Kalispell
(406) 755-1044
www.stagelineantiques.com
Go back to US 93; turn north and drive out of Kalispell. After you cross West Reserve, continue driving north until you come to milepost 118. Turn east onto Tronstad Road and drive to the intersection with Whitefish Stage Road, turn south, and go approximately 0.12 mile to Stageline Antiques on the west side of the road.

This pleasant country setting was simply made for a country store, and that's exactly what owners Bob and Chris Tolbert have created. Over the course of three decades they have amassed a collection of antiques guaranteed to thrill not only any children you may have in tow, but also your own inner child. This is the oldest antiques store in the Flathead Valley.

For fans of Coca-Cola, this a must stop. Signs for that product and others crowd together on the exteriors of the garage and store. (The Tolberts collect Coca-Cola advertising themselves.) A good selection of gas pumps, restored by Bob, stand on the grounds as another reminder of the era of mom-and-pop stores. Inside, expect to see tools of the trade from way back when— scales, bean counters, and old brass cash registers, for examples. A particularly unusual piece is an old drugstore counter that has "Prescriptions" written on it. Another find is an 1880s restored walnut watchmaker's cabinet.

When the Tolberts opened the store in 1968, they carried antique wood-burning kitchen cookstoves; you'll still find wood- and coal-burning stoves today, dating from the late 1800s through the 1920s. Old toys and cars from the 1920s through the 1960s, including Bob's assortment of restored pedal toys, fill glass cases. And you might come across a rare 1926 Stutz pedal car.

Stageline Antiques is also the place to search for soda-fountain and game-room collectibles, such as a 1957 Wurlitzer jukebox. And if you'd like to take home a unique brass lighting fixture, Bob has restored a number of those. A nostalgic highlight at Stageline Antiques is the hand-carved, 1890s wooden carousel horse. You can learn a great deal more about the inventory by prowling around their website.

The country store is open year-round 6 days a week, Mon through Sat.

COCK-A-DOODLE-DOO!
12 Lupfer Ave., Whitefish
(406) 862-0776

If your whimsy is folk art, your penchant is for primitives, or your heart beats for American country, you should stop at Cock-a-doodle-doo! in Whitefish, just off Baker Avenue. What better symbol for Americana than a rooster crowing to one and all the delights of this treasure-filled antiques business, housed in a little red barn trimmed in white. Located in the alley behind owner Karen Monaghan's house, the shop was designed to look like an East Coast carriage house. The cheeky rooster on the shop's exterior proclaims the store is open 6 days a week.

The scent of candles and potpourri greets you as you enter, and in winter Karen keeps a pot of tea or coffee warming to take away the chill from diehard antiquers. From shelves to floor, every square inch of this shop bursts with American country appeal. Country primitives, traditional handmade crafts, and reclaimed architectural pieces lend the enterprise distinction. Old cupboards and shelves with peeling paint hold decoys, crockery, and hand-pieced table runners. Look for crocheted rugs and old quilts, which add their own brand of homespun flavor. If you've been searching for a gateleg or drop-leaf table, you may find them here, either with peeling paint or newly painted. Vintage 1930s and 1940s tablecloths may be spied, as well, rolled up and tucked in a crock or basket.

Karen is constantly bringing in new country accessories and giftware that blend well with her antiques, such as Ohio-made crockery bowl sets and Amish doorknobs. Also look for architecturally inspired accessories—all made from pieces of old houses—or you might find a mirror to hang on your wall or other charming piece to take home.

Cock-a-doodle-doo! is open seasonally in July and Aug and on select weekends. To check before you go, you can e-mail Karen at kmonaghan@bigsky.net or call her at the number above. Karen is also the organizer of the Big Sky Country Antique Fair—see the Insiders' Tip in this chapter.

i Should you find yourself a Flat-head Valley "golf widow," shopping for antiques makes a great daytime pursuit for whiling away some time.

OLD TOWN ANTIQUES
13 O'Brien Ave., Whitefish
(406) 863-9633

Right across the alley from Karen's shop is a tall, yellow home that was designed by owner Andrea Dunnigan to look like an old row house. Don't miss this shop, where, in addition to antiques, you will find locally made reproduction furniture and new home decor items.

The primitive reproductions made by local craftsmen, who fashion them from old wood salvaged in the area. Barnwood from local homesteads has been given new life as wall cupboards and wood plate racks. Other pieces have been constructed using tongue-and-groove wood removed from the old Whitefish Masonic Temple when it was remodeled. "All pieces have some history to them," Andrea says.

She designs her reproduction furniture and a local carpenter builds it—some of it on-site. Andrea also has garage-sale finds refinished. A trip to Old Town Antiques might net you a cupboard with a salvaged window as a door. Other furniture to look for includes daybeds, reproduction cabinets, and harvest tables. If you fall in love with a table but it's not the size you need, she can probably have one like it built to fit your dining space. Some tables are constructed of salvaged wood, some made with new wood. Tables can be painted to look old or done in a natural finish, whichever fits your style.

Upstairs, Andrea runs the textiles part of her business, where she sews pillows and table linens using vintage drapery panels from the 1920s through the 1950s. The bright pillows and table runners make strikingly colorful accents when placed among her rustic wood furniture. Andrea also sews handmade pillows from natural linen.

Many of the store's items go to clientele furnishing second homes, Andrea says. An eclectic piece from Old Town Antiques will make a handsome addition to your cabin, cottage, or country home—even if you have only one!

Old Town Antiques is open year-round Tues through Sat.

KIDSTUFF

For a kid visiting the mountains in summer, what could be more fun than skipping rocks and splashing around in the cool water of a lake or stream? How about a simulated bobsled ride, a trip in a chairlift, or the ultimate in summer fun—traveling to a high mountain pass and making snowballs in July! In winter, of course, snow is the thing everywhere. Skiing, snowboarding, sledding, ice-skating—and snowballs—will keep Mom and Dad out in the cold along with the kids. Hot chocolate might entice you to come inside long enough to get warm, but then you're out the door again.

Glacier National Park and the Flathead Valley both offer myriad activities for kids in the summer. Glacier isn't all that accessible in winter, and many attractions in the Flathead close from late September until May or June. But summer always makes its return, bringing with it the promise of fast-moving water and the possibility of an abundant crop of wild huckleberries.

From "A" to "Z," the following are suggestions for some of the most kid-friendly activities in the area; let interest, ability, and stamina be your guides.

✳A AVALANCHE LAKE TRAIL & TRAIL OF THE CEDARS

On Going-to-the-Sun Road, about 5 miles east of Lake McDonald Lodge, is one of the best short family hikes in Glacier National Park. The trail leads from the Avalanche picnic area and campground about 2 miles on a gentle slope to a clear glacial lake. On a hot day, you may be tempted to splash around in the water at the end of the trail, but remember that it's fed by meltwater from the glacier above and is very, very cold. Be aware that the lake's wide shore can be crowded. Park Service naturalists also guide hikes to **Avalanche Lake**—check the *Glacier Explorer* newspaper for the schedule.

If the 2-mile hike seems a bit much for your clan, and you prefer to just stretch your legs, the 1-mile, wheelchair-accessible **Trail of the Cedars** is a good choice. It, too, starts from the Avalanche picnic area and heads through a magical grove of trees with trunks 4 to 7 feet in diameter.

B BIG MOUNTAIN

In summer or winter, Big Mountain is a place you simply *must* visit while in Glacier Country. (Don't be confused by the new name, Whitefish Mountain Resort—the mountain is still Big Mountain!) It doesn't have to be January for this ski area to be fun and exciting; in fact, some of the summer activities rival alpine skiing for their fun factor.

Hiking and **mountain biking** can be done on the mountain by persons of just about any age and ability level—you can either bring your own bikes or rent them (and helmets) here. Special programs for kids are available; call (406) 862-2900 for more information.

Other kid-friendly activities include the scenic lift ride to the **Summit Nature Center.** The lift—called the **Big Mountain Express**—makes the trip to the top, 2,000 feet of vertical gain, in about 10 minutes. A restaurant and picnic area are located at the **Summit House**—where you can also feast on the views. The Nature Center, run by the USDA Forest Service, has interpretive displays on wildlife and habitats, complete with a children's activities corner. Kids 7 to 12 are encouraged to become Junior Forest Rangers, a free honor that includes a special badge and certificate. And families are invited to borrow an **Outdoor Adventure Pack,** which includes field guides and other materials to help make outdoor explorations more educational. The center is open daily from 10 a.m. to 5 p.m., from late June through early Sept; its phone number is (406) 862-1972.

Additional activities at hand are the **Walk in the Treetops** (a 2½-hour guided nature walk through subalpine forest taking place along an elevated boardwalk), Zip Line Tours, and the occasional concert.

The **Whitefish Mountain Resort** is located at the top of Big Mountain Road, just outside of Whitefish. To get there, take US 93 north through town and follow it as it turns west. Turn right onto Baker Avenue and pass over the viaduct. It turns into Wisconsin Avenue; follow it all the way to Big Mountain Road, which is marked with a flashing yellow light.

C CORAM'S AMAZING FUN CENTER

If wandering through the **Glacier Maze** at this popular US 2 attraction doesn't interest you, **miniature golf, go-karts,** and **squirting bumper boats** might tickle your fancy. You can't miss the Amazing Fun Center—though you may miss the town of Coram if you don't look carefully—as you travel on US 2 to and from Glacier National Park and the Flathead Valley; you'll spot the giant wooden walls of the maze.

D DEPOT PARK

Stop to admire the restored Kalispell train depot while the kids frolic in this grassy park. The shaded area with benches is perfect for a picnic—and if you're lucky, you'll catch a live performance at the gazebo. The park is located at the corner of Center Street and US 93 (Main Street) in Kalispell.

E EVEN IN THE RAIN!

Should you get a rainy day, **Flathead County Library** branches are open 6 days a week in Kalispell, Whitefish, and Columbia Falls, and 5 days a week in Bigfork. Each library has a kids' section specially designed for easy browsing by the younger set. "Story hours" happen on a regular basis, too; call ahead to see what's on. And the Whitefish library has a fireplace you may want to cozy up to, as well! Phone numbers are: Kalispell, (406) 758-5820; Columbia Falls, (406) 892-5919; Whitefish, (406) 862-6657; and Bigfork, (406) 837-6976. For more information on the library system, check out www.flathead countylibrary.org on the Internet.

F FLATHEAD LAKE

Flathead Lake is the largest freshwater lake west of Minnesota, and there are six state parks to enjoy along its waters (one of them, Wildhorse Island State Park, is accessible only by boat). The **fishing, picnicking,** and **swimming** are all terrific. There's plenty of **water activities:** Sailboats, motorboats, canoes, sailboards, and other watercraft can be rented at several locations; short cruises, evening cruises, and day trips are available from touring companies, as well. See the Kalispell, Attractions, and Polson chapters in this book for more information.

G GRIZZLY BEARS

If you're lucky, you may see a grizzly bear (from a distance!) while you're in Glacier National Park. But even if you don't, you'll know you're in bear country—everything from the Montana Grizzlies and Lady Griz sports teams to ministorage businesses and dog schools are named for the bears. See how many "bears," of any kind, you can count in Montana.

Real grizzlies come in a variety of sizes and colors. They can be blonde, brown, or nearly black. You can distinguish them from black bears by their distinctive faces (their noses turn up at the end of a rather dished-in profile) and by the large hump between their shoulders.

Make plenty of noise while you're hiking the trails to warn bears of your presence, so that they can get out of your way before you get close to them. Talking loudly, clapping your hands, singing a song, or even yelling once in a while are good ways to make noise. A growing number of people carry pepper spray in case of an encounter. See the Close-up on bear safety on p. 186 for more information.

H HUCKLEBERRIES

You'll notice huckleberry products—jams, jellies, pancake syrup, barbecue sauces, wines, vinegars, and more—all over western Montana, but the self-proclaimed center of the huckleberry universe is the town of Hungry Horse. These small purple fruits, a wild relative of the domestic blueberry, are a true Montana delicacy, and it would be a shame to miss out on their juicy, messy goodness. At the **Huckleberry Patch Restaurant and Gift Shop** on US 2 in Hungry Horse, you'll find all things huckleberry, including an excellent huckleberry pie.

The Outdoor Recreation chapter has more information about seeking out the purple fruits yourself, though the location of prized patches is often a secret passed down from generation to generation. Personnel at USDA Forest Service ranger stations in the area can give you a good idea of where to look if you're in the area at peak berry time—generally late July and Aug. Be aware that bears are awfully fond of the berries, too, so huckleberry-picking should be a group endeavor! Make lots of noise while you're picking, and let the bears have the berries if you happen to meet up at one of their favorite patches.

I ICE

To a certain extent, ice—really, really big and heavy ice—is what Glacier National Park is all about. Those peaks and valleys were formed by glaciers scouring the land and carving knifelike edges on the tops of mountains. In Glacier National Park you can play in the runoff water from melting glaciers, and you can actually walk out on glaciers yourself (given sufficient skill level and stamina in your group). One excellent place to see **glaciers** is the **Swiftcurrent Valley** on the east side of the park. Step out on the boat dock behind **Many Glacier Hotel** to view **Grinnell** and **Salamander Glaciers,** or take a scenic boat cruise and get a closer look from Swiftcurrent Lake.

J JEWEL BASIN

This **hiking** area in the Swan Mountains shines even when compared to the recreational opportunities in Glacier National Park. There are more than two dozen lakes and 35 miles of hiking trails in the 15,000-acre area, making it excellent for day hikes and short backpacking trips. This is a great place to introduce your kids to the backcountry experience.

Two good hikes for families lead to **Picnic Lakes** and to **Birch Lake.** Either is suitable for a day hike or short backpack outing. The Picnic Lakes are 2.5 miles from the trailhead at Camp Misery on Forest Trail 8. Birch Lake is accessed from Forest Trail 717 and Forest Trail 7. A trail map is located at the parking area, and a forest ranger is frequently on hand to answer questions.

To get to Jewel Basin, take US 93 from Kalispell 7 miles south and turn east toward Bigfork onto Highway 82. Turn south at Highway 35 and proceed to the flashing light, where you will turn east onto Highway 83. At another flashing light, turn north onto Echo Lake Road. Signs will lead you to the Jewel Basin parking lot and trailheads.

K KEHOE'S AGATE SHOP

On a rainy day, or even on a sunny one when you've just had enough scenery and fresh air, this little shop in what used to be the town of Holt is a great place to visit with the kids. In addition to its colorful polished agates, the rustic shop—built in 1932—has a collection of petrified wood, minerals, gems, fossils, and thunder eggs collected from all over the world. To get there from Bigfork, turn west from Grand Avenue onto Holt Drive at the flashing yellow light. Signs will lead you to the agate shop in 2.3 miles. The road ends at the shop, so you won't miss it.

L LICENSE-PLATE GAME

Montana's big spaces and steep mountains mean lots of roads and lots of time spent in the car. Luckily, traffic arrives from enough places to make the time-tested license-plate game fun for kids. See who can spot license plates from the most states and provinces. To make it more interesting, assign point values to the states based on their area or population, or their distance from Montana. The winner gets to decide what activity to try next.

M MOUNTAIN GOATS

Though there are many places in Glacier Country where you might spot one of these agile creatures, one of your best options is 3 miles east of the town of Essex on US 2. There you'll find a parking lot on the south side of the road, with a trail leading to an overlook. On the steep cliffs above the Middle Fork of the Flathead River, you'll have a good chance of seeing billy goats, nannies, and kids, as well as elk and deer. The animals are attracted to the mineral deposits on the cliffs—most of their time here is spent in licking the rocks.

N NATIONAL PARK SERVICE

The National Park Service offers guided hikes and regularly scheduled interpretive talks throughout Glacier National Park. Check at a visitor center for the Junior Ranger Program and find out more about kid-friendly activities listed in the *Glacier Explorer* newspaper.

You can also call (406) 888-7800 for more information on schedules and topics.

O ÓHPSKUNAKÁXI

The Blackfeet name for the area around Many Glacier Hotel is Óhpskunakáxi, meaning "waterfalls," and this is one of the best places in the park to see the tumbling water up close. One of the best short hikes for families is to **Apikuni Falls,** a 0.7-mile walk with spectacular mountain views, colorful wildflowers, and the occasional Columbian ground squirrel to interest you along the way. The falls, and the potential of seeing pikas, a small, furry, short-eared relative of the rabbit, are rewards for the steep but enjoyable trek. To get to the hike, take Many Glacier Road 1 mile east of the hotel to the trailhead parking lot on the north side of the road near Apikuni Creek bridge.

✳P POLEBRIDGE MERCANTILE

If you have a vehicle up to the rigors of the trip, a visit to Polebridge—where you can see part of the West that is still wild—is one your kids will truly enjoy. The drive up the North Fork Road is a bumpy and dusty one, but the fresh-baked goods at the **Polebridge Mercantile** and the possibility of seeing bears, wolves, moose, elk, deer, mountain lions, and fields of wildflowers make it worthwhile.

Q SHHH . . . QUIET

Quiet hours in campgrounds are intended to help everyone get a good night's sleep and be ready for the next day's adventures. Particularly at the campgrounds in Glacier National Park and at the busy state parks around Flathead Lake, crowds mean noise.

Observing quiet hours from 10 p.m. to 6 a.m. keeps everyone happy.

R REDROCK FALLS

This easy 1.8-mile hike in Glacier National Park is a great one for stretching the legs and viewing **waterfalls** in the Many Glacier area. Sedimentary red rocks line the way, and you can also still see a burn area from a major 1936 fire on your way to the falls. Be aware that the icy pools at the bottom of the falls are not ideal for wading—the rocks are slippery and the water is extremely cold. To get to the trailhead, go to the parking area across from the Swiftcurrent Camp store in the Many Glacier Valley. The hike starts at the parking area.

S SKIPPING ROCKS

Many an hour has been whiled away by children and adults skipping rocks, and the shores of Lake McDonald offer a great spot for this most serious of fun pursuits. Behind Lake McDonald Lodge is a boat dock—where you can rent boats and buy tickets for the guided lake tours—and beside the dock are some fine large rocks for sitting on, with the little skippers scattered about nearby.

T TYRANNOSAUR AT ALBERTA VISITOR CENTRE

Could anything be more fun than visiting the **Tyrannosaurus rex** skeleton at the **Alberta Visitor Centre**? Well, how about a simulated bobsled ride? It may be hard to tear your kids away from the exhibits at this visitor center, designed to introduce visitors to Canada's Waterton Lakes National Park. You don't have to cross the border to get there; the center is in West Glacier, just off US 2. See the Attractions chapter for more information.

U UMBRELLA WEATHER?

Though outdoor recreation is the area's main attraction, there are, of course, times when inclement conditions drive even the hardiest of adventurers inside. Two great options for indoor family outings in Kalispell are the **Hockaday Museum of Art** and the **Conrad Mansion.** See The Arts and Attractions chapters, respectively, for more information.

V VORTEX

The **House of Mystery** has to be the strangest attraction in Glacier Country, and it's guaranteed that your kids will love it. It's located on US 2 between Columbia Falls and Hungry Horse, and you'll see the billboards for it before you actually locate the small house where seemingly everyone is stopped. Why is it a mystery? The folks who run it claim that the area around the house is in a gravitational vortex, causing the trees to grow sideways. The odd angles of the house may convince you . . . though whether it's the work of mysterious forces or optical illusion is something your kids will have fun trying to determine.

W WILD HORSE ISLAND

You may not see wild horses at this state park in Flathead Lake, but there are plenty of other attractions to entice you to rent a boat so you can set foot on shore, or to board the *Polson Princess* for a ride around the island. The island got its name from the Flathead and Pend d'Oreille Indians, who are said to have used the island to protect their horses from raids by the Blackfeet. There are no facilities on the island, though the wildlife doesn't seem to mind. You may see the plentiful bighorn sheep, among other critters.

i Spending the Christmas holidays in the Flathead? You might want to know that Santa's sleigh flies over the valley each year, on some evening in December that no one can predict. Suddenly you'll look up and see a lighted sleigh moving through the sky. (You may hear that this has something to do with ALERT, the Kalispell Regional Medical Center rescue helicopter, but Santa has connections in many important places.) Children (as well as adults) love it, and it's just one more reason to be good before Christmas!

X XEROPHYLLUM TENAX

The tall stalks with fluffy cream-colored heads that you may see throughout Glacier and the Flathead are called **beargrass,** but not because Xerophyllum tenax actually has anything to do with bears. Lewis and Clark—who skirted the eastern edge of this territory during their explorations of the Louisiana Purchase—named it beargrass because bears were often seen in its vicinity, and they assumed the bears ate it. Now we know that beargrass has more to do with elk, which eat the whole plant, and with mountain goats, which eat the parts untouched by winter's snow. Native Americans wove baskets and clothing from the plant, which can grow to be 5 feet tall. The fluffy head of the flower is generally about the size of a large fist. Be aware that the leaves, which lie in bunches close to the ground, are slippery . . . so watch your step.

Y YAAK

The Yaak, which is short for the **Yaak River** drainage, is a rugged and remote, off-the-grid area occupying the extreme northwest corner of Montana. It's worth making a day trip from Kalispell to explore it. The kids will love the waterfalls, wildlife, and winding, timber-embraced roads.

✳Z ZIP LINE

The **Zip Line Tours** at the Whitefish Mountain Resort are a summer favorite for the bigger kids—those who've reached at least 54 inches in height. Strap on a harness, click in to the cable trolley, and get ready for some real fun!

ANNUAL EVENTS

At Glacier Country's annual events—big and small, on sunny summer days and in the snow—you can expect to see residents coming out in full force and visitors joining in on the fun. Fiddling festivals, arts in the parks, rodeos, powwows, and the ubiquitous huckleberry fests fill up the calendars of events and demand everyone's attention. The following listings, organized by month, are just a sampling of some of the more time-tested events held in the shadows of Glacier Country's glorious mountains and on the shores of its lakes.

JANUARY

Winter in Montana is cold, snowy . . . and wonderful. So Montanans tend to spend as much time outdoors as possible, and the annual events schedule reflects that tendency. Winterfest in Seeley Lake is one of the most consistent offerings, but you can find cross-country ski races, downhill skiing events, snowmobile runs, and winter games of all sorts nearly every weekend.

WINTERFEST
Seeley Lake
(406) 677-2880
www.seeleylakechamber.com
Located a few miles south of the southern end of the Swan Valley, the community of Seeley Lake comes alive for their annual celebration of winter. Activities include ice-sculpture judging, dogsled rides, and snow softball, topped off by that midwinter tradition—fireworks. There's also cross-country skiing just outside of town on the Seeley Creek Trails, one of the best Nordic skiing venues in the northern Rockies. The dates for Winterfest vary every year, so call the chamber of commerce at the number above or visit the website for information.

FEBRUARY

It's still cold out, so how about a nice evening torchlight parade and art walk? The folks in Whitefish cook up a special event every year in early February, and have since 1960—the ✴**Whitefish Winter Carnival.** Call (406) 862-3501 or visit www.whitefishwintercarnival .com for more information about the happenings. For some reason, February also seems to lead to thoughts of fine things to eat and drink, and this is the month of wine and food festivals and chocolate fairs throughout the Flathead.

✴SNOW JOKE HALF-MARATHON
Seeley Lake
www.cheetahherders.com/snowjoke
.html
For more than 30 years, the loosely organized Seeley Lake running club known as the Cheetah Herders—almost everything about this group and its events is tongue-in-cheek—has been hosting the annual Snow Joke Half-Marathon. But the 13.1-mile loop around Seeley Lake really is no joke; the pavement can often be snow- and/or ice-covered, so shoes with good traction are highly recommended. Afterward, overall and

🔍 Close-up

Free Your Heels, Free Your Mind

Over the past 30 years, the venerable telemark turn has seen a huge revival in the United States and Europe. Telemark skiers use "free-heel" equipment: Their ski bindings connect only the toe, not the heel, of the ski boot to the ski. With this greater mobility—and instability—telemarkers are able to ski upslope as well as down, and so the equipment is used as a means for winter enthusiasts to explore hilly backcountry terrain away from the designated ski areas. Crested Butte, Colorado, and Whitefish, here in Montana, have been two of the primary centers of telemarking in America. On the gentlest slopes of the Whitefish Mountain and Blacktail ski resorts, you'll see folks trying it out, starting to carve their turns with knees bent and one ski shooting ahead the other. People get addicted to the graceful turn—it's challenging and eventually becomes fluid, almost like a dance over the snow. Like all sports, telemark has its upper-end practitioners, and telemark racing rivals alpine racing for the money and time its racers put into it. The Whitefish Mountain Resort is regularly a stop on the World Cup Telemark racing circuit, and in 2010, the resort's slopes hosted the US National Championships. Check out the schedule of events; big races often take place in March. It's a great time to be in town, as "tele" racers come in from Sweden, Norway, Switzerland, Germany, Austria, and other countries to compete. You'll see them walking around town in their racing colors as they visit local bars and restaurants . . . and you'll really want to see them up on the hill, the best at what they do.

divisional winners are draped in fur sashes and inducted into the Royal Order of Cheetah Rangers.

MARCH

March may be spring some places in the world, but in the Flathead snow is still the main source of entertainment. Be sure to check out local cross-country, telemark, and downhill ski races. This is also a good month to catch performances and concerts at local theaters. There's plenty to do, both indoors and out!

APRIL

Well, in April the ski areas generally close and the snow recedes. Too bad. We'll have to

venture elsewhere for our fun . . . how about a storytelling weekend in Cut Bank?

MONTANA STORYTELLING ROUNDUP
Cut Bank High School
101 Third Ave. Southeast, Cut Bank
(406) 873-0276
The town of Cut Bank lies immediately outside the Blackfeet Indian Reservation, at the eastern extent of what Travel Montana, the state's official tourism branch, considers to be Glacier Country. Every year, over a weekend in late Apr, around a dozen entertainers from throughout the West gather in Cut Bank for this unique event. More than 3,500 people sit in to listen to live cowboy poetry, stories (ghost and otherwise), folk music,

Indian tales, fun and funny history lessons, and more. Great for the entire family!

MAY

Now it's starting to look like spring! You can celebrate the arrival of warm weather with a trip to the Cherry Blossom Festival at Yellow Bay, by hitting the water in a kayak race in Bigfork, or by attending one of the several other May events not listed here.

CHERRY BLOSSOM FESTIVAL
Yellow Bay Club House, south of Bigfork
(406) 982-3437
This area is famous for its cherries, and this festival will surely make you think of the warm summer to come. It's a fund-raiser for the Yellow Bay Ladies Auxiliary, and includes craft vendors, a bake sale, live music, and more.

✳WHITEWATER FESTIVAL
Bigfork
(406) 892-2256 or (406) 752-2880
The water will be really cold—and really fast—over Memorial Day weekend, so bring your wet suit and something warm for post-water fun. There's a slalom race for beginners, as well as a slalom for experts along the infamous Wild Mile of the Swan River. Also on tap for the weekend: a down-river race, a triathlon, and entertainment at the local pubs and elsewhere.

JUNE

Summer's festivals are just heating up, but there are plenty of offerings as the days get longer and warmer. Hit the water and the trail, but remember it's still early in the summer season and come prepared for all kinds of weather conditions. One of the most

exciting events of the year—the opening of Going-to-the-Sun Road—usually takes place in June. It's a great time to see the park teeming with wildlife and showing its spring colors in banks of wildflowers.

JULY

Make sure you get your spring yard work done, because with all of the offerings of the season you won't have much time on the weekends to do much more than mow. Starting in July and continuing through Aug, this is the busiest time of year in Glacier Country.

WHITEFISH ARTS FESTIVAL
(406) 862-5875
www.whitefishartsfestival.org
The Whitefish Arts Festival turned 30 in 2010. The event is a feast for the eyes and the palate, featuring nearly 100 artists from the Flathead Valley and beyond, as well as food vendors, local musicians and entertainers, and other fun stuff. The festival takes place in Parkside Credit Union Park, at the corner of Spokane Avenue and Railway Street. It serves as a fund-raiser for the Whitefish Christian Academy.

ARTS IN THE PARK
Kalispell
(406) 755-5268
This juried art show held annually in Kalispell's lovely Depot Park benefits the Hockaday Museum of Art in Kalispell. Fine arts and crafts, entertainment, and food are featured.

BLUE MOON NRA RODEO
Columbia Falls
www.northernrodeo.com

Bareback, saddle-bronc, and bull riding are all a part of rodeo action, and you'll find plenty of it here at the Blue Moon Rodeo. The Northern Rodeo Association sanctions the event, so top performers are expected in all categories. Other July Glacier Country rodeo events, also part of the series, take place in Babb and Eureka.

KSANKA STANDING ARROW POWWOW
Elmo
(406) 849-5659

This is a great place to experience the culture of the Kootenai Indians, who share the Flathead Reservation with the Salish Indians. The event is held at the Kootenai headquarters in Elmo, on the west side of Flathead Lake. Dancing is the main event of the powwow.

MAIN STREET CHERRY FESTIVAL
Polson
(406) 883-5800

A family event featuring more than 125 vendors, including arts and crafts, food, live entertainment, children's activities, homemade cherry pies, jewelry, woodworking, and more (including the always-popular cherry-spitting contest). Local businesses offer specials in their stores.

ARLEE POWWOW
Arlee
www.arleepowwow.com

The 112th Arlee Powwow took place in 2010, so it's well into its second century. The event is sponsored by the Confederated Salish and Kootenai tribes and takes place in Arlee, at the southern end of the Flathead Reservation. Dancing is the main feature of the powwow, and dancers wear traditional and nontraditional costumes. Stick games,

Native American crafts, clothing, and food items—such as the delicious fry bread—are also features of the powwow.

LEWIS AND CLARK FESTIVAL
Cut Bank
(406) 873-2201

When you're on and around the Blackfeet Indian Reservation, be sure to take some time to reflect on one of the most important expeditions in American history, that of Lewis and Clark and their Corps of Discovery. Not far south of Cut Bank, which is just east of the Blackfeet Indian Reservation, is the Two Medicine Fight Site (not open to the public), where the only bloodshed to occur between the expedition and any Native American group happened on July 27, 1806. This event commemorates that tragic day, but also includes a parade, costume contest, concerts, a chili cook-off, a horseshoes tournament, and more. Camp Disappointment, the northernmost point reached by any of Lewis and Clark's men, is also nearby, 12 miles northeast of Browning.

✳NORTH AMERICAN INDIAN DAYS
Browning
(406) 338-7406
www.browningmontana.com/naid.html

This nationally recognized powwow is the highlight of the year on the Blackfeet Indian Reservation to the east of Glacier National Park. Dancers and visitors come from around the country to the capital of the reservation at Browning; a parade, sporting events, and a rodeo are also held during the weekend. The Museum of the Plains Indian is located in Browning and will provide good background for your powwow experience.

AUGUST

✳NORTHWEST MONTANA FAIR AND RODEO
Flathead County Fairgrounds

A highlight of summer in the Flathead Valley, the fair stretches over 5 days in late Aug and offers everything from farm animals and 4-H projects to a rodeo, pig wrestling, and carnival rides. In between are horse races, fireworks displays, and all sorts of exhibits. There's even a demolition derby. Visit www.nwmtfair.com to learn more.

HUCKLEBERRY DAYS
Whitefish
(406) 862-3501

This annual ode to the tiny bright purple treasures that Montanans call huckleberries is filled with pie-eating contests, a huckleberry cook-off, and an arts and crafts fair. If you return home without a purple tongue and purple fingers, you simply have not devoured enough of the magical berries. For shame!

BIGFORK FESTIVAL OF THE ARTS
Bigfork
(406) 881-4636
www.bigforkfestivalofthearts.com

After more than 30 years, this event continues to offer fun music, good food, and fine arts and crafts in the setting of a village that *Sunset Magazine* named one of the most picturesque towns in the Northwest.

SANDPIPER OUTDOOR FESTIVAL OF THE ARTS
Polson
(406) 471-5243
www.sandpiperartgallery.com

Held on the courthouse lawn in Polson, thousands flock to town for this fine arts and crafts festival that has been a Polson tradition for more than 30 years. It also features food booths and live entertainment.

WHITEFISH LAKE TRIATHLON
Whitefish
(406) 752-2880

This popular competition is a sprint-distance triathlon, with a half-mile swim, 20-kilometer bike leg, and 5-kilometer run. Afterward, there's burgers, beverages, and more than $1,000 in prizes.

SEPTEMBER

LIBBY NORDICFEST
Libby
(406) 293-2440
www.libbynordicfest.org

A short drive west from the main corridor of activity in the Flathead Valley, this traditional Nordicfest is worth the trip down US 2 for food, dancing, wood-carving workshops, and the extremely popular quilt show. They also serve lutefisk, just in case you've been craving a taste of that delicacy.

FLATHEAD QUILTERS GUILD SHOW AND QUILT AUCTION
Flathead County Fairgrounds
(406) 892-5864

Almost 30 years old, this major quilt show has become a well-established Flathead County event. It's a great chance to pick up a handmade piece of Montana history!

OCTOBER

✳GLACIER JAZZ STAMPEDE
Kalispell
(406) 755-6088
www.glacierjazzstampede.com

This jazz festival, one of the largest music gatherings of any style in Montana, brings visitors from around the country to hear 4 days' worth of traditional and Dixieland jazz. Food, crafts, and sidewalk sales can also be found at festival venues.

NOVEMBER

November is the time to start praying for snow and gearing up for the return of winter. Kalispell is the first to offer a Christmas parade, and more will follow in the month to come.

DECEMBER

The holiday season is upon us, and most communities offer lights and celebrations. Think snow at this time of the year; (almost) everybody wants a white Christmas and a powder-filled New Year.

NIGHT OF LIGHTS PARADE
Columbia Falls
(406) 892-7529

**HOLIDAY PARADE, ART WALK, AND
  TREE LIGHTING CEREMONY**
Bigfork
(406) 837-5888

**SANTA'S CHRISTMAS EVE TORCHLIGHT
  PARADE**
Whitefish Mountain Resort
Big Mountain, Whitefish
(406) 862-2900

OUTDOOR RECREATION

This wondrous land in the northern Rocky Mountains was known by the Blackfeet Indians as the "backbone of the world." A jewel in the Crown of the Continent, Glacier National Park and surroundings is a mecca for outdoor recreationists of all stripes. In this chapter you'll be guided to some of the best recreational opportunities in the region—which is to say, in the world—and offered some hints on how to help keep the area's pristine beauty intact for future visitors. Certain precautions to take while recreating in the great outdoors are also included.

THE ENVIRONMENT

With Glacier National Park at its core, Glacier Country is a geologic mosaic that was created by natural forces over the span of some three billion years. Once a vast inland sea, sediment and sea life deposited in layers on the bottom formed the limestone we see today. Volcanic activity subsequently thrust up mountains to great heights; then the mountains underwent upheavals that slid older layers of rock over younger ones.

This "block overthrust faulting" created the steep rock faces on the eastern front and the somewhat gentler slopes on the western side. The massive glaciers that retreated around 14,000 to 10,000 years ago sculpted some slopes more steeply, while rounding other hills and filling in low spots with glacial till.

Nature's work continued over many millennia with storms, floods, avalanches, wind, and fire. The resulting landscape we see today is home to the plants and animals that make this region's ecosystem unique in all the world.

The variety of plant and animal communities reflects the broad ranges of climate, geology, topography, and soils. Elevations range from a low of 3,150 feet at the juncture of the North Fork and Middle Fork of the Flathead River to 10,466 feet at the summit of Mount Cleveland. This elevation differential of more than 7,000 feet alone influences life zones to a great degree. From the temperate rain forest of the Lake McDonald Valley one can travel to an arctic tundralike environment simply by driving to Logan Pass, elevation 6,646 feet. Variations in the relative quantities of moisture, wind, sun, and shade at each elevation further influence and create local microclimates.

The area we are considering comprises three million acres of nearly unbroken wilderness. Roughly bounded by Waterton Lakes National Park on the north, Highway 83 on the west, US 89 on the east, and Highway 200 on the south, the region encompasses Glacier National Park and the Great Bear, Bob Marshall, and Scapegoat wilderness areas in the Flathead and Lewis and Clark National Forests. A million acres are in Glacier National Park, 2.36 million acres in the Flathead National Forest, and the remainder under state and private ownership. The Swan Range runs north-south uncut by a road for 100 miles. In other words, there's plenty of wild country to explore here.

Within this wild circle endures one of the world's largest intact temperate ecosystems. Populations of most plants and animals—carnivores and herbivores, predators and prey, and the plants that sustain them—remain from before Euro-American explorers and trappers first ventured in 200 years ago. In Glacier and Waterton Lakes National Parks alone live more than 1,000 varieties of plants, 25 major tree species, 264 bird species, nearly 60 kinds of mammals, and 17 species of fish.

The larger predators include grizzly and black bears, mountain lions (or cougars), gray wolves, coyotes, foxes, lynx, badgers, martens, and mink. Larger prey animals include moose, elk, white-tailed and mule deer, mountain goats, and bighorn sheep. These are accompanied by their smaller neighbors such as beavers, snowshoe hares, pine squirrels, deer mice, and meadow voles. Even the nearly exterminated bison that once roamed the plains by the thousands is represented by a captive herd in Waterton Lakes National Park. And the Flathead River system is one of the few watersheds in the country that still support self-sustaining, genetically pure populations of native westslope cutthroat and bull trout.

The Continental Divide—The Great Divide—the north-to-south mountainous spine bisecting the region, exerts a major influence on weather, capturing rainfall from warm, moisture-laden air masses moving in from the coastal states on the western side of the mountains. The mountains also restrict the westward flow of cold, continental arctic air masses from east of the Rockies.

The eastern slopes are dry, hot in summer and bitterly cold in winter, and windy, and beyond them lies the vast upland prairie that once supported the great bison herds. In the high country, weather can be extremely changeable, and both sunshine and snow are possible at any time of the year.

Water has been and continues to be another powerful force shaping the landscape and influencing habitat. The Flathead River's three forks drain Glacier National Park, thousands of acres of the Flathead National Forest, and part of British Columbia. The US Congress designated 219 miles of these waters as part of the National Wild and Scenic Rivers System. Sometimes heavy spring rains, a deep mountain snowpack, and warm temperatures that hasten snowmelt combine to swell one or more of the forks and the main river beyond their banks. The riverbed constantly changes as the waters eat away the banks in some places and deposit soil and debris at others. The Stillwater, Whitefish, and Swan Rivers wind their way through forests, agricultural fields, and urban areas. The St. Mary River heads north, carrying Glacier's waters toward Hudson Bay. Numerous swift mountain creeks carve through rocky channels to reach forest and meadows below.

Disturbances to the land, both natural and human-caused, also greatly influence plant and animal communities. This landscape has evolved with fire as a constant force for change and renewal. Frequent lowintensity surface fires kill small trees and shrubs and leave the more fireresistant trees largely intact. Many tree and plant species, especially the pines—ponderosa, lodgepole, western white, and whitebark—and western larch depend on fire to perpetuate their existence. Lodgepole pine, which maintains its seed in fire-resistant cones for several years, is often abundant on sites where whole stands have been burned. Some seeds remain dormant in the soil for decades and sprout after a moderately hot fire. Aspen, huckleberry, fireweed, and grasses quickly move in to revegetate a burned area. Grizzly bears and elk feed on many of these "pioneer species." Native Americans intentionally burned prairies and pine-forest understory plants to improve grazing conditions for deer, elk, and bison.

Introduction of nonnative species, most notably fish and noxious weeds, has also disrupted natural habitats. Native fish have suffered from habitat loss, food competition, and disease from the presence of these "exotics." Noxious weeds, introduced largely by Euro-American settlers in crop or pasture seeds over the past century, are so aggressive they have infested millions of acres, choking out native plants and destroying fish, wildlife, and livestock habitat. Spotted knapweed, leafy spurge, and St. John's Wort are among more than a dozen noxious weeds targeted by weed-control programs of western Montana counties, which require landowners to eradicate weeds from their property.

PLANT & ANIMAL COMMUNITIES

With an abundance of streams, rivers, lakes, and wetlands in the broad Flathead Valley, the riparian zone is one of the area's most prominent habitats. In valley bottoms at about 3,000 feet in elevation, black cottonwood, willow, alder, and red-osier dogwood dominate the tree and shrub species growing along the waters, often mixed with a smattering of conifers and quaking aspen. Biologists estimate that 82 species of wildlife depend on these riparian marshes and forests, including

enormous numbers of migratory birds, along with resident eagles and osprey. Spotted sandpipers bob along shorelines; red-winged and yellow-headed blackbirds share the cat-tail marshes and sloughs with muskrats, beavers, and raccoons. River otters, weasels, and mink can also be found here, and even the rare northern-bog lemming has been spotted in Lake McDonald's marshes. White-tailed deer find good browse in the grasses, sedges, and shrubs. The haunting cry of the common loon, long gone in many states, still adds its magical notes to nature's symphonies on large and small lakes across Glacier Country. And the brightly colored harlequin duck is a brilliant presence on the rushing, cold mountain streams in and around Glacier National Park during the bird's breeding period.

i If you plan on backcountry camping in Glacier Country, you should carefully select gear to minimize bulk and weight but maximize safety and comfort. Your comfort level will be greatly enhanced, obviously, if you take clothing that keeps you warm and dry, and that can be layered. Wear clothing next to the skin that wicks away moisture and dries quickly. Bring a portable camp chair so that you can relax comfortably in camp. An empty stuff sack can easily be converted into a pillow by stuffing it with extra clothing. Consider wearing gaiters to keep rocks, brush, and snow out of your boots. Sometimes a mosquito net is a welcome addition to your backcountry gear arsenal. These are just a few tips to keep in mind.

From 3,000 to 4,000 feet, quaking aspen, paper birch, and black cottonwood continue to dominate valley bottoms, especially in

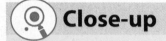

Close-up

The Fires of 2003

On July 17, 2003, one of the most dramatic fire seasons in northwest Montana's history began with a lightning storm at about 2 a.m. Both the **Wedge Canyon** and **Trapper Fires** started that night—one in the Flathead National Forest north of Columbia Falls, and another in the remote center of Glacier National Park. It was an early start to the fire season, and fuel moisture levels were at historic lows—some standing live trees had been sucked of their moisture to a greater degree than kiln-dried wood. Soon, most of northwest Montana was covered in smoke so dense that much of the time the fires could not even be seen.

Only one week after the Wedge and Trapper Fires began, the **Robert Fire** took off. Unlike the other fires that summer, the Robert Fire—which eventually reached 57,570 acres—was human caused. An unattended campfire, abandoned just north of Columbia Falls, began to spread and then blew up in a matter of hours. The Robert Fire jumped both the Outside North Fork Road and the North Fork of the Flathead River, running east directly toward the town of West Glacier. A Type 1 team was brought down from Alaska to attempt containment of this fire, and some fairly risky firefighting tactics were successfully used to stop the fire's advance toward West Glacier. Firefighters began backburns, also called burnouts, north of the fire in the Apgar Mountains; the convection column raised by the burnout created its own wind so strong that it sucked the Robert Fire north, diverting it from its own path toward the town. During this time the whole McDonald drainage had to be evacuated—visitors, Park Service employees, and inholders alike. (Inholders are those who established their property rights before the national park was created. The National Park Service has purchased many of these former inholdings, while others remain under private ownership within park boundaries.)

Meanwhile, the **Trapper Fire** blew up, racing toward the Continental Divide, requiring the evacuation of Granite Park Chalet—a story in its own right. The Many Glacier

riparian areas, often encircling grassy fields and forming a transition to the higher coniferous forests. Their yellow and gold autumn foliage stands out against the green of conifers. Also found here are serviceberry, chokecherry, mountain maple, red-osier dogwood, and alder. Wild geranium, arnica, and Oregon grape grace the forest floor. This is habitat for white-tailed deer, moose, and wolves. Montana's state bird, the western meadowlark, shares the open areas with LeConte's sparrow and the savannah sparrow. The low- to mid-elevation (3,000 to 4,000 feet west of the Continental Divide; 4,000 to 5,000 to the east) dry montane forest is typified by Douglas fir, ponderosa pine, lodgepole pine, and limber pine, with understory species such as ninebark and mountain maple. These forests often have open crowns with a grassy understory that provides winter habitat for mule deer, elk, and bighorn sheep. In stands of old growth, predators like the goshawk can be seen on the hunt.

The wetter mid-montane forest reflects the Pacific maritime weather influence in the lush growth of vegetation. Western red cedar and western hemlock are common trees, along with Douglas fir, western

Valley was evacuated for a week. But with some strategic helicopter bucket drops, the spot fires that hung poised above the east side were quenched, and soon the Many Glacier drainage was reopened to the public.

As if this weren't enough—in mid-August, the **Middle Fork complex of fires** began along US 2. Again, lightning-caused fire provided some fantastic viewing for those traveling in the area. US 2, which was never closed, turned into a popular venue for watching what sometimes seemed like erupting volcanoes. More fires began south of the park, as well. The Bob Marshall Wilderness and Swan Range saw their share of activity, and residents in the Hungry Horse were also evacuated as fires glowed on the sides of Columbia Mountain.

Smoke flowed into the Flathead Valley, making air quality so bad that the county government urged people with respiratory conditions to temporarily leave the area. At times the smoke was so thick it seemed to penetrate every home and vehicle. But on September 8, the rains came . . . long, steady rains that finally reduced the fires to smoldering ashes.

The statistics showing the extent of some of the fires are impressive: Wedge Canyon, 53,315 acres; Robert Complex, 57,570 acres; Rampage Complex, 24,488 acres; Middle Fork Complex, 11,851 acres; Trapper, 19,150 acres. The Robert Complex of fires alone required seven 20-person fire crews, 3 helicopters, 21 engines, 12 water tenders, and 557 total personnel. More than 12 agencies cooperated in the firefighting effort.

As you drive throughout northwest Montana, look for the signs of fire on the land. Fire is part of the natural cycle here: The apparent destruction it does is followed the next spring by a return of new life to the land. Patterns of regrowth—called mosaic—can be seen as you drive over Going-to-the-Sun Road in Glacier Park. Watch for evidence of the Heaven's Peak Fire of 1936, the fires of 1967, and now, the fires of 2003.

larch, and spruce. The understory is typically luxuriant with many ferns, wildflowers, shrubs, and mosses. This habitat is typical of the McDonald Creek drainage, ranging from 3,100 to 4,000 feet above sea level. In the old-growth forests you'll see such birds as western tanagers, Swainson's and varied thrushes, Townsend's warblers, Hammond's flycatchers, and brown creepers, as well as birds that prey on the smaller winged things, like sharp-shinned and Cooper's hawks. The snowshoe hare is common here, too, and the lynx that preys on this hare is reported to be staging a comeback. A magnificent stand of old-growth western red cedar can be seen at Avalanche Campground and on the shoreline of McDonald Lake's upper end. The 1910 fire destroyed a much larger population of this species.

In the subalpine forest (above 5,000 feet) spruce and subalpine fir dominate, along with whitebark pine in higher elevations. Douglas fir is common on southfacing slopes. Near the upper limits, trees thin out and mingle with treeless communities, creating parklands holding spectacular displays of wildflowers, mosses, and lichens. East of the Continental Divide at these elevations, subalpine fir and lodgepole pine dominate. Mule deer, pine martens, and black bears inhabit these forests on both sides of the divide.

In the highest elevations of Glacier Country, the plants and animals of the alpine community have adapted to the long, cold winters and cool, short growing seasons. Only a few trees and shrubs can survive, such as arctic willow, dwarf birch, and fir, hugging the ground and stunted by the searing winds and frigid temperatures. Mosses and lichens cling to bare rock; alpine bogs resemble a miniature landscape for a kingdom of little people. Alpine meadows astound the eye for a few weeks in July and August with a spectrum of wildflowers, including heather, gentian, beargrass, and glacier lily. The rare dwarf alpine poppy is unique to this area, occurring in both Glacier and Waterton Lakes National Parks. Grizzly bears dig for glacier lily and spring beauty bulbs. Ptarmigan, pikas, hoary marmots, wolverines, and mountain goats are at home in this rarified environment. Bighorn sheep wander through the high meadows and golden eagles nest on the cliffs. Logan Pass, the Hidden Lake Trail, and the Highline Trail provide the easiest way to get up close and personal with this habitat.

Returning to the lower elevations, remnants of the native grasslands that once covered the Great Plains now occur mainly in broad, arid, low-elevation basins. Bluebunch wheatgrass, fescues, and needlegrasses dominate these areas. Although found primarily on the park's east side, they move quickly into areas soon after a forest fire, as they did in the Polebridge area after the Red Bench Fire burned large tracts of forest in 1988. Wildflowers thrive in these grasslands, their blossoming peaking in May

and June at the lower elevations. Common species include yarrow, fleabane, potentilla, spirea, locoweed, and lupine; another, wild geranium, is a major food item for elk and white-tailed deer. This is also the habitat for badgers, coyotes, savannah sparrows, chipping sparrows, northern harriers, and prairie falcons. East of the divide, Two Dog Flats provides a splendid grassland wildflower display that peaks in June, with pasqueflower, lupine, Indian paintbrush, gaillardia, asters, and shooting stars all in abundance. Exotic weed species have invaded many of these prairies, especially east of the divide where forage grasses have been extensively planted for livestock grazing. Sagebrush, symbol of the romantic West in so many classic movies, also grows in this environment. It's common east of the divide, and is also found in a few spots west of the divide, such as Round Prairie and other areas along the Inside North Fork Road.

The residents of Glacier Country depend on the area's wealth of natural treasures to support certain economic activities, including farming, ranching, timber harvesting, tourism, and outdoor recreation. People are striving to maintain their freedoms and "frontier lifestyles" while also preserving the area's wildness, clean air and water, and pristine landscapes. Farmers and ranchers struggle to maintain their family operations as cities and towns expand outward, threatening to engulf them. Park visitors and area businesspeople debate road access and development within the park. Families and businesses dependent on timber cutting in the national forests, as well as wilderness advocates and forest recreationists, apply diverse pressures on the Forest Service in such matters as road access and timber-harvest methods and quantities.

Amidst ongoing conflicts about how best to manage these public lands and resources, local governments and private groups work to achieve a balance between preservation and development. The Flathead Basin Commission, created by the Montana State Legislature in 1983 to monitor and protect Flathead Lake's water quality, has been working with Canadian, US, and state and local agencies to collect data and develop methods for guarding the waters in this important watershed. Volunteers monitor pollution levels on 30 lakes that flow into the basin, as landowners and land managers are encouraged to use best management practices to reduce runoff into streams and rivers feeding the lake. The commission addresses such far-ranging problems and challenges as climate change, invasive species, new marina proposals, and how best to work together in the trans-boundary area (known as the North Fork of the Flathead in the United States, and simply as the Flathead in Canada).

Private groups such as the Flathead Land Trust, The Nature Conservancy, and the Montana Land Reliance work with private landowners to protect agricultural and wildlands from development and provide additional habitat for plants and animals. Organizations like the Flathead Audubon Society, the Montana Native Plant Society, and the Glacier Institute conduct field trips, classes, and meetings to educate the public about plants, birds, and habitats. The Flathead National Forest, Glacier National Park, and the Montana Department of Fish, Wildlife and Parks all have public adult and school educational programs, as well. Through a variety of public meetings, forums, and workshops, and active involvement in development and conservation issues, Citizens for a Better Flathead promotes "Smart Growth," so that population growth and development occur in such a way that they minimize the impact on the region's resources and values.

This chapter will suggest an array of ways in which you can experience this immensely varied, fascinating country—from simply walking a few steps away from your vehicle to see a stunning vista or look more closely at a wildflower, to taking an all-day hike, raft trip, or ski tour into a wilderness setting. It includes information to guide you to a few of the region's most special places, and also recommends additional information sources to deepen your familiarity with Glacier Country.

NATURE VIEWING

Fascinating plants and animals are just about everywhere in Glacier Country, and they can be yours to view in many cases with very little travel and effort. The general habitats described in the environment section give you an idea of where you are likely to see which animals. Nature observation is particularly exciting here because there is such an array of wildlife concentrated in a small geographic area. An observant person can see many animal species with the naked eye; with the aid of binoculars or a spotting scope, the opportunities magnify to a tremendous degree.

Your "want-to-see" list probably includes mountain goats, elk, bald eagles, moose, and grizzly bears. The many creeks, rivers, lakes, and wetlands provide prime habitat for migratory waterfowl, songbirds, and osprey, while beaver, river otters, and mink are some of the mammals you might spot there. Wildflower lovers, meanwhile, will revel in the variety of species included in the spectacular displays of color in alpine settings along Going-to-the-Sun Road. In this section are listed a few specific places you're most likely to see the starring attractions such as mountain goats and bighorn sheep.

Wildlife-Watching Tips

You can make wildlife watching safe and fun for yourself and safe (if not fun) for the animals you watch by observing a few basic rules. You'll enjoy the animals the most by observing them undisturbed in their activities. Wear subdued, natural colors. Be as unobtrusive as possible; move slowly and quietly, and hide behind the cover of boulders or vegetation. (This is *not* the case for observing bears, however.) Learn as much about the wildlife species as possible before attempting to observe them, such as where and what time of day they are most likely to appear. Most large mammals are the most active and "spottable" while feeding in the early morning and late evening. Keep your distance; use binoculars or a spotting scope to "get close." If you're shooting photographs, use a long lens. Don't feed the animals! An excellent pamphlet titled *A Guide to Ultimate Wildlife Watching* expands on these points and can be obtained from the USDA Forest Service or Montana Fish, Wildlife and Parks (addresses listed at the end of this chapter). Also watch along the highways for signs bearing the brown and white binoculars logo and the words WILDLIFE VIEWING AREA, with an arrow pointing to the site.

Grizzly Bears

These large bruins roam open woods and meadows during the summer and fall, foraging for their diet of grasses, roots, berries, insects, and occasionally young elk or deer. They also feed on carrion at kill sites of mountain lions and other carnivores. In spring, grizzlies are commonly seen browsing the newly emerging vegetation at the edges of avalanche chutes along Going-to-the-Sun Road and in the lower meadows of the St. Mary and Two Medicine Valleys. In July and August, look for griz in the alpine meadows and in the Logan Pass vicinity, where they might be seen digging for bulbs of glacier lilies and spring beauties. Grizzly bears are also oftentimes seen along the park's west side, along the North Fork of the Flathead. They are as fond of huckleberries as humans are, and in summer and early fall you might see them raking berries into their mouths to help fatten themselves up for the winter. Bears are unpredictable and may attack without apparent provocation. Always observe the bear-country precautions described in the "Be 'Bear Aware' " Close-up found in the Columbia Falls & the US 2 Corridor chapter.

Rocky Mountain Bighorn Sheep

These large ungulates, the males of the species sporting massive horns, prefer high rolling valleys and tough-to-access rocky slopes and cliffs on the park's eastern side, where buffeting winds keep the ground snow-free in winter. They graze on grasses, shrubs, and forbs, and during harsh winters can be viewed in the lower valleys. Although sometimes seen on Going-to-the-Sun Road, especially at Logan Pass and along the Highline Trail in early summer, the best places to see bighorns are on the east side, especially in the Many Glacier Valley: Be sure to look up as you hike the trails to Iceberg Lake, Ptarmigan Tunnel, or Grinnell Glacier. During the fall mating season, listen for the cracking sound of the males' head-butting activities. (A small herd of bighorns can also be seen on a visit to Wild Horse Island on Flathead Lake.)

Mountain Goats

One of the most easily observed mammals in the park, these daredevil cliff hangers favor precipitous places where they can evade predators. In the winter, the shaggy white beasts seek south-facing slopes where they can forage shrubs, grasses, sedges, lichens, and forbs. Logan Pass is almost a sure bet for seeing goats, and they become traffic stoppers on Going-to-the-Sun Road, where their white coats are easily spotted on the cliffs above the road. Hikers often encounter them at Gunsight Pass. Goat Lick, along US 2 near Essex, is another popular place to watch for mountain goats, where they hang out just across the Flathead River and are sometimes visible from the parking area or from the Goat Lick, a short trail walk from the road.

Elk or Wapiti

If you visit Glacier Country in autumn you might be lucky enough to hear the bugling of the male elk as they herd their harems and challenge other males during the breeding season. These larger cousins of the deer prefer coniferous forests interspersed with openings such as logged or burned areas and open grasslands bordered by shrubs and trees. They spend summers in high-elevation mountain meadows and timber stands, and are often difficult to see at this time of year. In winter, spring, and fall, elk may be seen in the St. Mary Flats area near the park visitor center, at Two Dog Flats and the Many Glacier Valley, and in the southeast corner of the park near East Glacier. On the west side, sightings are not uncommon in a wintering area along US 2 east of Belton Hills, in the North Fork Valley, and in the grasslands along the Quarter Circle Bridge

Road near Apgar. Check with a ranger about current viewing possibilities.

Gray Wolves

Wolves have made a comeback in Glacier Country after being virtually wiped out in the early 20th century. Park biologists believe at least two packs have established themselves in the park, along with two more in the national forest outside the park. Most sightings are reported in the North Fork Valley, and it's often possible to find their large paw prints in the sand along the river and along the Inside North Fork Road at Hidden Meadow, where the large canines prey on small rodents and other critters. They shy away from humans, so consider yourself lucky if you actually see a wolf. Listen for their howls at night on the park's west side or in the Whitefish Range; there's nothing quite as thrilling as an evening chorus of wolves on a moonlit night in the Montana wilderness.

> **i** The most mysterious animal of all in Glacier National Park may be the brown mountain goat . . . well, it has horns like a goat, but it's brown with a whitish rump patch. It's true: You'll rarely see this animal in a guidebook—it's the female bighorn sheep. While most mammal guides include a picture of the bighorn ram—with its highly recognizable, curling horns—they usually neglect the ewe, which looks very much the same but grows a set of short, spiky horns instead (which in fact look like the horns of a goat). In the spring and summer, the females with their young live separately from the bachelor bands of males, who thus are not around to provide a clue as to what this exotic beast might be.

Pacific Harlequin Ducks

For a few weeks in mid-April into May, onlookers can watch the entertaining courtship of these small, dark-gray-and-white ducks on the frigid mountain streams in and near Glacier Park. They return from their winter home on the Pacific coast to the same streams where they hatched, to mate and raise another brood. Their attempts to maneuver the rapids are made more comical by their clownlike plumage. This is a special viewing opportunity that attracts many locals, year after year. The ducks can also be seen in the Big Creek drainage.

Bald Eagles

Even if you live where these birds are common, the sight of our national symbol always gives pause to the viewer, especially in a setting as grand as Glacier Country. Its large size and bright white head against its dark body make the bald eagle easy to spot. You may even identify a nest. Look for the birds near water, particularly along the North Fork of the Flathead River and near major lakes, including Lake McDonald, Two Medicine, and St. Mary Lakes in Glacier Park.

Wildlife Management Areas (WMAs)

Montana has set aside areas across the state to provide winter range for deer and elk, and breeding areas for waterfowl and upland game. Besides helping maintain healthy populations of these animals, these WMAs are great places to view a variety of wildlife and plants. Some are closed during wintering and breeding seasons, and many wetland areas are closed during the spring nesting season. Signs at the parking areas and trailheads specify closure dates.

Flathead Waterfowl Production Area— Somers Bay

The north shore of Flathead Lake is a duck and goose paradise, and pretty close to heaven for the other species that dwell or pass through here. Starting at the fishing access on Somers Bay, where waterbirds can be seen almost anytime of year, there is a nearly continuous strip of meadows and marshes extending east almost to Bigfork. It's a great place to see red-winged and yellow-headed blackbirds, flickers, geese, ducks, and other waterfowl and the occasional deer. You'll find trails and small, informal parking areas. You can stroll through the varied habitats or take a picnic and enjoy sitting with the sun in your face and a breeze from the lake in your hair. This area is closed during the breeding season between March 1 and July 1.

Smith Lake Waterfowl Production Area

Located 7 miles west of Kalispell and south of US 2, this 1,040-acre area encompasses a lake and an extensive marsh complex. It's a great place to view shorebirds, including phalaropes and yellowlegs, and waterfowl such as mallards, widgeons, pintails, and gadwalls. Also active here are Canada geese, grebes, gulls, tundra swans, and American bitterns. In the spring, look for sandhill cranes in the western grassy meadows, and for bluebirds nesting in boxes along the approach road. The area is closed from March 1 to July 1.

✴Wild Horse Island

Bighorn sheep, mule deer, coyotes, bald eagles, ospreys, and a small herd of wild horses live on this island in Flathead Lake. Mature forests of Douglas fir and ponderosa pine, along with abundant grassy uplands, also support goshawks, coyotes, marmots, mink, and numerous songbirds. Hiking trails lead to good viewing places.

✳ *Creston National Fish Hatchery*

At this 74-acre hatchery located along a beautiful spring creek, you can see up to a million rainbow and cutthroat trout and learn how they reproduce in captivity. The facility raises and produces eggs for propagation in stocked streams and lakes. Bird watching for fish-eating species is also excellent—ospreys, great blue herons, and kingfishers, for instance. Canada geese nest near the picnic area and their young can be seen in the summer. The hatchery is open daily from 9 a.m. to 3 p.m., and you can hike the area's nature trail at any time.

Swan River National Wildlife Refuge

This 1,568-acre refuge is best visited by canoe, but a walk along Bog Road (generally impassible to vehicles) can yield sightings of a fair share of the refuge's 171 bird species, including bald eagles, great blue herons, Canada geese, wood ducks, and yellowlegs. Keep an eye out also for a glimpse of some of the large mammals found here seasonally, including elk, deer, moose, and grizzly and black bears. The refuge lies at the southern end of Swan Lake, and is closed during the nesting season, from March 1 to July 1. Signs on the highway will alert you to the entrance road.

Wildflower Viewing

"There is no color known to man that is not reproduced from its most vivid hues to the most delicate tints by the plants and rocks of Glacier Park," writes Flathead Valley fixture George Ostrom in his book, *Glacier's Secrets.* He adds, "If I were a painter, I'd go bananas ten times a day running into this kind of arrangement of flowers, lichens, and colored rocks." Ostrom expresses so well the thrill of coming upon the multitude of colorful plants in Glacier Country. People simply cannot believe how stunningly beautiful they are until they behold them with their own eyes. Be prepared for spectacular summer displays in the alpine meadows, but don't overlook the cheery brightness of the first buttercups in early spring or the last of the Indian paintbrush to bloom in fall. Because wildflowers are generally limited to a short flowering period, refer to the following list for suggestions as to when you are most likely to see certain plants, and for particular locations where they are known to grow.

May

Some of spring's first wildflowers appear this month in Wayfarers and Lone Pine State Parks and on the Columbia Mountain Trail near Columbia Falls. Among the flowers you may see are buttercups, glacier lilies, bluebells, and wild crocus.

June

Violets, pyrola, foamflower, and queen's cup bead lily come into bloom in the cedar-hemlock forests around Lake McDonald. Wildflowers of the prairies and foothills begin to peak in June, as well—look for pink shooting star and "lakes" of blue camas on the park's east side. The more colorful members of the fescue-wheatgrass grasslands, such as yarrow, purple fleabane, St. John's Wort, cinquefoil, spirea, lupine, and wild geranium, put on bold displays at many locations, notably at lower elevations along Going-to-the-Sun Road, in the Polebridge area, and at Two Dog Flats on Going-to-the-Sun Road southwest of St. Mary.

July & August

The Danny On Trail on Big Mountain, Jewel Basin, and Logan Pass are prime areas for viewing the spectacular but brief displays of alpine wildflowers. At elevations between 6,000 and 7,000 feet, blooms of every color include those of heather, gentian, Indian paintbrush, beargrass, and glacier lily. At Logan Pass you may find the rare dwarf alpine poppy. Stop in at the Flathead National Forest's Summit Nature Center at the top of the Whitefish Mountain Resort for information on nature programs held in and around the resort.

August & Early September

Roadsides everywhere are in bloom. The backroads, such as the North Fork Road, Camas Road, Hungry Horse Reservoir roads, and open areas along national forest roads, treat you to the last of the season's Indian paintbrush, goldenrod, and asters, and the beginning of the reds and golds of autumn.

Huckleberry Picking: A Bear Necessity

The area's exalted huckleberry is either more or less than you may expect. For some people hailing from wild blueberry country, such as Maine, northern Michigan, and Minnesota, the huckleberry is overrated. For others, the huck's wild tartness is far superior to the sweetness of its eastern cousin. For those who have never tasted either, the huckleberry is an unsurpassed blue-black globe of flavor and aroma, well worth the effort to pick or the price to purchase.

Huckleberries provided sustenance in lean times for travelers, including Lewis and Clark's Corps of Discovery in 1805, and both Native American and white residents during the Depression, when entire families would move to the harvest sites and camp out, picking and "putting up" the berries. And the huckleberry holds both culinary and ceremonial significance for the Salish and Kootenai peoples, who dried the berries for use in stews and pemmican.

The huckleberry industry, which has grown in recent years, produces dozens of products, including preserves, pies, syrups, candies, and cosmetics. Most visitors obtain their huckleberries the easy way, by purchasing them from local purveyors, but if you want to try your hand at picking them yourself, here are some tips:

The best picking is usually found in areas opened up by forest fire or timber cutting, or along old roads. You can tell where the berries are prolific by where a lot of cars are parked! Try forest trails or abandoned logging roads when easily accessible spots get picked over or seem too crowded.

The huckleberry shrub prefers north-facing slopes between 3,500 and 7,000 feet in elevation, in the moist, acid soils typical of coniferous forests. It grows from about a foot to 6 feet tall and has short, elliptical leaves. The white or pinkish, bell-shaped flowers mature into plump blue-black berries. They usually begin ripening from mid-July to mid-August, depending on the elevation and the recent weather.

A battle of the berries may be in the making, as humans take more and more of the harvest and bears are left with scarcely enough to fatten up for winter hibernation. In 1998, a lean huckleberry year made worse for the bears by determined human pickers, drove grizzlies in unusual numbers into residential areas in search of food, which led to the destruction of several grizzly bears. So save some berries for the bears!

i Weather less than ideal? If you sense cabin fever setting in, the Flathead Valley offers a pair of excellent facilities for burning off that extra energy indoors: The Whitefish Community Aquatic & Health Center—aka The Wave—in Whitefish (1250 Baker Ave.; 406-862-2444; www.whitefish wave.com) and The Summit Medical Fitness Center in Kalispell (205 Sunnyview Lane; 406-751-4100; www .summithealthcenter.com). You can take an early morning swim, join a yoga class, or jog around the track. Call ahead to inquire about specific hours, day-pass fees, and amenities offered at each facility.

ON THE TRAIL—HIKING

Good old-fashioned walking and bicycling are two of the most economical and convenient ways to explore Glacier Country, with its infinite variety of environments and hundreds of miles of trails. Truly there is a trail for hikers and bikers of any fitness or skill level who want to leave their vehicles and immerse themselves in this extraordinary natural environment.

This section and the next will introduce you to a few of the best, easy-to-reach hiking and biking opportunities in the region, while also listing resources that can provide equipment, tips, and maps and other information.

Hiking opportunities encompass trails suitable for every type of visitor, from walkers and stroller-pushers, to backpackers and even those in wheelchairs. The trails described here range from less than a mile to several miles in length; the latter are those that can be accomplished in no more than a long day, even for slower sojourners. For very short hikes in towns, check the individual

city park descriptions. For longer day hikes and backpacking adventures, consult Hiking Glacier and Waterton Lakes National Parks and Wild Montana (see the For More Information chapter). If you decide after you get here to do some backpacking, you can find equipment rentals and maps to ensure a satisfying backcountry experience. Check the resource list at the end of this chapter.

Safety & Comfort

Good, sturdy shoes or hiking boots and proper clothing are a must for enjoyable, safe hiking. Even in midsummer when the hot, dry days resemble Arizona weather, in the mountains the weather can change quickly to penetrating cold, wind, rain, and even snow. In the mountains, hypothermia is possible even in the summer. When hiking or bicycling, always carry a hat, mittens, and clothing that is warm and wind and water repellent. Also carry more water than you think you'll drink; keeping hydrated is critical to maintaining stamina and avoiding both heatstroke and hypothermia. A small backpack or fanny pack stocked with a first-aid kit, water, and high-energy snacks such as nuts, fresh or dried fruit, and granola bars is indispensable for any hike, other than those taking you only a few minutes away from your vehicle. Be sure to pack out all food wrappers, as well as fruit peels and cores, because even though biodegradable, they attract animals—including bears—to the trailsides. Observe signs or rangers' warnings of bear activity and take appropriate precautions. (See the "Be 'Bear Aware'" Close-up in the Columbia Falls & the US 2 Corridor chapter.)

You can drive to many of the higher-altitude trailheads, so don't forget that at several thousand feet above sea level, oxygen is less available and people with breathing or heart problems should be cautious.

Hiking Opportunities

National Forest Trails

The hundreds of miles of trail are mapped and described in a packet available from the Flathead National Forest supervisor's office in Kalispell and the district rangers' offices located in several outlying communities.

Big Mountain
✳WHITEFISH MOUNTAIN RESORT, WHITEFISH

Big Mountain's summit provides an array of hiking possibilities, dishing out some of the most exquisite scenery in Glacier Country. Because the summit is snow-free only for a few months of the year, it's a real treat to see the displays of alpine wildflowers and open meadows during July and August. Hiking season at lower elevations begins in May or June, but on the summit it begins in late June and lasts through Sept (Oct in some years). The lift stops operation in late September and begins again when the ski season starts in early December.

The Danny On Memorial National Recreation Trail is one of the most popular hiking trails for people seeking premier views, easy accessibility, and options for varied length and difficulty. It was named in memory of a Forest Service silviculturist and nature photographer known for his beautiful pictures of the area, who died in a skiing accident on Big Mountain. It is actually 6 different hikes totaling 5.6 miles. More ambitious hikers ascend from the trailhead right above the Chalet in the village, a distance of 3.8 miles that takes about 2 hours. Others ride the gondola up to the Summit House and hike down. Two

of the connecting trails are the East Rim Trail, which is a half-mile loop path along the summit, and the 3.8-mile Flower Point Hike back to the lift. Trail maps are available at the chair lift and the Summit House, and at the Chalet at Big Mountain Village.

ℹ️ A small first-aid kit is essential for backcountry outings in Glacier Country. Your kit should contain enough items to control bleeding and to fashion and secure dressings and splints—athletic and duct tape is useful here. Moleskin or duct tape can effectively treat blisters, a common problem on the trail. Be prepared to improvise, using the contents of your backpack or other gear. For example, a trekking pole can easily convert into a splint. It's a good idea to obtain first-aid training before you travel to learn how to treat injuries in the field.

LONE PINE STATE PARK

Just 10 minutes southwest of downtown Kalispell, this park's trails offer panoramic views of Kalispell, much of the Flathead Valley, and into Glacier Park. The 0.75-mile Overlook Trail begins near the visitor center. It's a wheelchair-accessible, self-guided interpretive trail leading to the Flathead Valley Overlook. The park also has an archery range, and 2.5 miles of multiuse trails for hiking, biking, and horseback riding with benches along the way for resting and reflection. From Kalispell, go west on US 2 to Meridian Road, then south on Meridian to Foy's Lake Road. Proceed for 4 miles and turn left at the park sign. There's a day-use fee of $5 per vehicle for nonresidents.

☀ JEWEL BASIN

This popular hiker-only area is noted for beautiful scenery featuring alpine lakes, mountain streams, meadows, rocky peaks, dense conifer woods, and wildflower displays. Trails can be chosen for nearly every age and ability. Many hikers aim for the high peaks that dominate the 15,340-acre area, but open country on the lower slopes affords splendid views for the more casual walker or those with children. Mountain bikes and horses are excluded from the area. However, be aware that Jewel Basin is being "loved to death," and USDA Forest Service managers trying to protect the resource have introduced regulations to help reduce visitor impacts: Dogs must be leashed, and groups hiking the area are limited to no more than 12 people. If you seek solitude, check with the rangers' office to learn where there might be fewer people hiking that day. Located at the north end of the Swan Range between Kalispell and Hungry Horse Reservoir, the parking lot accessing the trails is reached by taking Echo Lake Road from Highway 83 and following the signs to Jewel Basin.

Glacier National Park

Most high-elevation trails in Glacier Park are hikeable only from midsummer, after the snows have melted, into early fall. So be prepared to take an alternate route if ice and snow are still factors.

☀ APGAR LOOKOUT TRAIL

West Side: This short but moderately difficult trail ends at Apgar Lookout, 5,236 feet above sea level, and rewards you with views of Lake McDonald and the full length of the Livingston Range. It begins on a primitive road, then leads over switchbacks across the foothills, giving glimpses of Great Northern Mountain, the Flathead Range, and Swan Range. To reach the trailhead, turn just inside the park's west entrance at the sign for the Glacier Institute Field Camp. Follow it to the T, turn right, and go a short distance to a V-intersection and take the left fork at the sign for Quarter-Circle Bridge. Go about a mile beyond the bridge and look for trailhead signs. Since some of this area was burned over in the 2003 fires, the trail offers more open views that it did previously.

AVALANCHE LAKE

West Side: This lovely, relatively easy 2-mile trek begins in giant old-growth cedars on the wheelchair-accessible Trail-of-the-Cedars boardwalk, continues on a moderately steep trail along Avalanche Gorge on well-timbered hillsides, and emerges at the alpine lake nestled in a cirque among the peaks. This is an especially satisfying hike to take with a ranger-naturalist; interpretive walks are scheduled regularly throughout the season. See the *Glacier Explorer* for times and designated meeting place.

FORESTS & FIRE NATURE TRAIL

West Side: If you happen to have hiked the Huckleberry Nature Trail before the summer of 2001, your drive to the trailhead will be the same, but the hike will be completely different! The former Huckleberry Nature Trail wound through a forest mosaic as it explored the processes of fire and regrowth following the 1967 Huckleberry Mountain Fire. However, the Moose Fire of 2001 reburned this area, so now another dimension has been added to the experience. The Park Service has renamed the

0.9-mile loop trail to reflect this fact, and has also produced a new trail brochure. This is a great spot to learn how plant and animal communities respond to fire. To find the trailhead, go south on the paved road between the Camas Creek Entrance Station and the Glacier National Park entrance sign. The road leads to a large parking area.

HIDDEN LAKE & HIDDEN LAKE OVERLOOK TRAILS

West Side: The 3-mile (6-mile round-trip) hike from the Logan Pass Visitor Center to Hidden Lake whisks you quickly into Glacier's high country on a moderately easy trail. It climbs to Hidden Lake Pass, where Mount Reynolds and Bearhat Mountain dominate the skyline and Hidden Lake lies below. The trail to the overlook then drops nearly 700 feet to the north shore of the lake—or, you can go only the mile and a half to the Hidden Lake Overlook (3 miles round-trip on the boardwalk) and observe the intriguing tiny alpine wildflowers along the way. Whichever you choose, this is a rare opportunity to experience an alpine ecosystem's plants and animals while savoring views in every direction. Interpretive information is available at the visitor center.

✳HIGHLINE TRAIL TO THE LOOP

West Side: Only a little bit of climbing, and a great deal of dazzling scenery, await you on this hike, because you set out from the top of Logan Pass. The Highline Trail runs some 30 miles along the Continental Divide from the pass into the Waterton Valley in Canada, connecting along the way to several other trails penetrating deep into the backcountry. The trail begins across the road from the Logan Pass Visitor Center at an elevation of 6,646 and runs mostly level for the first 3

miles to Haystack Butte, making it suitable for an out-and-back trip of various lengths. From Haystack Butte, the trail continues for another 4 miles along the divide to Granite Park Chalet, where it intersects with the Loop Trail—which descends 2,300 feet over 4 miles to the Loop parking lot on Going-to-the-Sun Road. Veteran hikers caution that this long downhill can be hard on the knees. Check into the schedule for the hiker's shuttle at the visitor center—you may be able to leave your car at the Loop, take the shuttle to Logan Pass, then hike back to your car.

PTARMIGAN TUNNEL

East Side: Some of the best park scenery is yours to enjoy on this popular trail. Allow a full day for the sometimes steep, 4-mile hike that begins at Swiftcurrent and follows one of the best-engineered trails in the park which includes a tunnel blasted through the mountain. Go through it to catch a view of the remote Belly River drainage, and be aware that hikers often spot grizzlies along this trail.

ST. MARY FALLS, VIRGINIA FALLS & BARING FALLS TRAILS

East Side: With trailhead parking areas situated along Going-to-the-Sun Road, this area offers interconnecting trails. You can choose to make a short hike to a single falls, or hike to them all. These enjoyable walks provide views of St. Mary Lake, impressive mountain peaks, and creeks, gorges, and waterfalls. From the St. Mary Falls pullout, you can hike the 1.2 miles to that falls and then go the additional 0.7 mile to Virginia Falls. The Baring Falls trailhead is located on Going-to-the-Sun Road about 0.3 mile west of Baring Creek, and the St. Mary Falls Trail pullout is on the south side of the road about 6.5 miles east of Logan Pass and a mile west of Sunrift Gorge.

If you make the hike from Sun Point to Virginia Falls, you'll be doing what was once called the Trail of the Water Ouzel. Water ouzels, or dippers, are tiny gray birds that often live near and feed in waterfalls, and you have a very good chance of seeing them along this route.

Hiking Equipment Rental

ROCKY MOUNTAIN OUTFITTER
135 Main St., Kalispell
(406) 752-2446
www.rockymountainoutfitter.com
This shop specializes in gear, clothing, and information for the hiker and backpacker. They offer limited rental of backpacking tents and stoves (but no personal gear like sleeping bags or packs), and have a good selection of books and maps to aid you in planning your adventure. The knowledgeable staff can advise you on the best places to go for hikers of various fitness and ability levels.

ON THE TRAIL—BIKING

The Flathead County parks and recreation board created a **PATHS** (People, Athletics, Travel, Health, and Safety) advisory committee that developed a comprehensive trail-network strategy to guide the future. Their mission: "The PATHS committee envisions a safe and convenient network of nonmotorized trails connecting Flathead County communities, schools, parks, and public lands for the benefit of our families, our economy, and our environment." Goals include creating a connected network of pathways and on-road facilities that link residential areas,

schools, parks, recreation areas, public lands, retail/business centers, and community event centers; providing high-quality nonmotorized trails on public lands; and ensuring connectivity between new recreational trails, existing trails in Flathead National Forest and Glacier National Park, and the rest of the county trail network.

In other words, over the next couple of decades the bicycling in Glacier Country should only get better and better. For now, vacationers who bring or rent bikes and want a short jaunt in town can head for Woodland and Lawrence Parks in Kalispell, both of which have pedestrian-bike paths. There are also trail segments in Whitefish and in Columbia Falls.

The new historical trail in Somers is especially attractive for families with young children. This 1.5-mile paved hike-bike path, the first completed component of a planned 23-mile-long trail, provides a friendly place to meet local strollers and bikers, young and old. You can't miss the trailhead in Somers, with its large overhead sign announcing the Great Northern Historical Trail. Park along the road and enter the trailhead next to Tiebuckers Pub & Eatery (see the Kalispell chapter). You get panoramic views across the Flathead Valley to the Whitefish and Swan Mountain Ranges. The varied habitat along the open meadows, conifer-covered cliff-sides, and watery slough make it a great place to see songbirds, waterfowl, small mammals, and wildflowers. The nonmotorized trail is well-used by locals, who stroll, jog, bike, or in-line skate along it.

Fat-tired mountain bikes make great sense in this extraordinary outdoor expanse, and that's the kind of cycling that's most popular. The following lists a few of the more accessible and popular destinations for cyclists.

Biking in the National Forest

Miles and miles of national-forest roads provide perhaps the best biking in Glacier Country, as they lead into some of the most scenic and uncrowded areas of these wildlands. Bikes are allowed on all roads and most trails, except those in Glacier National Park and in designated wilderness areas.

✳ *The Great Divide Mountain Bike Route*

The Great Divide Mountain Bike Route is a 2,708-mile off-pavement bicycle touring, or "bikepacking," route that stretches along the Continental Divide from Banff, Alberta, to Antelope Wells on the New Mexico–Chihuahua border. The route, mapped in the 1990s by Michael McCoy (the author of this book), links existing jeep tracks, logging roads, and singletrack trails.

On entering the United States, the route climbs from the pastoral Tobacco Valley outside Eureka, Montana, into the wild Whitefish Range, through old-growth forest and much younger clear-cuts where cyclists are nearly as likely to encounter a grizzly bear as they are another human. After winding through the valley of the North Fork of the Flathead, the route recrosses the Whitefish Range to emerge at Whitefish. Over mountains and through valleys it continues north to south in Montana; indeed, it teeter-totters with mountains and valleys throughout Idaho, Wyoming, Colorado, and New Mexico as well, crossing the Continental Divide more than two dozen times as it leads from Canada to the bottom of the contiguous United States.

In Montana a few other names on the Great Divide map are the Mission Mountains and the Seeley-Swan Valley; the Swan Mountains and the Blackfoot Valley; the Pioneer Mountains and the valley of Grasshopper Creek; the Tendoy Mountains and the Red Rock River Valley; and, finally, the Centennial and Henrys Lake Mountains, the doorway to Idaho. The Great Divide also passes directly through Helena and Butte, the two largest cities on the entire route.

For information on riding the Great Divide Mountain Bike Route, contact the Missoula-based **Adventure Cycling Association** at (800) 755-2453 or www.adventure cycling.org.

Big Mountain

You and your bike can ride the Whitefish Mountain Resort chairlift to the top of Big Mountain, then let gravity aid you in zipping down the trails. More than 20 miles of singletracks lead riders to stunning views of the Canadian Rockies, Glacier National Park, and the Flathead Valley. Summit Trail is an 8-mile singletrack between the top and the village. Another 12 miles of trails begin at the base of Chair 2. There are 20 miles of trails lower down the mountain that wind through forests and meadows accessed from the Outpost. No trail fees are charged, but there is a fee to ride the lift with your bike. Rentals, complete with helmets, water bottles, and trail maps are available at the hike-bike shop, conveniently located in the village.

The North Fork

A couple of good rides along the western boundary of Glacier National Park include the climb to Hornet Peak Lookout (you'll probably need to stash your bike and walk the final trail mile), and the cruise from

Polebridge to Kintla Lake in Glacier. Ask for more details at Glacier Cyclery, listed below.

Tally Lake Ranger District

The Tally Lake District, north of Whitefish, has a network of easily accessible trails and roads suitable for riders of various experience and fitness levels. Beginning mid-May to mid-June (depending on the year), you can spend the day biking, picnicking, and observing the wildlife and birds attracted to the waters and wetland habitat of Tally Lake. District personnel and volunteers have mapped a number of good rides ranging from beginner to advanced difficulty levels. Mostly loops, they traverse a combination of singletracks and logging roads at around 4,800 feet in elevation, and with little vehicle traffic. The 22-mile Reid Divide Trail, beginning and ending at Tally Lake, is a stellar ride. It follows the ridge for about 10 miles on a surface of mostly soft-packed forest duff before dropping back down to the lake. Bikers have spotted varied wildlife, including moose, black bears, and porcupines. A map is available at the district office and at Glacier Cyclery.

Glacier National Park

Hundreds of cyclists throughout the country, and even the world, have Going-to-the-Sun Road listed high on their "bicycling bucket list" of rides to do. Indeed, cycling there and elsewhere in Glacier National Park can be fun, but roads are narrow and winding with little or no shoulder, as well as congested during the main visitor season. June 15 through Labor Day bicycling is prohibited from 11 a.m. to 4 p.m. daily on Going-to-the-Sun Road, in both directions from Apgar to Sprague Creek Campground and eastbound (uphill) from Logan Creek to Logan Pass.

There are no restrictions east of Logan Pass. It generally takes about 45 minutes from Sprague Creek to Logan Creek and 3 hours from Logan Creek to Logan Pass.

Bicycles may be used only on established roads and designated routes. Bike travel is prohibited on all Glacier hiking trails except for the paved Apgar hike-bike path. The dirt/gravel roads on the west side of the park—the Inside North Fork Road, Bowman Lake Road, and Kintla Lake Road—are good options for mountain bike rides. (Note that Waterton Lakes National Park permits cycling not only on roads, but also on several singletrack hiking trails.)

i Make sure your bicycle is in good condition, with lights and reflectors. Take a repair kit, a pump, and an extra tube. Wear a helmet and stay alert for vehicles, road hazards, and wildlife at all times. Observe the same advice about gear, water, food, etc. as for hikers. Because most grizzly attacks are by bears that have been startled, be especially careful when traveling at high speeds, and make plenty of noise when traveling through timber and brush.

Bike Rentals

✳GLACIER CYCLERY
336 East Second St., Whitefish
(406) 862-6446
www.glaciercyclery.com

"We sell more than bikes; we sell a good time." So goes the motto of Glacier Cyclery, where they've been selling good times for almost 30 years. Here you can rent full suspension and hardtail mountain bikes, touring bikes, and kids' bikes by the half day, full day, or week. The $30 hardtail mountain bike (or $39 for a fully suspended ride) daily rate

Hike or Bike—A Spring Treat

For a springtime bicycling indulgence available to those who are on the spot, check out the plowing report for Going-to-the-Sun Road in Glacier National Park. There are a couple of weeks each spring—usually late April or early May—when stretches of the road on the west side have been plowed, but the roadbed itself is still too damp to bear the weight of automobile traffic. During this period when the pavement is drying out, the park opens the road to hikers and bicyclists. It's a wonderful treat: You can drive as far as the road is open to cars—usually to Lake McDonald Lodge or Avalanche Creek—and then unload your bike and start riding! With just hikers and bicyclists on the road, there's a holiday feel as the pace is mellow; people stop to get out their binoculars to scan for wildlife, or to chat with friends and neighbors. How far you can go depends on the plowing progress, but sometimes you can bike as far as the Loop (which makes for a great downhill run back—be sure to wear your helmet and dress warmly!). Remember, though, the road is "officially" a trail at this time and not open to dogs.

includes a helmet, and a water bottle you can take home with you. These folks worked with the Tally Lake Ranger District to develop a map of the trails on the district, so they can steer you to the best local rides. They also rent panniers, trailers, and car racks.

MOUNTAIN MIKE'S RENTAL BIKES
417 Bridge St., Bigfork
(406) 837-2453
Mountain Mike's has daily and weekly bike rentals for the whole family, and also offers guided tours. The shop stocks accessories and parts and does repairs.

WHITEFISH MOUNTAIN RESORT BIKE RENTALS
Snow Ghost Outfitters, Big Mountain
(406) 862-1996
www.skiwhitefish.com
With more than 20 miles of mountain bike trails on Big Mountain, it's not surprising that they rent mountain bikes at the resort. Snow Ghost Outfitters is open in summer from 9:30 a.m. to 6 p.m. daily in the Morning Eagle building right on the resort boardwalk. They rent adult full-suspension bikes for $46 a day ($39 for a half day); and children's mountain bikes for $19 a day. Helmets and maps are included with rentals; if you have your own bike but no helmet, you can rent just a helmet for $5 a day. The trails range from beginner to expert; the Runaway Train is billed as the most exciting free ride trail in the state. Lift access up the mountain is available for a fee; check the website for the latest information.

HORSEBACK RIDING

If a horseback trek in Glacier Country is indispensable to your experience in the still-wild West, stables are handily located in and near Glacier National Park. Outfitters offer trips ranging in duration from an hour to several days; rates go from about $35 per hour to $150 per day.

RAWHIDE TRAIL RIDES
12000 US 2 East, West Glacier
(406) 387-5727
https://glacierrawhide.com
Located close to Glacier Park, Rawhide Trading Post provides guided horse treks into the surrounding Flathead National Forest lands. They generally operate from mid-May to mid-Oct, depending on the season's weather. Rawhide also offers backcountry overnight trips and saddle-paddle trips in conjunction with river rafting. The stables are easy to locate behind the covered wagons at the trading post.

SWAN MOUNTAIN OUTFITTERS
(877) 888-5557
www.swanmountainoutfitters.com
Swan Mountain runs guided pack trips into the Bob Marshall Wilderness, and is also the only horse concession operating inside Glacier National Park, with corrals at 3 locations. Apgar Corral is near the park's west entrance and offers many rides suitable for beginners. The Lake McDonald Corral features trails through the rain forest as well as to Sperry Chalet. Rides from the Many Glacier Corral offer greatest opportunities to explore the backcountry on the back of a horse. The season is typically May through Sept, but can vary due to weather and trail conditions.

ON THE WATER

Like Norman Maclean wrote about western Montana, "a river runs through it"; in fact, many rivers run through it, and creeks, sloughs, lakes, and wetlands are abundant, as well. Wherever you look in Glacier Country, water, in its many forms, defines the landscape. Trying to imagine it without alpine lakes mirroring the mountains (themselves shaped by running water and by the movement of glaciers, or frozen water), creeks rushing to the Flathead River, and Flathead Lake's azure expanse is like trying to imagine the Arctic without icebergs or the Sahara without sand. These waters give passage to treasured places difficult, or impossible, to reach by land. They bring exhilaration and excitement where they boldly rush through rapids, and peace and tranquility where they quietly pool.

More and more adventures become available as a growing number of local businesses seek to provide the best and most up-to-date trips and equipment for the increasing number of recreationists attracted to these waters. Area kayaking and sailing events draw participants and spectators from near and far.

If you brought your own canoe, kayak, motorboat, or sailboat, you're set to hit the waters. If you didn't, rentals are available and generally quite affordable. If you're a lifelong landlubber, perhaps now is the time to get your feet wet with one of the established and reliable outfitting services, whose guides want to give you nothing but a wonderful experience on their home waters. Or, if it's fly fishing you've a hankering to try, you don't even necessarily need a watercraft—just a rod, reel, waders, assortment of artificial flies, and a bit of casting technique should "net" you the results you're hoping for.

Keeping Our Waters Wild & Wonderful

With more and more people discovering Glacier Country as a place to live and vacation, growing numbers are competing for space on the region's waters. The local, state, and federal agencies charged with managing the resources for the benefit of ecosystems and the humans who live and play in them need the cooperation of residents and visitors to ensure they remain enjoyable for generations to come. The primary agencies dealing with water recreation in the area are the Flathead National Forest, Glacier National Park, and Montana Fish, Wildlife and Parks (FWP). Each has plenty of handy resource materials available: regulations pamphlets, maps and guides, and other information to help make your water recreation safe and enjoyable. They are listed at the end of this section.

Warnings & Regulations

Glacier Country's streams and rivers vary greatly in their size and water conditions. High water from spring runoff usually begins in May and peaks in June on most river stretches. Unless you're going on a professionally outfitted trip, always check with the agency in charge and scout the area as much as possible beforehand. Whether you bring your own vessel or rent one, seek advice from local dealers, who get the latest scuttlebutt from local river runners about current conditions.

Glacier Country's changeable weather is particularly significant for lake boaters. High winds can gather momentum quickly on Flathead Lake and small craft are advised to always stay close enough to shore to get back safely. Personal flotation devices (PFDs, or life jackets) must be worn on flat-water trips as well as whitewater adventures.

If you are floating in the fall, check on hunting seasons and take precautions in national forest and Montana state lands when going ashore and walking away from the water course. Trespassing on private land when leaving the water can sometimes be a challenge to avoid. Public-access areas are usually well-defined, but many shorelines are under a mix of public and private ownerships, which are not always well-marked.

It's an under-appreciated fact that, despite legitimate concerns about bears and bear safety, water-related accidents are the number-one killer in Glacier National Park. At least one drowning occurred in both 2009 (Swiftcurrent Lake) and 2010 (Virginia Creek). In other years boaters have drowned after being taken by surprise in the spring by shifts in the rivers since the previous summer. High spring runoff has taken its toll, too; sometimes death has followed from hypothermia rather than drowning. Be careful—learn about the local conditions, go with experienced people, dress appropriately, and use the right gear.

Powerboats

Montana boating regulations require all motorboats and personal watercraft (PWC) such as Jet Skis to be registered and numbered, including out-of-state boats used here more than 90 consecutive days. These regulations also apply to sailboats 12 or more feet long.

Recent added regulations include more stringent wake restrictions for lakes in northwestern Montana. With a few exceptions all watercraft must maintain no-wake speeds within 200, or sometimes 300, feet of the shoreline of all lakes, and no-wake speeds altogether on lakes 35 acres or smaller.

Children 12 years and younger must be accompanied by someone at least 18 years old to operate a motorboat or PWC of more than 10 horsepower. Youths age 13 to 14 must have a Montana motorboat operator's safety certificate or be accompanied by someone who is at least age 18. Persons renting motorboats or PWCs of greater than 10 horsepower must be at least age 18. Strict regulations apply to boat operation, including wake restrictions, launching and mooring, harassment of wildlife, waste discharge, noise limitations, and more. PFDs and other safety accessories, such as fire extinguishers, are required in most circumstances. You can pick up a copy of these regulations at Montana Fish, Wildlife and Parks, along with the informative brochure titled *Ethics, Etiquette and the River Recreationist.*

If you choose to go on a guided trip or commercial boat cruise, the US Coast Guard reminds prospective riders that they are responsible for their own safety and should check out the record of operators of boat rides and cruises, and follow these guidelines: Before leaving the dock talk to the operator about the driver or guide's qualifications, and try to ascertain that the person in charge of your watercraft is not impaired by drugs or alcohol. Do they know first aid and CPR? A smart skipper will take time to give passengers a review of safety equipment and rules of conduct. Check out the equipment—PFDs, radio, fire extinguisher, and navigation lights—and learn how to use them. If you had to, could you start, stop, and steer the boat, or turn on navigation lights? Also inquire about the trip plan, the route, and the return time.

Paddling Montana, by Hank and Carol Fischer, *Three Forks of the Flathead—Wild & Scenic River Float Guide,* published by the Glacier Association, and a Flathead National Forest map should all be especially useful for planning your water recreation in Glacier Country. The map, besides showing river and lake access points on USDA Forest Service lands, provides a wealth of information on all public lands, including lists of lakes, camping, and other recreation areas with keys to services and opportunities at each.

With these in hand, here's a few suggestions for starters.

Glacier National Park

The lakes of Glacier provide some of the most peaceful and scenic paddling in the region, and provide access to intimate explorations of shorelines seldom reached by foot alone. Even on the lakes where tour boats cruise, an unhurried day of gliding over these crystal lakes on a sunny summer's day can be pleasure defined.

The park charges no fees for boating, but does enforce certain regulations (inquire for a set of them at headquarters or a visitor center; you'll also find them online at www.nps.gov/glac/planyourvisit/boating.htm). Canoes, kayaks, and sailboats are permitted on all park waters except upper McDonald Creek between Mineral Creek and Lake McDonald. These areas are closed to all types of boating and floating to protect nesting harlequin ducks. Personal watercraft such as Jet Skis are currently prohibited on all park waters. Privately owned, motorized boats are prohibited except on Lake McDonald, and St. Mary, Two Medicine, and Bowman Lakes, the latter two being limited to 10 horsepower or less. PFDs must be on board for each passenger and children must wear theirs while aboard. The park imposes both permanent and temporary shoreline closures in a few areas, usually to protect breeding wildlife. Always check with a ranger in advance to learn what's in force during your stay.

Canoes, rowboats, and low-power motorboats may be rented at Two Medicine, Many Glacier, and at Apgar and Lake McDonald Lodge on Lake McDonald. For those seeking a truly quiet, pristine canoeing spot and don't mind bumping along a primitive road to get there, try Kintla Lake on the park's west side. It's a watery jewel surrounded by heavily forested mountain slopes, with no motorboats allowed and only a small primitive campground on the shores.

Area Lakes & Rivers

All of the larger and many of the smaller lakes in Glacier Country feature one or more easily reached boat-access sites. Flathead Lake State Park has one at each of its five shoreline units, while at Whitefish Lake State Park you'll find a ramp on the southwest shore. Swan Lake's public access is located at the recreation area just north of the town of Swan Lake. Popular Forest Service access sites include Tally Lake northwest of Whitefish, Ashley Lake west of Kalispell, and numerous locations on Hungry Horse Reservoir reached from East Reservoir Road (turn off US 2 at Martin City) and West Reservoir Road leaving US 2 at the Hungry Horse Ranger Station. Motorized boats are permitted on these lakes, but check with Fish, Wildlife and Parks to learn if waterfowl-nesting-season restrictions are in force in some areas.

i Glacier National Park is not particularly dog friendly, and with good reason. Due largely to the presence of animals that will chase dogs (like bears and mountain lions) and animals that dogs will chase (like deer and elk), dogs must be on a leash no longer than 6 feet at all times in developed areas and along roads. Dogs are not permitted on trails at all. They also may not be left unattended in cars or tied to a stationary object like a picnic table. Kennels are available in the Flathead Valley if you plan to backpack or do extended day hiking in the park.

Flathead Lake Marine Trail

The Flathead Lake Marine Trail was designated specifically for kayaks, canoes, and small sailboats, with a network of access points and camping areas. You can plan a daylong or multiday outing around the lake, with stops at islands and secluded shoreline locales. Those intending to camp can pay overnight and vehicle-parking fees at Flathead Lake State Park. Pack-it-in, pack-it-out rules apply, and no pets are allowed on Wild Horse Island. Diamond-shaped signs mark landing areas. A trail map and guide is available from Fish, Wildlife and Parks, which reminds boaters that cold water can be a killer, and a wet or dry suit is recommended for most of the year.

The Flathead River

The Flathead River has a split personality. Each of its three branches, the North Fork, Middle Fork, and South Fork, offers distinct environments and adventures. Some or all of each fork is included in the National Wild and Scenic Rivers, for a total of 219 miles. The Middle Fork is suitable only for skilled rafters and kayakers or those with guides. The South Fork, which lies mostly in the Bob Marshall Wilderness, is accessible only by foot or horseback, except for one section in the central part at Cedar Flats River Access. This fork has class II and III waters with one gorge that is rated class V to VI and must be portaged. The North Fork arises in Canada and forms the western boundary of Glacier National Park. It has several public access points from both the Inside and Outside North Fork Roads. It flows clear and cold through conifer-covered mountains and is suitable mostly for intermediate and expert floaters. During spring runoff, which begins in May and can last into July, fast currents and logjams offer thrills, hazards, and challenges. The most pre-dictable conditions are usually from mid-July to Sept. The section between Polebridge and Big Creek is suitable for beginners, but only during low water and fair weather, and floaters should be watchful of riffles, logjams, and narrow channels.

For the first-time or short-time visitor, the Flathead's best offering is its main stem below the South Fork's junction just above Columbia Falls. After the spring runoff period is over, it flows rather leisurely on the remain-der of its journey to Flathead Lake through a braided channel among sloughs that provide habitat for waterfowl, raptors, and beaver. This stretch makes a good half- or full-day outing in good weather, with public access ramps found at Kokanee Bend, Pres-sentine Bar, and Old Steel Bridge.

Swan River

The Swan River flows northward 40 miles to Swan Lake from its Mission Mountain headwater lakes and numerous feeder streams, then gradually slows as it continues another 10 miles to its delta in Flathead Lake at Bigfork. The channel is heavily forested and bordered by rich wildlife habitat. The upper Swan is narrow and, even in its wider lower portions, logjams make it technically demanding and sometimes treacherous, especially in high water. But if the Swan's beauty seduces you to float your boat, two stretches are recommended for canoes and kayaks. At low water, 2 to 3 miles above Swan Lake the river slows and meanders at a pace suitable for beginners. Put in at the county bridge just above the Swan River National Wildlife Refuge, where waterfowl, shorebirds, deer, muskrats, and other wildlife are com-monly spotted. The Swan also attracts a lot of anglers, so you may see more people than

you expected, but it's still a quiet experience. Local floaters favor the 7-mile trip beginning at the bridge east of Ferndale, which is easy enough for beginners during low water in Aug and Sept. Leave the final "Wild Mile" to daredevil kayakers.

Swimming

Opportunities for water play are abundant in Glacier Country, whether it's swimming, wading, building sand castles on a river sandbar, or collecting colorful stones along the lakeshore. It's generally an informal affair and often the kids play along the river-bank while Mom and Dad fish. Many of the numerous public-access areas on lakes and rivers are free of charge and all you need is a bathing suit and (advisedly) protective footwear, as few areas have sandy beaches. All units of Flathead Lake State Park charge a day-use fee that includes the use of shore-lines, some of which have swimming areas roped off. For the most part, you can swim anywhere accessible from public lands. The water is gloriously clean and clear just about everywhere you look.

Popular swimming spots include areas along Flathead Lake, Whitefish Lake City Beach, Foys Lake, Whitefish Lake State Park, Lake McDonald, and Hungry Horse Reservoir. Woodland Park in Kalispell has a swimming pool, including a wading pool. Call (406) 758-7812 for hours and season. Columbia Falls also boasts a municipal pool; call (406) 892-3500 for hours and other information.

Sea-Kayaking Guides & Rentals

SILVER MOON KAYAK COMPANY
1215 North Somers Rd., Kalispell
(406) 752-3794
www.silvermoonkayak.com

Sea kayaking is booming in the Flathead Valley, and it's easy to see why. The sport offers a quiet, low-impact way to explore lakes and big rivers, and many boats have the capacity to support extended trips as well as day excursions. More and more of the boats around the Flathead are coming from Silver Moon Kayak Company, owned and operated by Bob Danford. Like other operations, Silver Moon offers a variety of boats for sale and rent, including Eddy-line, Boreal, and Venture brands; half- and full-day guided trips; moonlight tours (of course!); and instructional classes taught by ACA-certified instructors. Classes range from recreational paddling, all-women's classes ("BIBS"—Babes in Boats), to all-out Eskimo rolling, and class sizes are kept small to promote personal attention. Silver Moon also maintains a fully stocked kayak shop. No need to order, go home, and wait for your paddle gear to arrive; it's all here, right now!

WHITEFISH SEA KAYAKING
321 Columbia Ave., Whitefish
(406) 862-3513
Whitefish Sea Kayaking focuses on making kayak excursions in the immediate area—Whitefish Lake, the Whitefish River, and Flathead Lake—convenient and affordable. Owner Mark Roy carries Seaward and Current Designs boats, which are available for sale or rent. They rent for $25 per half day or $35 for a full day, and the company will drop off and pick up the boats for free in the Whitefish area. Whitefish Sea Kayaking also offers regular half- and full-day tours on the same lakes and river. Boaters bring their own snacks or lunches. Moonlight and custom tours are also available, as are lessons in rescue and advanced paddling skills.

Whitewater Kayak Rentals

ROCKY MOUNTAIN OUTFITTER (RMO)
135 Main St., Kalispell
(406) 752-2446
www.rockymountainoutfitter.com
RMO, established in 1976, rents demo white-water boats to those considering making a purchase.

Rafting Guides & Rentals

These folks love the rivers and want you to love them, too. They also are passionate about keeping the waterways and the plants and animals living there healthy and happy for generations to come. All are established companies employing experienced guides. Their prices for half- and full-day raft and kayak trips are within a few dollars of each other, with similar equipment and services provided. Charges for half-day raft trips run about $50 for adults and $40 for children. Full-day trips cost about $85 for adults, $60 for children. Some or all gear is provided. Trips with little or no whitewater are another option. The companies also offer hike-raft trips, hike-horseback outings, extended wilderness trips, fishing excursions, fly ins, and other enticing combination packages, each distinctive to the company offering it. If you're single or a couple, expect to share a raft with 4 to 6 others. The main tours feature some measure of whitewater, depending on the month and melting snowpacks feeding the rivers. Scenic cruises provide relaxing jaunts on quieter stretches; most companies require a 4-person minimum for these—although little seems hard and fast with these folks. They simply want to give you the best deal and the greatest experience possible.

GLACIER GUIDES/MONTANA RAFT COMPANY

P.O. Box 330, West Glacier 59936
(406) 387-5555, (800) 521-7238
www.glacierguides.com

Launched in 1987, Glacier Guides/Montana Raft Company is the only enterprise licensed to guide hiking trips in Glacier National Park, from day hikes to multi-day backpack trips. From May 15 to Sept 30, the company also guides whitewater trips on the Middle and North Forks of the Flathead River, using smaller rafts holding 6 to 8 people maximum. All-day tours feature a buffet lunch. The company also offers fishing trips on the Middle and North Forks. Their headquarters are located 1.5 miles west of the west entrance to Glacier.

*GLACIER RAFT COMPANY

Glacier Outdoor Center, West Glacier
(406) 888-5454, (800) 235-6781
www.glacierraftco.com

Established in 1976, Glacier Raft Company is the oldest continuously operating raft company in Montana. It also gained prominence as host and technical adviser for production of the Hollywood movie *The River Wild,* starring Meryl Streep and Kevin Bacon. Glacier Raft runs multiday, full-day, and half-day trips on both the North and Middle Forks as well as the main stem of the Flathead River. Eight riders on a raft is the norm, with a minimum of 4. Full-day trips include a barbecue lunch. They also rent inflatable kayaks for self-guided trips on the calmer stretches, and they provide shuttles.

GREAT NORTHERN WHITEWATER RAFT & RESORT

US 2, West Glacier
(406) 387-5340, (800) 735-7897
www.gnwhitewater.com

Great Northern's office is easy to spot 1 mile west of the Glacier Park entrance, by the red caboose on the hill. Now with nearly 35 years' experience, Great Northern specializes in trips down the Middle Fork of the Flathead River. They usually operate from mid-May into early Oct. In high water during spring, they use larger rafts holding 10 to 12 people; late-season trips, or summer floats when water levels are lower, use 6-person rafts. Morning trips come with a complimentary breakfast. They rent inflatable kayaks for self-guided trips on the Middle Fork only. With Swiss-style chalet rentals, raft trips, and fishing excursions, Great Northern can be your one-stop vacation center.

WILD RIVER ADVENTURES

11900 US 2 East
P.O. Box 272, West Glacier 59936
(406) 387-9453, (800) 700-7056
www.riverwild.com

In 2010, Wild River Adventures wrapped up its 25th year of guiding whitewater trips on the Middle and North Forks of the Flathead. The company has also teamed up with Flying Eagle Outfitters to offer "saddle/paddle" combo day adventures in and around Glacier Park, and they run fly-fishing excursions and offer fly-casting clinics. The season runs from May 15 to Sept 15. They are located 1 mile west of the West Glacier park entrance.

IN THE SNOW—SKIING & OTHER WINTER SPORTS

Winter in Glacier Country revolves around snow—how much, what kind, and how best to get out in it. Snow transforms the land into a winter wonderland and offers a slate of exciting outdoor adventures for young and old, timid and adventurous. Deep snow and frozen waterways make accessible many places in the park, national forests, and lakes that are difficult to reach at other times of the year. For many insiders who love it outside, winter is the best season and the chief reason they moved here.

Skiing, both alpine and Nordic, becomes the central preoccupation in many people's lives and in the area's economic life. The same folks you see biking and hiking in summer head for the slopes after work and on weekends. Snowboarding has skyrocketed in popularity, as has snowmobiling. There are more than 200 miles of groomed trails for snowmobiling in the Flathead Valley, but snowmobiles are not permitted anywhere in Glacier National Park. One of the things that makes the area so desirable is that the outdoor opportunities are so many and so close to the cities and towns. In fact, you can cross-country ski right in town in Kalispell, and just a couple of minutes away from downtown Whitefish.

i Glacier Country's steep terrain, heavy snowfall, and ever-changing weather are key elements for one of nature's most awesome and deadly occurrences—the snow avalanche. Responsible and prepared backcountry travelers should possess the skill and knowledge to assess avalanche conditions. Always carry shovels, probe poles, and avalanche beacons. Biweekly avalanche advisories are issued during winter by the Glacier Country Avalanche Center. Check www.glacieravalanche.org or call (406) 257-8204 for avalanche-condition updates.

As in other seasons, winter weather differs, often drastically, from one side of the Continental Divide to the other. On the west side, winters are generally cloudy, cool, and rather damp. Only occasionally does the mercury dip below zero, as the cloud cover and moderating influences of large water bodies like Lake McDonald and Flathead Lake keep temperatures in the teens and twenties. Areas east of the divide tend to be much colder, less snowy, and substantially windier. Driving can be tricky on either side, but especially on the east, as high winds pile the snow into deep drifts on the roadways, and whiteouts with near-zero visibility are not uncommon.

Locals will generalize about the weather, then tell you there really is no typical winter. The winter of 1996–97 deposited 12 feet of snow in the Flathead Valley, and cross-country ski trails stayed open into Apr. The very next year, snowfall was sparse, disappointing skiers, snowmobilers, and ski-resort operators alike. In 1998–99 the ski resorts reveled in frequent powder dumps, and cross-country skiing continued well into Mar even at the lowest elevations. Subsequently, a run of drier winters was followed by 2008, which proved to be a bonanza year for skiers, with excellent conditions over a long season.

Snow in the valley bottoms can be deep, or it can be disappointing. But even when there's little snow down below in the winter, you can almost always find plenty in the mountains above 5,000 feet. The mountains receive about 80 percent of their annual precipitation as snow; while those clouds hanging over the mountaintops are blotting out the sun, know that they are also depositing snow in the high country, building a snowpack that usually lasts well into summer. As late as June, cyclists with skis or snowshoes strapped to their backs can be seen heading up Going-to-the-Sun Road (before it opens to vehicles), where they will stash their bikes and take off into the remaining high-country snow.

With thousands of miles of forest roads and trails available to explore, backcountry snowmobiling ranks high on the list of winter activities. And don't forget, "flatlander" winter activities are also popular here, like rinks for ice-skating, in-town hills for sledding and tubing—and even mushers who will take you out for a dogsled ride.

Winter Safety Tips

Don't let winter's soft, snowy beauty dull your awareness of its potential hazards. Lack of awareness and planning can be fatal. Whether you are snowshoeing, skiing, snowmobiling, or hiking, when you're away from towns in Glacier Country, you are "out there" and on your own.

If you're venturing into the backcountry, travel with at least one partner, let someone know where you are going and when you expect to return, be sure you're in shape for the level of exertion you plan, check the weather and road conditions before heading out, and carry emergency-survival equipment and supplies.

The risk of hypothermia and frostbite hovers just beyond your mitts and parka, even when it doesn't seem that cold. It is the primary killer of outdoor enthusiasts. With hypothermia, a person's inner core is chilled, resulting in slowing of mental and physical responses. Be alert to common symptoms—drowsiness and confusion. Once hypothermia has set in, external sources of warmth are necessary to restore the victim to normal. To stave off hypothermia, drink plenty of liquids, stay dry, wear layers of warm clothing (removing them during exertion so that you don't become wet from sweat), and snack frequently.

To prevent frostbite, wear warm clothing and avoid exposing your skin in extremely cold and/or windy conditions. Be alert for whitening tissue and numbness in cheeks, noses, fingers, and toes, all of which are especially prone to frostbite.

Avalanche!

Avalanches can occur at any time during the winter. Snowmobilers are at greatest risk because their powerful and heavy machines can carry them into the highest and most-avalanche-prone reaches. They regularly outnumber other Montana snow recreationists in avalanche deaths.

An understanding of and familiarity with avalanche conditions and snow behavior are the snowmobiler's and skier's best defenses, but if caught in an avalanche a survival kit can save a life.

Experts advise the following:

- Avoid mountainous terrain after heavy snowfall or prolonged high winds.
- Avoid crossing steep slopes and steep-sided canyons.
- Keep to the windblown side of ridges, rather than the leeward side, where heavy snows are deposited by the wind.
- Learn avalanche danger signs.
- Carry and know how to use transceivers, probe poles, and shovels.

If caught in an avalanche:

- Try to remain calm so that you can remember what you're supposed to do.
- Attempt to stay on the surface and "swim" toward the side of the avalanche.
- As you come to a stop, try to paw an airspace around your face. If you aren't caught in the slide but a companion is, mark the place you last saw the victim, look for him or her downhill from there, and probe the area. Unless additional

help is very nearby, stay with the victim and keep searching. You may have no more than a half hour to try to save your companion's life.

To obtain information about avalanche conditions prior to setting out, consult the **Glacier Country Avalanche Center** at (406) 257-8204 or www.glacieravalanche.org. The For More Information chapter lists some helpful books on avalanche safety, as well.

Downhill Skiing

✳BLACKTAIL MOUNTAIN SKI AREA
P.O. Box 1090, Lakeside 59922
(406) 844-0999
www.blacktailmountain.com

"Uncrowded, affordable, and friendly" are words commonly used by skiers and snowboarders to describe Glacier Country's newest downhill ski area. The spectacular views and first-rate slopes of Blacktail Mountain make the 14-mile drive through national forest from Lakeside well worth the effort. As you reach the top on a wide, well-maintained USDA Forest Service road, vistas greet you across Flathead Lake and the Flathead Valley to the Swan and Mission Mountain Ranges. The road heads west from US 93 leaving just south of Lakeside. It takes 30 to 45 minutes to drive from Kalispell to the summit and lodge.

Blacktail first opened in Dec 1998, after a flurry of construction activity to complete the development on 1,000 acres of national forest lands. It straddles the mountain's 6,780-foot summit, which receives average yearly snowfall of 250 inches. An "upside-down" resort, skiers park at the top and descend from the "base" lodge to access the lifts at the lower terminal some 1,440 vertical feet below. More than two dozen groomed runs add up to approximately 14 miles of trails, offering a full range of challenges for every level of skier. Seventy percent of the slopes are rated intermediate, and for the rad bunch there's the Independence Terrain Park—so this is a very family-friendly ski area.

Blacktail attracts many who seek affordable alpine skiing in a relaxed setting with all the expected amenities. There's reasonably priced day care for the kids, who can also take skiing or snowboarding lessons from qualified instructors. You can also savor the views and the food at one of the two restaurants, or have a hot drink in the lounge after you've conquered the slopes.

During Blacktail's season, from late Nov or early Dec into Apr (depending on conditions), the resort is open Wed through Sun and holidays 9:30 a.m. to 4:30 p.m., including the Christmas season. It offers 2 double chair lifts, 1 triple lift, and 1 beginner's platter. Daily ski-rental package prices are $22 for adults, $16 for children, and $22 for snowboards and gear. A steal of a deal for adults is the Thrifty Thursdays, when you can ski all day for just $25 (excluding holidays). Or, if you happen to hit Blacktail on your birthday, you can ski for free! Call or check the website for additional information on day-pass and season-pass prices. If you prefer cross-country skiing, be aware that the North Shore Nordic Club maintains a system of groomed trails below the mountain off Blacktail Road (see below and/or visit www.northshorenordic .org for more detailed information).

WHITEFISH MOUNTAIN RESORT
P.O. Box 1400, Whitefish 59937
(406) 862-2900, (800) 858-3930
www.skiwhitefish.com

Whitefish Mountain Resort attracts winter sports enthusiasts from throughout the United States and Canada. It is among North

America's largest ski and summer resorts, with more than 3,000 acres of skiable terrain and 94 marked trails, with the addition of huge amounts of free-form tree and bowl skiing. And the view from the mountain's alone is worth the price of admission! Snow storms annually shower the peak with around 300 inches of the white stuff. *Ski Magazine* readers consistently rank the resort number 1 in Montana and among the nation's top 20. In the magazine's 2010 rankings, for instance, Whitefish Mountain nabbed 19th place, ahead of such Colorado heavyweights as Keystone, Winter Park, and Crested Butte.

Renowned for its powder—though it's not quite as light as the powder blanketing the higher Rockies to the south, in Wyoming, Colorado, and Utah—the 60-plus-year-old resort offers a top-notch experience for every level of skier. An atmosphere of happy exuberance fills the village area as skiers, snowboarders, tubers, and sightseers debark busses and cars, purchase their lift tickets, and circulate between the chairlifts and slopes and the restaurants, pubs, and shops. Just 5 miles from downtown Whitefish, "the village" attracts not only skiers and 'boarders, but also locals and visitors simply wanting to immerse themselves in the lively scene.

A variety of lifts, including 3 high-speed quads and 2 slower quads, 5 triple chairs, and a pair of T-bars, whisk winter recreationists to their desired location on the mountain, whether they're novice or expert schussers.

The 2010–11 daily rates were $64 for adults, $34 for juniors (ages 7 through 12), $56 for youth (13 through 18), $52 for seniors (65 through 69), and free for "super seniors" over 70 and children under 6. A variety of season passes are also available.

Incurable powder hounds can hitch a snowcat ride from Olney, 18 miles north of Whitefish, high into a particularly storm-battered locale in the Whitefish Range to ski open glades and tree stands all day long. The cost is $325 per person. Groups generally ski 8 to 10 runs per day.

Back at the resort, lighted slopes extend the skiing hours on Fri and Sat from mid-Dec through mid-Mar from 4 to 8:30 p.m. The price for night skiing is $16. The ski school has many programs, and rental equipment is available for alpine and Nordic skiing and snowshoeing. There's also a day-care center. Whitefish Mountain Resort's ski season runs from early Dec until the second week of Apr, with the lifts running daily from 9 a.m. to 4 p.m. The free SNOW Bus operates between Whitefish and the Whitefish Mountain Resort Village, making it a piece of cake to get to and from the ski hill.

Cross-Country Skiing & Snowshoeing

BUFFALO HILL GOLF CLUB
1176 North Main St.
P.O. Box 1116, Kalispell 59903
(406) 756-4545
Located a stone's throw from downtown Kalispell, the club opens its 27-hole golf course to cross-country skiers when snow conditions permit, usually from Dec 1 to Mar 1. Beginners and intermediate skiers will enjoy a relaxed tour on the gentle slopes, along the Stillwater River with views of the mountains. Trails are not groomed, but it's free, and skied-in track lead to the best slopes and scenery. It makes a good choice when you have only a short time to get your blood racing. Warm your toes and tummies with food and beverages at the cozy club-house, open daily from 8:30 a.m. to 5 p.m.

GLACIER NORDIC CENTER AND
OUTBACK
Ski Shack
1200 US 93, Whitefish
(406) 862-9498 (Nov 1 through Mar 31)
Located at the Whitefish Lake Golf Club a mile west of downtown Whitefish, the Glacier Nordic Center offers conveniently accessible, affordable skiing. Some 12 kilometers (7.5 miles) of generally gently sloping trails wind around the golf course, with great views of the Whitefish Range. It's a perfect course for beginners and intermediates, but the racers in town also train there because of its convenient location. The Glacier Nordic Club sponsors the center and tries to groom the trails daily for both ski skating and classic skiing. Nearly 2 miles of trail are lighted nightly with hundreds of 10-watt bulbs, making for a pleasant after-dinner outing. Glacier Nordic Ski School offers instruction programs, including classes for kids and seniors, skate skiing, and classic skiing. The club asks skiers for a donation, which, along with club memberships, helps covers the cost of grooming and equipment. No dogs or snowshoes are permitted.

The on-site Outback Ski Shack rents ski equipment packages for half and full days (24 hours). Call or visit the shack for current rates. Certified instructors offer lessons here, and the nearby Grouse Mountain Lodge is a full-service dining and lodging facility. The center's trails are generally open from mid-Dec through mid-Mar.

GLACIER OUTDOOR CENTER
US 2, West Glacier
(406) 888-5454, (800) 235-6781
www.glacierraftco.com
The location of Glacier Raft Company's summer operations, this full-service outdoor center rents its logs cabins the year around. In winter they groomed 10 kilometers (6 miles) of cross-country ski trails for both classic and skate skiing. The trails meander over 100 acres of rolling terrain just outside West Glacier. Rental ski and snowshoe equipment is available; a day pass costs $8 for humans, and just $2 for dogs! They also offer guided half-day and full-day interpretive ski tours in Glacier National Park.

*IZAAK WALTON INN
US 2, at Milepost 180, Essex
290 Izaak Walton Inn Rd.
(406) 888-5700
www.izaakwaltoninn.com
More than 30 kilometers (20 miles) of scenic backcountry trails await your skinny skis at this historic lodge between West Glacier and Marias Pass. Considered one of the top cross-country ski resort destinations in the Rockies, the inn's trails wind through a largely forested, sheltered terrain, and are broken out as 30 percent easiest, 50 percent more difficult, and 20 percent most difficult. The trails range from between 3,800 and 4,800 feet in elevation.

The inn was built in 1939 to house winter snow removal crews working on the Great Northern Railway tracks. Railroad workers still hole up there, and the track complex behind the building evokes the excitement and romance of a long-distance train ride through the Wild West. Helper engines still push trains over the pass from the rail yard, and plenty of vacationers still arrive by Amtrak train for their ski holiday. A new bridge across the railroad tracks offers convenient, safe passage to the ski areas.

Railroad buffs, especially, will enjoy the yard activity and memorabilia such as sig-

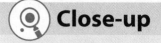

Close-up

Emergency Gear

Glacier National Park and the surrounding wildlands provide unbounded recreational opportunities for the outdoor enthusiast. However, hidden amid the scenic grandeur of the area are risks and hazards that can be deadly. Precipitous terrain, swift and cold water, wild animals, and ever-changing weather are all factors that contribute to the wildness of the area.

It's imperative that you engage in outdoor activities compatible with the skill levels and physical capabilities of everyone in your group. Always evaluate your group members and assess the hazards before heading out. Avoid traveling solo, and advise family or friends of your route and planned time of return.

Responsible backcountry travelers are always prepared for the unexpected. Specific equipment to bring should be governed by the type of outing you'll be engaging in, but consider the following as standard-issue emergency gear:

Map and Compass or GPS. A topographic map of your area, as well as a compass. Whatever you bring, be sure you know how to use it.

First-Aid Kit. Being able to treat injuries and illness in the field can make a big difference in the relative well-being of someone in your party. Emergency medical services may not be readily available.

Emergency Signaling Device. Be prepared to signal both aerial and ground search-and-rescue personnel. Helpful items include a whistle, a signal mirror, and an emergency signal that sends up smoke.

Fire Starter. Survival could depend on your ability to make a fire. Consider taking a candle and cigarette lighter. Fine steel wool or pieces of a cedar shake make good fire kindling.

Adequate Food and Water. Calorie intake and proper hydration are essential to your comfort and safety. Boil, filter, or treat backcountry surface water to avoid such ailments as giardiasis. Carry more high-energy snacks than you think you'll need.

Reliable Wind and Rain Gear. This is hypothermia country. A sturdy rain and wind parka and pants are musts to enable you to stay warm and dry.

Bivouac Bag or Space Blanket. Be prepared for an unplanned night in the mountains. These items can help provide some protection from the elements. Also carry a piece of foam pad to provide insulation between your body and the ground.

Layered Clothing. Dressing, and undressing, in layers of clothing affords you greater capacity to regulate your temperature.

High technology has surfaced in the backcountry in many ways, including in the form of satellite phones. Many look at these devices as an intrusion into the "wilderness experience," while others wouldn't consider leaving home without the "dial-a-rescue" potential. However, keep in mind that they could lead to a false sense of security—a satellite phone can't take the place of common sense and adequate skill and training.

nal lanterns, historic posters, and dining-car menus rounding out the inn's decor.

The high elevations, with earlier and heavier snows than much of the surrounding region, yield a lengthy season, generally from late Nov to mid-Apr. Don't be surprised to find that you have the trails nearly to yourself. This area is perfect for snowshoeing, as well, and several trails are marked specifically for that activity. Around every bend in the trail lies a postcard view of distant snow-covered peaks, or a more intimate scene of a snow-banked mountain creek. A favorite with advanced skiers is the half-mile loop along the Flathead River, and lights lining the Starlight Trail allow for night skiing.

You can rent skis, snowshoes, and ski sleds here. They also offer ski lessons and guided trips via either skis or snowshoes into Glacier Park. A $12 daily pass admits you to all trails (overnight guests ski for free). Season and family passes are also available.

WHITEFISH MOUNTAIN RESORT
NORDIC CENTER
Big Mountain Road, Whitefish
(406) 862-1900, (800) 858-5439
www.skiwhitefish.com
Take to the wide trails hovering around the 5,000-foot level that let the beginner enjoy the easy ones and the advanced skier take the challenge of steep runs, all winding through conifer woods. These trails are some of the first in the area to receive snow. The Nordic Center, with its large parking area and activity area, is reached by Big Mountain Road. Groomers sweep and set tracks daily on the 15 kilometers (9 miles) of trails with both classic and skating lanes. The ski shop sells the $15 trail passes, rents skis and boots, and arranges lessons and tours. They also rent snowshoes and can instruct you

on their proper use. Snowshoe lanes and trails run around the cross-country area. The season extends from early Dec until early or mid-Apr.

Flathead National Forest Trails

The immensity of this region, and the vast network of Flathead National Forest roads, beckon the dedicated backcountry skier to endless discoveries. Most of the roads remain unplowed and are used by both skiers and snowmobilers. The Tally Lake, Swan Lake, and Hungry Horse districts offer groomed ski trails where snowmobiles are prohibited. Forest Service maps, which identify the roads suitable for skiing, are available from the supervisor's office in Kalispell or the individual district offices. For general recreation information call (406) 758-5204.

BLACKTAIL MOUNTAIN
Swan Lake Ranger District
(406) 837-0783
www.northshorenordic.org
The North Shore Nordic Club maintains a system of groomed trails below the ski area off Blacktail Road. Some 25 miles of groomed or packed forest trails lead you along scenic ridges and slopes with panoramic views of Flathead and Mary Ronan Lakes and the Mission and Swan Mountains. Trailheads and parking areas for the lower and upper trails are about 6 and 8 miles from Lakeside on Blacktail Mountain Road. At roughly 5,500 feet in elevation, the area offers trails ranging from quite level and easy to roller-coasting and more difficult. Contact the district for a ski report.

JEWEL BASIN
Hungry Horse Ranger District
(406) 387-3800

This spectacular and popular backcountry use area boasts more than 15,000 acres of high mountain country and 35 miles of trails, some suitable for backcountry skiing. Take Echo Lake Road from Highway 83 northeast of Bigfork and follow the signs to Jewel Basin. Call for more information.

ROUND MEADOWS
Tally Lake Ranger District
(406) 758-5200

Off the beaten track in the Flathead National Forest, 15 miles northwest of Whitefish, Round Meadows has some 12 kilometers (7 miles) of intermittently groomed trails open between mid-Dec and mid-Mar. Mostly beginner and intermediate slopes wind through woods and meadows. Snowmobiles and dogs are prohibited. Logging activity may restrict or close some trails. Call for information and grooming updates.

Essex Area

Several miles of touring trails lie along the Middle Fork of the Flathead River across from the Izaak Walton Inn. The inn grooms the trails intermittently and has USDA Forest Service trail maps available.

Glacier National Park Winter Activities

Winter magnifies Glacier Park's special brand of beautiful magic. The snow-covered roads become silent pathways leading into the heart of scenic areas, far away from crowds and cars. Skiers and snowshoers make the park their haven, with new residents exploring virgin territory, conferencegoers taking some time out for a little exercise, and vacationers unwinding from the high-speed and heavy-adrenaline activities of the Whitefish Mountain Resort. The park prohibits snowmobiles anywhere within its boundaries.

Check at park headquarters, (406) 888-7800, for snow conditions. A cross-country skiing brochure with map and descriptions is available at the **Apgar Visitor Center,** open winter weekends from 9 a.m. to 4 p.m. Call (406) 888-7939.

APGAR-WEST GLACIER

Several routes lead from 2 parking areas in this area: one at the horse barn reached by taking the first left off Going-to-the-Sun Road after the entrance station, and the other at the barricade on Camas Road just beyond the McDonald Creek Bridge. The trails range from 2 or 3 miles round-trip to nearly 12 miles. The park brochure mentioned above describes them in detail.

MONTANA'S DUCK LAKE LODGE
P.O. Box 210, Duck Lake Road, Babb
59411
(406) 338-5770
www.montanasducklakelodge.com

East of Glacier, tourist activities come to a near-dead stop during the winter. The visitor is greeted in many places by boarded-up inns, restaurants, and shops. In Babb, however, on the Blackfeet Indian Reservation, Montana's Duck Lake Lodge offers year-round accommodations—including rooms, meals, and information about winter recreation in the area. If you're happy with unpretentious, down-home comfort, this spot will suit you just fine. It's located only 2 miles from Duck Lake, renowned for its enormous rainbow trout. Ice fishing is popular and it's a short drive to cross-country skiing in Glacier National Park. With these activities and 350 acres of lands to explore by snowmobile, the lodge makes a good winter getaway east of the Continental Divide.

GLACIER ADVENTURE GUIDES
P.O. Box 4833, Whitefish 59937
(406) 892-2173
www.glacieradventureguides.com

How would you like to spend a winter's day in Glacier's backcountry with a professional guide who'll safely escort you to prime locations and interpret the wondrous landscapes encountered? This outfit's guides are skilled in winter mountaineering, avalanche safety, and first aid, and they can take you on a trip appropriate for your group's interests and abilities: day tours, backcountry tours with overnights in an igloo or snow cave, and evening tours on full-moon nights. They offer outings via snowshoes as well as skis. Call for details on pricing and scheduling.

POLEBRIDGE

From the Polebridge Ranger Station parking area, a quartet of popular routes follow unplowed gravel roads to these destinations: Big Prairie (4 miles round-trip), Covey Meadow Loop (3 miles), Bowman Lake (12 miles round-trip), and Lone Pine Prairie (6 miles round-trip). Except for the Bowman Lake route, which is hilly and potentially icy, these routes are suitable for families with small children. To reach the ranger station, take the North Fork Road leading from Columbia Falls toward the Canadian border (but first check on road conditions, especially after a heavy snowfall).

ST. MARY

From the special parking area near the Hudson Bay District Office (just south of the town of St. Mary), several routes, including short loops, lead into level areas and rolling hills with views of St. Mary Lake and the Red Eagle Valley. Some are specially designated and marked. The Red Eagle Loops comprise three short routes winding through meadows and aspen and conifer stands, while longer trails lead to Red Eagle Lake and along Divide Creek.

TWO MEDICINE VALLEY

Two Medicine Road, which usually remains unplowed, is used as a ski trail with several destinations, long and short, easy and strenuous, through this highly scenic valley. Start at the end of the plowed road, usually 4 miles north of East Glacier near the junction of Highway 49. Because of the common east-slope winds, certain areas may be blown free of snow, so anticipate possibly needing to remove your skis now and then.

UPPER LAKE MCDONALD

Going-to-the-Sun Road is kept plowed to McDonald Lodge, where it is barricaded. From there skiers and snowshoers follow such popular routes as the 4-mile round-trip to McDonald Falls and, beyond the falls, the trip to Sacred Dancing Cascade.

For even more information on cross-country skiing, have a look at the PDF brochure titled *Cross Country Skiing Montana's Flathead Valley*, at www.fcvb.org/brochures/xcountry.pdf.

Snowmobiling

A snowmobiler's paradise, Glacier Country boasts more than 200 miles of groomed snowmobile trails and nearly 2,000 miles of ungroomed Forest Service roads that can lead you into great hill climbing, powder play, and spectacular ridgetop views of Glacier National Park, the Flathead Valley, and the Canadian Rockies. Snowmobile organizations are instrumental in keeping the trails maintained and groomed during the long season in the high country. They educate other riders about safety, outdoor survival, and avalanche awareness to keep the sport enjoyable for all. One of the area's most popular places to snowmobile is the Marias Pass Trail Complex, where trails meander along the Continental Divide, back and forth between Flathead and Glacier Counties. Well-marked trailheads and parking areas border US 2 at the pass. Maps are available from the Cutbank Snowgoers or the Lewis and Clark National Forest (see listings below).

FLATHEAD SNOWMOBILE ASSOCIATION
P.O. Box 5041, Kalispell 59903
www.flatheadsnowmobiler.com
This membership organization works to educate the public about the sport of snowmobiling, and to enhance and publicize the riding opportunities in and above the Flathead, while promoting safe family recreation. They are also a member of the Montana Snowmobiling Association (MSA), which is a useful source for finding snowmobiling events and contact information for other area snowmobiling clubs (www.m-s-a .org/clubs.cfm).

LEWIS AND CLARK NATIONAL FOREST
1101 Fifteenth St. North, P.O. Box 869, Great Falls 59403
(406) 791-7700
The Cutbank Snowgoers groom trails east of the Continental Divide and the trails on Marias Pass that traverse both the Flathead and the Lewis and Clark National Forests.

WHITEFISH MOUNTAIN RESORT SNOWMOBILE TOURS
P.O. Box 1400, Whitefish 59937
(406) 862-2900, (800) 858-3930
www.skiwhitefish.com

You say you're not a skier, but you ache for a snowy mountaintop adventure? A guided snowmobile excursion leaving from the Whitefish Mountain Resort summit is a good bet for an unforgettable experience. Terrific views—of Glacier, the Flathead, the Swan Range, the Canadian Rockies, and more— and endless photo opportunities are yours to be had on these thrill-filled trips. After a brief safety session, you'll don your helmet and zoom off into the wild in the company of a certified snowmobile guide. Half-day (3-hour) tours begin at 9 a.m. and 1 p.m. daily in the winter and cost approximately $175. Full-day (6-hour) trips begin daily at 9 a.m. and cost $250. Drivers must be at least 16 years old; kids 12 and under ride for free with a paying adult.

Other Winter Sports/Activities

Dogsled Rides
＊DOG SLED ADVENTURES
P.O. Box 34, Olney 59927
(406) 881-BARK (2275)
www.dogsledadventuresmt.com
Located 20 miles north of Whitefish on US 93, 2 miles north of Olney, Dogsled Adventures has been owned and operated by musher Jeff Ulsamer since 1979.

Dog sledding is an unusual and extraordinarily fun way to spend a day in Glacier Country. Dog Sled Adventures takes you on a 1¼-hour trip along a 12-mile loop through the Stillwater State Forest, courtesy of a team of fast and friendly Alaskan huskies, many of them rescued dogs. Afterwards, you'll be pampered with hot chocolate and cookies by the fire, as you enjoy the exchange of tall "tails." Wear warm clothes, including hat and mittens, and bring sunglasses. If it's extremely cold, you'll be wrapped in a warm cocoon of down and elk skins. After the trip you can pet the dogs! Calling ahead is mandatory; rides are arranged only after a reservation is made. The cost is $90 for adults and $45 for children. Snow conditions permitting, the tours run from late Nov to mid-Apr. If you happen to be staying up at the Whitefish Mountain Resort, on Tues and Thur free transportation is provided from there to the Olney operation and back. Call the resort at (406) 862-2919 for reservations.

Ice-Skating

Frozen lakes and ponds abound in a Glacier Country winter, but you won't see many ice-skaters on them, because the bodies of water are typically covered with snow—with the possible exception of those on the Blackfeet Indian Reservation, where winds often keep lake surfaces clear. Skaters can take advantage of at least 2 public rinks. One of them is at Kalispell's Woodland Park, where the rink has a warming hut and offers rentals and lessons during Dec and Jan. See the Kalispell section of the Attractions chapter for more information on Woodland Park.

STUMPTOWN ICE DEN
725 Wisconsin Ave., Whitefish
(406) 863-2477

This rink is just outside Whitefish on the way to the Whitefish Mountain Resort. Whitefish Parks and Recreation runs the facility, which is open for public skating daily on a variable daily schedule from Sept through late Mar. Hockey leagues and skating classes also use the ice, so be sure to check on the schedule. Stumptown Ice Den offers rentals, skate sharpening, and instruction. Admission to open skating is $5 per session for those 6 and older, and skate rental is $2.50. Children 5 and younger skate for free when accompanied by a paying skater.

i Snow conditions on the east side of Glacier National Park vary considerably, and in some places the wind can blow a cross-country ski route clear of snow at any time. Call the East Glacier Ranger Station to inquire about snow conditions, at (406) 226-4473. Some routes cross onto the Blackfeet Indian Reservation. The tribe requires a free cross-country skiing permit, obtainable at the tribal fish and game office in Browning.

HUNTING & FISHING
Hunting

The long-standing tradition of hunting wild game to fill the winter larder still burns strongly in Glacier Country, as elsewhere in Montana. The homesteading way of life counted the harvest of meat and fish from the woods and rivers vital to supplementing field crops, garden produce, and purchased food. The abundance of fur-bearing mammals—especially beaver—is what brought the first non-Native people to the mountains, and Northwestern Montana is still one of the places where individuals can legally trap certain species. Shotgunners find upland game birds plentiful here, especially ring-necked pheasant, Hungarian partridge, and several species of grouse. Waterfowl like ducks and geese are abundant, too, with Canada geese so common that some hunters refer to them as "flying carp."

Realistically, though, Glacier Country's hunting is somewhat limited compared to many areas of the state, because so much of the land here is either in Glacier National Park, where no hunting is allowed, or on the Blackfeet or Flathead Indian Reservations, where the public hunting opportunities are minimal and strictly regulated. A large share of the national forest lands in Glacier Country are roadless wilderness areas that require backpacking or horseback riding to reach the game. The remaining, more accessible national forest acreages, state lands, and some private properties do provide opportunities to hunt game birds and such critters as elk, white-tail deer, mule deer, and black bear. Some big-game hunting hotspots include the northern Swan Range, the national forest lands west of the North Fork of the Flathead, and the Yaak River drainage of the Purcell Mountains farther west still. Moose, bighorn sheep, and mountain goat hunting permits are granted through special drawings.

If you want to visit Glacier Country for a hunting trip, going on a guided trip with a licensed outfitter is a good option. A roster of active outfitters is available from the Montana Outfitters and Guides Association, listed at the end of this chapter. Licenses and permits are obtained from the Montana Department of Fish, Wildlife and Parks (FWP) offices or from license agents. People using Montana State Trust lands for hunting, fishing, or simply walking must also have a state recreational-use license, also available at offices of FWP and the Montana Department of Natural Resources and Conservation. Regulations and dates of seasons change from year to year, so it's wise to get a copy of the most current information from FWP, or from the Flathead or Blackfeet reservation.

Fishing

Although not acclaimed as a fishing destination on par with, say, the Yellowstone region, Glacier Country does indeed fulfill the dreams of many anglers, both local and visiting, with tasty trout and a fun diversion amid scenic splendor. An abundance of lakes, rivers, and streams attracts a dedicated bunch of local anglers on a regular basis, rain or shine, heat or cold. Trophy lake trout, or mackinaw, thrill plenty of anglers, and catch-and-release fly fishermen also can find some great stream fishing.

Montana's Fishing Access Sites program provides recreational opportunities for both residents and visitors. These sites have parking areas, usually feature either vault or flush toilets, and are well marked with the brown and white, hook-and-fish logo on road signs leading from the main highways.

Fishing license requirements for Montana residents are as follows: younger than age 12, no license is required; youths ages 12 through 14 need only a conservation license; people ages 15 through 61 must purchase both a conservation and fishing license; and those age 62 and older need only the conservation license. The conservation license costs $8 for residents and $10 for nonresidents; the fishing license, $18 for the season for residents and $60 for out-of-staters. Nonresidents younger than age 15 need no license if they are with a licensed adult, but the combined catch limit is the same as for a single license holder. The two-day nonresident license is $15. Full details can be found at http://fwp.mt.gov/fishing/regulations. No license is required for fishing in Glacier National Park. Call (406) 888-7800 or check the website for information about fishing regulations there. Resource agencies of the Flathead and Blackfeet Indian Reservations require special permits to fish there.

Streams and rivers in western Montana open for fishing on the third Sat of May and close Nov 30. Lakes and reservoirs are open year-round, with a few exceptions.

Catch & Release

Check with Fish, Wildlife and Parks for current information on the experimental bull trout angling season on Hungry Horse Reservoir, the South Fork of the Flathead, and Lake Kookanusa. Pictures and descriptions of the fish are available at FWP and fishing shops. Certain other species are restricted to catch and release on some streams and lakes. Check the current fishing regulations for such restrictions.

If you practice catch-and-release fishing, experts advise that you should use certain techniques to reduce stress on fish. Use hook-removal tools and, if you must handle the fish, use soft, wet gloves, or at least wet your hands.

- Use barbless hooks for fast and easy hook removal.
- Artificial lures and flies cause far less mortality than bait.
- Play the fish as rapidly as possible, not to its total exhaustion.
- Don't squeeze the fish or put your fingers in its gills when removing the hook. If its deeply hooked, cut the line as close to the mouth as possible; don't yank the hook out.
- Release the fish only after its equilibrium appears to be regained. If necessary, gently hold the fish upright facing upstream and move it slowly back and forth.

Fishing the Lakes

High mountain lakes generally are icebound until mid-June or early July. Trails to some may not be clear of snow until midsummer or later. Inquire about conditions at the agency in charge of the public lands where the lake you want to fish is located, or at a local sporting-goods shop. Be prepared for biting insects and unpredictable weather. In Glacier National Park, Lake McDonald and St. Mary Lake are more renowned for their beauty than for their fish. The best fishing lakes are said to be on the east side—but, not surprisingly, on both sides of the Continental Divide the very best fishing is in the more remote lakes that require a substantial hike to access. That said, here are a few of the lakes and streams accessible by vehicle or a short, easy hike, where the fishing can be respectable to quite good.

AVALANCHE LAKE, GLACIER NATIONAL PARK

In its splendid alpine setting surrounded by cloud-scratching peaks, Avalanche Lake is an easy 2-mile hike from Avalanche Campground on Going-to-the-Sun Road. Cutthroat trout is the main species here, and 8- to 10-inch fish are in good supply mainly in June and July.

BOWMAN LAKE, GLACIER NATIONAL PARK

The best time to catch the resident lake trout, kokanee salmon, and cutthroat trout in Bowman Lake is right after spring breakup and in the fall. The boat access ramp lies just beyond the campground, which is about 7 miles from the Polebridge Ranger Station up a bumpy dirt road.

CHURCH SLOUGH

Church Slough, a large oxbow lake adjacent to the Flathead River, lies along Lower Valley Road about 6 miles southeast of Kalispell. It is popular with local anglers for its populations of largemouth bass, northern pike, and yellow perch. A boat helps a lot here.

Echo Lake

Like Church Slough, Echo Lake is known for its largemouth bass, northern pike, and yellow perch, as well as for its sunfish. You can launch your boat at the state ramp at Echo Lake Marina; parking and shore access are limited. The best fishing is in the spring and fall.

Flathead Lake

Flathead Lake seldom freezes over, so year-round fishing attracts anglers seeking trophy lake trout as well as whitefish and yellow perch. Somers Bay, Woods Bay, and state park units all have boat launches. There's a small fee at the state parks for day use or camping, and parking areas are set aside for boat trailers. Somers and Wayfarers State Parks are wheelchair accessible.

Hidden Lake, Glacier National Park

Set in a beautiful alpine cirque, Hidden Lake is a scenic spot for pursuing Yellowstone cutthroat trout. The moderately strenuous 3-mile hike from Logan Pass offers spectacular scenery, and as a dividend you're likely to see mountain goats on the way. The lakeshore is accessible for easy bank fishing. As is always a good idea, be sure to bring along polarized sunglasses to make it easier to see through the bright reflections on the water. Bears are known to frequent the lake's outlet, so sometimes the trail is closed to human traffic.

Josephine Lake, Glacier National Park

June and July are the best months to catch the brook trout and kokanee salmon in this small lake just a 1.5-mile walk from the Many Glacier Hotel. If you have a light canoe or inflatable kayak, you might want to haul it along.

✳ Kintla Lake, Glacier National Park

Continue about 12 miles past the Bowman Lake turnoff on the Inside North Fork Road to find one of the prettiest lakes in Glacier National Park. The fishing is reasonably good, to boot. Boat fishing is best, but shore fishing is also possible away from the road and campground. Kintla Lake supports cutthroat, lake trout, and some kokanee.

Swan Lake

Swan Lake attracts a lot of anglers with boats, who launch from their cabins or from the ramp at the state recreation area just north of the town of Swan Lake. From May through Oct kokanee salmon, rainbow trout, westslope cutthroat, and northern pike can be taken. Early morning and late evening are best for fishing; during the heat of the day the lake is often abuzz with water-skiers and PWC (personal watercraft) riders.

Swiftcurrent Lake, Glacier National Park

You could practically throw a line into this lake from your room at the Many Glacier Hotel. But for best results do your angling in June or July from a boat and try to net some of the lake's pan-sized brook trout.

Tally Lake

On the Tally Lake Ranger District northwest of Whitefish, Tally Lake, at nearly 500 feet in depth, is Montana's deepest natural lake. The fishing is not the greatest, but it's a perfect spot for a family outing when some want to fish and others want to bike, hike, or just picnic. There's a boat launch at the campground. Cutthroat, rainbow, kokanee, and northern pike are some of the fish species inhabiting the lake.

TWO MEDICINE LAKES, GLACIER NATIONAL PARK

The beauty of these lakes—lower, main, and upper—makes them a joy to fish, and you have a fairly good chance of catching rainbow and brook trout. Most run under 15 inches. The best fishing is in June and July.

Creeks & Rivers

The forks of the Flathead River offer a wide variety of fishing opportunities. The Stillwater and Whitefish Rivers are slow and bordered by pastures and urban development, but there are a few places where people fish successfully for northern pike and rainbow trout in the spring. On the Swan River the inexperienced boater or angler will have the safest, most satisfying experience in the company of a guide. Brush and logs make it difficult and sometimes dangerous to navigate or wade, and private land ownership closes off a lot of the shore access.

Anglers seeking a more serious fishing experience in Glacier Country are advised to hire a guide or consult the extensive array of books about Montana fishing that give detailed descriptions of the waters, fish, lures or bait, and techniques recommended for best results.

FLATHEAD RIVER

The Flathead River system is vast, and much of it, especially the Middle Fork and South Fork, lies deep in the wilderness—where the most interesting fishing occurs, according to veteran anglers. The North Fork, which is road-accessible along much of its way, supports bull trout, westslope cutthroat, and mountain whitefish populations. The

4-hour float from Big Creek to Glacier Rim is popular with locals. The main Flathead channel below Columbia Falls to Kalispell offers reasonably good populations of westslope cutthroat, mountain whitefish, and rainbow trout especially between Pressentine and the Old Steel Bridge.

Fishing Charters

Flathead Lake charter fishing doesn't usually start up until early May when the lake is full. During the winter months and on into Apr, water levels are typically so low that larger boats can't get to the water. The Flathead Lake charters use downriggers to place lures at the desired depth in order to attract mackinaw (lake trout), whose large size makes them the preferred species with most anglers. The outfitters do not generally sell licenses, so to avoid delays call ahead and arrange to buy your license elsewhere the day before.

A ABLE FISHING CHARTERS AND TOURS
P.O. Box 355, Lakeside
(406) 844-0888
www.aablefishing.com
A Able has been running charters for more than 20 years. They utilize both large and small covered boats with bathroom facilities for their fishing charters on Flathead Lake, and take all comers, including children, and have had guests in their 80s. No experience is necessary to catch fish. Charter costs include all equipment and a snack or meal depending on trip length. Half-day (5-hour) small-boat trips for 1 or 2 people are $350. The full day (9-hour) outing costs $700 for 1 or 2 people; a flat fee of $50 is charged for each additional person. The company does not mix groups—you make up your own group. They also offer nonfishing scenic cruises.

BAGLEY GUIDE SERVICE FISHING CHARTERS
Woods Bay Marina, Bigfork
(406) 837-3618
www.bagleyguideservice.com
Owner Dusty Bagley brings years of Flathead Lake fishing experience, top-of-the-line watercraft, and state-of-the-art equipment to his charter fishing cruises. He says trophy lake trout weighing 20 pounds are common, and that some 30-pounders are hauled in each year. The outfit offers half-day and full-day trips for up to 6 people; half-day rates range from $350 to $450 (depending on the number of people), while full-day trips cost from $700 to $900. Bagley's main boat is a 24-foot North River Seahawk Offshore. His charters operate out of Woods Bay Marina, located about 4 miles south of Bigfork.

GLACIER ANGLERS
US 2, West Glacier
(406) 888-5454, (800) 235-6781
www.glacierraftco.com
A branch of Glacier Raft Company, this full-service fly shop and outdoor store is located 0.5 mile west of West Glacier. The shop features fishing and outdoor gear, rentals, and gifts. Inquire about their half-day, full-day, and multiday guided fishing trips on the Middle Fork and North Fork of the Flathead. They also offer an hour-long casting clinic at a private pond. Glacier Raft Company also rents fully furnished deluxe log cabins overlooking the mountains of Glacier National Park. Visit the website for current trip rates.

LAKESTREAM FLY FISHING SHOP
334 Central Ave., Whitefish
(406) 862-1298
www.lakestream.com

Some of Lakestream's most popular trips are their drift-boat floats on the forks of the Flathead River. They also guide anglers down rivers located farther afield, including the Missouri, Blackfoot, and Clark Fork; they dabble in big-water fishing as well, on Whitefish and Rogers Lakes. Equipment, including waders, rods, and reels, is included in the trip price unless nonstandard gear is requested. Their experienced guides have the patience of Job; their main goal is to show you a good day on the water, whether or not you catch fish. You can view the full range of trips and trip prices at the company's website.

THE NORTHERN ROCKIES OUTFITTER
270 Bayou Rd., Kalispell
(406) 756-2544
www.northernrockiesoutfit.com
Owners Rich and Marcy Birdsell offer guests a variety of fishing opportunities based on years of experience guiding and instructing fly-fishing. Trips include Flathead River drift-boat floats for rainbow and native cutthroat trout, mountain-lake fishing, and hike-in mountain-stream fishing. Lake trips go mainly to the Badger-Two Medicine area on Glacier Park's east side for wade-walk or float-tube fishing. Half-day Flathead River float trips cost $325 for 1 or 2 people; full-day trips, $425. Call for current prices of other trips.

GOLF

Glacier Country golf courses don't have to toot their own horns, because plenty of others are doing it for them. *Golf Digest* has named the Flathead Valley among the top-50 best golf destinations in the world. The magazine described the Flathead as having "terrific courses, excellent weather, welcoming locals, unparalleled natural beauty, and prices that seem too good to be true."

You can find a course suited to your golfing goals, whether it's simply to enjoy a few relaxing hours amid unsurpassed scenery with friends or family, or to test your mettle on a challenging 18-hole layout in the company of scratch players. The mild weather on the west side often allows for an extended season, and it's not all that uncommon to see players out on the course in late Nov and again by Mar. All courses listed here are open to the public. As expected in a popular retirement area such as the Flathead, several clubs are affiliated with golf communities; in some instances, golf clubs and area hotels have teamed up to provide special deals for stay-and-play packages.

Yardages cited are for the men's white tees. All courses prohibit pets and metal spikes. **Flathead Valley Golf Association** provides a central reservation service for 10 courses; you can call them at (800) 392-9795 or check out their website at www.golf montana.net.

BIG MOUNTAIN GOLF CLUB
3320 US 93 North, Kalispell
(406) 751-1950, (800) 255-5641
www.golfmt.com

This 18-hole course combines the best of a traditional Montana-style park course and classic Scottish links, with its tree-lined fairways, undulating waves of native grasses, and natural water hazards. *Golf Digest* rated it the fourth best course in Montana for 2009–10. The lack of trees on the opening 9 reveals its conversion from a 250-acre potato field. The 6,180-yard, par-72 course is characterized by deep roughs and lots of fairway mounding against a backdrop of the

Whitefish and Swan Mountain ranges. The club also has a restaurant and PGA golf shop.

*BUFFALO HILL GOLF CLUB
1176 North Main St., P.O. Box 1116,
Kalispell 55903
(406) 756-4530, (888) 342-6319
www.golfbuffalohill.com

Buffalo Hill, the Flathead Valley's most popular golf course, ranks consistently on *Golf Digest*'s list of top courses and places to play. The 27-hole, target-oriented course keeps golfers returning to play in one of the most picturesque settings anywhere. Along with spectacular views of the Swan and Whitefish Mountains, and holes along the Stillwater River, golfers often see moose and other wildlife. The buffalo herd of the original owner is no longer there, but the name evokes its history. The original, standalone Cameron Nine is a 2,996-yard, regulation par-36 course. The 6,199-yard, par-72 Championship 18, designed by Robert Muir Graves in classic 1930s style, retains its multilevel greens and offers challenges you can increase from the back tees. Buffalo Hill's rustic log clubhouse encloses the pro shop and full-service lounge and restaurant.

EAGLE BEND GOLF CLUB
279 Eagle Bend Dr., P.O. Box 1257,
Bigfork 55911
(406) 837-7310, (800) 255-5641
www.golfmt.com

Golf Digest consistently rates this 27-hole resort course the No. 1 golf course in Montana and among the top 50 in the nation. Flowing in and around trophy homes and condominiums, the original 18 holes enclose the natural features of rocky cliffs and mammoth outcroppings; stands of Douglas firs and cattail marshes blend with landscaping in a graceful mix of human and natural elements. The 360-degree scenic feast includes views of Glacier's peaks and the Salish Mountains east of Flathead Lake. The 6,297-yard, par-72 course attracts high handicappers and scratch golfers alike, who seek their personal array of challenges. The "Nicklaus Nine" provides a stand-alone course running along the lake and ponds. A pro shop and the Grill at Eagle Bend share the large clubhouse near the entrance.

GLACIER PARK LODGE GOLF COURSE
East Glacier Park
(406) 892-2525
www.glacierparkinc.com
History and scenery combine to make playing this 9-hole golf course a unique experience. It was built by the Great Northern Railway's James J. Hill in 1927, making it the oldest grass-greens course in the state of Montana. The par-36 course lies within the boundaries of the Blackfeet Indian Reservation, and each of the 9 holes is named after a past chief of the Blackfeet Nation. The course runs 3,300 yards, and has soe unexpected tight and blind shots. Sitting east of the Continental Divide, Glacier Park Lodge experiences the vagaries of eastern-slope weather, including stiff winds, but displays magnificent views from its fairways lined with lodgepole pine and quaking aspen. There's also a par-27 pitch-and-putt course. The season runs from mid-May through Sept, weather permitting.

GLACIER VIEW GOLF CLUB
River Bend Drive, West Glacier
(406) 888-5471
www.glacierviewgolf.com
Situated just across the river from Glacier National Park, Glacier View Golf Course has earned its reputation as a friendly, family-oriented course. The 4,875-yard, par-69 course is characterized by open fairways and small greens. To create more challenges, they have gone to a 3-tee system and roughed things up with water and sand. It's a pretty little golf course with extremely reasonable greens fees—perfect for the traveling golfer who'd like to play the links in the morning and then search for lynx and other wildlife in Glacier Park in the afternoon.

MEADOW LAKE GOLF RESORT
490 St. Andrews Dr., Columbia Falls
(406) 892-2111
www.meadowlakegolf.com
Although mainly known for the premier natural setting and scenic beauty of its location just minutes from Glacier National Park, Meadow Lake is no pushover, according to those who've play there. Narrow, tree-lined fairways and plentiful water hazards combine to create challenges that helped the par-72 course get rated by *Golf Digest* as one of the top-6 places to play in Montana, and earn a "must play" course rating from *Golf Magazine*. The 18-hole course has a par of 72 and measures 6,416 yards.

✳POLSON BAY GOLF COURSE
111 Bayview Dr., Polson
(406) 883-8230
www.polsonbaygolf.com
This vintage golf course situated on Flathead Lake's southern shore features spectacular views of the lake and the Swan and Mission Mountain ranges. The original 9, known as the Olde Course, opened in 1936. The holes on this stand-alone course tend to be short with tight, conifer-lined fairways and small greens. The newer 18-hole, 6,271-yard Championship Course plays longer and in a

more open setting. The Bay Club Bar & Grill is a great place for a sandwich mid-round if you're playing the Championship Course, or after you've bagged your 9 holes on the Olde Course.

VILLAGE GREENS GOLF CLUB
500 Palmer Dr., Kalispell
(406) 752-4666
www.montanagolf.com
Affordability and superb groundskeeping attract many golfers to this course in suburban Kalispell known for its fine bentgrass greens. Both nines on the 5,907-yard, par-70 course have an abundance of water, plenty of fairway mounding, and big white-sand bunkers. Spike's 19th Hole serves up a full menu of sandwiches and beverages, both adult and otherwise.

WHITEFISH LAKE GOLF CLUB
US 93 North, Whitefish
(406) 862-4000
www.golfwhitefish.com
Montana's first 36-hole golf complex provides awesome views of Whitefish Lake and the Whitefish Range, including Big Mountain. Both of the tight, tree-lined 18-hole courses tend to reward accuracy over distance.

Whitefish Lake's establishment was a product of politicking during the 1930s for the New Deal's Works Progress Administration. WPA agreed to fund a landing strip, and the citizens of Whitefish, who wanted a golf course, were willing to put up matching money. Pilots and golfers ended up sharing some of the expanses of green that served as both fairways and emergency landing strips, and the occasional conflicts that flared between the two are immortalized in the Stumptown Historical Society records. The log clubhouse lends a 1930s vintage atmosphere to the first-class dinner restaurant. The North 18, par-72 course measures 6,138 yards. The 6,141-yard South 18, completed in the 1990s, plays at par 71.

FLATHEAD LAKE STATE PARK

The six units of this state park offer great venues for outdoor recreation, from fishing and wading to hiking and biking. All have boat launch ramps. More information on these and other state parks may be found at www.fwp.mt.gov/parks, or you can call (406) 752-5501.

✳Big Arm

Situated on the western shore, this 217-acre park supports beefy, mature ponderosa pines, and is a popular launching point for Wild Horse Island. There are 36 campsites, rental yurts, a nature trail, a hiking and horseback trail, and a mountain bike trail. It sits on the Flathead Indian Reservation, so to fish at the park you'll need both a Montana fishing license and a Confederated Salish Kootenai tribal fishing license.

Finley Point

Located at the south end of the lake, this 28-acre park features a marina for boats up to 25 feet long and 16 RV campsites. This park, too, is located on the Flathead Indian Reservation.

Wayfarers

On the eastern shore, this 67-acre park south of Bigfork is a favorite place for swimming and camping. There are 30 campsites located here, with 7 tent-only sites.

West Shore

Also on the western shore, the park's rock outcrops provide spectacular views of the lake and surrounding mountains. With 26 campsites, 129-acre West Shore is popular with boaters and anglers; the beach is rocky, but you can still swim here. Praised as the most private park on Flathead Lake, it is graced with a mature forest of fir, pine, and larch.

Wild Horse Island

Wild Horse Island's 2,164 acres offer great hiking and wildlife viewing. You can get there only by boat, but the solitude and chance to see bighorn sheep, mule deer, bald eagles, and wild horses make it worth the effort. No camping is permitted at this day-use only park. Be aware that there's a lot of private property along shoreline perimeter.

Yellow Bay

Located on the eastern shore amid the cherry orchards, Yellow Bay, at just 15 acres in size, offers a wide, sandy beach for swimming, along with boating, fishing, and bird watching. It has about a half dozen campsites, including 4 walk-in tent sites.

RESOURCE AGENCIES & ORGANIZATIONS

Government Agencies

BLACKFEET NATION
1 Agency Sq., Browning 59417
(406) 338-7521
www.blackfeetnation.com

CONFEDERATED SALISH & KOOTENAI TRIBES
42487 Complex Blvd., Pablo 59855
(406) 675-2700
www.cskt.org

FISHING OUTFITTERS ASSOCIATION OF MONTANA
P.O. Box 67, Gallatin Gateway 59730
(406) 763-5436
www.foam-montana.org

FLATHEAD NATIONAL FOREST SUPERVISOR'S OFFICE
650 Wolfpack Way, Kalispell 59901
(406) 758-5204
www.fs.fed.us/r1/flathead

GLACIER NATIONAL PARK
P.O. Box 128, West Glacier 59936
(406) 888-7800 (general information)
www.nps.gov/glac/index.htm

HELENA HEADQUARTERS
1420 East Sixth Ave.
P.O. Box 200701, Helena 59620
(406) 444-2535
www.fwp.mt.gov

MONTANA BOARD OF OUTFITTERS
111 North Jackson, Helena 59620
(406) 444-3738

MONTANA DEPARTMENT OF NATURAL RESOURCES AND CONSERVATION
Kalispell Unit
655 Timberwolf Pkwy., Suite 1, Kalispell 55901
(406) 751-2240
www.dnrc.mt.gov

MONTANA FISH, WILDLIFE AND PARKS
Region I
490 North Meridian Rd., Kalispell 59901
(406) 752-5501
http://fwp.mt.gov

MONTANA OUTFITTERS AND GUIDES ASSOCIATION
5 Microwave Hill Rd., Suite 1, Montana City 59634
(406) 449-3578
www.montanaoutfitters.org

Other Resources

THE GLACIER INSTITUTE
137 Main St., P.O. Box 1887, Kalispell 59903
(406) 755-1211
www.glacierinstitute.org
Since 1983 this environmental education institution has been providing hands-on, field-based exploration opportunities to people from throughout the world. The institute offers year-round courses on the plants, animals, and ecology of Glacier National Park and surrounding locale. For short-term visitors to the area, a daylong or weekend workshop is a fine way to get off the beaten track and learn from experts about this fascinating ecosystem. You can choose from such topics as Glacier's harlequins, owls of Glacier, Glacier's grizzlies, or prairie wildflowers. They also offer summer youth field science camps and seminars for kids ages 7 through 13.

KALISPELL

With the population sitting at just under 20,000, Kalispell retains a small-town feel yet is big enough to rank as Montana's seventh-largest city and the biggest community in the four counties of northwest Montana. It's a splendid mix of the best of urban and rural. During your time here, you'll find yourself enjoying such traditional city delights as shopping, restaurants, and museums, as well as those qualities more associated with Montana's rural roots—fairs, rodeos, horseback riding, and fishing, along with a general air of peace and tranquility.

OVERVIEW

Kalispell is the county seat and business center of Flathead County. It is located at the intersection of US 93 and US 2, just 45 minutes from Glacier National Park and 10 minutes from Flathead Lake. Though it may lack the distinct identity of smaller communities like Bigfork and Whitefish, Kalispell prides itself on being a town that provides a quality of life that simply can't be beat. The town was once named by *Mountain Sports and Living* magazine as the Best Mountain Town in America, taking into account its proximity to the Whitefish Mountain Resort and Blacktail Mountain ski areas and to Glacier National Park, as well as its superb health-care facilities, quality schools, and unsurpassed outdoor recreational opportunities.

Kalispell is also rich in history, a frontier town founded in 1891 by Charles E. Conrad. This Missouri River trader combined a colorful, rugged spirit with the good old-fashioned horse sense that made him a rich man. Conrad's huge wooden home, built in 1895 and occupied by members of the Conrad family until 1975, has been restored to its Victorian elegance and is open to the public

as the Conrad Mansion (see the Attractions chapter). One of the city's most popular tourist stops, it provides a lesson in just how much more "civilized" the frontier could be than Hollywood's westerns would lead us to believe. The mansion is one of the main stops on a self-guided walking tour of historic buildings that begins at the Hockaday Museum of Art in downtown Kalispell.

Another exciting piece of the historic legacy of Kalispell is the Museum at Central School, which opened in 1999. This impressive stone structure was built in the 1890s as a school, and it later served as office space and classroom space for Flathead Valley Community College before being closed for about 10 years and barely escaping the demolishing crew. The efforts of the Northwest Montana Historical Society led to the preservation of the building, which has been extensively renovated and now hosts exhibits, lectures, and community events.

Downtown Kalispell has suffered some of the same vicissitudes that other Main Streets throughout America have seen over the past few decades. The business community has expanded beyond the city limits in recent years, first toward Evergreen, east of Kalispell on US 2. This is the home of such popular mega-stores as Wal-Mart, as well as car lots, fast-food restaurants, and other businesses. More recently, "Little Missoula" has popped up near the intersection of Reserve and US 93 north of town—so-called because the area now has many of the big-box stores Flathead residents used to drive to Missoula to visit. Nevertheless, downtown Kalispell is thriving. Unlike many other cities, Kalispell arranged a deal in the mid-1980s that led to the building of a mall not outside of town on a highway strip, but right on Main Street, just a block or two from the city's oldest historic businesses. That anchor has proved key to securing a future for the downtown. Today several new buildings have gone up, housing restaurants, clothing stores, and gift shops, and Kalispell's city center is more vibrant than it has been in many years.

To the south of Kalispell, two communities on Flathead Lake have distinct identities of their own, but they're enough to Kalispell that they are included here. Somers is the smaller of the two, with its public boat ramp and private marina helping to set the tone. This was a railroad town in earlier years, and many of the houses were built for railroad employees. A few of these have been converted to public use, such as Tiebuckers Pub & Eatery, which offers a mix of home cooking and gourmet meals in a rustic, rambling house. A few miles farther south on US 93 is Lakeside, which over the past few years has developed into one of the most popular destinations on Flathead Lake. Several resorts and motels offer boating and fishing opportunities during the summer, and the Blacktail

Mountain ski area gives the community a year-round appeal.

All in all, Kalispell and its surrounding communities can provide days of entertainment, education, and shopping for tourists. Still, many visitors find that even a long vacation offers insufficient time to enjoy everything Kalispell has to see and do. Those are the people who move here a few years after their vacations, helping make Kalispell and Flathead County one of the most thriving and cosmopolitan areas in Montana.

ACCOMMODATIONS

Hotels & Motels

Price Code

Keep in mind that some rates are based on availability. The average nightly peak-season rates for two adults at the hotels and motels listed in this section are indicated by a dollar sign ($) ranking detailed in the following chart. Many places offer lower off-season rates. The hotels and motels in this chapter accept all or most major credit cards.

$..................... **Less than $85**
$$ .... **$85 to $115**
$$$ .... **$115 to $150**
$$$$ .... **More than $150**

AERO INN $$$
1830 US 93 South
(406) 755-3798, (800) 843-6114
www.aeroinn.com
If you pilot your own small plane, there's really only one place to land for the night—the Aero Inn, located just off the municipal airport in Kalispell. And make no mistake, this airport really is IN Kalispell: It's located less than a half-mile south of the Flathead County Courthouse. The motel has 61 spacious guest rooms, along with an indoor

pool, hot tub, sauna, game room, continental breakfast, wheelchair-accessible facilities, high-speed Internet, and winter plug-ins for your car (and tie-downs for your plane!). There is also 24-hour front-desk service at this customer-friendly hotel.

BLUE AND WHITE MOTEL   **$$**
640 East Idaho St.
(406) 755-4311, (800) 382-3577
www.blu-white.com

This is one nonchain hotel that can still compete with the more familiar names. The Blue and White gets lots of repeat business from businesspeople and others who travel to Kalispell frequently. That's because of the friendly service and the excellent accommodations. There are 106 rooms with double- and queen-size beds, and wheelchair-accessible facilities are available upon request. There is a free continental breakfast and a small indoor swimming pool, sauna, and Jacuzzi. Pets are welcome, and winter plug-ins are available for engine-block heaters to help make certain your car starts on those cold Montana mornings. The large parking lots can handle RVs, trucks, trailers, and buses. The Blue and White is located next to Finnegan's, one of the few 24-hour restaurants in Kalispell.

HAMPTON INN   **$$$$**
1140 US 2 West
(406) 755-7900
http://hamptoninn.hilton.com

The Hampton Inn, a major hotel that targets business clientele in particular, has many conveniences that also make it perfect for families. All guest rooms feature an iron and ironing board, a small refrigerator, TV/VCR, video-game player, coffeemaker and coffee, hair dryer, HBO, high-speed Internet, and free local calls. The hotel also has a 24-hour indoor swimming pool and Jacuzzi, as well as a gift shop, coin-op laundry, business center, and exercise facility. Although there is no restaurant per se, a complimentary breakfast buffet featuring eggs, waffles, sausage, fresh fruit, and more is served every morning. Children younger than age 18 stay free, and the Hampton provides a free 24-hour airport shuttle service.

i Got a late start? Need to jump-start your drive? It seems like about every other corner in the towns of the Flathead Valley has a drive-up espresso shop: Java Joe's, Mountain Mocha, Juice 'n' Java, Java Junction, Big Mountain Buzz . . . they're all there, and more! Just keep your eye out.

✳**KALISPELL GRAND
   HOTEL**   **$$$–$$$$**
100 Main St.
(406) 755-8100, (800) 858-7422
www.kalispellgrand.com

The Kalispell Grand Hotel is a beautifully remodeled historic hotel located conveniently right in downtown Kalispell—and which goes out of its way to welcome not only you but your 4-legged friends as well. Noted writer Frank Bird Linderman leased and managed the hotel from 1924 to 1926, and he and his good friend Charlie Russell, "America's Cowboy Artist," would on occasion sit in the hotel's lobby and exchange thoughts and tall tales of the West. Today, a complimentary breakfast is served every morning in the Grand Lobby, which still has the look of a luxurious frontier hotel lobby with its high, pressed-tin ceilings and golden oak staircase. All rooms have high-speed Internet, and the Linderman suites feature oversized jetted tubs. The 3-story brick hotel also connects to the **KB Sports Bar & Grill,** originally known as the Kalispell Bar, where live music is heard often on summer weekends. In season you can take a carriage ride through the downtown area, or simply stroll through an area rich in shops, restaurants, and history.

OUTLAW INN $$$
1701 US 93 South
(406) 755-6100
www.outlawhotel.com

The locally owned Outlaw Inn (also known as the Outlaw Hotel) is the granddaddy of convention centers in the Flathead Valley. It is the biggest—with 220 guest rooms and suites—and the most comprehensive, with three options for dining and extensive convention facilities. A healthy, hot breakfast buffet is included. Fitness-center facilities are available to guests, along with an indoor pool and 3 Jacuzzis. The restaurant and lounge, the **Outlaw Steak House,** includes a large casino area.

RED LION HOTEL KALISPELL $$$$
20 North Main St.
(406) 751-5050
www.redlion.com

This large hotel offers a perfect compromise for tourist couples who can't decide between shopping and sightseeing. After a full day at Glacier Park or on Flathead Lake, you can return to one of the 170 rooms or suites and freshen up for dinner, after which you can walk into the adjacent Kalispell Center Mall for an evening of bargain hunting at the 50 or so stores. Back at the hotel you can swim in the indoor solarium pool or relax in the sauna or whirlpools. The Magic Diamond Casino offers fun and drink. When you arise

the next morning, the Roaring Start Breakfast Buffet will do as the name promises; there's also food available 24 hours a day at **Cafe2Go.** The Red Lion hosts the Glacier Jazz Stampede each fall and is a popular convention center, too, with more than 10,000 square feet of meeting and banquet space.

SOMERS BAY LOG CABIN LODGING $$$$
5496 US 93 South, Somers
(406) 857-3881, (888) 443-3881
www.somersbaycabins.com

Despite the look of old-timey cabins, Somers Bay Log Cabin Lodging is one of the newer accommodations in the Flathead Lake area. Built in the spring of 1998, Somers Bay Log Cabin Lodging features both studio units and bedroom/loft cabins. Each features a queen-size log bed and a queen-size sofa sleeper and comes equipped with a kitchenette that has microwave, stove top, refrigerator, coffeemaker, and dishes. There is extra parking for boats and trailers, so you can use the cabin as the base for your lake fun. Flathead Lake State Park boat access is within walking distance.

SUPER 8 $$$
1341 First Ave. East
(406) 755-1888, (800) 800-8000
www.super8.com

The Kalispell Super 8 motel is a safe bet for travelers who are looking for pleasant accommodations on a budget. Don't hesitate to ask for those little extras such as first-aid supplies, irons and ironing boards, hair dryers, and other essential toiletries you may have forgotten. The accent here is not on frills, but on friendly service, which makes it a popular choice for business travelers. There is also daily laundry and dry cleaning pickup and delivery. Pets are allowed, the motel has high-speed Internet, and the room price includes a continental breakfast.

WHITE BIRCH MOTEL & RV PARK $$
17 Shady Lane
(406) 752-4008, (888) 275-2275
www.whitebirchmotelandrv.com
White Birch is an offbeat little motel in a parklike setting on a creek. This location, set back from Highway 35 just 0.75 mile from US 2, is a bit out of the way, yet it's just minutes from all amenities. All rooms have a coffeepot, complimentary coffee and refrigerator, plus three come with kitchens. A coin-operated laundry is also available on-site. The motel is open year-round, and the RV park, which opened in 1996, operates from May through Oct. It offers tent sites and electricity-only sites, as well as full hookups. The RV facility features modern restrooms and showers with wheelchair access.

Campgrounds & RV Parks

Price Code
$	Less than $10
$$	$10 to $16
$$$	$16 to $24
$$$$	More than $24

GLACIER PINES RV PARK $$$
1850 Montana Hwy. 35 East
(406) 752-2760, (800) 533-4029
www.glacierpines.com
Glacier Pines RV Park, occupying a wooded location about 5 minutes from Kalispell, offers 30 tent sites and 140 RV sites with full hookups. There is no maximum size limit or time limit. Available on-site are a store, laundry, showers, a heated swimming pool, horseshoes, and other recreational facilities, including a play area.

ROCKY MOUNTAIN "HI" RV PARK & CAMPGROUND $$$-$$$$
825 Helena Flats Rd.
(406) 755-9573, (800) 968-5637
www.glaciercamping.com
Rocky Mountain "Hi" is the only privately owned RV park in the Kalispell area that is not on a highway. Signs point the way from either Highway 35 or US 2 toward this quiet park that features mature shade trees and cable television hookups. All sizes of RVs can be accommodated in the 5 dozen spots, and there are also 18 tent sites. The kids will enjoy the large Western-style play town and playing field. In addition, there's an on-site store, along with camp showers, a recreation room, and rental cabins.

SPRUCE PARK ON THE RIVER $$$-$$$$
1985 Hwy. 35
(406) 752-6321, (888) 752-6321
www.spruceparkrv.com
You'll find 30 tent sites and 120 RV sites at Spruce Park, which is located near the Flathead River and features fishing, 30- or 50-amp service, volleyball and basketball courts, and a playground for the kids. The park is located 3 miles east of Kalispell and open from Mar through Nov. Pets are welcome.

Bed-and-Breakfasts

Price Code
$	Less than $85
$$	$85 to $115
$$$	$115 to $150
$$$$	More than $150

Bed-and-breakfast inns can be found on the highways and back streets throughout Montana. One way to track them down is by consulting the **Montana Bed and Breakfast**

Association website (www.mtbba.com) for current listings. Many B&Bs have come and gone in the Flathead Valley, but the ones listed throughout this guide are now well established. While most are traditional B&Bs—homes converted to offer lodging—many have unique twists, and all have interesting histories. Be sure to check them out!

FULL CIRCLE FARM   **$$**
1230 Truman Creek Rd., Kila
(406) 257-8133

Situated 12 miles from Kalispell, the full name of this place occupying a former commercial herb farm is A Slice of Heaven in the Mountains at Full Circle Farm. The guest house is the lovingly renovated Kila Church, which retains its original charm but has been transformed into a modern cottage in a quiet wooded setting. Amenities include queen-size bed (and pull-out couch), dining and living area, full kitchen, full bath, microwave, and gas barbecue. (Note that this is not a true bed-and-breakfast, since meals are not served.) Pets are welcome, and accommodations are also available for horses, with a corral that includes a feed bunk and water. The guest house is open from May 1 through Oct 31.

OUTLOOK INN BED
**   AND BREAKFAST**   **$$$**
175 Boon Rd., Somers
(406) 857-2060, (888) 857-8439
www.outlookinnbandb.com

The Outlook Inn is located on a promontory across US 93 from Flathead Lake in Somers. This spacious yet cozy lodgelike home sits on 7 private acres and offers 4 guest rooms, with all of the amenities you expect from a fine establishment. Curl up in front of the river-rock fireplace with a good book, or relax in your room with the private jetted tub or

double shower. The house features a huge log deck overlooking the lake and Rocky Mountains as well as a variety of locally produced art. You can walk to fine dining in minutes, or step out the door and go for a stroll in the wooded hills. In the winter you can cross-country ski from the inn (be sure to inquire about winter rates).

RESTAURANTS

Price Code

The following listings rate restaurants according to a 4-symbol price key, representing the average cost of dinner for two people. The code excludes the price of beverages, tax, and gratuity.

$....................... $10 to $20
$$ .... $20 to $28
$$$ .... $28 to $35
$$$$ .... More than $35

Family Friendly Dining

ALLEY CONNECTION   **$**
22 First St. West
(406) 752-7077

The Alley Connection is something of a local tradition in Flathead County. Today it's joined by several other Oriental-style restaurants, but the Alley is still the best. Specialties include Szechuan pork and chicken, egg foo young, as well as a hearty wonton soup that includes a generous helping of pork and greens along with both fried and noodle wontons. And even if you don't usually like sweet and sour, you may want to try it here (a favorite is the wontons!), because it has a distinct flavor that is a particular treat. Individual combination dinners are also available, such as the one featuring soup of the day, egg roll, sweet and sour wontons, chicken chow mein, and combination fried

Close-up

Lewis & Clark

Lewis and Clark's **Corps of Discovery** barely set foot in a corner of the area covered by this book . . . but their brief visit had lasting effects. On their journey west, as most everyone knows, Lewis and Clark followed the Missouri River. In west-central Montana, they came to the junction of two major rivers, and it wasn't clear to them which was the main channel. Part of the group scouted up the northern channel, and the men under Lewis's and Clark's command became convinced that this was the way to proceed. But both leaders felt the other channel was the primary river—it ran clearer than the other, as the captains surmised a river coming from the mountains should. They were right. The other waterway proved to be what we now call the **Marias River**—named by Lewis after his cousin, Maria Wood—which drains the southeastern corner of Glacier National Park. Had the explorers discovered Marias Pass, where US 2 crosses the Continental Divide today, they might have significantly shortened their westward journey. But to follow the Missouri was their plan; and, anyway, the Blackfeet guarded Marias Pass against all comers even then.

When they were homebound for St. Louis, Lewis and Clark split their expedition into two groups in order to explore more territory. Lewis's group returned to travel up the Marias River in late July 1806, hoping that it would go north, thus extending the United States' claim to the territories rich in beaver, among other resources. But the river turned west. **Camp Disappointment**, now within the boundaries of the Blackfeet Indian Reservation, was the northernmost point the party reached. In the following days, Lewis's group would camp with a Blackfeet hunting party. When the Blackfeet attempted to take the rifles from two of Lewis's sleeping men, a fight erupted and one, or possibly two, Blackfeet was killed. Lewis's men rode back to the Marias as fast as they could to warn the remaining party members still there of a possible Blackfeet reprisal.

While Lewis and Clark's journey touched only a corner of Glacier Country, their time at the Great Falls of the Missouri has captured many people's imagination. The **Lewis and Clark National Historic Trail Interpretive Center in Great Falls** (see the last website below), run by the USDA Forest Service, is an outstanding visitor center that focuses on not only the explorers and their mission but also on the many Native groups they encountered. The significances of Lewis and Clark's mission are many; it's highly recommended that you take the time to stop and discover a few of them. Great Falls and Cut Bank, as well as Missoula and other towns in southwest Montana, are all educational stops on the **Lewis and Clark National Historic Trail.** If you're searching for the Lewis and Clark "information highway," look no further than www.fs.fed.us/r1/lewisclark/lcic.htm.

rice. Lunches are a real deal, and you can also get American menu selections for kids.

✳BOJANGLES DINER $
1319 US 2 West
(406) 755-3222

This is one of those family dining establishments that locals eat at, but tourists tend to pass up for more familiar places like McDonalds or Wendy's. Don't make that mistake. Not only is the menu full of good food, it's also full of references to the 1950s. In fact the whole restaurant is a throwback to simpler times. A cutout of Marilyn Monroe greets you at the front door, and the walls are filled with 1950s-era memorabilia such as license plates, movie tie-ins, and—of course—Elvis. Hamburgers are named after pop singers such as Jerry Lee Lewis (lots of jalapeños), Neil Sedaka, Gene Vincent, and Buddy Holly (no frills, just the plain burger). Open 7 days a week for breakfast and lunch (breakfast is served all day), and an added attraction for the kids is a model train that runs along a rail that is set up on beams atop the walls.

CHARLIE WONG INTERNATIONAL CUISINE $
2316 US 2 East
(406) 257-1377

Charlie Wong's is located in Evergreen, the suburb east of Kalispell's city limits where much of the business development has taken place over the past few years. If you get through shopping at Wal-Mart, it's a short drive to this restaurant, where you can get both Asian specialties and a handful of American entrees. Always popular is the kung pao chicken, but you can't go wrong with this menu. Hot entrees can be ordered mild or medium, too, so don't be shy about trying something new.

CISLO'S $
2046 US 2 East
(406) 756-7330

Cislo's is the closest thing to Mel's Diner from the old TV show *Alice* that you will find in Kalispell. It features a crew of tough but lovable waitresses, and a menu right out of the 1950s. Look for the open-face hot turkey and hot beef sandwiches, the chili burger, and the club sandwich, but don't be afraid to try just about anything on the menu. This is

home cooking that won't disappoint. And be sure to save room for dessert, which usually features 5 or 6 fresh-baked pies. One interesting side note: Cislo's used to be located where the Staples office-supply superstore is now situated, a bit closer to Kalispell; but when Cislo's lost their lease, they didn't lose their restaurant. They just loaded it up on top of a truck and hauled it down the highway to its current spot. Now that's one tough little restaurant (but the turkey and beef are tender).

FRONTIER ROADHOUSE RESORT & GOLF CLUB $$
100 Hwy. 206
(406) 755-0111
www.frontierroadhouse.com

Even though the Frontier is on a golf course and features a large bar in the dining room, it still ranks high as a family-friendly eatery. The menu features many low-priced entrees—so although there's no separate children's menu, there are plenty of choices kids will enjoy (spaghetti, hamburgers, and chili). The main menu features barbecue, along with items like Southern fried catfish and Cajun pasta. There's also a great selection of appetizers, like fried green tomatoes and crispy fried oysters. The Frontier features one of the best views of any nonlakeside restaurant in the Flathead Valley; you dine practically underneath the Swan Range at the east end of the valley. And, for the family that golfs together, the Frontier features a very reasonably priced 9-hole executive (par 30) course.

J. D. MORRELL'S BISTRO $$
227 South Main St.
(406) 257-9195

The food at J. D. Morrell's is so good for you—with all those fresh veggies and homemade

Close-up

Before & After Lewis & Clark . . .

Well before the 1805 arrival of Lewis and Clark in Montana, the influence of Europeans was changing the mountains and plains of the West. Lewis and Clark took earlier maps of the area with them, including one based on **David Thompson**'s explorations. Thompson worked for the Hudson's Bay Company and did a tremendous amount of exploring in the Canadian West, but he also followed the Columbia River and traveled through the Flathead Valley. *Sources of the River: Tracking David Thompson across Western North America,* by Jack Nisbet, is a wonderful account of this man's astonishing adventures. Thompson survived a broken leg, crossed northerly Howse Pass in the winter on snowshoes, traded with the Native tribes along the way, canoed from Quebec west through Lake Superior—and generally led an unpredictable but exciting life.

Another author worth checking out is **John C. Jackson**. His *Children of the Fur Trade: Forgotten Metis of the Pacific Northwest* also chronicles the early years of European contact in the West. Many white men took Native wives, and their offspring were the metis, a group that simultaneously connected the two worlds and failed to fit into either. Jackson's more recent *Piikani Blackfeet: A Culture under Siege* tells the history of the Blackfeet tribe from earliest oral accounts to the present day.

After Lewis and Clark came through, life in the West began to change radically for the Native people. Accounts of Blackfeet mythologies can be found in **George Bird Grinnell**'s *Blackfoot Lodge Tales;* Grinnell was a white man who negotiated on behalf of the Blackfeet when they ceded what is now the east side of Glacier National Park to the US government in 1895. He is also known as the father of Glacier National Park, but he was enough of a friend of the Blackfeet that they gave him a Blackfeet name, "Fishercap," because he wore a hat made from the skin of a fisher.

Walter McClintock was another white man who lived for a time with the Blackfeet. His book, *The Old North Trail, or Life, Legends and Religion of the Blackfeet Indians,* is generally considered an accurate account of his experiences with them. The Old North Trail was the route the Blackfeet and other tribes used to pass north and south along the eastern front of the Rocky Mountains. Traces of it can still be found today in the foothills of the Blackfeet Reservation.

---

bread and all—that's it's hard to believe how indulgent even a little lunch here can make you feel. The sandwiches are luscious; the soups, amazing: mojo sausage and potato, carrot ginger, mushroom sherry with wild rice, and Jamaican veggie, for starters. And they have Coke in glass bottles. What more can you ask for?

LOS CAPORALES $$
1600 US 93 South
(406) 752-6800

Los Caporales features authentic Mexican food from south of the border—*way* south, from the region around Guadalajara, west of Mexico City, where the owners came from. So, you'll find the menu items to be a bit different from those typically served at Mexican restaurants, but the difference (which includes a lot of grilled foods) is worth savoring. Try the carnitas de res from the beef menu for a tasty Mexican stir-fry of sirloin strips, peppers, tomatoes, and mushrooms in a spicy seasoning mix. Or, if chicken is your fancy, order the arroz con pollo, which features chunks of chicken breast with onions, tomatoes, and mushrooms, this time in a tasty red sauce and melted cheese, all served over a bed of rice. The less adventurous can choose from more standard Mexican fare, such as combination dinners of enchiladas, tacos, tostadas, chiles rellenos, chimichangas, and burritos. Kids can opt for a grilled cheese and fries, children's-size portions of Mexican food, or a hamburger.

MACKENZIE RIVER PIZZA CO. $$
2230 US 93 South
(406) 756-0060
www.mackenzieriverpizza.com
MacKenzie River is a Montana-based company, with around 10 locations in the state. They know how to do pizza right. You can get just about anything you want on top, from artichokes to garlic plus all the traditional favorites like pepperoni and sausage. They also dish up top-notch sandwiches and salads. Meals are served at rustic-style tables, or you can grab your pizza pie and run with it.

SIZZLER RESTAURANT $
1250 US 2 West
(406) 257-9555
This franchise eatery is a favorite for families in the Kalispell area. The local owners go the extra mile for their customers, and they have been great innovators throughout the years. Sizzler is a steak house, of course, but you can get much more than the trademark

sirloin steak here. The restaurant has one of the best all-you-can-eat salad bars in town, with everything from fresh fruit to tacos to pasta and soups, and the separate dessert bar is an especially sweet find. Kids have their own all-you-can-eat food bar featuring macaroni and cheese, pasta, chicken nuggets, and fruit. The place is usually packed, but they never have to turn anyone away, thanks to rapid service.

SOMERS BAY CAFE $
47 Somers Rd., Somers
(406) 857-2660
This little cafe housed in the old Somers State Bank building is open the year around for breakfast, lunch, and dinner. The interior is cozy, and the walls are decorated with historic photos and artifacts from the early logging and railroading days. On a sunny summer day, though, you'll want to have lunch on the deck. The burgers are hearty and the chicken breast sandwich filling; really, though, it would be hard to go wrong with just about anything on this straightforward and satisfactory menu.

Fine Dining

CAPERS $$$
121 Main St.
(406) 755-7687
www.capersmontana.com
Chef-owned Capers is an undisputed leader in the realm of Kalispell fine dining. Chef Doug Day is a master of presentation and gastronomy, and everything in his restaurant shows the extra effort of a great dining establishment. Organic ingredients, Pacific Northwest seafood, Angus beef, and Montana buffalo anchor the menu.

Openers might include steamed Whidbey Island clams or lemon zest ravioli.

Entrees on the menu change every couple of weeks, but they might include anything from grilled prime tenderloin of pork to seared Alaskan weathervane scallops. Brick oven pizza are another house specialty. After dinner your wait person will tempt you with desserts of a staggering array. Capers serves dinner Tues through Sat only, starting at 5 p.m. Reservations are not required, but highly recommended on the weekends.

> **i** Don't expect Las Vegas–style gambling at Montana's casinos. Most establishments have keno, slots, and poker machines only.

THE KNEAD CAFE $$
25 Second Ave. West
(406) 755-7510
www.theknead.com

Open for breakfast and lunch 7 days a week, The Knead Cafe bills itself as a "spirited fusion of food, art, and music." The menu is an eclectic combination of health food, such as tabouli and eggplant, and American deli traditions, such as the reuben sandwich. The restaurant features a bright modern decor, along with a small deck for outdoor seating when in season. This place is a find well worth finding.

MONTANA GRILL ON FLATHEAD LAKE $$$$
5480 US 93 South, Somers
(406) 857-3889

This restaurant features fine dining in fine surroundings, both indoors and out. The restaurant and bar are housed in a timber-built structure that makes "log home" seem like a synonym for palace. And the views looking out across Somers Bay can't be beat. The menu, meanwhile, is varied and

delightful. A range of past appetizers has included the likes of baked artichoke and baked penne with shrimp. Seafood and freshwater fish entrees are extensive, including fillet of salmon and rainbow trout. Other regional dining choices might include grilled elk steak and baby back ribs. Lighter entrees are also on the menu; items like fettuccine and grilled eggplant, while featured desserts such as flaming bananas foster or cherries jubilee might magically appear on your table before the evening ends.

✳NORTH BAY GRILLE $$$
139 First Ave. West
(406) 755-4441
www.nbgrille.com

The North Bay Grille combines elegant food with a casual atmosphere, for an extraordinarily comfortable dining experience. The dark wood paneling will relax you as you peruse the menu. Open for lunch and dinner, both menus focus on small plates: for lunch, selections like Maryland-style crab cakes and sesame-smeared ahi tuna; and, for dinner, such choices as goat cheese tempura and barbecued pork quesadillas. North Bay Grille is open Mon through Fri for lunch and 7 days a week for dinner.

> **i** Kalispell takes its name from a Salish Indian group that inhabited the area, the Kalispels.

OUTLAW STEAKHOUSE $$$
1701 US 93 South
(406) 755-61008160

This restaurant, a Kalispell mainstay for nearly 4 decades, is located in the Outlaw Inn. The interior is quiet and darkly lit, making it a pleasant place for an intimate dinner. Prime rib, lobster tail, and Cajun shrimp set the tone for a satisfying and memorable meal. Also on site is the Bulldog Pub, where beer and burgers are the primary gustatory attractions.

ROSARIO'S IN LAKESIDE $$$
7125 US 93 South, Lakeside
(406) 844-2888

Lakeside has many pleasures for the vacationing family, not the least of which is Rosario's restaurant, located on the second floor of an old marina building. Through the lakeside windows, you look out over weathered docks and pilings at Flathead Lake and the Swan and Mission Mountains in the background. Turning back to the restaurant, you can watch the chef hard at work in the kitchen, keeping customers satisfied with many specials and standard delights such as veal francaise, sautéed scallops of veal smothered in butter garlic lemon sherry sauce, and pollo alla rollatini, which is chicken cutlets stuffed with prosciutto ham, mushrooms, mozzarella, and ground veal in a marsala mushroom sauce. More traditional fare like veal parmigiana and fettuccine alfredo can also be ordered.

TIEBUCKERS PUB & EATERY $$$
75 Somers Rd., Somers
(406) 857-3335

Tiebuckers is a restaurant with a real history. The building that houses the establishment dates from 1928 and for many years was both a depot for the Great Northern Railway and headquarters for the Somers Lumber Company. It first transformed into a restaurant in the 1960s, then went on hiatus, and was reopened as a restaurant by Barry and Julie Smith several years ago. Many of the recipes pay homage to Julie's grandfather, Joe Di Cristina, such as the chicken basted

in Grandpa's Sauce, an oil and vinegar blend, then barbecued for an hour and steamed to retain natural juices. Tiebuckers is also noted for its pork ribs and combo platters. Kids meals are available for those age 12 and younger. Dinner is served starting at 5 p.m. Tues through Sat. Live music can be enjoyed on some weekends. The associated pub, which features a turn-of-the-20th-century bar, was the first in Montana to pour cask-conditioned ales since the days of Prohibition.

NIGHTLIFE

KALISPELL BAR
110 Main St.
(406) 257-7035

This place was the earthy Kalispell Bar from the 1950s until 2000, when the owners transformed it into the more upscale Painted Horse Grill. But what goes around sometimes comes around, and late in 2009 the venerable drinking spot once again became the Kalispell Bar, funkier than the Painted Horse but less rowdy than the Kalispell Bar of yore. A "family-friendly sports bar with a full lunch and dinner menu" is how general manager Jeff Epperly described it to a *Flathead Beacon* reporter. (Epperly was a star basketball player at Flathead High School in the 1980s and also played for Montana State University.) It's located in the historic Kalispell Grand Hotel complex, and owned by Butch and Janet Clark, who also own the Kalispell Grand and the adjacent Kalispell Casino. Burgers, steaks, and bar food are on the menu for lunch and dinner.

MONTANA NUGGET CASINO
740 West Idaho St.
(406) 756-8100

The Montana Nugget is the perfect place to go to acquaint yourself with the Montana casino lifestyle. The ding-ding-ding of video poker machines hitting the jackpot merges with the sounds of a sports announcer on one of the many television sets, the country tunes coming over the loudspeaker, and the waitresses calling out another order. One side of the large open building is dedicated to dining, but plenty of room is devoted to gambling activities, and there's usually a poker game in progress if you want to take a shot at trying your luck against some genuine Montana characters on their home turf.

✳MOOSE'S SALOON
173 North Main St.
(406) 755-2337
Visiting Kalispell and not ducking into Moose's at least once is sort of like going to New York City and not visiting Central Park. Established in 1957, Moose's Saloon is the real McCoy, a genuine hangout, with a square bar often crowded with customers who are old friends and others just getting to know each other. It's reminiscent of the bar on the *Cheers* TV show, complete with lots of colorful regulars. The table area is dark and atmospheric; the floor, covered with sawdust and peanut shells, since Moose's provides complimentary nuts to munch on with your drinks. Lots of folks in the Flathead Valley consider the pizza at Moose's to be the best in the West. You can also order from a variety of sandwiches, along with other munchies from the kitchen. Next door at Moostley Moose's, you can pick up a souvenir t-shirt or ball cap.

PADDY'S TOUCHDOWN LOUNGE
153 Meridian Rd.
(406) 260-4333
Long the location of the Finish Line bar, this renovated tavern was transformed into Paddy's Touchdown Lounge, a sports bar-restaurant combo, in June of 2010. Co-owner Pat Kelly's goal was to create a comfortable atmosphere with plenty of good food and an abundance of TV screens. Sandwiches and burgers are lunchtime mainstays, along with specialty pub grub like shepherd's pie, fish and chips, and Paddy's Reuben. The same goes for dinner, with the addition of steaks and pastas, and pizzas can be ordered any time of day, from 11 a.m. until midnight every day except Sun. The place is divided into 3 sections: the bar, the family dining area, and a casino.

SHOPPING

DEPOT PARK SQUARE
Junction of Main and First Streets East
Kalispell
This complex of stores in 3 buildings is a delightful alternative to mall shopping, and it's just across the street from the Kalispell Center Mall, so it also makes a nice complement. Some of the stores here are The Athlete's Foot shoe store, featuring gear for the sports minded; Golf USA; the Avalanche Creek Cafe; and the Kalispell Chamber of Commerce offices. The pedestrian-mall quality of the 3 buildings and the easy parking have helped to bring a fresh feel to downtown Kalispell.

IMAGINATION STATION
132 Main St.
(406) 755-5668
If possible, this branch of Whitefish's Imagination Station is even more fun than the original. It's prettier, say the owners—they learned from their first experience. And it has some special features, too: A small upstairs

is dedicated to teachers' materials, theme books, bulletin boards, and posters. Downstairs, the store is chock full of all kinds of toys—from pirates to kites to Thomas the Train engine sets—as well as "classic" toys parents will delight in remembering and introducing to a younger generation. Stop on by and have a look around. It's a fun shop for all ages, open 9:30 a.m. to 6 p.m. Mon through Sat.

KALISPELL CENTER MALL
20 North Main St.
(406) 752-6660
www.kalispellcentermall.com
Though not as big as the malls in many larger urban areas, Kalispell Center Mall has three dozen stores to keep tourists and locals busy for an afternoon or more. The anchor stores are JCPenney and Herberger's, with an emphasis at both on clothes for all family members. Among the other businesses in the mall are Anna's Greek Gyros & Pizza, Glacier Candy, Riddle's Jewelry, Northwest Bounty Restaurant, RadioShack, and Payless ShoeSource. A distinctive feature of the mall is that it connects to the Red Lion Kalispell Hotel, so you can shop all day long, then drop into your bed at night. For some, a dream vacation.

ROCKY MOUNTAIN OUTFITTER
135 Main St.
(406) 752-2446
www.rockymountainoutfitter.com
While Sportsman & Ski Haus (see below) caters to the general outdoorsy public, RMO is more devoted to self-powered sports: backpacking; climbing; kayaking; and backcountry, cross-country, and skate skiing. The staff is knowledgeable and friendly—and knows what's happening in the wilds around the Flathead Valley, whether it's water levels in the rivers or recent avalanche reports. Spend a little time in this store, and you'll probably catch the drift of what's really going on out there in the woods!

SASSAFRAS ART CO-OP
120 Main St.
(406) 752-2433
Just walking around this shop is a blast, with so many different kinds of beautiful crafts, arts, and the materials to make them all displayed side by side. Sassafras is a collective—artists and craftspeople rent out a space in the store, so watercolor paintings are juxtaposed with handmade dolls, yarn from Montana sheep, artsy china-mosaic mirrors, fun woven placemats and napkins, Western-style ironware, nostalgia items, and much more (even a few pianos). It's a feast for the eyes! Each artist has business cards available, so if you want to you can follow up with a particular person. You might want to keep your eyes on your watch, though—time can slip away quickly in this enjoyable place.

SPORTSMAN & SKI HAUS
145 Hutton Ranch Rd.
(406) 755-6484
www.sportsmanskihaus.com
If you've come all the way to Montana, you may as well enjoy the great outdoors, and that's where Sportsman & Ski Haus comes in. This is the department store of sporting-goods in the Flathead, and they are now installed in a beautiful new building in that section of Kalispell known as "Little Missoula." With thorough inventories for hunting and fishing, camping, and water sports, as well as an extensive line of footwear and outdoor clothing, you can get everything you need for your family expedition here, down to

and including the live bait. It's open Mon through Sat from 9 a.m. to 9 p.m., and Sun from 10 a.m. to 6 p.m.

STRAWBERRY PATCH
404 West Center St.
(406) 752-2660
This popular shopping spot was located in the Gateway West Mall for many years, but when that establishment closed, the Strawberry Patch wound up in a beautiful new facility across the street from Kalispell Center Mall. Strawberry Patch is a quintessential gift store, carrying a line of merchandise that ranges from collectibles to local items like jellies and sauces from the Bigfork Inn, along with their popular selection of fudges. And if you wish Christmas was every day, you'll find the corner nook of decorations and Christmas collectibles to suit your fancy. You'll also see brightly colored dishes and decorative items of every type. Prices range from hundreds of dollars for certain items to a dollar or two for candles.

WESTERN OUTDOOR
48 Main St.
(406) 756-5818
If you have a little buckaroo or cowgirl in tow, you might want to head on over to the Western Outdoor Store for some genuine Western-wear souvenirs that will last for years. There's a complete lineup of clothing for little pardners, from boots to cowboy hats, and there's rarely been a little one who could resist a shiny new belt buckle. Plenty of Western fashions for grown-up boys and girls are stocked, as well. The sizable place also includes a rack of cowboy hats that runs clear around the store. Up on the walls you can inspect hundreds of boards featuring cattle brands used by ranchers across Montana, some dating to the 1800s. The store, occupying the 1896 McIntosh Opera House building, phased out saddles a few years ago, but you can still buy a full line of cowboy accessories: halters, bridles, saddle pads, spurs, and even bullwhips. When you've spent enough money on wrangling gear, you can mosey on down the stairs to the Kalispell Antiques Market, which is located on the lower level.

WHITEFISH

Originally a railroad and logging town, Whitefish has evolved into a delightful resort community whose residents and visitors enjoy small-town charm, plenty of big-city amenities, and world-class outdoor recreation. The town sits at the northwest end of the Flathead Valley, just south of the Whitefish Range and Big Mountain and at the foot of 7-mile-long Whitefish Lake. The town itself is a busy retail and business center that has maintained its low-key, history-influenced character: You'll feel at ease strolling in and out of small shops or chatting with the staff in restaurants. In the summer, flower gardens and hanging baskets embellish virtually every corner and shop; in the winter, holiday decorations add color and warmth to the season's festivities. And Whitefish folk like to do things—just watch the vehicles going up and down the road. Whether they're pulling a horse trailer or snowmobiles, or carrying skis, bikes, or boats, you'll get the idea pretty quickly: Whitefish is a great place to play in the great outdoors.

For a small town, Whitefish offers a surprising range of places to stay, eat, and shop. It bustles in both winter and summer; fall and spring are quieter times to visit. The downtown core is quite compact and easy to explore on foot: Within a few blocks you'll find everything from the Stumptown Historical Society to the new city library and cultural arts center, small retail shops and restaurants, standard services (post office, fax, banks, etc.), and city parks. In the outlying areas are other lodgings, shops, restaurants, and larger resorts associated with the Whitefish Mountain Resort or the golf courses, for example, but even these are only minutes from town.

ACCOMMODATIONS

Price Code

Lodging code per night for two people:

$	**Less than $85**
$$	**$85 to $115**
$$$	**$115 to $150**
$$$$	**More than $150**

PINE LODGE $$$–$$$$
920 Spokane Ave.
(406) 862-7600, (800) 305-7463
www.thepinelodge.com
The Pine Lodge is neatly wedged between US 93 (Spokane Avenue) and the Whitefish

River, which means that, while it's on the main road into town, the areas at the back of the lodge—the lobby, swimming pool, deck, and many rooms—overlook the willows and water. And should you opt for a 1-bedroom suite, you'll be pleasantly surprised by the northern view as well, as these rooms face the Whitefish Mountain Resort.

All Pine Lodge rooms include remote-controlled television, telephone, and bath. Standard rooms, deluxe rooms, minisuites, and 1-bedroom suites offer a range of amenities, from spas to gas fireplaces and balconies, for between $142 and $225 per night for 2 people during the peak season. The Pine Lodge features an exercise room, indoor/outdoor heated swimming pool, outdoor hot tub, guest laundry, and a meeting room for up to 50 people. Complimentary continental breakfast is served each morning. Nonsmoking rooms and floors are available.

ROCKY MOUNTAIN LODGE $$$–$$$$
6510 US 93 South
(406) 862-2569, (800) 862-2569
www.rockymtnlodge.com
Best Western Rocky Mountain Lodge is one of the newer hotels in Whitefish. Its 79 rooms include executive rooms and minisuites, which offer a king-size bed and gas fireplace, wet bar with small refrigerator, sink, and microwave, Jacuzzi or garden tub, a sofa bed, and fax/modem port. Standard rooms feature king- or queen-size beds, and 12 annex rooms are located in a motel-style detached building where you can drive right up next to the room, like at old-fashioned motels. Other amenities include an outdoor heated pool and Jacuzzi, laundry, exercise room, and meeting and banquet facilities. Guests enjoy a complimentary deluxe continental breakfast each morning.

Peak season room rates range from a high of $198 per night for minisuites to as little as $115 per night for annex rooms. Pets are permitted in some rooms for an additional fee.

Bed-and-Breakfasts

The Garden Wall Inn is a private home that its owners have opened up to guests. Good Medicine Lodge and Hidden Moose Lodge are small inns offering the same personal attention and full breakfast you would expect of a bed-and-breakfast.

✳THE GARDEN WALL INN $$$$
504 Spokane Ave.
(406) 862-3440, (888) 530-1700
www.gardenwallinn.com
"Luxurious," "gracious," and "comfortable" are three words that may well spring to mind soon after you enter The Garden Wall Inn, in business since 1987. This beautifully restored 1920s house is now furnished with period antiques; the attentive but not intrusive service will charm your stay. You'll find a rose decorating the coffee tray in your room each morning, a very civilized half hour before the scrumptious gourmet breakfast featuring locally grown and/or produced foods. And after your day's adventures, you might spend some time soaking in a claw-foot tub, then sip sherry and enjoy hors d'oeuvres before the fireplace.

The Garden Wall Inn—named for the Garden Wall, the part of the Continental Divide that runs just north of Logan Pass in Glacier National Park—displays many details that reveal the owners' love of that nearby national park and for that of the sport of skiing. Historic photos of Glacier, Blue Willow china originally used in the park hotels, first-edition copies of books about the park, even the Audubon prints on the walls all speak of Glacier (the Audubon Society was founded by George Bird Grinnell, probably the single person most responsible for creation of the park). Between owners Mike and Rhonda Fitzgerald and chef and co-owner Chris Schustrom, you'll find a tremendous knowledge of the outdoors, whether you're interested in hiking, skiing, fly-fishing, or kayaking. They also know the Flathead Valley well and will be happy to point you in the right direction for shopping, dining, or exploring. The Garden Wall Inn is located just 2 blocks from downtown Whitefish, giving you easy access to the town's services and attractions. The inn's 5 bedrooms range in price from $155 to $195 per night for 2 people; a suite may be arranged for $255 per night for up to 4 people. All rooms have private baths. Pets and smoking are not permitted.

GOOD MEDICINE LODGE $$$–$$$$
537 Wisconsin Ave.
(406) 862-5488, (800) 860-5488
www.goodmedicinelodge.com

"Good Medicine," indeed—you'll find this place the perfect prescription for rest and relaxation. Location, interiors, furnishings, breakfast—every detail reflects Good Medicine Lodge's attention to your well-being. Built of cedar timbers, the lodge glows with the warmth of wood, accented with fabrics influenced by Native American designs. The lobby and great room invite you to curl up and read by the fire, help yourself to freshly baked cookies, or get ready to soak in the hot tub just out the door. In summer you'll enjoy stepping into the garden or relaxing under the broad covered porches of the L-shaped lodge. And, summer or winter, you'll find a big, buffet-style breakfast awaiting you each morning: fresh muffins, breads, and cobblers, cereals, granola, yogurt, meats and cheeses, coffee, tea, and juice.

The 9 rooms (6 standard and 3 suites) all have private baths, air-conditioning, phones, and custom-made log beds. Most rooms have balconies with mountain views. The rooms offer either a queen-size or twin bed arrangement, and the largest suite can sleep 5. The master suite, which has its own loft, gas stove, whirlpool tub, Swiss shower, and balcony, helped Good Medicine earn a rave review as one of America's 10 "most romantic inns." In addition, the lodge has a ski room with boot and glove driers as well as a guest laundry.

Rates range from $150 to $250 per night for 2 people during the peak season, depending on the room. The lodge is located about 6 blocks north of downtown Whitefish on the road to the Whitefish Mountain Resort.

HIDDEN MOOSE LODGE $$$–$$$$
1735 East Lakeshore Dr.
(406) 862-6516, (888) 733-6667
www.hiddenmooselodge.com

The great room's log-framed cathedral ceiling and massive fireplace made of local rock bespeak the warm, rustic feeling of the Hidden Moose Lodge. Antique skis adorn the walls, bringing the outside inside; a mix of colors, patterns, and textures in the fabrics and custom-made log furniture add richness to the interior of all the lodge rooms. The Hidden Moose Lodge is built into the side of a hill and surrounded by pine, birch, and aspen trees. Every once in a while the "hidden moose" emerges for a stroll—and you may also see deer and the occasional bear wandering behind the lodge. But if the wilderness is at your backyard, civilization makes its presence known, too—terraced rock gardens and hanging flower baskets brighten the entrance all summer long.

Hosts Kim and Kent Taylor have designed their lodge with all the comforts foremost in mind. Many rooms have their own entrance, and quite a few boast Jacuzzi tubs. All have a private deck, private bath, and phone, cable TV, and DVD player. Breakfast is hearty—most guests say they don't need lunch!—and can include such scrumptious items as huckleberry buttermilk pancakes or Hidden Moose chorizo quiche. Afternoon refreshments include wine, cheese, and nonalcoholic beverages. Guests are invited to use the lodge's mountain bikes and canoe, as well.

The Hidden Moose Lodge is located on the road to the Whitefish Mountain Resort, 1.5 miles out of downtown Whitefish. Rates for the "Montana-themed" rooms include the full breakfast; for 2 people, prices range from $125 to $175 per night, depending on room size and amenities.

Resorts, Guest Ranches & Lodges

GAYNOR'S RESORTS $$–$$$
1992 K M Ranch Rd.
(406) 862-3802
www.gaynorsresorts.com
Overlooking a bend in the Stillwater River, Gaynor's Resorts offer a unique opportunity to enjoy ranch life in the Montana countryside—yet the luxury cabins offer all the amenities of home, and within a 15-minute drive of Whitefish. In fact, they proved so popular that the Gaynors expanded and now also offer their Cabins-in-the-Woods, located a few minutes from the main ranch.

It's hard to describe the peace and beauty of this place. Here you can forget your worries completely as you take in the quiet and big views. The river attracts songbirds and waterfowl, and mountain bluebirds nest in boxes along the fence. The ranch is set back from the road, which has very little traffic, and state forest land—with both riding and hiking trails—lies just across the way.

Whether you've spent your day exploring Glacier, skiing at Whitefish Mountain Resort, golfing, or otherwise enjoying the area, you'll feel like you're coming home when you return to the Gaynors' each

evening. You'll have your own river view to the west, where you can put up your feet and enjoy the sunset.

You may also choose to make the ranch itself the focus of your vacation. Sleeping in and enjoying a cup of coffee by the river is a great way to start the day, but there's plenty of exploring to do here, too. Gaynor's offers customized trail rides, tailored to your experience and limited to your own group. Special rides are available for children. During your stay you are welcome to explore the entire ranch property. Its open pastures are home to several ranch horses as well as others that are boarded at the ranch. Those traveling with their own horses may board them here in spacious stalls or large outdoor paddocks. Your hosts, Don and Nancy Gaynor, will be happy to help you with your plans.

Cabins, which come equipped with pots and pans, washer/dryer, and more, can accommodate 2 to 10 people. There's a 3-night minimum stay in summer and 2-night minimum in winter. Rates vary by season, and range from $169 to $300 per night. Smoking is not allowed indoors; if you have pets traveling with you, inquire ahead of time about the pet policy.

i To ski or not to ski? That is the question. Find out what conditions are to help with the answer—call (406) 862-SNOW for the Whitefish Mountain Resort snow report, updated daily during ski season at 7 a.m.

GROUSE MOUNTAIN LODGE $$$
2 Fairway Dr.
(406) 862-3000, (800) 321-8822
www.grousemountainlodge.com
Here is lodging in the grand style—everything you could think of, and more. With its

river-rock fireplaces, warm polished wood, and robust elk-antler chandeliers, you'll know you're in Montana. The 145 rooms are stylish and comfortable, and some include Jacuzzis, kitchens, and/or loft bedrooms. The lodge restaurant (see The Grill under Restaurants) is one of the finest in town and is open for breakfast, lunch, and dinner. The Whitefish Lake Golf Course is out your door; in the winter its fairways are groomed for cross-country and skate skiing. And the lodge has an indoor swimming pool and hot tubs.

Grouse Mountain Lodge also has conference facilities for groups as large as 300 people. Banquet and catering services will provide just the level of support you need, whether that's coffee and rolls or a sit-down dinner.

Room rates, which vary by the season, begin at $109 to $205 per night for 2 people. Be sure to inquire about both ski and golf packages. ·

HAYMOON RANCH RESORT $$$$
1845 Hodgson Rd.
(406) 862-1471
www.haymoonresort.com
Nestled on 20 private acres 3 miles outside of Whitefish, the Haymoon Ranch Resort is a vacation dreamscape occupying an estate-like setting. The cabins and lodging quarters feature antiques and handmade new furniture, original art by local artists, and class touches like special herbal lavender Haymoon toiletries. Outside, in summer the grounds explode with perennial and herb gardens, which embellish acres of manicured lawn perfect for "barefooting." On-site activities include horseshoes, volleyball, croquet, marshmallow roasts, ping-pong, and hot-tubbing. Nightly rates at peak season range from $179 for the Deermoon Quarters

to $1,299 for the Flowermoon Lodge, which at a sprawling 3,500 square feet can sleep as many as 20—making it ideal for a family reunion or other large gathering of friends.

THE LODGE AT
WHITEFISH LAKE $$$–$$$$
1380 Wisconsin Ave.
(406) 865-4000, (877) 887-4026
www.lodgeatwhitefishlake.com
The Lodge at Whitefish Lake, new in 2005 but inspired by the grand lodges of an earlier era, makes maximum use of its beautiful waterfront location on Whitefish Lake. It is unique among the area's commercial lodgings in being right on the water, and that gives it a special focus. The 1-, 2-, and 3-bedroom condo suites all have private balconies overlooking the lake; and the resort's private beach has a swimming area (as well as an outdoor pool, 2 spas, and an indoor spa). The new Viking Lodge, located east of the main lodge, is a day-use and overnighting facility overlooking 30 acres of wetland that the owners, the Averill family, have preserved under a conservation easement in partnership with the Whitefish Lake Institute.

The full-service marina operates a boat-rental service—try an afternoon picnicking on a pontoon boat! Or rent a speedboat for waterskiing, a sea kayak, or a canoe. Ski and bike lockers as well as a guest laundry are available.

Looking for an afternoon or evening cruise? Step aboard the lodge's *Lady of the Lake,* a 31-foot motor yacht, for a turn around Whitefish Lake. The Lady is also available for private charters.

The luxurious lakeside condo suites have full-size living rooms, gas fireplaces, fully equipped kitchens with a breakfast bar and dining room, air-conditioning, and cable TV.

A standard view studio suite goes for around $285 per night during the peak season, while a lakefront studio is $395. Lakefront suites are priced at $472 per night, and you can keep going up from there—for instance, a 5-bedroom lakeside condominium for $1,199. King rooms in the Viking Lodge are priced at $249 per night.

The Lodge at Whitefish Lake is located on the road to the Whitefish Mountain Resort, about a 5-minute drive from downtown Whitefish. Be sure to inquire about special ski and golf packages.

NORTH FORTY RESORT $$–$$$
3765 Hwy. 40, P.O. Box 4250, Whitefish 59937
(406) 862-7740, (800) 775-1740
www.northforty.com

What could be more Montana than staying in a log cabin in the woods? A beautiful 40 acres of tall pines at the North Forty Resort shelter 22 log cabins (14 individual family cabins and 8 duplexes) that combine rustic decor with modern amenities. Each of these newly built cabins has a fully equipped kitchen, gas fireplace, and its own porch, picnic table, and grill. Two hot tubs and a sauna building are centrally located. The cabins are arranged in small groups, so the North Forty would also make the perfect location to hold a family reunion or other get-together. A walking and cross-country ski trail begins at the north end of the property.

The resort's Snowberry Center, constructed in the same rustic log style as the cabins, is available for meetings and other group functions involving as many as 65 people. With a full kitchen, large windows, gas fireplace, and large outside patio, it can provide a spacious setting for your family reunion, celebration, or other meeting.

Cabin rates vary from $199 per night for 2 people to $259 for a duplex cabin that will sleep as many as 8. All cabins are nonsmoking. Inquire in advance about the resort's pet policy.

WHITEFISH MOUNTAIN RESORT $$–$$$$
P.O. Box 1400, Whitefish 59937
(406) 862-2900, (800) 858-4152
www.skiwhitefish.com

The Big Mountain was, of course, initially a ski hill—but nowadays it's a good deal more than that, as signaled by its recent name change to Whitefish Mountain Resort. Winter visitors still focus on skiing—and, with more than 3,000 acres of skiable terrain, the mountain has something to offer alpine skiers and snowboarders of every ability. Other activities include cross-country skiing and skate skiing on the groomed track, and backcountry snowcat skiing. And summertime now brings incredible outdoor fun, too—hiking, mountain biking, zip-lining, huckleberry picking, and more—including live music and other special events (see the Outdoor Recreation chapter).

The Whitefish Mountain Resort central reservation office handles reservations for most lodgings on the mountain. The various facilities cover a wide range of accommodations and prices, and all are available as part of lodging/lift ticket packages. All include a spa or sauna and laundry. Many businesses here close briefly in both the spring and fall off-seasons, so be sure to check dates of availability. Nightly rates will be higher during the holidays. Whitefish Mountain Resort is expanding rapidly; check the website for the most up-to-date and comprehensive information on lodging.

- **Anapurna.** $$$–$$$$. Studios to 4-bedroom condos are located near the General Store and Sherpa Pool complex. Rates range from $125 to $630.
- **The Edelweiss.** $$$–$$$$. These charming condos are located in the heart of Big Mountain Village. Rates range from $125 to $400 per unit.
- **Hibernation House.** $–$$$. An overnight stay at this economy lodge includes a full skier's breakfast. Shuttle to the ski hill is available, or you can ski to your door. Rates vary from $68 to $135 for a value room.
- **Kintla Lodge.** $$$$. The Kintla Lodge offers deluxe condos and shops right at the base of the ski hill, along with underground parking and elevator access. Rooms run from $125 to $250, while condo units range from $225 to $625.
- **Morning Eagle.** $$$$. These luxury condos offer from 1 to 3 bedrooms in the center of the resort village. Prices range from $200 to $625.
- **Tamarack Loop.** $$$–$$$$. These condos feature anywhere from 1 to 5 bedrooms; the overnight prices vary accordingly, from $130 to $700.
- **Townhomes.** $$$$. These 3-, 4-, and 5-bedroom units range in price from $400 to $1,200 per night.
- **Winter Lane Properties.** $$$$. Many of these condos, chalets, and duplexes are within walking distance of the slopes. Some include hot tubs. Rates range from $175 to $400.

Also operating independently on Big Mountain:

- **Kandahar Lodge.** $$$. This traditional-style ski lodge features a fine restaurant open for dinner in a family atmosphere. Rates range from $169 to $529,

depending on the room chosen and the number of people staying there. Call (800) 862-6094 or visit www.kandahar lodge.com.

> **i** Technically, "alpine" refers to the terrain above the tree line; "subalpine" refers to the area right at tree line—where trees grow, but just barely; where conditions like wind, temperature, snowpack, poor quality of soil, or just plain rockiness limit their size and distribution. Logan Pass, for example, is technically subalpine, since stunted subalpine fir trees do grow there. The climate is so tough on them, however, that they are twisted and dwarfed into formations called "krummholz"—German for "crooked wood"—a very good description of trees at tree line.

Campgrounds & RV Parks

Price Code

$	Less than $10
$$	$10 to $16
$$$	$16 to $24
$$$$	More than $24

TALLY LAKE CAMPGROUND $–$$$
Tally Lake, approximately 14 miles west of Whitefish
(406) 863-5400

Tally Lake is on the Tally Lake District of the Flathead National Forest and the campground is administered by that office. The campground itself is some 14 miles west of town at the far end of the lake. It has 40 sites and 2 group camping areas. Technically, the campground is open all year, but the Tally Lake Road is not plowed in winter and there is no fee for those who want to snowmobile or ski into the area to camp. Full services,

The Western Larch

In the mountains surrounding Whitefish—and in the North Fork Valley, the Swan Valley, and elsewhere in Glacier Country—you'll see lots of forest, obviously, as well as plenty of clearcuts. Some older clearcuts have assumed the character of natural openings; you may actually be glad for them, as they often facilitate long-distance views that otherwise would be obscured by trees.

Speaking of trees, one species you can't help noticing in northwest Montana is the beautiful **western larch** *(Larix occidentalis)*. The tree has a rich reddish-brown trunk that grows tall and impossibly straight. David Thompson, early into these parts as a fur trader for the North West Company, wrote about one immense western larch he ran across in the Kootenai River country in 1808, with a "thirteen feet girth and one hundred and fifty feet clean growth" ("clean growth" meaning the trunk below where branches begin growing).

The largest of several Pacific Northwest tamarack species, the western larch is one of a rare breed of deciduous conifers; that is, it sheds its needles each autumn. After turning positively golden, the needles drift to earth, glimmering in the sun like fairy dust and magically carpeting the forest floor with color. The trees appear dead and somber in winter, but come spring fresh larch needle growth provides the otherwise dark-green forest with wonderfully bright splashes of spring green. Mature western larch are particularly impressive: Fully two-thirds of their height can consist of clear, straight trunk, before limbs start branching out on the upper third. Individual trees can grow as tall as 200 feet, although 150 feet is more common.

The straight grain and relatively dense wood of the western larch makes it the favorite of savvy firewood cutters in these parts. Its strong, decay-resistant qualities also make the tree ideal for use in items such as telephone poles and mine timbers. Prehistoric Indians brewed a tea from its bark (purportedly as a treatment for tuberculosis, coughs, and colds), chewed its solidified pitch like gum, took advantage of its solid wood for fashioning bowls, and used the tree's rotted wood for smoking buckskins. It's also said that the Kootenai Indians preferred the larch for the center pole in performing sun-dance ceremonies. Tribes east of the Rockies typically employed cottonwoods for the purpose.

including running water, pit toilets, garbage pickup, and a dock on the lake, become available in mid-May. Trails will be worked and opened in late May or June, depending on snow conditions. Services end Sept 30, and after that time campers must again pack in their own supplies and pack out their own garbage.

Campground fees are $15 per vehicle per night, with $5 extra for each additional vehicle per site. A $4 day-use fee is charged for others using the area. A covered pavilion that will accommodate up to 100 people can be rented for a $75 fee. For group reservations, call (877) 444-6777.

✳WHITEFISH LAKE STATE PARK $
US 93 North
(406) 752-5501
www.stateparks.com/whitefish_lake__
campground.html
This small state park, within a 10-minute drive of downtown, is right on Whitefish Lake. Its tall trees and lakeshore offer a pleasant change of pace for those who want to day trip or to camp overnight. Picnic tables are close to the lake. A boat ramp and parking for trailers provide access to the water. Dogs are permitted but must be on a leash. Resident day-use fees are prepaid with state vehicle registration; nonresident day-use fee is $5.

The 25 campsites are scattered throughout the trees a little above the water. A maximum of 6 people and 2 camper units may occupy a site, where space allows. Fires may be made in provided grates only; firewood is available for purchase during the summer months. Fees for the summer season are $15 per night (camping is available May 1 through Sept 30). One trailer site is wheelchair accessible. The maximum stay is 7 nights. Commercial or large groups require a permit; call Montana Fish, Wildlife and Parks at the number above.

The park is located just west of town on US 93 North. Follow the signs along the road beginning just west of the Grouse Mountain Lodge.

WHITEFISH RV PARK $
6400 US 93 South
(406) 862-7275
www.whitefishrvpark.com
The Whitefish RV Park offers 57 full hookups, 14 of which have pull-through parking. This newer facility is just off the highway into town, yet is quiet and pleasantly landscaped with trees and grass. A dump station, restrooms and showers, playground, and laundry will make your stay as convenient as being at home. A major grocery store, services, and restaurants are within easy walking distance. Pets are welcome and there's a pet-exercising area. Cable TV hookups are available at all sites for free, and telephone/Internet hookups are available at many sites. Tent-camping areas are also available.

The Whitefish RV Park is open year-round. Rates for full hookups are $36 per night (add $5 for 50-amp service); partial hookups are $32 per night (plus $3 for each additional person over 2 people). Weekly and monthly rates are also available. Tent rates are $24 per night, plus $5 per person for each person over 2 people. No monthly tenters are permitted.

And More . . .

FIVE-STAR RENTALS $–$$$$
704 Baker Ave.
(406) 862-5994
www.fivestarrentals.com
If you're planning to be in the Flathead Valley for at least a week—whether it's for your vacation, honeymoon, family reunion, corporate retreat, or whatever—you might try a different approach to lodging. Five Star Rentals offers a wide variety of listings, encompassing everything from secluded cabins in the woods to Whitefish Lake homes and condos to mountain retreats. All properties are fully furnished and equipped for a great vacation. Special amenities vary and may include barbecues, decks, fireplaces, docks and canoes at water properties, hot tubs, and steam rooms. Every property is unique, and some offer 5-star views.

Sizes range from cozy, 1-bedroom cabins to spacious 5-bedroom homes, and prices range from $1,000 to $5,000 per week.

RESTAURANTS

Price Code

Restaurant price code, for two people exclusive of beverages, tips, and tax:

$....................	$10 to $20
$$	$20 to $28
$$$	$28 to $35
$$$$	More than $35

Family Friendly Dining

THE BUFFALO CAFE
& NIGHTLY GRILL   **$–$$**
514 Third St. East
(406) 862-2833
www.buffalocafewhitefish.com
Opened in 1979 originally in Bigfork, the Buffalo Cafe is a northwest Montana institution. It's a favorite place for locals to get together and catch up on what's going on around town. Despite increased competition from newer places in the last few years, the Buffalo remains the place to eat before skiing: Its substantial breakfasts—whether a buffalo pie, huevos, or the pancake of the day—stand up to a good day's fun in the snow.

"The Buff" is open daily for breakfast and lunch from 7 a.m. (8 a.m. Sun) to 2 p.m. The Nightly Grill opens for budget dinners Mon through Sat from 5 to 9 p.m.

PESCADO BLANCO: MOUNTAIN
MEXICAN KITCHEN   **$$–$$$**
235 First St.
(406) 862-3290
www.pescadoblanco.com
A "white fish" by any other name, even in Spanish . . . The first thing you'll learn about Pescado Blanco's offerings is that they're not like other Mexican you've had. They call it Mountain Mexican Kitchen, or a fusion cuisine—from southern Mexico to northern Montana. Whatever its origins, it's been a great success. Pescado Blanco opens nightly for dinner from 5 to 10 p.m., with a menu full of familiar names: enchiladas, quesadillas, and taquitos all make their appearance. But then you'll start to notice ingredients like elk chorizo, pumpkin seed pesto, honey-cumin glaze . . . and the fun begins. Entrees run from $14.95 to $20.95. Pescado Blanco also has a short Bambinos menu for kids that includes a small drink for $6.95. Orders to go are an option.

WASABI SUSHI BAR AND
GINGER GRILL   **$$–$$$**
419 Second St. East
(406) 863-9283
www.wasabimt.com
For 10 years now, the Wasabi Sushi Grill has been introducing Whitefish residents and visitors to items like tempura fried fusion rolls, red quinoa veggie rolls, lamb Adadaba, and wasabi pad thai. The place opens for appetizers and dinner at 5 p.m. Mon through Sat, with the addition of Sun during the peak seasons.

Fine Dining

CAFE KANDAHAR   **$$$$**
Kandahar Lodge
3824 Big Mountain Rd.
(406) 862-6247
www.cafekandahar.com
An informal but elegant atmosphere makes the Cafe Kandahar an excellent place for a special dinner, whether you've been skiing at the Whitefish Mountain Resort or not. The menu is as fine as you'll find anywhere: The James Beard Foundation recently

recognized Chef Andy Blanton as a nominee for the "Best Chef Northwest" award, which takes in not only Montana, but Alaska, Washington, Idaho, Oregon, and Wyoming. Everything is prepared with style and presented beautifully; the motto here is "thoughtfully constructed cuisine," and a lot of the ingredients come from local farmers and ranchers. The service is quick, helpful, and not obtrusive, making for an altogether delightful evening. Cafe Kandahar is open for dinner only, nightly from 5:30 to 9:30 p.m. Reservations are strongly recommended.

THE GRILL $$$$
Grouse Mountain Lodge
2 Fairway Dr.
(406) 862-3000
www.grousemountainlodge.com

Grouse Mountain's The Grill evokes a certain slice of Western life. The restaurant combines pine decor, a fine sound system, and flat-screen TVs with Montana touches—an elk keeps his eye on the dining room, as do a flight of pheasants on the far wall. The Grill features fine cuts of beef as well as chicken and baby back ribs; fresh Northwest sockeye salmon baked on a plank is another specialty. Unique side dishes such as sweet potato fries complement the main course. Whatever you choose, you're sure to enjoy the fine dining and distinctive ambience of Grouse Mountain Lodge. During warm weather, you can opt to dine outside on the Deck & Patio, an extension of The Grill. The Grill is open for breakfast, lunch, and dinner. Reservations are recommended for dinner.

MCGARRY'S ROADHOUSE $$$–$$$$
510 Wisconsin Ave.
(406) 862-6223
www.mcgarrysroadhouse.com

McGarry's, featuring "Flavors of Montana, Flavors of the World," came to the Whitefish dining scene when its owners moved here from Whidbey Island, Washington, in 2003. They brought with them years of experience in the restaurant and hotel business. Their goal was to create a warm and classy but comfortable restaurant offering an eclectic menu that draws on many regional cuisines—and they have succeeded. A touch of Mexican here, a Vietnamese spider (aka tempura!) there, and a Bison meatloaf on the other side. The menu will make you choose between many good things! Daily specials feature fresh seafood, and the wine list is extensive. Entrees run from $11.95 to $27.95.

*TUPELO GRILLE $$$–$$$$
17 Central Ave.
(406) 862-6136
www.tupelogrille.com

Cajun-style cooking may not be what you expect to find in Montana, but here it is! And Tupelo Grille (named for Elvis's hometown in Mississippi) is one of the most often recommended restaurants in Whitefish—known for its excellence and the consistently high quality of its dinners. *Bon Appetit* magazine said: "Whether you're a Whitefish native or a visitor to Glacier National Park, Tupelo Grille should be on your itinerary." Just walking into the place you'll enjoy the mix of aromas. The menu features everything from seafood to fried catfish, crawfish, blackened chicken breast, slow-cooked pot roast, and pastas, and each dinner is beautifully presented. Tupelo Grille opens for dinner at 5:30 p.m. each evening. The restaurant is small, and reservations are requested for groups of 6 or more. Entrees run from $18 to $29.

WHITEFISH LAKE RESTAURANT $$$$
Whitefish Golf Club
1200 US 93 North
(406) 862-5285
www.whitefishlakerestaurant.com

Also known as just "the Golf Course," the Whitefish Lake Restaurant has an authenticity to it that's hard to match. Built in 1936, the rustic, warm dining room's stone fireplace and heavy log beams give it a relaxed, elegant ambience. The service is professional but not fussy, and the food is consistently excellent—the restaurant is known for its prime rib, featured on Sun, Wed, Fri, and Sat nights (while it lasts), as well as for its seafood and its Iowa rack of lamb. It's where locals go to celebrate special occasions, so be sure to call for reservations—this fine-dining establishment can be busy. Even so, you'll never feel crowded or rushed.

You'll find the restaurant at the Whitefish Lake Golf Club, less than a mile out of town on US 93 North as the road heads west toward Eureka. In winter, watch for the two huge evergreens decorated with colored lights from top to bottom. The restaurant is set back from the road a ways. Entrees range from $19 to $40. It also opens for lunch daily at 11 a.m., and a club menu for more casual dining is served in the clubhouse after 3 p.m.

And More . . .

✳HELLROARING SALOON
  AND EATERY   **$$**
Whitefish Mountain Resort
(406) 862-6364
http://hellroaringsaloon.com

The Hellroaring Saloon, occupying the original 1949 chalet in Whitefish Mountain Resort Village, features the sort of ambience money can't buy. It takes time, and thousands of contented skiers, to make a ski-hill restaurant feel this way. Old skis grace the paneled walls (if you're "of a certain age," you may remember when you had bindings like that), famous skiers have autographed the posters, a fire crackles in the fireplace, and Warren Miller movies and other ski flicks play discreetly in the corners of the bar. The nachos are mountainous, the chili famous, and the beer cold and locally brewed. In the spring-skiing season, the porch is the place to be for soaking up the sun. The Hellroaring Saloon and Eatery is open for lunch and après ski in the winter. It also operates through the summer months for dinner Tues through Sun (5 to 9 p.m.), shutting down briefly during the spring and fall. Entrees run from $5 to $12.

NIGHTLIFE

Whitefish is a hopping town in a low-key sort of way. The Great Northern Bar is a landmark in its own right—you'll hear phrases like "it's just a block from the Northern" when you ask directions. Add in the string of other watering holes located on Central Avenue, right downtown, and you're sure to find a spot to put up your feet and enjoy a brew. The Great Northern and some of the others feature live music on weekends.

Since the 1998 completion of the I. A. O'Shaughnessy Performing Arts Center, Whitefish has proudly claimed a central location for performances of all sorts. The O'Shaughnessy is the home of the Whitefish Theatre Company, which stages plays throughout the year, but also hosts an eclectic series of musical performances. Lately the center has been screening some foreign films and big-screen productions. Check the marquee out front or www.whitefishtheatreco.org for current events.

The **Glacier Symphony and Chorale** presents a full schedule of concerts throughout the school year. Generally the Sat night performance is at the Whitefish Central School auditorium; visit www.gsc music.org or call the office at (406) 257-3241 for current information.

The Whitefish Reading Series brings both nationally recognized and local authors into town for public presentations, with usually about one talk a month during the school year. The best place to check on the current schedule is at **BookWorks,** located at 244 Spokane Ave. in Whitefish, (406) 862-4980.

The **Whitefish Mountain Resort,** of course, is the source of endless fun and frivolity, whether it's suds at the Bierstube, the end-of-ski-season furniture races down snow-covered slopes, or summer concerts outdoors. Give the resort information center a call at (406) 862-2900 for current events.

i **The first Thursday of each month from May through October, Whitefish holds its "First Thursdays" gallery nights. Eighteen different galleries in downtown Whitefish open their doors from 6 to 9 p.m. and invite you to explore their exhibits. Warm summer nights and a festival atmosphere make this the perfect way to enjoy your evening! Participating galleries and more information are available at www .whitefishgallerynights.org.**

Last but not least, something you won't find in too many other places. Late Oct is the off-season for the Flathead Valley, but if you do happen to be in town you'll find yourself in the midst of an incredible event—Halloween, Whitefish style. As in other communities, you'll see the kiddies out trick-or-treating in the late afternoon. But Whitefish adults also take Halloween seriously. Later in the evening head downtown to experience the huge Halloween party in progress. You won't recognize anyone, that's for sure—many come in full head-to-toe costumes. Be sure to pick up at least a witch hat or a big nose, or you'll definitely feel underdressed.

SHOPPING

You'll enjoy strolling through Whitefish shops, whether you're window-shopping or in search of that perfect gift for someone back home. Whitefish has a compact, functional downtown, where you'll find everything from a hardware store to an auto dealership to fairly upscale boutiques. Do take your time to stroll around town. Of course, downtown Whitefish also offers services such as banks, post office, UPS and other delivery services, a public library, and print shops. What follows is just a sampling of shops that are well worth browsing through:

1. **BookWorks** (244 Spokane Ave., 406-862-4980) is an independently owned bookstore. Front tables feature local writers, books focusing on the West and Western issues, and current best-sellers. The store also has an excellent selection of children's books. And be sure to check the front doors for posters featuring upcoming cultural events.

2. **Imagination Station** (221 Central Ave., 406-862-5668). If you've discovered your child's favorite toy was left at home, here's the place to go. The Imagination Station carries all sorts of great toys, games, you name it, and adults will enjoy looking around as much as kids. And now there's a Kalispell branch at 132 Main St. as well.

3. **Lakestream Fly Fishing Shop** (334 Central Ave., 406-862-1298) is just what you'd expect of a fly-fishing shop in Montana—all the gear you can imagine and a knowledgeable staff as well. Even nonfisherfolk will enjoy strolling through Lakestream, which has a nice selection of outdoor clothing and a comfortable ambience. You can check them out online at www .lakestream.com.

4. **Sage & Cedar** (214 Central Ave., 406-862-9411) is a fun place to spend some time. The shop specializes in bath supplies—soaps, shampoo, lotions, oils, and so on. But here's the twist: You can have your own combinations mixed for you. As you walk in there's a rack where you can smell the various scenting oils—from such standards as rose, gardenia, and lavender to such "western" favorites as sage, "Montana morning," or "rain," to some fun food smells (try a whiff of chocolate or pear!) Now you choose what sort of base you want scented, and suddenly you can have rose shampoo, sage hand lotion, and chocolate bubblebath. Fun for gifts, and fun for yourself.

5. **Sportsman & Ski Haus** (Mountain Mall; 406-862-3111; www.sportsmanskihaus .com) is the major source for outdoor gear in Whitefish. You'll find national brands in outdoor clothing and footwear, and equipment for everything from boating to skiing and backpacking.

6. **Third Street Market** (Third and Spokane, 406-862-5054) earns a mention for the change of pace it brings to Whitefish. This health-food store offers a variety of organic, locally grown, and bulk groceries. It also has a big section of vitamins and other supplements as well as books on related topics.

COLUMBIA FALLS & THE US 2 CORRIDOR

Columbia Falls is the "Gateway to Glacier," and you'll find this is true in many respects. This little community sits at the northeast corner of the Flathead Valley, where the Flathead River flows out of the mountains through Bad Rock Canyon. Since both US 2 and the railroad follow the river valley, if you're traveling into Glacier from west of the Continental Divide, you will almost certainly pass through this little town.

OVERVIEW

Driving through Columbia Falls you may notice that there's no natural waterfall here. At least two different stories exist to explain the town's name: The more interesting one has to do with the expansion of the Great Northern Railway. As investors began buying up land along the projected route, they anticipated that J. J. Hill would put the next depot west of Belton (West Glacier) at a town then known as Columbia, Montana. On hearing of the land rush, in a fit of perversity Hill decided to have the next depot at Whitefish, and turned to his employees and roared, "Columbia falls!"

While the railroad may not have chosen Columbia Falls for its operations, other major industries have. Both the Columbia Falls Aluminum Company (CFAC) and Plum Creek Timber Company have employed many people over the years. Tourism is growing as an industry here, too—many visitors choose to stay in this part of the valley because of its easy access to Glacier National Park. Therefore, new restaurants and accommodations seem to spring up each year.

The US 2 corridor is a scenic drive in its own right. Leaving Columbia Falls and

heading east, you'll start by driving through Bad Rock Canyon. Take a few moments to pull over at Berne Park along the cliffs and read the roadside markers about the wilderness and this ancient route through the mountains. The road is right beside the water for a ways; soon you'll cross the bridge over the South Fork of the Flathead River, which carries water running out the Hungry Horse Dam (see the Attractions chapter) from the Hungry Horse Reservoir. As you drive through Coram, you'll get your first glimpse of the peaks that hover above Lake McDonald: Stanton Mountain appears briefly right over the highway. Once you reach West Glacier, US 2 follows the Middle Fork of the Flathead River through a beautiful gorge and valley up to the Continental Divide and out onto the Great Plains (see the scenic loop drive described in the Attractions chapter). You'll find lots to explore all along the way.

Within this Columbia Falls and US 2 corridor chapter, businesses are listed by category, beginning with those in Columbia Falls and then from west to east, as if you were driving the highway from Columbia Falls to East Glacier.

ACCOMMODATIONS

Price Code

Keep in mind that some rates are based on availability. The average nightly rates for two adults at the hotels and motels listed in this section are indicated by a dollar sign ($) ranking in the following chart.

$................. Less than $85
$$ .... $85 to $115
$$$ .... $115 to $150
$$$$ .... More than $150

Hotels & Motels

THE GLACIER HIGHLAND $–$$
12555 US 2 East, West Glacier
(406) 888-5427, (800) 766-0811
www.glacierhighland.com

The Glacier Highland has undergone some major renovations over the past few years—if you stayed here a dozen years ago and weren't too impressed, it's time to give it another try. For those making their first trip to the area, the Highland provides a great base for exploring all the area has to offer. It's located right at the west entrance to Glacier National Park, with easy access to hiking, rafting, horseback riding, and everything else along Going-to-the-Sun Road as well as Amtrak and US 2. In the evening you'll want to come home, mellow out in the hot tub, have dinner at the restaurant, and head for your queen-size bed. Knotty-pine panels give a warm, rustic glow to these affordable rooms.

All rooms have satellite TV. The summer rate for a room with one queen-size bed is $80; 2 queen-size beds, $90; and 2 queen-size beds and a twin, $95. Winter rates are less, so be sure to inquire. The Glacier Highland also handles car rentals during the summer months.

GLACIER PARK MOTEL &
  CAMPGROUND $$–$$$
7285 US 2 East, Columbia Falls
(406) 892-7686
www.glacierparkmotelandcampground
.com

This 23-unit motel, now part of a larger complex including RV park, camping cabins, tipis and wall tents, laundry, and convenience store, was formerly known by the lengthy name of Western Inn Glacier Mountain Shadows Resort. In addition to its comfortable rooms, the motel offers an outdoor pool and 2 spas. For convenience, its location is hard to beat: it's only a 20-minute drive to Glacier National Park, but all the amenities and activities of the Flathead Valley are nearby. Kids take note: right across the road is the Big Sky Waterslide. Rooms run from $110 to $125 a night, based on double occupancy. Family suites ($125 to $165) that sleep as many as 6 are also available, and the place is super pet-friendly.

GLACIER PARK SUPER 8 $–$$
7336 US 2 East, Columbia Falls
(406) 892-0888, (800) 800-8000

You may think all Super 8s are alike, but you'll change your mind after walking into the lobby at this one. The entrance displays a remarkable collection of mounted animals—if you didn't see it in the woods, you'll probably find it here. But, as across the country, Super 8 supplies clean, comfortable rooms for travelers at a reasonable rate. The 32 rooms include some special rooms with Jacuzzis or kitchenettes. Both non-smoking and wheelchair-accessible rooms are available. The motel includes a spa, copy machine, fax, and meeting room; all rooms have their own television with HBO, ESPN, and Disney channels. Complimentary continental breakfast is served each morning. Room rates range from $50 in the winter to $95 in the summer for 2 people per night, depending on the size of the room and included amenities.

Bed-and-Breakfasts

BAD ROCK B&B　　　　　　　　$$$–$$$$
480 Bad Rock Dr.
(406) 892-2829, (888) 892-2829
www.badrock.com

Your hosts, Serena and Mark Jackson, invite you to enjoy this elegant Big Sky home. Bad Rock B&B sits in open meadows framed with towering pines, and every window offers huge views of the Swan and Whitefish Mountain ranges.

Bad Rock has Big Sky flair. The bedrooms are large; one has its own balcony for sunset viewing. The living room offers a fireplace and comfortable sofas and chairs for reading or spending time with other visitors. Downstairs is a gathering room, with a guest bar stocked with juice, wine, beer, and snacks. Bad Rock also makes exploring easy. Each room has a copy of the *Bad Rock Bible,* 70 pages of detailed descriptions of things to do and places to go. They also loan all kinds of gear to guests—from fanny packs to kayaks and bicycles.

A little back from the main house across the lawn, you'll find Bad Rock Junction, described as "a mini-town of western log houses styled after those built by Scandinavian settlers in the 1850s." The 4 guest rooms here, each named for a lake in Glacier National Park, along with the newer Swan Mountain Cabin, feature handmade lodgepole pine furniture, gas fireplaces, and large private baths. Each has its own entrance.

A full breakfast is included with all rooms. Breakfast is hearty—depending on the day of the week, you'll be treated to creations such as spinach quiche, bacon-wrapped polenta, fluffy Belgian waffles with strawberries, or Montana potato pie.

Rates vary with the season. Rooms in the house range from $125 to $195 per night for 2; rooms at Bad Rock Junction run from $125 to $250. All rooms have private bath and telephone. The entire complex may also be rented.

✳GLACIER B&B　　　　　　　　$–$$
220 Beta Rd., Hungry Horse 59919
(406) 387-4551

Visiting the Glacier B&B is an experience. In spring and summer the yard is edged all around with tulips, poppies, peonies, and lots and lots of roses—you won't even have to bend over to smell the fragrance! Indoors you'll find yet more flowers, along with an impressive collection of mounted fish and game trophies. Host Bob Johnson is a fisherman and hunter of many years' experience, and he has bagged elk, lynx, bobcat, buffalo, wild turkey, and more—as well as plenty of fish species—and every mount has a story behind it. Bob knows the state and its backcountry well, and he can tell some fascinating tales.

Bob's log home and separate cabins offer comfortable and gracious accommodations. Each of the 4 lodge rooms has its own bath. One includes a king-size bed and Jacuzzi; another rents as a suite with a kitchenette. The common living room and dining room are brightened with skylights by day and the fireplace by evening. A big deck overlooks the yard and gardens, and a full breakfast is served each morning between 6 and 8 a.m.

The Glacier B&B is open year-round. In the summer, rooms rent for $75 to $100 per night for 2 people, with a $10 charge for each additional person. Rates for winter, when breakfast is not served, are substantially less. The cabins, which accommodate up to 3 people, go for $110 per night in the summer (breakfast not included).

GLACIER PARK INN B&B   **$$$–$$$$**
9128 US 2 East
P.O. Box 190753, Hungry Horse 59919
(406) 387-5099
www.glacierparkinn.com
Located just 9 miles west of West Glacier, the Glacier Park Inn is a newly remodeled, octagonal shaped home that features 5 rooms, each with a private bath. One of them, the Many Glacier Family Area, can accommodate as many as 6 guests. After its location so close to the park, Glacier Park Inn's biggest draw is certainly the view from its location on the Middle Fork of the Flathead River—you might decide just hanging out on the deck is enough of a vacation in itself! But your hosts, Mary and Mark Robertson, will be happy to hook you up with all sorts of outdoor activities if you've a bit more energy than that. Room rates range from $120 to $200 per night. The entire facility may also be rented by the day or week.

⁕THE WAY LESS
   TRAVELED B&B   **$$–$$$**
North Fork Road, Polebridge
(406) 261-5880
www.thewaylesstraveled.com
The Way Less Traveled is definitely not a place you will just happen by as you drive from point A to point B in Glacier Country. The 3-room B&B is nestled in the woods 17 miles north of Polebridge just 3 miles from the Canadian border, giving it distinction as the northernmost bed-and-breakfast enterprise in the state of Montana. Hosts Nancy and Paul Winkler can give you some great ideas on where to go hiking or mountain biking in the North Fork, which is a real Montana backwoods holdout (much like the Yaak area, lying about 60 miles due west of the North Fork). Come winter, activities include snowshoeing, cross-country skiing, and curling up by the fire with a good book and a steaming mug of gourmet hot chocolate. The rooms here rent for between $90 and $110 per night.

Guest Ranches, Resorts & Lodges

⁕BELTON CHALET   **$$$–$$$$**
US 2, West Glacier
(406) 888-5000, (888) BELTON-5
www.beltonchalet.com
The original Belton Chalet was completed in 1910, the same year Congress established Glacier National Park. The balconies and gables typify the Swiss-chalet design of the Great Northern's train stations and hotels throughout the park. Built as a railroad inn, the Belton Chalet also served as the park's first winter headquarters. It closed as a hotel during World War II and only in recent years was it fully renovated and restored to its original beauty.

The "chalet" now consists of the 25-room Belton Lodge and a pair of private cottages named "Lewis" and "Clark." There's a wide range of lodging options: from a chalet room with a communal bath, to the honeymoon suite with its private balcony and antique clawfoot tub, or one of the separate cottages. The enterprise also includes the **Grill Dining Room & Tap Room,** serving drinks and dinner 7 days a week from late May through early Oct, and Fri through Sun during the winter (early Dec through late Mar).

(Q) Close-up

Be "Bear Aware"

Glacier National Park is at the core of an immense wilderness ecosystem that provides one of the last remaining refuges in the Lower 48 for the grizzly bear. As such, numerous risks and rewards are associated with a visit to this area, and an encounter with a wild animal—including bears—is always possible when you're in the out of doors. Bears are naturally wary of humans, but they can also be unpredictable and may attack without warning.

Visitors to Glacier Country have been injured and killed by bears, and, in some cases, humans' careless actions have resulted in the bears' removal. Your knowledge of bear habitat and behavior can help reduce your chances of a dangerous encounter—thereby keeping both you and the bears more safe.

The following practices are well-accepted means to increase your margin of safety in bear country:

- **Never Hike Alone.** Solo hikers have been involved in a number of tragic bear encounters. Hiking in a group reduces the chances that you'll be attacked (especially if you hike with people who are slower runners than you!).

- **Make Noise.** Use your vocal cords liberally when hiking or camping, in order to alert bears and other wild animals to your presence. Bear bells are a popular noisemaker, as well. Use extra caution, and make extra noise, in brushy areas, on blind curves, and when wind or running water might mask the sound of your approach.

- **Stay on the Trail.** Visibility is usually better on the trail, and human activity is generally more common than off the trails, thus giving you a greater margin of safety.

- **Hike When it is Safest.** Bears can be active both day and night, but tend to be out and about more at dawn or dusk and during the night.

- **Avoid Bears' Prime Food Sources.** Bears will vigorously defend food sources. Never approach a smelly animal carcass and beware of other areas with abundant food sources such as berries, bulbs, grasses, and flowers.

- **Be Alert for Bear Sign.** Fresh bear scat (dung), tracks, or signs of digging may indicate a bear is in the area. Be extra careful and extra loud.

- **Enjoy Wildlife at a Distance.** Never intentionally approach or feed wildlife, and be aware of one of the most dangerous situations; a female bear with cubs. If you encounter such a scenario, immediately leave the area. If you have no other choice, turn around and go back down the trail.

- **Secure Food, Garbage, and Cookware Properly.** These items should always be hung or stashed out of reach of bears except at mealtimes (your mealtimes, that is). Check with the National Park Service or USDA Forest Service for specific regulations and for the locations of bear-proof storage boxes.

- **Respect Closures.** Trail and campground closures resulting from bear danger are common in Glacier. It is both unsafe and illegal to enter a closed area, so heed the signs for your own safety.

The Belton Chalet is located in the heart of West Glacier, just a step across the road from the West Glacier Amtrak depot and a 2-minute drive from the west entrance to Glacier National Park. Hiking, horseback riding, bus tours, whitewater rafting, cross-country skiing, and snowshoeing are all readily accessible.

Summer room rates for 2 people per night run from $155 to $180. Cabins, which sleep up to 6, rent for $325, and require a minimum 2-night stay during the peak season. Rates are discounted during the spring and fall shoulder seasons and in the winter, when only the cottages are available to rent.

IZAAK WALTON INN $$–$$$$
P.O. Box 653, Essex 59916
(406) 888-5700
www.izaakwaltoninn.com

History comes alive at the Izaak Walton Inn, built in 1939 to house Great Northern Railway crews working the trains that traveled over Marias Pass. It's located right on the rail line, and today's guests enjoy waving to Amtrak passengers as the trains pass by. The only flag stop on Amtrak's Empire Builder route—Seattle to Chicago—is at Essex, moments from the inn's door. The association with the railroad is evident throughout the inn—in the bar downstairs, for example, are fascinating photos of historic engines, avalanches over the tracks, and even train wrecks. And the whistle and rumble of passing trains will bring you back to the present, while dreaming of the past.

All rail history aside, the Izaak Walton Inn is as cozy a getaway as you'll find. When you see the very inviting lobby, you'll want to find a good book and curl up by the fire, or perhaps spend some time chatting with your fellow guests. The Dining Car Restaurant—open for breakfast, lunch, and dinner—is charming and bright. All rooms have been remodeled in recent years to include a private bath, but the original character of the inn is firmly intact.

During winter, the Izaak Walton Inn offers a stellar network of groomed cross-country ski trails, which become walking paths in the summer. The resort is perched on the edge of the Great Bear/Bob Marshall Wilderness and just across the river from Glacier National Park, close to millions of acres of hiking, riding, snowshoeing, and ski-touring terrain. The inn's trained guides will show you the backcountry on skis in the winter, and the inn will be happy to help you arrange raft trips, bus tours through the park, or guided hikes during the summer.

Basic, double-occupancy rooms run from $117 to $168 per night. The inn also offers family rooms beginning at $235 per night. Four "caboose cottages"—renovated cabooses with heat, full kitchen, and bath—go for $230 per night and require a minimum 2-night stay. The Inn also offers 3-, 4-, and 5-day packages that include 2 or 3 meals per day in addition to a choice of guided outdoor activities, from whitewater rafting in summer to guided snowshoe treks in winter.

GREAT NORTHERN WHITEWATER
RAFT & RESORT $$–$$$$
P.O. Box 270, West Glacier 59936
(406) 387-5340, (800) 735-7897
www.gnwhitewater.com

You won't miss the Great Northern Whitewater Resort—the bright red caboose and Swiss log chalets will grab your attention as you drive by. The resort is located just 1 mile west of West Glacier, providing easy access to everything the area has to offer. The chalet balconies offer beautiful views of Desert and Strawberry Mountains, as well as the little nubbin known as Chocolate Drop—it's about the shape of a Hershey's Kiss! The charming log chalets are furnished and have fully equipped kitchens. The 3 larger chalets feature gas fireplaces. All are nonpet and nonsmoking.

The Great Northern also is headquarters for all sorts of outdoor activities. Full- and half-day whitewater raft trips, kayak clinics, and fishing trips can be arranged. Fly-fishing "school" is an option for those just getting their feet wet. If you're looking for a longer trip, the Great Northern offers extended 2- and 3-day whitewater trips. And, at the end of your adventures, you can relax in the swim spa back at the resort.

The chalets accommodate 6 to 8 persons (with 2 or 3 queen-size beds and a sleeper sofa) and vary in price according to the season. The smaller chalets, Two Bear and Osprey, range from $99 to $260 per night. The larger chalets, Wapiti, Moose, and Tatonka, range from $150 to $295 per night. During the peak seasons, late June through late Aug and the week of Christmas, a 3-night minimum stay is required.

MEADOW LAKE RESORT $$$–$$$$
100 St. Andrews Dr.
(406) 892-7601, (800) 321-GOLF
www.meadowlake.com
Located on Meadow Lake Golf Course, this large resort maintains inn rooms, condo suites, and 1- and 2-bedroom condos, as well as 2- to 5-bedroom vacation homes. It's built on gentle hills and many trees grace the fairways, so it feels almost like a very pretty neighborhood. The 18-hole golf course sets the tone, but, in addition to the pro shop and market, you'll find a recreation center with Nautilus and aerobic machines, pools, and spas. "Troop Meadow Lake" provides supervised children's activities throughout the week, and there's a children's playground, too. **Truby's,** long a favorite in downtown Whitefish, recently picked up and moved to Meadow Lake Resort, where they serve their famous brick-oven pizzas as well as other favorites—wild-caught salmon, chicken-fried steak, and barbecued chicken, for starters. Truby's is open for lunch and dinner 7 days a week.

The Spa at Meadow Lake boasts of being the premier spa facility in all of northwest Montana, and it features 4 treatment rooms and a relaxation room. Meadow Lake provides a good base location for exploring Glacier Country. Glacier National Park is about a 25-minute drive to the east, the Whitefish Mountain Resort lies about 25 minutes to the west, and Flathead Lake is roughly 30 minutes away to the south.

A room at the Meadow Lake Inn runs from $139 to $189, depending on the season. Condos range from $139 to $365, depending on size and season. Vacation homes, with 2 to 5 bedrooms, run from $160 to $620 per night. The new Glacier Village luxury condos go for between $145 and $475.

SILVERWOLF CHALETS $$$
P.O. Box 115, West Glacier 59936
(406) 387-4448
www.silverwolfchalets.com
"Designer log cabins for two"—10 log chalets tailored for two make up the Silverwolf. You'll find each perfect little cabin has its own queen-size log bed with handmade quilt, gas fireplace, private bath, and a cupboard tastefully concealing a microwave, small refrigerator, and coffeemaker. Breakfast is brought to your cabin, but if you don't want to stay indoors on a beautiful day, you

can of course step out and enjoy your gourmet Colombian coffee on your own porch.

The cabins are nestled in a landscaped and forested setting that fosters privacy and quiet. The resort caters to adults, and pets and smoking are not allowed on the premises. One cabin is wheelchair accessible, and one has 2 oversized single beds. The Silverwolf is open from mid-May until mid-Oct. Rates vary by season and range from $136 to $168 for 2 people per night.

TIMBER WOLF RESORT   **$-$$**
P.O. Box 190800, 9105 US 2 East, Hungry Horse 59919
(406) 387-9653
www.timberwolfresort.com
With RV and tent sites, rustic and deluxe cabins, and a bed-and-breakfast, the Timber Wolf Resort has just about everything in terms of overnighting options. The 20-acre property is practically a small town in the middle of the summer—complete with its own convenience store and gathering room—but the grounds are so spacious, hilly, and nicely wooded that no one feels crowded.

If it's an RV site you're looking for, the resort has 12 full hookup sites going for $36 per night, and 12 with just electric, for $30 per night. Both pull-through and back-in sites are available. Tent sites cost $24 per night.

Sleeping cabins, dubbed either a Ranger, Mountaineer, or Pioneer cabin, range from rustic to deluxe. Rustic cabins renting for $48 per night have a double bunk bed, but are otherwise unfurnished; bring your own linens or sleeping bag, or you can rent from the resort. Deluxe cabins are furnished and have a double bunk bed with linens, heat, and electricity. These cabins rent for $52 to $84 per night.

The Timber Wolf also operates two B&B lodge rooms with a shared bath. Queen-size beds with handmade quilts will keep you cozy, and you'll enjoy the peak-season amenities of satellite TV and in-room phone. Lodge rooms rent for $95 per night.

The Timber Wolf Resort offers some beautiful views toward Glacier National Park and Columbia Mountain in the Swan Range. You'll find the practical details fall into place, too: The resort includes coin-op showers (and you can rent towels), laundry, gift shop, a gazebo with 3 barbecue grills, a children's play area, and picnic tables. All buildings are nonsmoking; be sure to inquire about the pet policy. The Timber Wolf's heated cabins and lodge rooms are open the year around, while the rest of the resort operates during the summer months only.

Campgrounds & RV Parks

Price Code
$.................. Less than $10
$$ .... $10 to $16
$$$ .... $16 to $24
$$$$ .... More than $24

CANYON RV AND CAMPGROUND   **$**
P.O. Box 7, 9540 US 2 East, Hungry Horse 59919
(406) 387-9393
www.montanacampground.com
Canyon RV and Campground is located just east of Hungry Horse and its property runs right along the Middle Fork of the Flathead River, providing both views and fishing access. The campground has quite a variety of sites—"No rig too big" is their way of saying that they can accommodate any RV. There are 10 tent sites available, and Canyon also has six 12 x 12 sleeping cabins (bring-your-own-bedding). Hot showers, a

dump station, and a small store are all found on-site.

Canyon RV is open from May 1 to Sept 30. Tent sites run $25 per night; the 51 RV sites range from $27 with no hookup to $37 for full service. Sleeping cabins rent for $63 per night. All rates are based on 2 people; if more are involved, so too may be additional fees. Pets are permitted on leash (though they're not allowed in the cabins). Reservations are recommended for July and Aug.

COLUMBIA FALLS RV PARK $
**P.O. Box 508, 1000 Third Ave. East,
Columbia Falls 59912
(406) 892-1122, (888) 401-7268
www.columbiafallsrvpark.com**

Columbia Falls RV Park really is at the Gateway to Glacier National Park, right on US 2 where it leaves Columbia Falls and heads up toward the park. The RV park itself includes a laundry, showers, bathrooms, store, and a gift shop featuring local crafts, but if there's something you can't find here, Columbia Falls is right out your back door with both retail and dining establishments. And, when it comes time to fire up the grill, there's an outstanding family-owned custom meat shop right next door.

This facility features 51 pull-through RV sites and 13 back-in sites. All have water, sewer, and electric hookups and begin at $35 per night (pay for 6 nights and the 7th night is free). Cable is available at some sites. Several secluded tent sites are also available and begin at $24 per night. Pets are allowed on a leash, and owners must clean up after them. Reservations recommended during the summer season.

DEVIL CREEK CAMPGROUND $
**Mile marker 190, US 2
Hungry Horse Ranger District
Flathead National Forest, Hungry Horse
(406) 387-3800**

The 14 sites of Devil Creek Campground are open from around Memorial Day (depending on snow conditions) to mid-Sept. Drinking water and vault toilets are available, and a campground host is in residence during the summer. Forest Service Trail #167 (Devil Creek) is nearby. Some double-wide or long sites will accommodate RVs, although there are no hookups. There's no garbage pickup, so all campers must pack it in, pack it out. Because this is grizzly habitat, all food (including pet food and garbage) must be kept in a hard-sided vehicle whenever it is not being prepared. Horses are not permitted in the campground.

A fee of $10 per night is charged during the summer. Reservations are not accepted. For late-season visitors, the campground is open without charge until closed by weather, but water is not available and outhouses are not regularly cleaned. The campground is approximately 8 miles east of Essex and 7 miles west of Marias Pass along US 2.

GLACIER MEADOW CAMPGROUND $
**P.O. Box 124, East Glacier 59434
Between mile markers 191 and 192
US 2 East
(406) 226-4479
www.glaciermeadowrvpark.com**

Situated on an expansive 58 acres of private property, this campground occupies a beautiful meadow but also edges into the trees, thereby offering both sun and shade throughout the summer months. Campers of all sorts are welcome, including those with horses in tow (boarding is available).

Glacier Meadow has wide, long pull-through sites, sites with electric and water hookups, back-in sites with electric only, and tent sites. It also can accommodate groups of all sizes—up to 1,000 people! A playground, shower house, dump station, and covered pavilion will all make your stay comfortable and convenient. A small store sells propane, ice, and other essentials. And if you want to travel the information highway while staying put, the enterprise has wireless Internet.

Glacier Meadow Campground is open from May 15 to Sept 15, weather permitting. Rates for 2 people run from approximately $20 for tenters to $34 for RVs. Add $5 for each additional person over 10 years old. Because this is grizzly habitat, all food (including pet food and garbage) must be kept in a hard-sided vehicle whenever it's not being prepared. Pets are permitted on leash; owners are expected to clean up after their pets. Reservations are recommended, especially for groups.

MOUNTAIN MEADOWS RV PARK AND CAMPGROUND $
P.O. Box 190442, 9125 US 2 East, Hungry Horse 59919
(406) 387-9125
www.mmrvpark.com

The literature for Mountain Meadows RV Park and Campground describes it as "Montana's Most Beautiful Campground"—and, once you drive in, you may well agree. RV sites are spacious for those with slide-outs and awnings, and will accommodate motorhomes 40-plus feet long. But the setting is what makes it special: The campground is on a gently sloping hill with many trees, yet it looks out over the valley. A lovely little pond, stocked with rainbow trout, graces a meadow that offers big

views toward Columbia Mountain, Teakettle Mountain, and Bad Rock Canyon.

Mountain Meadows provides just about every conceivable service. All sites have picnic tables and campfire/barbecue grills. Restrooms and hot showers are clean. The laundry room is open 24 hours a day. A dump station and mobile pump-out service are available, and the campground store sells souvenirs, ice cream, snacks, milk, pop, ice, firewood, and fishing tackle, as well as camping and RV supplies. You can even rent a fishing pole. Leashed pets are OK.

Mountain Meadows is open from May 1 until Sept 30. Reservations are strongly recommended for July and Aug. Full hookups are $38 per night; sites with water and electric hookups only (no sewer) are $35 per night. No tent sites are available, but rustic camping cabins are, and they begin at $55 per night.

SUMMIT CAMPGROUND $
Marias Pass, US 2
Rocky Mountain Ranger District
Lewis and Clark National Forest Choteau
(406) 466-5341

This small Forest Service campground is conveniently located at Marias Pass, 12 miles west of East Glacier on US 2. The site is wooded, which you'll be grateful for, as the Continental Divide can be a windy place to camp. Nevertheless, it's a wonderful site—not only for Memorial Square and its monuments, but also for the imposing peaks just across the highway: Summit and Little Dog Mountains. If it's geology that rocks your clock, take a few moments to scan these peaks: You'll be able to pick out the Lewis Overthrust Fault, where younger rocks rode up and over the older rocks beneath. The fault line looks like a dark band in the side of the mountains, almost as if there were a road halfway up the slope. North of US 2, you're in Glacier National Park. Three Bears Lake is an easy hike in from the road, and the trail then continues both east and west below the mountains. Be sure to make lots of noise—although you're not far from a major highway, this is indisputably bear country.

Summit Campground's 17 sites are generally open from about Memorial Day (depending on the snowpack) to Labor Day, and a campground host is on-site to help if you have questions or concerns. Several sites will accommodate RVs up to 35 feet long, but there are no hookups. The campground has drinking water and vault toilets; additional amenities include fire grates and picnic tables. Because this is grizzly habitat, all food (including pet food and garbage) must be kept in a hard-sided vehicle whenever it is not being prepared. Sites are $10 per night. Be aware that Summit Campground can be very busy and often fills between July 4 and Labor Day.

TIMBER WOLF RESORT $
P.O. Box 190800, 9105 US 2 East, Hungry Horse 59919
(406) 387-9653
www.timberwolfresort.com
If you're looking for an RV site, this resort has a cool two dozen of them, 12 with full hookups for $36 per night, and 12 with just electric for $30 per night. Both pull-through and back-in sites are available. Tent sites cost $24 per night. If you want to make an off-season visit, the campground water is turned on in May and off in Oct depending on weather, but with advance notice the owners will even plow a spot for your RV!

The Timber Wolf Resort offers some beautiful views toward Glacier National Park

and Columbia Mountain in the Swan Range. The resort includes showers, laundry, convenience and gift shop, a gazebo with 3 barbecue grills, a children's play area, and picnic tables. All buildings are nonsmoking; inquire in advance about their pet policy.

RESTAURANTS

Price Code
The following listings rate restaurants according to a 4-symbol price key, representing the average cost of dinner for two people. The code excludes the price of beverages, tax, and gratuity.

$.....................	**$10 to $20**
$$	**$20 to $28**
$$$	**$28 to $35**
$$$$	**More than $35**

THE BACK ROOM $–$$
522 Ninth St. West, Columbia Falls
(406) 892-3131
http://backroom.dropzite.com
The Back Room is definitely a locals' spot—no fuss, no muss. But if you're ready for good home cookin', this is the place to go. The specialty is pork ribs, smoked on-site, but also recommended are the locally cut steaks, rotisserie chicken, pasta and pizza, and seafood. Most dinners come with all the Back Room "trimmings": baby red potatoes, coleslaw, baked beans, and fry bread with whipped honey butter. Not for the faint of heart or diminutive of stomach! The portions are generous—lots of folks will be taking home doggie bags and enjoying the leftovers tomorrow.

Back Room dinner entrees run from around $5 to $15; 10-, 13-, and 15-inch pizzas go for $10 to $16 or so. The Back Room also sells its specialty spice and barbecue sauce to take home. Both seniors' and kids' menus are available, and take-out orders are, too. The Back Room is open from 4 to 9 p.m. Mon through Sat, and opens at 2 p.m. on Sun.

i Wolves were once the most widely distributed mammal in North America, but they were exterminated throughout much of the continent. In Montana, the last wolf was shot around 1930. Although occasionally individual animals wandered down through the state from Canada, not until 1986 was there pack—or family—activity here again. That's the year a female wolf crossed south over the international border and gave birth to a litter of pups in Glacier National Park. It was the beginning of a naturally occurring recolonization of the area that continues to this day. Your best chance of seeing—or hearing—wolves is up the North Fork of the Flathead River. A fair number of people will see tracks in this area; some will hear the wolves howling, and a very few lucky folks will actually see them.

BELTON CHALET $$–$$$$
US 2, West Glacier
(406) 888-5000, (888) BELTON-5
www.beltonchalet.com

The Belton Chalet's Grill Dining Room and Tap Room offer a glimpse into this beautifully renovated, historic lodge and are well worth stopping to see, so consider taking a few moments to check them out. The lunch menu includes soups, salads, and sandwiches, or you can order a box lunch to go. The Tap Room features Montana microbrewsl. If it's a sunny summer afternoon, you can sip yours on the deck. Salads, sandwiches, and appetizers in the Tap Room go for between $9 and $14, while entrees in the Grill Dining Room range from $20 to $34. Representative of the dinner menu are items like stuffed veal, Montana bison meatloaf, and locally raised jerk marinated pork loin.

CIMARRON DELI AND CATERING $
700 Ninth St. West, Columbia Falls
(406) 892-9000

This full-service deli includes a small seating area, but it's also a great place to pick up a picnic "to go"—the variety of fresh sandwiches made to your order, hot sandwiches, and homemade soup will give you lots to choose from. For example, check out the section on chicken—the "chicken coop"—which includes several different kinds of "hot chicks": Monterey, Lorraine, BBQ, Chipotle, Malibu, Southwest, and a chicken breast sandwich with lemon pepper. Also have a look at the equally long list of salads. Prices run from $5 to $10.50, and the deli carries a selection of beverages and desserts. Cimarron Deli also caters and creates party trays.

GLACIER GRILL AND PIZZA $$
10126 US 2 East, Coram
(406) 387-4223

The Glacier Grill and Pizza is the place to go in Coram . . . and it had gotten so popular and busy over the years that they recently expanded the building. Family friendly and comfortable, you'll enjoy taking the evening off and just mellowing out in this local favorite. Pizza is what it's all about, and the salads and wings are also great. Try a huckleberry shake! Unlike several restaurants up in West Glacier, the Glacier Grill is open year-round.

Close-up

Mountain Goats & Bighorn Sheep

It's no surprise that looking for animals is a favorite activity for visitors in Glacier National Park, and with minimal effort you're almost certain to at least see **mountain goats**. "Goat" is something of a misnomer; these animals are more closely related to the chamois of Europe than to any domestic goat. They can look ragged in the early summer when they are shedding the previous winter's extra fur, but by August or so they're sparkling white with their new, trim summer coats. Some Native Americans called them the white buffalo, and even today mountain goats sometimes trigger reports of polar bears at Logan Pass!

A symbol of the mountains (and of the Great Northern Railway), the goat is perfectly adapted to its high mountain home. Its hooves are sharp on the rim, for good purchase in soft rock and snow, but they are spongy in the middle, giving the goat traction on hard, flat rock. Its shoulders are massive, allowing it to climb and descend amazingly steep slopes. The animal's fur is dense, with an outer layer for protection from rain and snow and an inner layer for insulation. Goats live in the cliffs, which are their harbor—few predators can follow them along the steep faces and narrow ledges that they traverse with such apparent ease. When winter comes they may move to lower, lee-side cliffs, but they continue to prefer the steep terrain. With the summer grasses gone, goats lick lichens from the rocks with tongues as rough as sandpaper: so the saying goes, "goats like lickin' lichen"!

Scan the steep, rocky cliffs of the park to see goats. Logan Pass, Many Glacier, and Two Medicine all have the rugged terrain these mountain dwellers prefer.

Bighorn sheep range often overlaps with that of mountain goats. While goats tend toward the higher cliffs, sheep favor the open, grassy slopes just below them. They depend more on their speed to outrun predators. Sometimes goats and sheep will graze close together, and their young have even been known to play together at an early age.

Bighorn sheep are brown with a cream-colored rump patch; the rams carry their namesake curling horns. The bigger the curl, the older the ram. Females are smaller and sport spike horns, similar to those worn by goats of both sexes. Sheep are more of a herd animal than goats are; in the summertime, the ewes form bands and go off to have their young, while rams form bachelor bands that often move to higher country. As fall comes on, however, all groups reconvene and move to lower elevations where the winter is just a little bit milder.

Currently there is no precise count of sheep or goats in Glacier. Clearly, though, there are more goats than sheep. Good places to look for sheep include Logan Pass, across from the visitor center on the slopes of Pollock Mountain; the slopes of Piegan Mountain, just up from Siyeh Bend on Going-to-the-Sun Road; the Many Glacier Valley; the Highline Trail between Logan Pass and Granite Park; and the Two Medicine Valley.

THE GLACIER HIGHLAND $
US 2 East, West Glacier
(406) 888-5427
www.glacierhighland.com

The Glacier Highland's restaurant offers home-cooked food at affordable prices. Open for breakfast, lunch, and dinner from May through Oct, hearty hikers' breakfast items include pancakes, eggs, and Black Forest ham. Lunch and dinner feature sandwiches, soups, burgers, and Rocky Mountain trout. If you have any room left afterward, you'll want to top it off with pie, huckleberry no doubt—or maybe the huck pie is the reason to stop by in the first place. The Glacier Highland is located directly across from the Amtrak station in West Glacier, minutes from the west entrance to Glacier National Park.

IZAAK WALTON INN $$–$$$
P.O. Box 653, Essex 59916
(406) 888-5700
www.izaakwaltoninn.com

Even if overnighting at the singular Izaak Walton Inn is not on your itinerary, if you're driving by on US 2 you should at least swing in for a meal. The Dining Car Restaurant is open for breakfast (suggested: huckleberry pancakes with thick-sliced bacon), lunch (buffalo French dip), and dinner (huckleberry glazed pork shanks), and makes a great excuse to stop and explore this fascinating historic inn.

The dining room is charming, its dark wood, flowers, and train motifs intermingling to create a cozy and relaxed ambience. The menu features "comfort foods"—including Montana specialties like buffalo meats and, of course, huckleberries (the huckleberry cobbler gets rave reviews). Before or after an active day outdoors, this is the perfect place to fuel up or wind down. It's open from 7:30 a.m. to 8 p.m.; dinner entrees range from $15 to $26.

*TIEN'S PLACE $
329 Ninth St. West, Columbia Falls
(406) 892-1585

After escaping communist Vietnam in a fishing boat packed elbow-to-elbow with other children, Tien Pham ended up in Columbia Falls in March of 1984. The 12-year-old didn't know where he was, it was strangely cold, and he had never before seen that white stuff covering the ground. He had been adopted through the Lutheran Social Services by locals Bob and Judy Windauer.

Today, Tien's Oriental restaurant, which he launched in 2003, serves everything from spicy kung pao chicken to Philly cheesesteak sandwiches to diverse combo platters made up of an array of Asian dishes. And Tien Pham Windauer gives back in spades to the community that has supported him and helped make his restaurant a success.

Tien's is perhaps like the Oriental restaurant you frequent back home—not fancy, but the food's great and it doesn't take long to get it. Conveniently located, it makes an easy stop on your way home from a day of exploring, or you can call in advance and pick up your order to go.

Lunch is from 11 a.m. to 3 p.m. and features a variety of specials—standards like lemon chicken, but also Asian BBQ chicken or beef, and vegetarian dishes. Appetizers, soups, and quite a few a la carte items can also be ordered, and the menu includes burgers for those who prefer to leave their chopsticks in the wrapper.

Dinner is from 4:30 to 9 p.m. Sun through Thur and from 4:30 to 9:30 p.m. on Fri and Sat nights. The dinner menu is more extensive than the lunch menu and includes beef, pork, chicken, seafood, and combination plates. Tien's Place also offers "international selections," which are preset dinner menus meant to be ordered for the whole table and priced per person. A small dessert list finishes the menu—and, of course, a fortune cookie.

WEST GLACIER RESTAURANT
AND BAR $
West Glacier
(406) 888-5359

After a great day rafting the Middle Fork—or hiking to Apgar Lookout, perhaps—you'll enjoy not having to drive far to find a good dinner. The West Glacier Restaurant, part of the West Glacier Village complex, is just outside the park boundary in West Glacier, ready with breakfast, lunch, and dinner. The relaxed, family atmosphere makes it a great place to rev up or wind down. And you're sure to find a huckleberry treat (ice cream, pie, soda) to complete your day in Glacier Country. The West Glacier Restaurant is open from mid-May to late Sept.

NIGHTLIFE

The nightlife is a little bit sleepy in this neck of the woods, but there are a few spots where you're sure to enjoy putting your feet up or letting down your hair. The West Glacier Bar (adjacent to the West Glacier Restaurant) will often have a crowd on the porch in the evening, folks like rafters just off the river swapping stories about getting soaked. The Tap Room at the renovated Belton Chalet offers a cozy atmosphere and an outdoor deck; it's a great place to stop for a beer or cocktail. If it's winter, after a day of cross-country skiing or snowshoeing you can do no better than chugging in to the

Flag Stop Bar at the Izaak Walton Inn for a cup of "fortified" hot chocolate.

Or, if you're down in the Flathead Valley and feeling adventurous, try the Blue Moon Nite Club. It's a slice of Montana life and a landmark—located at the junction of US 2 and Highway 40, about halfway between Columbia Falls and Whitefish, which everyone around here refers to as the Blue Moon junction. This grill, casino, and nightclub has it all: live music, karaoke, special events, and dancing.

SHOPPING

Breathtaking views and the great outdoors take priority for most visitors to Glacier Country, no doubt, but you should also pay visits to these indoor places.

GLACIER ASSOCIATION
US 2, West Glacier
(406) 888-5756
www.glacierassociation.org

Located in the historic Belton depot in West Glacier, the Glacier Association is a cooperating partner of Glacier National Park. It sells books, videos, maps, posters, and more on subjects related to the park, and profits generated are used to enhance the park's educational programs. All that serious stuff aside, the association's store is a great place to shop! For anyone who's enjoyed their time in the mountains, this beautiful shop offers a huge selection of books covering geology, history, Native American culture, plants, and animals—everything from *Alces alces shirasi* (aka the moose) to *Zigadenus elegans* (the lovingly named mountain death camas). Other items include field guides, photo books, and children's books. And you'll have a hard time deciding which beautiful poster to take home to frame your visit to

Glacier. Open from 8 a.m. until 4:30 p.m. Mon through Fri.

IZAAK WALTON INN
P.O. Box 653, Essex 59916
(406) 888-5700
www.izaakwaltoninn.com
The Izaak Walton Inn has a small but enticing gift shop selling a variety of items all related to Glacier National Park, the inn itself, or the Great Northern Railway. You'll find teddy bears, locally crafted silver and antler jewelry, Christmas ornaments, maps and books, ball caps, t-shirts, outerwear, and more. The inn has even arranged for the reproduction of the Great Northern Railway's "Glory of the West" china pattern, used on the Empire Builder route from 1940 to 1957. This is a fun place to spend some time. The owners have been clever and selective in choosing the souvenirs they offer for sale.

BIGFORK

Bigfork, "Where Flathead Lake Begins, is located at the northeast corner of the big pond. It's a combination of the perfect Montana small town, the perfect lakeside village, the perfect tourist destination, and the perfect artists' colony. When you get right down to it, what visitors and residents all seem to agree on is that Bigfork is, well, *perfect*.

Bigfork is located on Highway 35, which hugs the eastern shore of Flathead Lake from Polson in the south to just north of Bigfork. The community sits at the mouth of the Swan River where it empties into Flathead Lake, the largest natural freshwater lake west of Minnesota. The lake and the river provide the crux of the recreational opportunities in Bigfork—with fishing for mackinaw, rainbow, cutthroat, perch, bass, and northern pike all available nearby—but the town is also just 17 miles from Kalispell and 45 miles from Glacier National Park, so there's a lot more to do in a day than go boating or fishing. East of Bigfork is the 950,000-acre Bob Marshall Wilderness, a favorite of local backcountry hikers and horsemen. The Jewel Basin Hiking Area is also nearby, with 38 miles of trails that are easy for almost anyone to navigate by foot. The east shore of Flathead Lake is also noted for its cherry orchards, which provide excuses for plenty of "pit stops" by motorists in July and August.

OVERVIEW

The population varies considerably depending on the time of year. Summertime is the high season here, and with Flathead Lake at full pool, the population in this little town soars from 3,500 to as many as 10,000. But in any case, with its economy supported by tourism, Bigfork offers a splendid variety of diversions, from canoeing to bowling, horseback riding to live theater, jet skiing to shopping. Eagle Bend is a world-class golf course not far from downtown, and there's always a new restaurant to try in what is arguably the culinary capital of Glacier Country.

The evolution of Bigfork into something of an artistic mecca goes hand in hand with the opening in 1960 of the Bigfork Summer Playhouse. That repertory company, which was then housed in a rustic building but now performs in air-conditioned comfort in the Bigfork Center for the Performing Arts, started to draw creative people to Bigfork. The tourist trade built up steadily as well, leading to many opportunities for new businesses. Today Electric Avenue—Bigfork's main commercial street—is a bustling row of artists' studios, galleries, gift shops, bookstores, and restaurants. The playhouse's repertory company puts on shows from late May through early Sept. And during some of the annual festivities, such as the Fourth of July or the Bigfork Festival of the Arts, the atmosphere is truly electric, although even on a nonfestival day in summer Electric Avenue lives up to its name (which derives from a small power plant nearby). Sliter Park, located at the end of Electric Avenue and across the old steel bridge, is the venue for live outdoor performances during the summer.

After the larch needles fall, more of a secret is that Bigfork is also a good spot to plan for winter recreation. For one thing, the lake has a modifying effect on the climate, so most winters here are milder than typical for a latitude this far north. And discounted rates at resorts and other lodging facilities are common during the off-season. Here you have the same access to the Flathead National Forest for cross-country skiing and snowmobiling that you would have from elsewhere in the valley, and both the Whitefish Mountain Resort and Blacktail Mountain Ski Area are less than an hour away.

Also definitely worth taking in if time permits is the extraordinarily scenic drive from Bigfork to Swan Lake and Seeley Lake on Highway 83. This trip through what's known locally as the Seeley-Swan Valley typically results in quite a bit of wildlife viewing, especially at dawn and dusk when deer can perhaps too commonly be seen crossing the highway (in other words, drive carefully). Swan Lake and Seeley Lake are both lakes and towns on their respective lakes, the community of Seeley Lake being substantially larger than Swan Lake. The lakes themselves offer excellent recreational opportunities.

ACCOMMODATIONS

Hotels & Motels

Price Code

Keep in mind that some rates are based on availability. The average peak-season nightly rates for two adults at the hotels and motels listed in this section are indicated by a dollar sign ($) ranking in the following chart.

$.................	**Less than $85**
$$	**$85 to $115**
$$$	**$115 to $150**
$$$$	**More than $150**

BIGFORK TIMBERS MOTEL   **$$**
8540 Hwy. 35
(406) 837-6200, (800) 821-4546
The Timbers Motel is the most moderately priced accommodation in Bigfork. It is within walking distance of the village and very close to Wayfarers State Park. There's also trolley bus service to the village during the summer season. The Timbers offers 40 rooms, along with continental breakfast, cable and HBO, and complimentary in-room coffee. The motel also features an outdoor pool in the summer, and a sauna and hot tub year-round. Pets are permitted with a deposit.

WOODS BAY RESORT   **$$-$$$**
26481 East Lakeshore Dr.
(406) 837-3333
www.woodsbayresort.com
Woods Bay is a small lakeside community located on Flathead Lake just 4 miles south of Bigfork, and this small facility offers 6 motel rooms, 5 cabins with kitchens, and 6 RV spots with full hookups. Owners Brad and Susan Western promote the friendly atmosphere; accommodations are clean and comfortable and there's beach access. Cabins are available on a monthly basis in the winter.

Resorts & Guest Ranches

FLATHEAD LAKE LODGE   **$$$$**
P.O. Box 248, Hwy. 35, Bigfork 59911
(406) 837-4391
www.flatheadlakelodge.com

If you're looking for an upscale yet traditional Western experience, consider trying Flathead Lake Lodge, a famous 2,000-acre family-operated dude ranch that attracts celebrities and wealthy businesspeople from around the world, as well as ordinary families that save up for an extraordinary vacation. The 2011 rate for an adult for a week is $3,206, but for that sum you get much more than lodging. All meals and recreation are included in the package, and in the case of Flathead Lake Lodge that means 3 superb meals a day plus horseback riding, rodeo action, cookouts, water sports, use of sailboats, canoes, and fishing boats, waterskiing, lake cruises, a heated pool, tennis courts, volleyball, hiking wilderness and primitive areas, and many other ranch activities. The Averill family has operated the resort for more than 60 years, and they've bid "happy trails" to many hundreds of satisfied guests. It's a real Western vacation in a setting of unmatched luxury and beauty. The ranch offers week-long vacations with everyone arriving and departing on the same day, but you can't just call up and get in the next week. Reservations are often made years in advance, and the lodge boasts a 50 to 60 percent return of guests year after year. It has been featured by *Better Homes & Gardens, Travel + Leisure, Bon Appetite, Good Morning America,* and many others.

✳MARINA CAY RESORT $$$$
180 Vista Lane
(406) 837-5861, (800) 433-6516
www.marinacay.com
This resort is a deluxe facility on Bigfork Bay, just up the hill from the village. Accommodations range from an economy room for 1 or 2 people only with no view to a waterfront marina suite with king-size bed and private

Jacuzzi. One-, two-, and three-bedroom condo rentals are also available. Marina Cay features an outdoor pool and whirlpool, as well as a full-service marina where you can rent a ski boat, Jet Ski, canoe, or other watercraft. Guided fishing charters will escort you to just the right spot to catch "the big one." After you come back for the night, you can enjoy one of three restaurants and several bars and lounges. Visit Marina Cay in the off-season for significant savings. Rates during the high season range from $140 to $499, but they're discounted 25 percent or more from the last week of Sept to the middle of May.

Bed-and-Breakfasts

CANDLEWYCKE INN B&B
311 Aero Lane, Bigfork
(406) 837-6406
www.candlewyckeinn.com
The Candlewycke Inn, hidden in a wooded, wonderfully secluded location not far from town, has 5 rooms for rent, including the Wilderness queen room, the Botanical deluxe Jacuzzi king, and the Country Heaven king. A full gourmet breakfast is part of the package, and arrangements can be made for dinner, as well, if you make reservations before noon. Popular entrees include lamb shanks with Mediterranean couscous, mojito grilled chicken, and citrus-glazed salmon. Room rates are $150 to $165 during the peak season.

COYOTE ROADHOUSE INN &
RIVERHOUSE CABINS $$$–$$$$
602 Three Eagle Lane
(406) 837-4250
This seasonal bed-and-breakfast establishment is an offshoot of the Coyote Roadhouse Restaurant. Owner and chef Gary Hastings decided he wanted to offer intimate

dining experiences to guests, so he started the Roadhouse Inn, which takes maximum advantage of the woodsy setting and adds fine food of a high order. There are 5 cabins on the scenic Swan River with private docks. Barbecues, canoes, and bicycles are available for an extra charge. The Coyote Roadhouse Inn is located near Ferndale off Highway 209 on a scenic portion of the Swan River. This is a great place to get away if you enjoy quiet walks along the river. Nightly rates are $125 to $175; if you want to stay for an entire week, the cost will run from $875 to $1,225.

O'DUACHAIN COUNTRY INN $$$
675 North Ferndale Dr.
(406) 837-6851
www.montanainn.com

Best known for total comfort and Montana charm, this 3-level log home and 2-story guest house is located on 5 acres just 5 miles from Bigfork. The grounds include many rustic features as well as birds like peacocks and waterfowl, which can be seen on the pond. Bill Knoll and Mary Corcoran Knoll are the owners of the O'Duachain (pronounced O-Do-CANE), which was established in 1985 by Tom and Margot Doohan. The breakfast menu still includes Margot's Stuffed Irish Toast, as well as homemade maple nut cereal with fruit puree, and lots of different teas and coffees. The facility offers suites and rooms with private baths. The guest house also has balconies and patios with incredible views. If you're looking for stiff European charm, the Knolls warn, this is not the place for you. They'll make you feel right at home!

SWAN RIVER INN $$$–$$$$
360 Grand Dr., Bigfork
(406) 837-2328
www.swanriverinn.com

The Swan River Inn has expanded to include 8 themed luxury suites at the inn, 3 suites located about a quarter mile away, and a trio of country houses for rent outside Bigfork. The inn is affiliated with the **Swan River Inn Cafe,** a very popular restaurant. Room service is available in the inn rooms, so you can take advantage of the elegant and healthy menu at the restaurant. Antiques grace all the rooms, which have different themes such as Victorian, Art Deco, Arabian Nights, and rustic Western, each offering a unique interpretation of luxury. Summer rates begin at $145 and go up from there.

i Pepper spray as a defense against aggressive bears has gained in popularity for both park rangers and visitors. Be aware that wind, rain, and distance all influence the spray's effectiveness, as does the spray's product shelf life. Don't let carrying pepper spray give you a false sense of security, however, and don't substitute it for taking safety precautions in bear country. Also be sure to request instructions on its proper use when you purchase the spray, which is widely available at sporting goods stores in northwest Montana.

Campgrounds & RV Parks

Price Code
$................. Less than $10
$$ .... $10 to $16
$$$ .... $16 to $24
$$$$ .... More than $24

FLATHEAD LAKE STATE PARK $
490 North Meridian Rd., Kalispell
(406) 752-5501
http://fwp.mt.gov/parks

The park consists of 6 scenic units bordering Flathead Lake, two of which are on the east shore near Bigfork. With the exception of Wild Horse Island, all units feature economical camping, fishing, boating, and swimming. Closest to Bigfork is 67-acre Wayfarers (406-752-5501) just outside of town, which features 30 campsites, including 7 tent-only sites. The park has flush toilets and a group picnic shelter, as well as trailer and boat sewage dump stations. The Yellow Bay facility is 15 acres and the campground has 4 walk-in tent sites. Flush and vault toilets and coin-operated showers are available. All individual campsites are available on a first-come, first-served basis. Plan to arrive early, as most sites fill up by 4 p.m. on weekends during July and Aug. Maximum stay is 14 days. The day-use fee for nonresidents at both parks is $5; campsites are $15 per night for residents and nonresidents.

OUTBACK MONTANA $$$
27202 East Lakeshore Dr.
(406) 837-6973, (888) 900-6973
There are 70 pull-through RV sites at Outback Montana (located 4 miles south of Bigfork), some with full hookup and others with electric and water only. Several dry-camp tent sites are also available. You'll appreciate that there's more of an emphasis on privacy than at many RV parks, with fenced terraces, patios, and picnic tables. Pets are allowed with certain restrictions—check ahead for details. Families will enjoy such activities as tetherball, badminton, and horseshoes in the delightful outdoor setting. The fee for sites with full hookup ranges from $21 to $27 per night, while sites with partial hookup are $15. Tent sites go for $12.

**WOODS BAY MARINA
  AND RV RESORT** $$$$
624 Yenne Point Rd.
(406) 837-6191
www.woodsbay.com
From May to Oct 1, you can drive your RV right up to Flathead Lake at the Woods Bay Marina, in operation since 1980, and enjoy a lake vacation for just $35 a night (full hookup) or $30 a night (partial—just water and electric). Weekly and monthly rates are also available. If you're pulling a boat, you'll enjoy the advantage of having the boat docked within feet of your hookup. Four tent sites are also available at $12 per site for one person and $5 for each additional person. Free hot showers and a laundry facility are nearby. Gas and repairs are available for boats on-site, and a market sells food, tackle, and other essentials. Fishing and lake tour guides can be hired from the marina as well. The resort is situated 3.5 miles south of Bigfork off Highway 35.

RESTAURANTS

Price Code

For two people, meal exclusive of beverages, tip, and tax.

$	$10 to $20
$$	$20 to $28
$$$	$28 to $35
$$$$	More than $35

Family-Friendly Dining

BROOKIE'S COOKIES $–$$
191 Mill St.
(406) 837-CHIP, (800) 697-6487
Just around the corner from Electric Avenue near the Swan River is a place to swing into for all kinds of munchies, from famous chocolate chip cookies to cinnamon rolls, triple

berry muffins, and more. In 2010, owner Greg Edwards, who took over Brookies in 2007 (with no previous baking experience beyond warming up frozen pizzas, he says!), decided to expand his culinary horizons; now every evening the bakery transforms into the Kickin' Chicken Bar and Grille, serving barbecue meat and an array of side dishes. With a full liquor license, the night operation also offers a full slate of beers and cocktails. It's a great place to hang.

CHAMPS SPORTS PUB AND GRILL $$
180 Vista Lane
(406) 837-5861, (800) 433-6516

Though Champs is a sports bar, it's also a fine place to enjoy a family meal because it features a fun kids' menu and large lunch and dinner specials. Large televisions air sports coverage and trivia games, and the bar serves local microbrews for Mom and Dad to enjoy. Champs is part of Marina Cay Resort, for which you'll find another listing in the Nightlife section.

DEL NORTE $
355 Grand Dr.
(406) 837-0076

A great place to go with the kids is Del Norte, located right across the street from the bay in Bigfork. The menu features plenty of authentic Mexican specialties as well as burgers and other American food and takeout. Even if the kids don't care for the Mexican cuisine, they'll definitely enjoy the ice cream, which comes in both hard and soft varieties and in lots of flavors, including huckleberry. Del Norte is open daily.

✴SWAN RIVER INN CAFE & DINNER HOUSE $$$
360 Grand Dr.
(406) 837-2328
www.swanriverinn.com

This is a great compromise for families looking for something in between fine dining and diner food. The Swan River Inn's European and American menu caters to a healthy diet, with plenty of specialties to pique the appetite. You can get steak and eggs for breakfast to prep you for a busy day fishing on the lake, and then come back and have a gourmet dinner. Outdoor seating is available with one of the best views of Bigfork Bay anywhere. (They like to say that the breathtaking sunsets are served as dinner's sixth course.) All meals are made from scratch, and you'll enjoy the homey atmosphere and emphasis on service. The hours of operation were in transition at the time of this writing; call the inn for the latest scoop. Lodging rooms are available for rent in the same building.

WILD MILE RESTAURANT & DELI $–$$
435 Bridge St.
(406) 837-3354
www.wildmiledeli.com

The Wild Mile serves breakfast, lunch, and dinner, as well as offering 30 beer choices. It's best known for its German fare: bratwurst, brockwurst, braunschweiger on rye, and more. The restaurant is located near the famous Wild Mile of the Swan River, the scene of a popular kayaking competition every spring. It's open Mon through Sat from 9 a.m. to 8 p.m.; closed Sun.

Fine Dining

BIGFORK INN $$$–$$$$
604 Electric Ave.
(406) 837-6680
www.bigforkinn.com

The Bigfork Inn is one of the defining spots in this lakeside community. Built in 1937 after a fire destroyed the Bigfork Hotel, it features a mountain-chalet style echoing the architecture of structures in Glacier National Park. The inn, which serves dinner only, is open year-round 7 days a week, with fine dining from an extensive menu that features pasta, veal, prime rib, fresh fish, and steak. The outdoor patio is open for summer dining, and dancing happens on Fri and Sat nights to the traditional jazz sounds of the Company Brass. The lounge opens at 4:30 p.m., and meals are served beginning at 5 p.m.

BRIDGE STREET GALLERY & CAFE $$
408 Bridge St.
(406) 837-5825

Bridge Street offers a unique combination of art and delectables, with brunch, lunch, and dinner served daily. During the summer you can eat outdoors on the deck or inside, but the latter is where the action is. The walls of Bridge Street are covered with art that's for sale; a rotating series of exhibits are featured throughout the year, including the annual Christmas wreath contest, which includes a prize for best edible wreath. The cafe features a large selection of wines by the glass or bottle, and a private dining room is available for larger parties. Reservations are suggested.

COYOTE ROADHOUSE $$$
602 Three Eagle Lane
(406) 837-1233

Owner and chef Gary Hastings has a reputation as a perfectionist. He certainly deserves it, according to anyone who has ever eaten at the Coyote Roadhouse. This is a world-class restaurant that features a highly trained staff and a gourmet menu in a backwoods setting. You have to drive a little ways from Bigfork toward Ferndale on Highway 209, then follow the signs from Ferndale to the Roadhouse, which is located on a remote and scenic portion of the Swan River. Make a reservation before you show up at the front door, because it's a popular spot that often fills up despite its hidden location. Most nights look for such Cajun specialties as blackened redfish and many European specialties as well as fresh fish. Rooms are also available (see previous listing under Bed-and-Breakfasts for Coyote Roadhouse Inn).

✳SHOWTHYME $$$
548 Electric Ave.
(406) 837-0707
www.showthyme.com

The ShowThyme restaurant sits next door to the Bigfork Center for the Performing Arts, which explains the pun in the name. But whether or not you are making a stop before watching a show put on by the Bigfork Summer Playhouse, you can't go wrong stopping here. ShowThyme, located in a historic bank building, is simply one of the best restaurants the Flathead Valley; indeed, in the entire Northwest. Every night a variety of specials is available, from the featured rack of lamb to a variety of fresh fish and shellfish. The wait staff is trained to recite specials from memory and to take orders without benefit of a notepad. It makes for a nice challenge for the highly professional staff, and they rarely if ever get an order wrong. Save room for dessert, though you'll be hard-pressed to choose between the simple delight of the crème caramel and the decadent Benedictine chocolate truffle pie. Reservations are highly recommended for dining, which begins at 5 p.m. Tues through Sat.

NIGHTLIFE

GARDEN BAR
451 Electric Ave.
(406) 837-9914

Lots of folks park themselves in the Garden Bar after work and just hang out there for hours. Why not? There's great food from the grill, a pool table, pinball, electronic darts, TVs for sports viewing, live music on summer weekends, and video poker and keno machines. In the summer months don't forget to poke your head out back to see how the bar got its name. The outdoor patio and garden is a delightful place to kick back and sip a beer (at least 20 different microbrews on are tap at all times). The Garden Kitchen does a great job with burgers, but you can also get chicken, fish, salads, and hot dogs. By the way, if you aren't sure about whether the Garden Bar is right for you, this sign seen on the wall should be a good clue: THIS ESTABLISHMENT SERVES NO DRINKS WITH LITTLE TINY UMBRELLAS. It's a Montana tradition of three decades that shows no signs of slowing down.

MARINA CAY
180 Vista Lane
(406) 837-5861, (800) 433-6516
www.marinacay.com

Three popular night spots keep things kickin' at Marina Cay Resort. The poolside Tiki Bar serves up scrumptious snacks, festive drinks, and live evening music; the Piano Lounge offers an upscale mellow atmosphere with live piano music. You'll can get your favorite cocktail, rare whiskey, or aromatic cigar here. Finally, Champs Sports Pub & Grill serves casual dinners in the presence of plenty of TV screens.

✳PICK'S BOWLING CENTER
2849 Hwy. 82
(406) 837-2233
www.picksbowl.com

After the North Shore lanes closed in 2008, Bigfork's large legion of league bowlers went into withdrawal for several months—and they were overjoyed when Pick's Bowling Center opened early in 2009. Things get rolling here daily at 10 a.m. and keep going until 10 p.m. most weekdays, and later on weekends. Pick's has 20 lanes and hosts special events like "cosmic bowling" on weekends, when the place takes on the air of an upbeat nightclub. Also on site is Pick's Pizza and Grill, with food available beginning at 10 a.m.

THE VILLAGE WELL
260 River St.
(406) 837-5251

The Village Well is a popular nightspot where you can get pizza, sandwiches, chicken wings, burgers, and more, along with a selection of microbrew beers. On the roof deck you can drink under the stars during the summer season, and live music happens downstairs on the weekends. Pool, foosball, and darts make for alternative entertainment, and there's keno, as well.

SHOPPING

BIGFORK BAY GIFT & GEAR
491 Electric Ave.
(406) 837-5850

This is a good place to start your shopping, since they manage to stock a lot of merchandise in the space. You'll find a large selection

⊙ Close-up

Backcountry Cooking

Cooking and eating can be some of the most pleasurable aspects of a backcountry outing in Glacier National Park and the surrounding wilderness. The scenic grandeur alone provides a backdrop that can rival the ambience of the finest five-star restaurant. Backcountry meals are a fun social time, but just as importantly they provide the energy and sustenance to fuel vigorous activities.

Backcountry menus will be influenced by the personal preferences and dietary needs of your group. During a typical backcountry trip, you need not worry much about eating an excess of sugar, starch, or fats. Strenuous activities and higher elevations demand extra amounts, within reason, to provide needed energy. Preference should be given to high-energy-producing foods such as pasta, rice, beans, nuts, cheese, and wheat products.

Dried veggies and meats, or meat substitutes, are lightweight and add substance, color, and taste to perhaps otherwise bland pasta, rice, or potato dishes. A spice kit is a must for any backcountry connoisseur.

Food and cookware weight and bulk will impact your packing, particularly on extended trips. Lightweight freeze-dried food offers an attractive option and the advantage of quick preparation. You can reduce some weight and bulk by repacking food into reusable plastic bags. This also reduces litter to pack out.

Trail snacks are vital for backcountry travelers. Dried fruits, nuts, crackers and cheese, candy, and energy bars all provide helpful energy boosts.

By now you know that Glacier Park is the domain of black and grizzly bears, and your menu and cooking techniques must take this into account. Select foods that are low-odor; avoid strong-smelling recipes that may attract bears. Try not to spill food in the cooking area.

Proper food and garbage storage is important in bear country. Regulations require you to hang or store food, garbage, and cookware in backcountry campgrounds at all times except mealtimes. Never cook, eat, or store food in your tent; it may attract a bear into your camp. Wastewater from cleanup should be strained of food scraps and scattered, while the scraps should be packed out.

Campfires are permitted in approximately half of Glacier's backcountry campgrounds. Cooking over an open fire can be enjoyable; however, for the lowest impact, you should forgo the fire and use a lightweight camp stove. Many campers find that stoves cook food more quickly and evenly, anyway. In the case of bad weather or an emergency, a stove is a fast and reliable way to prepare hot drinks and food.

Backcountry rangers are perhaps the greatest culinary experts roaming Glacier's wildlands. Here is a favorite simple dinner entree from a backcountry ranger who chooses to remain anonymous:

Vigo brand Santa Fe pinto beans and rice with corn (available in the Mexican section at the grocery). Boil contents in three cups water for one minute. Simmer 20 minutes. Add 2 tablespoons butter or margarine. Garnish with grated cheese. Serve with pita bread. Feeds one hungry ranger.

of toys, lotions, stationery, T-shirts, and gift items. Such indispensables as Jelly Belly jelly beans are also readily at hand. The prices are reasonable and the faces friendly.

BIGFORK STATION
470 Electric Ave.
(406) 837-2332

A relatively recent addition to downtown Bigfork's scene is the Bigfork Station, a collection of shops in a new building reflecting the architecture of a turn-of-the-20th-century railroad station. Don't let it concern you that the railroad never came to Bigfork, just enjoy the ride. First stop is Roma's Eclectic on Electric, a funky shop full of delightful "don't-need-but-must-haves." Whether you are looking for glassware, gadgets, or gourmet cookware, you can find it here, right down to the moose-shaped cookie cutters. The shop is brightly lit and a pleasure to the eye. Moving on, Kathy McDonnell Jewelry, Montana Bear Food (huckleberry products, etc.), Buffalo Creek Clothing Company, Merry Gems (kids' clothing), Bigfork Bigphoto, and Art Fusion are all in or adjacent to the complex.

ELECTRIC AVENUE GIFTS
490 Electric Ave.
(406) 837-4994
www.electricavenuegifts.com

Open 7 days a week the year around, Electric Avenue Gifts specializes in service with a smile. First opened in 1983, the enterprise recently moved across the street from its former location into larger quarters previously occupied by Electric Avenue Books, next door to the Bigfork Summer Playhouse. Folk art, travel games, greeting cards, Christmas ornaments, nostalgic signs recreating old matchbook covers, scrapbook pillows,

"cherry fairies." In other words, if they don't carry it, chances are it's not made. Gift wrapping is always free, and the folks there are happy to pack and ship purchases home for you. Drop in and say hi!

✳EVA GATES HOMEMADE PRESERVES
456 Electric Ave.
(406) 837-4356, (800) 682-4283
www.evagates.com

Walk in the door of Eva Gates Homemade Preserves and you'll feel like you're back in grandma's kitchen decades ago. In fact, for 60 years the Gates family has been creating the aromatic and tasty preserves and syrups that are today highly prized. Back in 1949 Eva used her own grandmother's recipe, and today it is her grandchildren and great-grandchildren keeping up the family tradition. When you walk in the front door, you might see Gretchen Gates or one of her assistants in the process of doing the cooking. They welcome questions and love to share the secrets of their success. The syrups and preserves are made in 5-pint batches without additives or preservatives to keep them as fresh as possible. Gift baskets and special Christmas boxes are popular items for sale here. Jan through Mar, the store is closed on Sun.

> **i** Missing that special something from your Montana trip? Looking for a perfect gift? Eva Gates will ship homemade preserves, syrups, or sampler baskets all over the country. Huckleberry will always steal the show, but the raspberry, black cap, apple, strawberry, and cherry products are nothing to sneeze at! Contact Eva Gates at www.evagates.com.

✳**KEHOE'S AGATE SHOP**
1020 Holt Dr.
(406) 837-4467

Kehoe's shop lies just off the bank of the Flat-head River in old Holt, an early settlement that lasted from the 1880s to the 1920s. Just across the road from the shop is the old Holt general store, crumbling quietly as the years pass, and a little farther down the road are the remnants of an old ferry crossing. But Kehoe's Agate Shop looks much farther back in time, as it features a variety of gemstones, agates, and fossils dating back millions of years. Many were collected from around the world and ground or worked into a variety of shapes by James Kehoe Sr., a gemologist whose son, Jack, built the shop in 1932, using planks from the steamboat Helena. Jack's children, Leslie and James, took over the shop in 1992 and ran it until James died unexpectedly of a heart attack in 2008. But Leslie and James's widow, Kristen, vow to keep things going as ever. A sign next to the shop explains a little of the history of Holt, the ferry, and the Helena. Remnants of the Helena, including the pilothouse, are also on display. To find the shop, all you have to do is keep your eyes open. Almost every major highway in the area of Bigfork has a sign pointing you in the right direction.

POLSON

At the south end of Flathead Lake, midway between Kalispell and Missoula, sits the town of Polson, the first community in the area to be settled by whites. In fact, Polson is in the middle of the Flathead Indian Reservation. Although the Confederated Salish and Kootenai tribes have jurisdiction over some aspects of life here, everyday matters are handled pretty much as they are elsewhere in Montana. There's a sheriff and a county commission for Lake County, a city council for Polson, and people pay taxes to the state of Montana. But there are a few exceptions to the rule. The tribal authorities here, for instance, negotiated a separate gambling compact with the state government that allows somewhat higher payouts for gaming machines and more machines than are allowed in nonreservation casinos. A separate tribal license is also required for hunting and fishing.

OVERVIEW

Polson, which was named after pioneer rancher David Polson and was incorporated in 1910, is the largest city on the reservation, but it still boasts only a population of about 4,000 people. The city's early claim to fame was its steamboats, which for many years were the only means of reaching the north end of the lake and Kalispell. Today Polson offers a wide variety of activities, especially for those wanting to take advantage of the scenic wonders of Flathead Lake. Tour boats depart from the Polson dock for sightseeing on Flathead, including trips to Wild Horse Island, the lake's largest island and home to bighorn sheep and other wildlife. The fishing is, of course, remarkable throughout Flathead Lake, with sizable lake trout and whitefish being popular catches. When you're on the lake, keep an eye open for the legendary Flathead Lake Monster, an American cousin of the Loch Ness Monster, which, like its more famous counterpart, is often discussed and written about but rarely spotted.

If you travel south of Polson toward Missoula on US 93, attractions you should try to see include the Kerr Dam, located just south of town. The now defunct Montana Power Company built the dam on land leased from the tribes. Whitewater rafting is a popular activity on the Flathead River below the dam, and you'll also find scenic-vista pullouts and a picnic area. In the tribal capital of Pablo, you can stop at the People's Center to learn about local history and Native traditions. A little farther south you can witness the profound influence of the early European settlers on the area at the historic Mission Church at St. Ignatius, which features remarkable murals. Not far away is the gravel driving loop through the National Bison Range (outside Moiese), where bison, antelope, and other creatures big and small are plentiful and easier to photograph than in Glacier National Park.

If it's late summer, you can drive north of Polson on either US 93 or Highway 35 and procure produce at ample roadside stands, in the form of the area's famous sweet cherries. The trip to Glacier Park from Polson is less than 2 hours.

Life in Polson is rather low-key, perhaps as a result of the combined influences of the immense lake, the Native American spiritual traditions, and the relatively temperate weather. In any case, while you stay here, plan on spending some time in the downtown shops—which are laden with arts and antiques—and in the town's unassuming restaurants and taverns. Everyone is just a local here. You can blend in easily as you go a round at the Polson Bay Golf Club, watch the ensemble work of the Port Polson Players at a theater in the clubhouse, or enjoy the Montana State Old Time Fiddlers' Jam, held annually at the Polson High School on the fourth full weekend in July.

ACCOMMODATIONS

Hotels & Motels

Price Code

Keep in mind that some rates are based on availability. The average nightly rates for two adults at the hotels and motels listed in this section are indicated by a dollar sign ($) ranking in the following chart. Also, the hotels and motels in this chapter accept all or most major credit cards.

$ . . . . **Less than $85**
$$ . . . . **$85 to $115**
$$$ . . . . **$115 to $150**
$$$$ . . . . **More than $150**

BAYVIEW INN $–$$
914 US 93 East
(406) 883-3120, (800) 735-6862
www.bayview-inn.com
The Bayview Inn provides all the comforts of a modern motel. Built in 1984, it features queen-size beds, a lake view, and a view of the distant peaks of the Mission Mountains, usually snow-covered well into summer. Each of the 25 rooms includes a microwave and refrigerator, a real plus if you plan to stay in Polson for a few days. A continental breakfast is provided, the motel has Wi-Fi, and it's within walking distance of a full-service restaurant. Call ahead to inquire about the pet policy if you're planning to bring Barkus on your trip with you.

CHERRY HILL MOTEL
  AND CABINS $–$$
50713 US 93
(406) 883-2737
The Cherry Hill is indeed built on a hill that once supported cherry orchards. The motel overlooks the highway and the Polson Bay Golf Club, as well as Flathead Lake. Built in 1943, the facility was completely renovated in 1996. Now it has the best of both worlds, the quaint roadside motel-look of the 1950s, and the amenities of the modern day. The motel is actually a series of buildings that each house a couple of rooms and 2 cabins. Accommodations range from 2 bedrooms with a kitchenette to just a simple room. In addition to the large, grassy yard, there's an outdoor hot tub for use in summer, and gazebos and benches for a comfortable perch for a picnic with a great view. Advance reservations are strongly recommended in the summer.

PORT POLSON INN $$$–$$$$
502 US 93
(406) 883-5385, (800) 654-0682
www.portpolsoninn.com

Before KwaTaqNuk (see the Resorts and Guest Ranches section) came to town, this was the most popular lodging spot, and it's easy to see why. Many of the 44 rooms look out across the highway right onto Flathead Lake and the Mission Mountains beyond. You can enjoy the indoor and outdoor hot tubs, indoor sauna, and exercise facility. Although the outside of the motel has a 1960s look, the owners work hard to give the rooms a bed-and-breakfast feel, with flowers provided in the summertime and a continental breakfast offered. Also available are some themed rooms; plan ahead and you can stay in a cowboy-style room or one dedicated to Mickey Mouse! Rates during the peak season range from $150 to $300 nightly.

SUPER 8 $–$$
Junction of Highway 35 and US 93
(406) 883-6251, (800) 800-8000
www.super8.com

The Polson Super 8 offers all queen-size beds, a muffin and pastry bar for breakfast, bus/truck parking, and many nearby conveniences. The hotel features 44 rooms, including an executive suite. It's across the street from the 4Bs Restaurant, the Safeway grocery store, and a Wal-Mart. It's also within walking distance of a pair of lounge casinos. Pets are allowed with permission.

Resorts & Guest Ranches

Price Code

$	$70 to $120
$$	$120 to $170
$$$	$170 to $220
$$$$	More than $220

*BEST WESTERN KWATAQNUK RESORT $$
49708 US 93 East
(406) 883-3636, (800) 882-6363
www.kwataqnuk.com

This hotel and conference center is owned by the Confederated Salish and Kootenai tribes and is one of the great success stories of the tribal economy. It is the jewel in Polson's resplendent tourism crown. The KwaTaqNuk Resort features 112 rooms on 3 floors, a restaurant, convention facilities, a lounge and casino, an art gallery, a gift shop, indoor and outdoor pools, an indoor whirlpool, and a full-service marina. The convention facilities can accommodate groups up to 300 people. Jocko's Lounge offers good food and drink in a relaxed atmosphere. Unlike most of the hotels in Polson, KwaTaqNuk is built right on the lakeshore. The resort operates the *Shadow*, a 148-passenger tour boat that offers daily cruises of Flathead Lake during the summer months. The Bay Cruise departs at 10:30 a.m. for an hour-and-a-half adventure at the southern end of the lake. At 1:30 p.m., the Wild Horse Island Cruise departs for a 3-hour tour around the island. Or, you can board the *Shadow* for the 7:30 p.m. Twilight Cruise and watch the sunset from the water. For more information, call the resort number listed above.

MISSION MOUNTAIN RESORT $
257 Fulkerson Lane
(406) 883-1883
www.polsonmtresort.com

This getaway is located on an 80-acre sanctuary just 3 miles from Polson at the foot of the Mission Mountains. You can see Flathead Lake and the rest of the valley from this scenic perch, while enjoying pine-scented air and mountain living. The accommodations are relatively new and feature Western motifs. The 3 guest rooms and 2 guest cabins (sleeping 4) rent for a base rate of $75, with an additional $10 charged for each person beyond 2 guests. In the roomy and rustic lodge you can kick off your boots and relax, or sidle up to the 1800s-era soda fountain. Another specialty of the house is the Antique Emporium, featuring knickknacks of the olden days, along with local artwork and gifts. The grounds include miles of nature trails. Pets are not permitted, due to wildlife concerns.

SUNNY SHORES RESORT
   ## AND MARINA $
609 A St., Big Arm 59910
(406) 849-5622

If you're searching for a low-cost family vacation place that is strong on lake fun, you might consider the Sunny Shores Resort and Marina, located 12 miles north of Polson on US 93. The resort sits right on the lakeshore and features cabins and rental trailers as well as RV hookups. A small grocery store on-site sells refreshments and picnic supplies, as well as outboard fuel and oil. They also stock lures, tackle, and bait. You can rent a boat from the marina, or just rent a boat slip if you have your own vessel in tow. Evenings, when the boats pull in, you might enjoy a sing-along around a campfire or roasting some marshmallows. The resort specializes in family reunions, so you'll want to get your reservations in early to make sure space is available. "Family" at Sunny Shores includes your favorite pet.

Campgrounds & RV Parks

Price Code

$................. Less than $10
$$ .... $10 to $16
$$$ .... $16 to $24
$$$$ .... More than $24

EAGLE NEST RV RESORT $$$$
259 Eagle Nest Dr. on Highway 35
(406) 883-5904
www.eaglenestrv.com

Eagle Nest RV Resort has 7 acres of lawn and trees, offering spacious, shady, quiet campsites. You'll find 6 tent spaces and 56 spacious RV spaces with full hookups, 50-amp service, and roomy pull-throughs, which range from $25 to $40 by season. Tent sites are $30 per night 2 people in one tent. The facility, which borders Polson's 27-hole public golf course, has been around since 1993. Amenities include showers, a rec room, laundry, a gift store, a horseshoe pit, a playground, free Wi-Fi, and much more. Eagle Nest is open from Apr 15 through Oct 15 and also offers weekly, monthly, and seasonal rates.

FLATHEAD LAKE STATE PARK $
490 North Meridian Rd., Kalispell
(406) 752-5501
http://fwp.mt.gov/parks/visit

This park consists of 6 scenic units bordering Flathead Lake (one of them, an island, is completely surrounded by the lake!), two of which are within 15 miles of Polson. With the exception of Wild Horse Island, all units feature camping, fishing, boating, and swimming. Finley Point is on the east shore of Flathead Lake on Highway 35 and has 4 tent sites and 16 RV sites. It is open only during the summer. Big Arm is 14 miles north of Polson on US 93. At this facility, rental yurts sleeping up to 6 are available May 1 through Sept 30, partially furnished, at $45 per night. The camping fee in season is $15, and 14 days is the maximum length of stay permitted.

MONTANA PINES RESORT $$$
6913 East Shore Route (Highway 35)
(406) 887-2537

Close-up

✳Camp Tuffit

The word "rustic" could have been coined especially for **Camp Tuffit,** an old-style fishing resort on Lake Mary Ronan that's been run by the Thomas family for a century.

Lake Mary Ronan, named after the wife of an early Indian agent who stocked the lake with cutthroat trout in 1892, traditionally has had some of the best fishing in Montana. Charlie Thomas came to Lake Mary Ronan in 1914 and established the fishing camp that's now run by his grandchildren and great-grandchildren. Generations of fishing enthusiasts have come to the camp, and many return year after year to the rough-hewn cabins built by Charlie and named whimsically for old-time radio-show personalities, famous gold-mining camps, and so forth. Mention Camp Tuffit around northwest Montana, and chances are someone will wax eloquent about the beauty of the spot, the quality of the fishing, and the memories of the good times shared with friends and family.

The camp looks much the same as it does in old photographs that show the cabins and the lodge in the early days. A quality of timelessness may be one of the enduring appeals of Camp Tuffit. The personality of the founder still can be seen throughout the camp—in the cabins he built and the newspaper clippings about him, and even in the old piano, where modern fishing enthusiasts still pound out tunes.

Charlie Thomas built wooden boats for fishing; at one time he had as many as 65 hand-built boats plying the lake. The wooden boats have been retired now, replaced by aluminum craft, but some of Charlie's creations are still used as flower planters. Charlie was quite a marketing agent, too. He built colorful cutouts of mannequins sitting like fishermen in flat-bottomed boats. The signs, which said follow the boats to camp tuffit, at one time were posted on roads in Nevada, Idaho, Washington, and Montana. The Thomases maintain handmade signs on the road to the camp, and some of the originals are now in a storage shop, along with some of Charlie's hand-built boats.

Camp Tuffit got its name after a Kalispell physician told Charlie to take his ailing wife out into the woods to "tough it" for the summer. When the doctor planned a fishing trip at the lake, Charlie wrote "Camp Tuffit" on a piece of cardboard to guide him to the spot, and the name stuck. Charlie started building boats and cabins and welcoming guests, who rented a boat for $1 a day.

The resort's **Crawdad Cafe** serves breakfast, lunch, and dinner, and specializes in homemade pies. The cabins have been modernized through the years, but they maintain the old rustic flavor that guests seem to love. In addition to its 24 cabins, Tuffit has tenting sites and several trailer hookups. Return guests often reserve their favorite cabin by name.

Though the fishing at Lake Mary Ronan has been clouded some by an anonymous "bucket biologist" who illegally dumped perch into it a few years ago, Camp Tuffit retains its loyalty and its charm: a peaceful, rustic place where "progress" is suspended and the smiling presence of Charlie Thomas seems to linger as new generations tell fish stories around the campfire.

To reach Camp Tuffit, turn off US 93 at Dayton, about 40 miles south of Kalispell, and travel about 6.5 miles on a paved road until you see one of Charlie's signs directing you to the camp. Phone them at (406) 849-5220 or visit on the web at www.camp-tuffit.com.

Open spring through fall, Montana Pines Resort is located 7 miles north of Polson on Highway 35. The main building, which dates from 1930, was at one time a dairy barn. Today it is the centerpiece of a lovely 40-acre RV park that also has a restaurant and lounge. From the deck you get a great view of the Mission Mountains and have access to a lot of added attractions, as well, including a lounge/restaurant, game arcade, and 18-hole miniature golf course. In summer you can expect to enjoy live music on the outdoor stage, free hayrides, and more. Montana Pines maintains 60 RV sites and 40 tent sites. Pets are allowed, and you're welcome to use the showers and coin-laundry facilities. If you want to rough it in native fashion, a rental tepee is available nightly.

POLSON MOTORCOACH
& RV RESORT $$$$
200 Irvine Flats Rd.
(406) 883-2333
www.polsonrvresort.com
This resort, formerly a KOA affiliate, can be counted on for a first-rate RVing experience. The 25 acres of grounds are well kept, and the individual lots and common areas are professionally landscaped. As they say, motorhome owners "may rent for a single night, a month, or stay forever," because lots are for sale at the luxury resort. Amenities include Class-A RV accommodations, state-of-the-art hookups, basketball and volleyball facilities, miniature golf, and a pool and hot tub. Coming soon are a club house, fitness gym with a sauna and massage room, and a lot more. Visit the website for information on rates, which vary by season and length of stay.

RESTAURANTS

Price Code
For two people, meal exclusive of beverages, tip, and tax.

$.....................	$10 to $20
$$	$20 to $28
$$$	$28 to $35
$$$$	More than $35

Family Friendly Dining

THE DRIFTWOOD CAFE $
50249 US 93
(406) 883-2558
Breakfast is served all day at the Driftwood, a longtime locals' favorite. There's nothing fancy at this cafe, but they usually get it right, and the menu offers lots of choices. For breakfast, don't overlook the Hungry Man Special, comprised of 3 eggs, 3 pieces of toast, hash browns, and choice of 6 sticks of bacon, 6 ounces of ham, or sausage links for just $7.95. A variety of omelets and a kids' menu are also available. For lunch or dinner, you can't go wrong with the burgers, either beef or buffalo. Buffalo steaks and stews are a specialty of the house.

4BS RESTAURANT $
Junction of Highway 35 and US 93
(406) 883-6180
After suddenly shuttering operations in 2007 after 16 years in business, the 4Bs Restaurant in Polson just as suddenly reopened in May of 2010—featuring the menu of old, including their ultra-popular tomato soup. A Montana tradition, the 4Bs chain started in Missoula in 1947, and eventually just about every major city in Montana had one. The founding family, the Hainlines (Bill, wife Buddy, and kids Bill Jr. and Barbara, hence the four "Bs"), eventually sold many

of their properties to Town Pump, another Montana corporation. Arizona-based Star Buffet bought others, as well as the rights to the 4Bs name and recipes. That's why not much seems to have changed at the Polson 4Bs. The specialties are still friendly service, quickly served food (without being "fast food"), and a family-oriented setting. The children's menu is generous to a fault, with lots of selections—everything from hamburgers to pizza—and a price that can't be beat. Grown-ups eat almost as cheaply, with a tasty prime rib special selling for under $10, including choice of potato or rice, soup or salad, and a roll. The 4Bs is no longer open 24 hours a day, but it keeps cooking well into the evening—midnight on Fri and Sat and 10 p.m. on weekdays, with longer hours possible in the future.

HOT SPOT THAI CAFE   **$$–$$$**
1407 US 93
(406) 883-4444
www.hotspotthai.com
The Hot Spot Thai Cafe was a bit of a surprise when it first opened in Polson, but it's a local favorite now! Their food is authentic—and wonderful. About the "hot spot"—take a clue from the menu, which rates their entrees from "not hot" through "mild" and "medium hot" to "hot hot" and "scorching"! The menu is varied, including curries, teriyaki, stir fry, and peanut dishes, plus a range of beverages and dessert. Senior and kids' plates are also offered. To complement its roots in Thailand, the Hot Spot favors Montana Natural Beef and buys local produce whenever possible. And their deck offers a fantastic view of Flathead Lake. Or, you can even enjoy their food *on* the lake—call the Hot Spot to inquire about their special

4-course meal for parties of 4 to 10 aboard a guided tour boat.

✴RICHWINE'S BURGERVILLE
50567 US 93
(406) 883-2620
Burgerville has been a Polson institution since the 1950s, and the Richwine name has been at the forefront since 1962. The meat for their burgers—some say they're the best in Montana—is ground on-site in a meat room behind the restaurant. Try a Royal Burger (a single, double, or triple cheeseburger), their most popular item, named after Royal Morrison, the Polson football coach who founded Burgerville in the early 1950s before moving on to coach in Missoula. Burgerville typically opens sometime in Feb and closes again in the late fall. It's hard to miss: Just watch for the orange windmill and the neon cow wearing a police uniform.

Fine Dining

JOCKO'S   **$$$**
49708 US 93 East
(406) 883-3636, (800) 882-6363
www.kwataqnuk.com
The restaurant at the Best Western KwaTaq-Nuk Resort is one of your best bets for fine dining in Polson—whether it's breakfast, lunch, or dinner. A variety of beef and seafood selections grace the menu, along with vegetarian choices and an extensive wine list. In the summer the best seats are on the outdoor deck right above Flathead Lake and the resort's marina. Also during the summer you may enjoy the Sun brunch. Hotel guests can take advantage of the restaurant's room-service menu.

NIGHTLIFE

BEST WESTERN KWATAQNUK RESORT
49708 US 93 East
(406) 883-3636, (800) 882-6363
www.kwataqnuk.com

The casino in KwaTaqNuk is a bit closer to big-time gambling than most of the casinos in Montana. That's because the Confederated Salish and Kootenai tribes own the facility, and the tribes negotiated an agreement with the state of Montana that allows more liberal gaming than what's typical. The casino is open 24 hours a day.

> **i** Mountain streams may look beautiful and clean, and they sometimes are, but they can also carry giardia, a nasty parasite that will give you untold intestinal distress. Always boil water for at least a minute before drinking it, or use a filter approved for giardia.

SHOPPING

ALPINE PRODUCT DESIGN
306 Main St.
(406) 883-3500
www.alpinetipi.com

This is a one-of-a-kind store where you can procure a surprising made-in-Montana gift for the folks back home, but these are pricey gifts. For several hundred dollars each, a wide range of tepees are available, including the lodgepole frames and the outer canvas. Walk into the showroom and you'll see everything from a full-size tepee that reaches to the ceiling, to a child's tepee perfect for the backyard, all the way down to a more economical bird-feeder tepee that's just a foot tall. A map on the wall shows locations across the United States where children's tepees have been shipped, and Alpine does most of its business by mail order, so remember to pick up a catalog while you're there. If a tepee is too big for your yard, you might consider a windsock, another specialty item produced by Alpine.

FIRST RESORT
219 Main St.
(406) 883-2129
www.firstresortclothing.com

This shop is worth a visit, partly because it offers a full range of clothing for men and women, but perhaps even more so because of its unusual design. It was formerly known as the Flagship, and it retains the nautical design instituted then. There's a captain's wheel on the entryway, and inside the seagoing motif continues, with changing rooms done up as ship's cabins and the walls decorated with barrels, portholes, and gangplanks. In between you'll find Pendleton and other brand names, along with a healthy helping of sale merchandise. They also offer tuxedo rentals in case you feel like really doing it up.

✳THREE DOG DOWN OUTLET
61545 US 93 North
(406) 883-3696, (800) 364-3696
www.threedogdown.com

This little store just across the Flathead River from downtown Polson is a phenomenon. It's been written up in *Glamour* magazine, *Entrepreneur* magazine, the *Chicago Tribune*, and many other national publications, including the travel magazines published by Delta and American Airlines. Owner Bob Ricketts, a former opera singer, can only be considered a world-class eccentric (and marketing man), and his bizarre vision of an all-down outlet store in Polson, Montana, has proved to be something the world was ready for. The store buys wholesale directly from many of the world's top down manufacturers, and there are also products manufactured right in Polson. Custom orders such as pillows, comforters, and even medical bedding are handled on a regular basis. The store's name, by the way, is a reference to the Inuit tradition of describing the temperature on a cold night by how many dogs you need to sleep with to stay warm.

THE BLACKFEET RESERVATION: EAST GLACIER, BROWNING & ST. MARY

The Blackfeet Reservation, home to approximately 10,000 enrolled members of the Blackfeet tribe, is set on beautiful, open prairie where the Blackfeet hunted buffalo for hundreds of years prior to the arrival of the white man. From every vantage point you can see the peaks of what the Blackfeet call the Backbone of the World—the Continental Divide. The mountains have always influenced the Blackfeet, who recognize them as sacred places. In more practical terms, the mountains create the wind and weather that sweep across the northern plains and touch every living thing on them.

OVERVIEW

The towns of East Glacier, Browning, and St. Mary will be the focus for most visitors, and listings in each category of service are arranged in that order.

East Glacier (also known as East Glacier Park) is home to many small businesses, shops, and restaurants, and you'll enjoy walking around the little town situated where the mountains meet the prairie. (A bicycle makes a good alternative for getting around.) The area offers tremendous hiking opportunities. The Two Medicine subdistrict of Glacier National Park is only an 11-mile drive away, with its web of trails leading to places such as Dawson Pass, Cobalt Lake, Twin Falls, or Old Man Lake. Glacier Park Boat Company also offers boat tours on Two Medicine Lake. The Lubec and Autumn Creek Trails beginning along US 2 west of East Glacier will lead you along beautiful, aspen-covered foothills. Be sure to check with a ranger station for current trail conditions prior to setting out.

Browning is the center of the reservation, and there you'll find all basic services. It's also the home of the Museum of the Plains Indian (see the Attractions chapter). An excellent time to visit Browning is the weekend after the Fourth of July, during the North American Indian Days. This large pow-wow draws Native Americans not only from tribes across the West but also from Canada and as far away as Florida. The combination of food, dancing, music, Native dress, and blend of people from across the continent create a remarkable atmosphere. You can also tour the reservation with a Blackfeet guide—Sun Tours does a great job of sharing Blackfeet history and culture through the native perspective.

St. Mary is a tiny community that grows significantly in the summer season. It's located at the eastern end of Going-to-the-Sun Road, and every square foot of this little town has a magnificent view of the mountains. From here you'll have access to the entire east side of Glacier National Park without too much driving required—Many Glacier is 40 minutes away, Two Medicine 45 minutes away, and Cut Bank 20 minutes away, not to mention Going-to-the-Sun Road. St. Mary has a large array of services available in the summer but very few in winter—read the descriptions carefully if you're planning to travel in fall, winter, or spring, as many businesses close down altogether.

The Blackfeet tribe requires a Conservation and Recreation Use Permit for non-members of the tribe who wish to recreate on the reservation, whether that be hiking, mountain biking, or otherwise exploring off the paved roads. The permit can be obtained at local businesses, where you can also purchase a tribal fishing license. For more information, call Blackfeet Fish and Wildlife at (406) 338-7207 or visit www.blackfeetfish andwildlife.com. Take the time to explore— the Blackfeet Reservation possesses a unique and unforgettable beauty.

ACCOMMODATIONS

Price Code

Keep in mind that some rates are based on availability. The average nightly rates for two adults at the hotels and motels listed in this section are indicated by a dollar sign ($) ranking in the following chart. Also, the hotels and motels in this chapter accept all or most major credit cards. Please note: In addition to the 7 percent state accommodation tax, all lodgings on the Blackfeet Reservation must collect an additional tribal accommodation tax of 6 percent.

$. . . . . **Less than $85**
$$ . . . . **$85 to $115**
$$$ . . . . **$115 to $150**
$$$$ . . . . **More than $150**

Hotels & Motels

✳**DANCING BEARS INN** $–$$
40 Montana Ave., East Glacier Park 59434
(406) 226-4402
www.dancingbearsinn.com
Open the year around, Dancing Bears Inn offers comfortable rooms with lots of amenities. The inn is located just a block or two from restaurants, shops, and the Amtrak station.

**EAST GLACIER MOTEL
  AND CABINS** $–$$$
P.O. Box 93, 1107 Hwy. 49, East Glacier Park 59434
(406) 226-5593
www.eastglacier.com
This little spot offers 2 fairly different lodging experiences. The 6 spacious motel units include 2 queen-size or double beds, a full-size refrigerator, microwave, hot plate, sink, and table service for 4. They cost $77 plus tax per night for 2 people. Eleven cozy cabins and bungalows are also available to rent. These cute little buildings, adorned with window boxes overflowing with flowers, have been renovated to include new showers and beds. Kitchenettes include a small refrigerator, hot plate, sink, and table service for 4. Cabins have 1 or 2 bedrooms and will accommodate 2 to 5 people. Rates run from $55 to $125 for 2.

The East Glacier Motel and Cabins are within walking distance of several restaurants, car rentals, and other shops. A pleasant yard out front is a great spot to picnic or hold a family get-together. Inquire for shoulder season rates; the motel and cabins close for winter.

MOUNTAIN PINE MOTEL $
Highway 49, East Glacier Park 59434
(406) 226-4403
www.mtnpine.com
The Mountain Pine Motel offers 25 units (some have 2 bedrooms), most with queen-size beds, color TVs, and tub/shower combinations. It's conveniently located within walking distance of about everything in East Glacier, including shops, restaurants, and car rentals. All rooms are nonsmoking and run from $720 to $84 per night for 2 people between June 15 and Sept 15; inquire about the lower rates between May 1 and June 15 and between Sept 15 and Oct 1, after which the motel closes until spring.

i Browning has now joined many other reservation towns in opening its own Glacier Peaks Casino. Located at the junction of Highways 2 and 89, it's right next to the Museum of the Plains Indian and the neighboring powwow grounds. The Jackpot Restaurant is open 8 a.m. to 10 p.m. each day, with discounts for seniors. Make a virtual visit at www.glaciercash.com or call (406) 338-CASH or (877) 238-9946.

THE WHISTLING SWAN MOTEL $
P.O. Box 318, 314 US 2, East Glacier Park 59434
(406) 226-9227
www.whistlingswanmotel.com
The Whistling Swan is charming, tidy, and clean. One step into the lobby and you'll start to absorb the unrushed, comfortable feeling that pervades this little motel. Each of the 8 rooms has color cable TV, and your night's lodging includes free coffee the next morning at the **Two Medicine Grill** just down the street and operated by the same owners. The Whistling Swan has the great merit of being open all year. If you've ever been caught in a blizzard, you'll appreciate how nice it is to have a good spot to wait out the weather. Rates are $58 per night for a single room and $78 for a double.

Guest Ranches, Resorts & Lodges

✴GLACIER PARK LODGE $$$–$$$$
East Glacier Park
(406) 892-2525
www.glacierparkinc.com
The first of the lodges to be built by the Great Northern Railway, Glacier Park Lodge continues to serve as the eastern gateway to Glacier National Park. Located not far outside the borders of the park, high peaks rise behind the lodge, creating an unforgettable backdrop. Lovely, well-tended flower gardens line the way as you approach the historic building. Walking through the lodge doors, you'll be startled to see the huge logs that support the lobby ceiling: immense Douglas firs, still bark-covered, imported from the Pacific Northwest to grace this hall. The neighboring Blackfeet Indians referred to the building as the "Big Tree Lodge." In contrast with its historic past, Glacier Park Lodge also offers modern amenities in addition to its 161 rooms. The hotel features a heated swimming pool, a 9-hole golf course, a gift shop, the **Empire Bar,** the **Empire Cafe Espresso Stand,** the Remedies Day Spa, and the **Great Northern Dining Room** (see Restaurants). Those working the information desk will be happy to set you up with a bus tour or hayride.

MONTANA'S DUCK LAKE LODGE $
P.O. Box 218, Duck Lake Road, Babb 59411
(406) 338-5770
www.montanasducklakelodge.com

If you're looking for accommodations that are decidedly off the beaten path, consider Montana's Duck Lake Lodge. It caters to anglers who frequent nearby Duck Lake, known for its excellent fishing. The lodge also offers a restaurant, rooms to rent (as well as a cabin and 2 campers), RV spaces, and tenting on acres of beautiful terrain. The lodge contains 9 bedrooms that share 2 common bathrooms. Double-occupancy rooms rent for between $64 and $112 per night in the summer. (Call to inquire about winter rates and rooms for 3 or 4.) The unpretentious living room downstairs showcases a collection of game trophies, and the dining room is open each night, serving chicken, steak, and fish specials. And if you're overdue for some good pizza, here's a place to get it. Five RV sites have full hookups, available for $25 per night. Tent sites cost $10 per night. Pets are allowed.

ST. MARY LODGE AND
   RESORT $$–$$$$
St. Mary
(406) 732-4431 (summer);
(888) 778-6279
www.stmarylodgeandresort.com
St. Mary Lodge is located immediately at the eastern end of Going-to-the-Sun Road, just outside Glacier Park. This complex of guest facilities includes cabins, lodge rooms, luxury cottages, and camping tepees, as well as several eating establishments, an outdoor store, gift shop, grocery, and gas station. A total of 122 accommodations are spread among 7 facilities. Rates run from $119 to $399 per night. Most services are open from mid-May to early Oct.

Great Bear Lodge rooms and suites are standard motel-style accommodations with queen-size beds, private bath, satellite TV, wet bars, and air-conditioning; the suites also have fireplaces and Jacuzzis. The historic Glacier Cabins feature a living area with breakfast table, microwave, and small refrigerator; they have a queen-size bed in an adjacent sleeping area and a separate bedroom with 2 single beds and a private bathroom. St. Mary Lodge also operates the Sun Cabin (sleeps 4) and the Guest House (sleeps 6). These larger cabins feature a variety of amenities, including full kitchens and gas barbecues. The East and West Lodges offer traditional lodge-style accommodations.

The main lodge houses the **Snowgoose Grill** (see Restaurants) and the **Curly Bear Cafe,** and an extensive gift shop offering everything from teddy bears and Native American jewelry to huckleberry products and homemade fudge.

Campgrounds & RV Parks

Price Code
$................. Less than $10
$$ .... $10 to $16
$$$ .... $16 to $24
$$$$ .... More than $24

JOHNSON'S RV PARK AND
   CAMPGROUND $$$–$$$$
HC 72, Box 10, St. Mary 59417
(406) 732-4207
www.johnsonsofstmary.com
The Johnson family has quite a few enterprises going in St. Mary—all located with a view overlooking the St. Mary Lakes and the mountains. But you'll be glad for the hill and trees that shelter the campground from the east-side winds (the answer to one question on their FAQ list should tell you something: "No, the wind has never blown like this before"), and the grassy sites, picnic tables, and fire rings make for a very pleasant stay. Patriarch Lester Johnson passed away in

2008, but his kids, Hugo and Kristin, continue the family tradition, and 2010 marked their 60th year in business.

All 82 RV sites are pull-throughs. Sites without hookups are $28.50 per night, sites with electricity and water are $38.50, and sites with full hookups are $44 per night. Johnson's also has 75 tent spaces that cost $25 each per night. The campground boasts a covered pavilion with a complete outdoor kitchen, hot showers, a laundry, and a store.

The Johnsons also have a camping cabin, cottages, and a B&B-style room for rent, and Johnson's World Famous Historic Restaurant is part of the complex, as well.

Chief Mountain

If you drive between St. Mary and Waterton Lakes National Park in Canada, or come in to Babb over the Duck Lake Road from Browning, you can't help but notice a looming, flat-topped peak that seems to lead the other mountains out onto the prairie near the border: Chief Mountain. Chief Mountain has a long history and prehistory as a significant spiritual site. For thousands of years the Blackfeet have held sacred ceremonies here, and they continue to do so today. The Chief Mountain Highway—Highway 17—affords many striking views of this imposing peak. A few miles northwest of Babb, pull off the road at the scenic overlook to enjoy the panorama of both mountains and prairie.

ST. MARY KOA $
St. Mary
(406) 732-4122, (800) 562-1504
www.goglacier.com
St. Mary KOA is on the shores of the St. Mary River and Lower St. Mary Lake, just moments from the town of St. Mary and Going-to-the-Sun Road. It could justifiably call itself a resort—this KOA offers not only tent sites, a group tent site, RV sites, and "kamping kabins and kottages," but also canoe, paddleboat, and mountain bike rentals, a playground and game room, an evening barbecue, outdoor hot tubs and a pool, a grocery store and gift shop, and, of course, beautiful views of the mountains, river, and lake.

St. Mary KOA is open from May through Sept. Tent sites are $32 per night, while fully equipped RV sites go for $56. Kamping kabins range in price from $90 to $170; these sleeping cabins have electricity and heat but no running water or bath. Bring your own bedding; water is available nearby, and each cabin has its own picnic table and grill. Kamping kottages and kamping lodges run from $186 to $240 per night, and include a bath, shower, and fully equipped kitchen. Prices are based on 2-person occupancy except for the lodges. Off-peak season prices are slightly lower. Reservations are highly recommended. Pet sitting is available, and so is food service at the AOK Grill.

And More . . .

✳BACKPACKER'S INN $
P.O. Box 94, 29 Dawson Ave., East Glacier Park 59434
(406) 226-9392
www.serranosmexican.com
For those backpacking or otherwise traveling light and low-budget, the Backpacker's Inn provides simple, comfortable lodging

just minutes from US 2 and the East Glacier Amtrak station. The inn has 3 dormitory rooms (one men's, one women's, one coed) that open onto a quiet, grassy fenced yard that's a pleasant place to relax. Cost per person per night is $12; a sleeping bag and pillow can be rented for $2 for the duration of your stay. Private cabins are also available at a cost of $30 per night. Reservations are recommended and must be confirmed 24 hours in advance of your arrival. The Backpacker's Inn, open from May 1 to Sept 30, is operated by Serrano's, right next door—so there's good Mexican food in the neighborhood, too!

ℹ️ The fastest route from East Glacier to Many Glacier (and on to the Canadian border at Carway)—and the straightest one, for those with long vehicles or trailers—is US 2 from East Glacier to Browning and then Glacier County Highway 464, the Duck Lake Road, to Babb. This paved, well-maintained road heads due north over the prairie. As it swings to the west back toward the mountains, it presents a huge view of the park's eastern front. You'll join US 89 about 8 miles north of St. Mary and 1 mile south of Babb.

THE BROWN HOUSE $
402 Washington St., East Glacier Park
(406) 226-9385

The Brown House, which is a guest lodge and also an art studio featuring fine ceramics, photographs, and paintings, offers 3 lovely rooms to rent at the corner of Washington and Dawsons Streets. Each has its own entrance and full bathroom; one has a queen-size and twin bed, the other a double and twin. Both rooms are elegantly and comfortably appointed (the double bed is an antique 4-poster). One is a "penthouse"—the second story in East Glacier is enough height to give you some view of the mountains, as well as of the town. The rooms do not have phones but do have television. Cost per night is $50 to $75 for double occupancy. The Brown House is open for lodging from June through Sept, when reservations are a must.

BROWNIE'S HOSTEL $
P.O. Box 229, 1020 Hwy. 49, East Glacier Park 59434
(406) 226-4426

Brownie's Hostel offers low-cost, basic lodging for the young and young-at-heart who are traveling through the East Glacier area. This 2-story log building has 16 beds (linens provided), a kitchen, laundry, baggage storage, parking, and bike rentals. It's located just a bit over a mile from US 2, and the hostel will pick up guests from the Amtrak station by arrangement. Private rooms are also available. A bakery and convenience store operate in the first floor. Brownie's, a member of Hostelling International USA, is open from June 1 to mid-Oct, weather permitting. Lodging is $17 per person per night; reservations are essential between July 4 and Aug 15. Groups are welcome but must make reservations.

JACOBSON'S COTTAGES $–$$
1204 Hwy. 49, East Glacier Park 59434
(406) 226-4422, (888) 226-4422

Twelve immaculately clean, modern cottages set among the pines and aspens of East Glacier Park . . . that's Jacobson's. Each cottage is carpeted and has cable television, electric heat, and tub/shower combinations; one includes a fully equipped kitchen

🔍 Close-up

Massacre on the Marias

If the greatest Indian victory of the West fought against the US Army was the **Battle of the Little Bighorn,** a lesser known but perhaps more typical event was the Massacre on the Marias. This encounter between the US Army and a band of Pikuni Blackfeet occurred in the winter of 1870, and it took a long time for the truth about the event to make its way to Washington. In many ways its tale of revenge, mistakes, and alcohol is all too familiar in this era. The following account is based on James Welch's *Killing Custer* (1994).

It's hard to say where such stories begin, but let's start this one in 1847. A trader for the American Fur Company, Malcolm Clarke, married a Pikuni, Cutting-off-head Woman. She was a member of the Many Chiefs band, as was her cousin, Owl Child. This band was led by Mountain Chief, a leader who had resisted the incursion of whites into Blackfeet territory. With this union, Clarke secured his position as a trader among the Blackfeet and gained the respect of the tribal elders to whom he was now related by marriage. Sometime later, Clarke retired from trading and settled on a ranch on Prickly Pear Creek, north of Helena. He was able to live quite comfortably and was well established in the Helena community.

Owl Child, previous to Clarke's marriage to his cousin, had become something of an outcast from the Many Chiefs band. He'd been involved in a killing for which he was ostracized, and although he spent some time with the band, he often roamed, growing bitter toward both the whites and his own tribe. But in 1867 he, with some other of Cutting-off-head Woman's relatives, visited Clarke's ranch. During the night, Owl Child's horses were stolen. He blamed Clarke and in turn stole some of Clarke's horses.

Clarke and his son Horace soon pursued the stolen horses to Mountain Chief's camp, where they found Owl Child. "Horace struck Owl Child with a whip and called him a dog. Clarke called him an old woman, and the men left with their horses. Now, it is not good to insult and beat a young Pikuni in front of his people. Such an action requires revenge . . . ." (Welch, p. 27). On August 17, 1869, Owl Child and 25 young warriors attacked the Clarke ranch. They left Clarke dead and Horace seriously wounded.

In an area already tense with hostilities, this was the last straw for the whites. The most powerful men in Helena demanded total annihilation of the "savages." They demanded the presence of the army. Initially, Gen. Philip H. Sheridan—reputedly the first to say "the only good Indian is a dead Indian"—delayed, saying he didn't have enough forces to attempt an attack against the Blackfeet. But at the same time he had

("everything but the groceries"). Prices run from $70 to $95 per night; an additional charge of $5 per person above the age of 6 is also assessed. Several restaurants are within walking distance.

Open from May 1 into Oct, Jacobson's is located on Highway 49 on the north side of East Glacier. Look for the 2 red A-frame

office buildings and the beautiful borders of flowers.

RESTAURANTS

Price Code

The following listings rate restaurants according to a 4-symbol price key, representing the

a plan: a new tactic, tried in 1868 when Indians were attacked unprepared in their winter camp on the Washita River. No longer was war confined to warriors: Women, children, and old men were driven from their tents and gunned down in the open.

On New Year's Day, 1870, Gen. Alfred Sully met with four Blackfeet peace chiefs: Heavy Runner, Little Wolf, Big Lake, and Grey Eyes. He wanted to speak with Mountain Chief, who did not show up. Nevertheless, Sully informed the others that to avoid war, they must deliver the dead bodies of Owl Chief and his party—within two weeks. The chiefs agreed, knowing they were incapable of meeting this demand; and Sully also recognized the futility of the agreement. He returned to Gen. Sheridan.

When the two weeks were up, Sheridan's plan went into effect. Scouts reported that Mountain Chief's band was wintering on the Marias River. Colonel E. M. Baker, stationed at Fort Shaw on the Sun River, was ordered to attack the band. Sheridan's telegraph read, "If the lives and property of the citizens of Montana can best be protected by striking Mountain Chief's band, I want them struck. Tell Baker to strike them hard" (Welch, p. 30).

Just before dawn on January 23, 1870, the army soldiers were in place above the Indian camp. One of Baker's scouts, a half-white, half-Pikuni named Joe Kipp, suddenly recognized by the designs on the tepees that this was not Mountain Chief's camp, but Heavy Runner's. Clearly, Mountain Chief had gotten word of the army's intentions and cleared out; Heavy Runner's band had meanwhile moved into the desirable location. Scouts and troops from the expedition alike, as well as Horace Clarke, who accompanied the expedition, later stated that Colonel Baker was drunk at the time of the attack—perhaps not an uncommon state for those leading hard and dreary lives. But when Kipp informed him that this was the wrong band of Blackfeet, Baker replied, "That makes no difference, one band or another of them; they are all Piegans [Pikunis] and we will attack them." He then threatened to have Kipp shot if the scout moved from the spot.

When the gunfire began, Heavy Runner ran from his lodge, waving a piece of paper—the safe conduct signed by General Sully at the New Year's Day meeting. He was shot dead. Most able-bodied men were out hunting, and when, at the end, 173 had been killed, most of them were women, children, and the elderly, still in their lodges. Many of them were totally helpless—smallpox had hit the band that same winter, too. Ironically, at the same time, Owl Child was dying of the disease in Mountain Chief's camp some 17 miles away.

The Blackfeet never took up arms against the United States again.

---

average cost of dinner for two people. The code excludes the price of beverages, tax, and gratuity.

$........................... $10 to $20
$$ .... $20 to $28
$$$ .... $28 to $35
$$$$ .... More than $35

THE CATTLE BARON
  SUPPER CLUB $$–$$$$
Junction of US 89 and the Many Glacier Road, Babb
(406) 732-4033

The most amazing makeover of the late-20th century was possibly the transformation of the Babb Bar—once called the "fourth-roughest bar in the country"—into the Cattle Baron Supper Club. Tastefully decorated with an Indian motif, the Cattle Baron is rapidly becoming known for its mouthwatering steaks. Many patrons have described dinner here as the "best steak they've ever had," so don't miss this opportunity to taste some fine Montana beef.

The Cattle Baron is open all summer, and they continue to experiment with winter hours. So, regardless of the season, if you're in the neighborhood and the lights are on, be sure to stop by.

GLACIER VILLAGE RESTAURANT AND BUZZ'S BREW STATION $-$$
304 US 2 East, East Glacier Park
(406) 226-4464

The in-house bakery, gourmet desserts, and espresso will probably be the big draw to the Glacier Village Restaurant, in operation since the 1950s, but breakfast, lunch, and dinner are good reasons to stop, too. The menu features a variety of hot sandwiches, salads, and pastas, and includes kids' selections. Bag lunches can be ordered to go for about $8. Huckleberry products are a specialty, including such unexpected creations as huckleberry pork chops. They also have a photo gallery with some terrific historic images of the area. Like many East Glacier businesses, this restaurant is open only during the summer months.

GREAT NORTHERN DINING ROOM $$-$$$
Glacier Park Lodge, East Glacier Park
www.glacierparkinc.com
(406) 226-9311 (summer only)

A Western theme dominates the Great Northern, and its menu features beef, chicken, barbecued ribs, and fish entrees. The restaurant offers a full buffet for breakfast, a luncheon carvery, and for dinner either a Western buffet or a la carte options. Breakfast runs from 6:30 to 10 a.m., lunch from 11:30 a.m. to 2 p.m., and dinner from 5 to 9:30 p.m. Box lunches are available for about $9. Also within the Glacier Park Lodge are the Empire Bar and the Empire Cafe, the latter operating out of the lobby and serving coffee and espresso drinks.

✳THE PARK CAFE $$
US 89, St. Mary
(406) 732-4482
www.parkcafe.us

"Pies for Strength" is the motto at the Park Cafe, in business for 30 years. The place will automatically draw your eyes from the road, as it is bordered all around with a beautiful garden of columbines, poppies, lupine, and big, blue delphinium. Inside you'll find several tables and a counter, though on a sunny summer day you might go for one of the tables on the outdoor porch. A few minutes of looking at the menu and you'll realize you have a tough decision to make; don't worry, though, whatever you choose will be excellent. The Park Cafe prides itself on the quality of its ingredients, and every breakfast, lunch, and dinner is fresh, wholesome, and homemade. Vegetarian fare is available (check out the "gallinaceous green" salad), but whether you choose that or a sandwich, burger, or nachos (great salsa), be sure to save room for pie! The Park Cafe always has a great selection—from fruit to berry to pecan or ice-cream pies—and they're all homemade and delicious.

The Park is open from around Memorial Day to mid-Sept, from 7 a.m. to 10 p.m. The cafe doesn't take reservations, but when it gets busy in the evening they do keep a waiting list—and a few minutes on the porch with the delphinium isn't bad at all.

SERRANO'S $-$$$
29 Dawson Ave., East Glacier Park
(406) 226-9392
www.serranosmexican.com

This great Mexican eatery occupies a century-old historic log house that's been retrofitted to serve as one of East Glacier's favorite restaurants. Somehow the mix of Western log building and Mexican restaurant works out just right—and you'll find this is often a busy place. Serrano's serves dinner only, but dinner runs from mid-afternoon to 10 p.m., 7 days a week. The restaurant has a full menu of Mexican delights, from soups, salads, and a la carte items to full dinners like chile puerco and pollo picado. Serrano's is open from May 1 to Oct 1.

SNOWGOOSE GRILL $$$-$$$$
St. Mary Lodge, St. Mary
(406) 732-4431
www.stmarylodgeandresort.com

The Snowgoose Grill mixes fine dining with a wonderful view for a distinctive dining experience. As you settle into your chair, you'll admire Red Eagle, Little Chief, Mahtotopa, and Dusty Star Mountains as they march up the shore of St. Mary Lake. A few moments later the menu will tempt you with its unique combination of buffalo specialties—prime rib, steaks, sausage, burgers—pasta, wild game, and nightly specials. While you wait, a basket of sourdough scones and honey butter will occupy your taste buds. And then there's dessert—huckleberry delights and other choices to top off the evening.

The Snowgoose Grill serves breakfast, lunch, and dinner from mid-May to early Oct. To warm up for dinner, you can sip a huckleberry margarita in the Mountain Lounge. Also on site is the more casual and less expensive Curly Bear Cafe, serving items like buffalo burgers and Mexican food.

TWO MEDICINE GRILL $-$$
314 US 2, East Glacier Park
(406) 226-9227
www.whistlingswanmotel.com

The Two Medicine Grill isn't just a restaurant, it's the social hub of East Glacier. The counter in front and the 7 or so tables in back are the meeting place for everyone in town, especially during the winter months when this is usually the only restaurant open. Breakfast, lunch, and dinner are all reasonably priced. Cinnamon rolls, soups, and chili are homemade—and be sure to check out the buffalo burgers and sour-cream-and-chive french fries. The Two Medicine Grill is open from 6:30 a.m. to 7 p.m., 7 days a week. The website carries the diner's menus, so tap in and you can start thinking now about what you're going to order when you get there!

✳THE TWO SISTERS $-$$
US 89, about 4 miles north of St. Mary
(406) 732-5535
http://twosistersofmontana.com

Whether you're coming from Babb to the north or St. Mary to the south, you won't miss the Two Sisters—it's the brightest paint job on a building perhaps in all of Montana! Inside, where the decor is equally outrageous, you'll find a comfortable little cafe known for its homemade soups, dinner specials, cake, and pie. They have an espresso machine, too, so stop for a latte if you're about to hit the road for the Midwest, Calgary, or Yellowstone. The Two Sisters—named for owners Beth and Susan Higgins, members of the Blackfeet tribe—is open for

lunch and dinner from June to mid-Sept, 11
a.m. to 10 p.m.

WHISTLESTOP CAFE   **$-$$**
1024 Hwy. 49, East Glacier Park
(406) 226-9292
Ordering breakfast at the Whistlestop can
be tough, because you have to choose
between stuffed French toast, caramel apple
French toast, huckleberry French toast, the
omelet menu—and the marvelous cream
puffs, napoleons, eclairs, and other luscious
pastries on display. Or perhaps you'll just
have to come back for the dinner menu,
which includes barbecue chicken and ribs,
stuffed potatoes, and sandwiches, as well
as huckleberry pie. The Whistlestop is open
from June 1 to mid-Sept, for breakfast, lunch,
and dinner. Its covered outdoor patio is
a pleasant spot to stop for an afternoon
refreshment, as well.

SHOPPING

Some places you'll want to stop and explore
include the gift shop at the Museum of the
Plains Indian (open all year) in Browning,
which features Native American crafts and
jewelry, and the gift shop at St. Mary Lodge,
with its wide variety of high-quality gifts and
souvenirs from the region. Another shop to
pop into is the unique Spiral Spoon, makers
of hand-carved wooden spoons and ladles.
They're located at 1012 Highway 49 in East
Glacier. And the Brown House in East Glacier
is primarily a fine ceramics shop, but it also
features paintings and photos by local artists.

SWAN VALLEY

Travel the Swan Valley and try to imagine the wild and pristine landscape a century ago when the first homesteaders broke sod, loggers began eyeing the virgin timber, and the Native American tribes freely hunted its abundant game.

The beauty and grandeur that are so abundant here for decades have captivated residents and regular vacationers, who simply call the valley "The Swan." While they welcome you with old-fashioned Montana hospitality, they passionately guard their valley's relative isolation, undeveloped character, and simple, unhurried lifestyle.

The Swan is bounded by official wilderness areas—the 73,887-acre Mission Mountains Wilderness to the west and the 1,009,356-acre Bob Marshall Wilderness to the east. Most of the mountain and valley lands are under the jurisdiction of the Flathead National Forest or belong to Plum Creek, a large timber company. The majority of the remainder belongs to the state of Montana and private landowners. The Swan and Mission Mountains soar to rugged 8,000 to 9,000 foot heights, stretching for nearly 100 miles without a road crossing them. When you enter the Swan on its only paved road—the two-lane, north-south Highway 83—there's no turning off midway. But traffic is much less than on the major north-south highways to the east and west, and many pleasurable stops are found along the way.

THE RIVER & LAKE

The Ice Age's magic touched the landscape here, carving the basins for Swan Lake and more than 50 other lakes of various sizes. These crystal-clear, snow-fed lakes drain via creeks into the Swan River as it winds Northward from its headwaters near the Swan-Clearwater divide. The river's flow is interrupted by Swan Lake's 9-mile length; from the lake's outlet, it continues on before emptying into Flathead Lake at Bigfork. Nearly every mile a sparkling creek gurgles under a highway bridge to join the river.

Swan Lake is bounded on the east side by the highway and many privately owned vacation properties, and on the west mostly by national forest, where steep, timber-covered slopes come right down to the shores. Tremendous biological diversity exists here with the convergence of three main forest types: the northern boreal, Rocky Mountain, and Pacific maritime forests, with larch and Douglas fir predominating, along with ponderosa, lodgepole, and other pines and Engelmann spruce. Major predator and prey species abound, and the Swan is a birder's paradise. Keep a sharp eye out for deer crossing the highway, especially early in the morning and in the evening.

THE PEOPLE, THEN & NOW

Archaeologists believe humans began hunting and camping in the Swan River

Valley on the heels of the receding glaciers about 10,000 years ago. Excavations have unearthed evidence of their presence thought to date from around 5,500 years ago. By the 18th-century Indian tribes used the area for religious gatherings and sweat-lodge ceremonies, giving the Swan River its original name, Sweathouse River, to the lower stretch. The Flathead tribes—the Salish and Kootenai—retained treaty hunting privileges in the Swan when they moved to their present reservation from the Bitterroot Valley in 1872. They also peeled the ponderosa pines to harvest the sweet cambium layer under the bark for food. Scarred trees from the 1800s can still be seen in the forest, including a notable one at the Pony Creek campsite reached by Forest Road 10651.

Fur trappers gathering beaver and marten pelts since the late 1700s for the Northwest and Hudson's Bay Companies had severely diminished that resource by the mid-1800s. Gold prospectors also explored the Swan after gold had been discovered elsewhere in Montana, but no significant mining was done here.

The first decades of the 20th century brought many changes as timber cutting intensified, settlers began constructing cabins, and the wealthy discovered the Swan as a vacationing ground. By the late 1800s much of the land had been brought into the Forest Reserve System, precursor of the USDA Forest Service, and the first ranger station was built at Holland Lake. Later stations, log structures built at Swan Lake and Condon, remain standing in good condition. In 1937 these stations were consolidated at Bigfork in a compound of buildings constructed by the Civilian Conservation Corps.

The largest timber sale in the history of the Flathead National Forest is said to have taken place in the Swan Valley during this time. From 100,000 to 150,000 board feet of mostly western larch, with some Douglas fir and pine, were cut by the Somers Lumber Company. They barged a steam engine on Flathead Lake to a point south of Bigfork. From there they laid tracks just ahead of the engine, drove it onto the tracks, then lifted the tracks behind it and repositioned them in front, leap-frogging this way until reaching the present forest recreation area near the village of Swan Lake. The engine served the logging operation between 1914 and 1919. Some folks say it was purposely sunk in Swan Lake and remains there today, but others claim it was taken out the same way it was brought in, was used in other logging operations, and finally was retired to a site at the old depot in Columbia Falls. The village of Swan Lake appeared during this early period, with the establishment of a store, a post office, and schools.

Kootenai Lodge, a luxurious vacation resort built during the teens and twenties on the north shore of Swan Lake, stood in marked contrast to the simple lives and dwellings of the loggers and homesteaders. The purchase of 137 acres of land on the lake's north shore by Anaconda Copper Company attorneys Lewis Orvis Evans and Cornelius Francis Kelley initiated the first development and several decades of incomparable opulent living and entertaining. Kelley became Anaconda's president and Evans its general counsel, and the compound, which had groups of separate cabins for each family, as well as the massive main lodge, became known locally as "Kelley and Evans." They lavishly entertained the copper company elite, royalty, and other wealthy or famous people, including Charles Lindbergh, Holland's Queen Wilhelmina, Will Rogers, and Montana artist Charlie Russell. The resort

🔍 Close-up

Your Safety in Mountain Lion Country

Much of Glacier Country and the Swan Valley is **mountain lion** country, so it's good to acquaint yourself with the behavior of these large felines. You'll find that bears get a lot of press here, while mountain lions get relatively little. Lions in general are extremely secretive and rarely seen; yet, unlike bears (which generally attack only when surprised or when they have come to regard people's belongings as a source of food), mountain lions do on occasion stalk people as prey. In particular, children and small adults need to be cautious. Children should not be allowed to play alone in suspected cat country, and they should never be permitted to run ahead of adults on the trail. Hiking alone even by adults is not advised for many reasons, lions being one of them. Something to keep in mind is that cats like cover for stalking prey; treed or cliffy areas are good habitat for them, and you are less likely to find one out in an open meadow. Consider too that some things people do may attract cats: A small pet dog, for example, looks like lunch to a cat, and may not be the best hiking partner for this reason. (Some residents have been known to put out salt licks or hay to attract deer—and then are surprised when the deer attract lions.)

Individuals have been attacked by mountain lions in the region in recent years. In one case, a boy was jumped midday in Apgar Campground at the foot of Lake McDonald. In other instances cats have been found within the limits of Flathead Valley and Swan Valley towns. Farther afield—in the Canadian Rockies and California, for example—mountain lions in isolated incidents have attacked and killed recreationists, like cross-country skiers and mountain bikers. If you should find yourself being stalked by a cat, remain calm and remember first that cats are curious, indeed, and the animal may be just checking you out. Talk quietly to the animal but look big and unafraid: If you have a small child with you, pick the child up and carry him or her on your shoulders—you'll both look bigger, and you'll know where your child is. Back slowly away. Should attack seem imminent, find something you can defend yourself with—a stick, a rock—or something you can throw from your backpack. Do not run. Should you actually be rushed, yell and fight back; cats can be intimidated (note this is the opposite of the advice given for dealing with bears). Once again, an ounce of prevention is worth many pounds of cure, so make noise when you're hiking.

The chances of seeing a mountain lion are slim—if you do, more than likely, it will be a quick glimpse of magic as a long tail disappears before your eyes. Bobcats and lynx also inhabit Glacier Country, but are even more rarely seen.

engaged local craftsmen for more than a decade to construct the buildings of native stone, larch, cedar, and copper. During its heyday, Kootenai Lodge employed up to 70 local people as cooks, housekeepers, butlers, chauffeurs, gardeners, bartenders, launderers, and in other occupations. Many area residents descend from those Kootenai Lodge workers and carry on in memory the Kelley and Evans legend.

The lodge and some of the land is now privately owned and in the process of being developed as luxury real estate. The rest of the acreage was logged and subdivided after the Kelley descendants sold the place in 1968. A visible reminder of that glittering age remains in The Rock House, built in 1930 on the lake's west side by Evans's wife, Martha. Reached only by boat, it provided a retreat from the hustle and bustle of the main compound. The Evanses entertained guests and held an annual party for lodge employees there. The house is also a registered historic site. You can see it perched above a large rocky point from the first pullout going south between mile markers 73 and 74 that takes you to the lakeshore.

Today's Swan Valley retains its simple rural character despite modest population growth and subdivision of most of the old homesteads. Many retirees have settled here, bringing a diversity of skills and backgrounds to community life and contributing to the area's economy, which still largely depends on its natural resources and tourism. Traditional timber cutting on state and federal lands has slowed dramatically, as concerned citizens have become involved in forest-management decisions and as philosophy and policy have begun to change regarding how to maintain forest health.

Facing polarization of the community by these issues, a group of upper-valley residents in 1990 formed the Swan Citizens ad hoc Committee to pursue collaborative ways of involving all interest groups and finding solutions to environmental, economic, and social problems. In 1996 the group established the Swan Ecosystem Center, a research and education center based in the Forest Service Condon Work Center. Its visitor information center provides a wealth of information about the Swan Valley's diverse natural environment and is well worth a stop. It offers hands-on interpretive exhibits, take-away educational materials, and accurate local information about the recreational and other activities in the national and state forests. It also provides an interpretive demonstration forestry project and a self-guided nature trail that explains the changing forest ecosystem. (You can check out the center online at www.swanecosystemcenter.org).

Public lands in and above the valley provide hundreds of miles of roads and trails for biking, horseback riding, cross-country skiing, snowshoeing, and dogsled touring. Camping is permitted free of charge on all forest lands except in developed fee areas. Use of state lands for any recreational purpose requires a recreational license, which can be obtained from the state forest unit headquarters at milepost 58 on Highway 83 or the Kalispell Unit on US 93 in Kalispell.

ACCOMMODATIONS

Price Code

Keep in mind that some rates are based on availability. The average nightly rates for two adults at the hotels and motels listed in this section are indicated by a dollar sign ($) ranking in the following chart. Also, the hotels and motels in this chapter accept all or most major credit cards.

$................. Less than $85
$$ .... $85 to $115
$$$ .... $115 to $150
$$$$ .... More than $150

Hotels, Motels & Resorts

✳HOLLAND LAKE LODGE $$–$$$
1947 Holland Lake Rd.
(406) 754-2282, (877) 925-6343
www.hollandlakelodge.com

The Great Bear and "The Bob"

If you can swing it, consider taking a day (or longer) hike while in the Holland Lake area, for you're smack in the middle of one of the biggest concentrations of wilderness in the contiguous United States. Look at a map of the area, and you'll see that to the west lies the USFS-administered **Mission Mountains Wilderness** and the adjacent **Mission Mountains Tribal Wilderness,** which is within the Flathead Indian Reservation. The Missions offer a woolly, Alaskan-type wilderness experience, with trail-less bushwhacking required to get to many of its more remote areas and plenty of grizzly bears, too.

On the other side of the valley, to the east, is the **Bob Marshall Wilderness.** Adjoining "The Bob" on the southeast is the Scapegoat Wilderness, and, to the north, the Great Bear Wilderness. Combined, the triad of wilderness areas encompasses some 1.5 million acres. Add to that the nearly 1 million wilderness acres of Glacier National Park, which is separated from the Great Bear only by a road corridor, and you have a wilderness complex of 2.5 million acres. That's larger than Yellowstone National Park.

The Bob, crown jewel of Montana's wilderness areas, was named after Bob Marshall, a forester and pioneer leader of the American wilderness movement. Marshall hoofed hundreds of miles through the wild country surrounding the South Fork of the Flathead River, gathering information that he would turn into a recommended plan for preserving much of the area from development. In 1940, shortly after Marshall's untimely death, the federal government set aside for protection nearly a million acres surrounding the South Fork. After Congress passed the Wilderness Act in 1964, The Bob received additional protection as a component of the National Wilderness Preservation System.

The well-maintained trail between Holland Lake and Gordon Pass is a popular west-slope route into The Bob, used by both backpackers and horsepackers. A popular destination, rising some 25 miles northeast of Holland Lake as the raven flies, is the Chinese Wall, a 1,000-foot-high escarpment along which the Continental Divide runs for miles. Forming part of the boundary between The Bob and the Sun River Game Preserve, the Chinese Wall is home to animals that include bighorn sheep, shaggy-white mountain goats, and golden eagles, which nest along its lofty cliffs.

Holland Lake Lodge is, quite simply, old Montana at its best. It's an awe-inspiring wilderness setting right on beautiful Holland Lake in sight of Holland Falls tumbling down out of the Swan Mountains. Built in 1925, the main lodge houses 9 guest rooms, bar, restaurant, and common room with a large fireplace of local river stone. Guest cabins with bath that sleep 4 to 6 guests have been restored and improved. The lodge restaurant serves breakfast, lunch, and dinner. The dinner menu features premium center-cut filet mignon and other specialties, as well as lighter vegetarian cuisine. The full bar stocks a collection of specialty premium California wines. Winter and summer there's lots to do here, including hiking, horseback riding, canoeing, cross-country skiing, ice-skating, and snowshoeing. The lodge grooms cross-country ski trails, and unlimited backcountry skiing can be enjoyed on national forest roads and trails. Dogsled rides round out the winter opportunities. They rent canoes, skates, snowshoes, and other equipment. Located at one of the major gateways to the Bob Marshall Wilderness, the lodge provides a selection of pack trips into the Bob, including fall hunting trips and winter ski-touring adventures. The Holland Lake turnoff is at the south end of the valley and is well-marked with large signs. The lodge is open year-round, except from Apr to May 15 and Nov 5 to Dec 15.

LAUGHING HORSE LODGE $$–$$$
P.O. Box 5082, 71284 Hwy. 83, Swan Lake 59911
(406) 886-2080
www.laughinghorselodge.com
In the village of Swan Lake, close to the lake and national forest recreation areas, this resort inn offers guests access to all sorts of recreational activities. Log cabins provide rooms with a range of accommodations, all with private bath. Guests can lounge in a common room, with woodstove, library, games, music, and TV, as well as in the pub that serves microbrews and Northwest wines. The rustic dining room serves outstanding beef cuts and other fare. Pets with responsible owners are welcome. In summer they rent sit-on-top kayaks, fishing kayaks, and bikes. Laughing Horse is open from May 1 through Oct 31, and during the Christmas-New Year's holiday season.

SWAN LAKE GUEST CABINS $$–$$$$
Highway 83, Milepost 78, Swan Valley
(406) 837-1137, (888) 837-1557
This resort features newer log cabins with handmade log furniture, kitchenettes, and gas barbecues. It's located on a hill overlooking Swan Lake, in a secluded, private wilderness setting. Lake views are visible from the property, but the cabins face toward the woods, providing glimpses of the Swan Mountains. The cabins have a maximum capacity of 6. Small children are not encouraged because of the heavily wooded setting and the presence of bears and mountain lions. Here you can enjoy a sweat in the centrally located, wood-fired sauna.

SWAN RIVER LODGE $–$$
Highway 83, Milepost 46.5
(406) 754-2688
www.theswanriverlodge.com
The rustic log buildings on the north edge of Condon, formerly a Super 8 motel, are a welcome sight for travelers during the winter months when many other lodgings are closed. Open year-round, this motel stays very busy during summer with tourists and in the fall with hunters and loggers until the snow blocks road access. Fourteen of their 22 rooms are nonsmoking, they have one room with wheelchair access, and pets are permitted at no extra charge. They also have RV hookups and 2 corrals for horses.

Campgrounds & RV Parks
Price Code
$	Less than $10
$$	$10 to $16
$$$	$16 to $24
$$$$	More than $24

SWAN LAKE TRADING POST AND CAMPGROUND $$–$$$
22998 Montana Hwy. 83, Milepost 71, Swan Lake
(406) 886-2303
www.swanlaketradingandcampground
.com

In addition to the full grocery, prepared sandwiches, local crafts, T-shirts, magazines, paperback books, household supplies, and stove fuel available at this community gathering place, you'll find the town post office along with a small campground with pleasantly shaded tent sites, full RV hookups, camping cabins, showers, and laundry. RV sites with electric go for $24 per night, tent sites cost $15, and the rustic cabins rent for $40. "Comfy Camping," where the proprietors provide everything you need for a night of luxury camping—from a tent and bedding to a cooler, lantern, and stove—is $30 per night. See the listing in the Shopping section of this chapter for more information.

✳SWAN VALLEY CENTRE $$
Highway 83, Milepost 42, Condon
(406) 754-2397
www.seeleyswanpathfinder.com
/swancentrecabins

Swan Valley Centre is one of those places that can boast if they don't have it, you probably don't need it. Water and electric hookups are available for campers, but no septic service (well, maybe they don't have *everything*), they offer monthly parking for RV campers, and they also rent 3 rustic cabins. Showers and a laundry await the tired and dirty backpacker or equestrian just off the trail. While you're there you can stock up on groceries and fishing supplies in the old-fashioned general store and have a deli picnic at one of the outdoor tables. Visitors and

locals are welcome to fish from the property along the Swan River behind the center. See the listing in the Shopping section of this chapter for more information.

RESTAURANTS

Price Code
The following listings rate restaurants according to a 4-symbol price key, representing the average cost of dinner for two people. The code excludes the price of beverages, tax, and gratuity.

$	$10 to $20
$$	$20 to $28
$$$	$28 to $35
$$$$	More than $35

HOLLAND LAKE LODGE $$–$$$
1947 Holland Lake Rd.
(406) 754-2282, (800) 648-8859
www.hollandlakelodge.com

The wilderness setting of this fine restaurant at Holland Lake Lodge and the views of Holland Falls make the breakfasts, lunches, and dinners experiences for the senses. And the food lives up to the promise of the surroundings. The dinner menu features premium center-cut filet mignon, other specialties, and vegetarian courses. The full bar stocks premium California wines.

HUNGRY BEAR STEAK HOUSE $$–$$$
6287 Hwy. 83, Milepost 38 to 39
(406) 754-2240

Outside and in, this restaurant welcomes you in old-fashioned Montana style. The imposing log structure houses a high-ceilinged dining room, a separate bar with pool table, and a dance floor. Mounted animals and trophy heads of local game adorn the high

Close-up

Floating The Clearwater Canoe Trail

After turning west off Highway 83 at a point a few miles south of the Holland Lake Lodge road, Nancy and I began bumping down the track that leads to the put-in for the Clearwater Canoe Trail. A mile north of the turn we'd stopped in at the Seeley Lake Ranger Station, where a knowledgeable ranger had guaranteed us that this river "trail" is suitable for any level of canoeist. In fact, he told us, the USDA Forest Service designated it for precisely that quality: The agency wanted to promote a stretch of river that nearly anyone can safely and enjoyably navigate. Unlike many streams in the region, the channel on this stretch of the Clearwater River is deep enough that beavers haven't managed to close it off by constructing dams, and log jams don't commonly block the river's flow the way they do on many area streams.

We were very pleased to hear from an official that the **Clearwater Canoe Trail** is negotiable by neophytes, because that's certainly what we were. At the parking area, ¾ of a mile from the highway, we wrestled the bright red canoe, generously lent to us by a friend in Missoula, off the top of the Jeep. Then we gently set it down close to the launching point while we retrieved lunch, binoculars, spare clothing, and other necessities from the car. After we donned our life jackets, Nancy crawled into the bow and I pushed us adrift, jumping into the stern just before the water deepened dramatically.

We paddled from the brackish backwaters put-in area into the main channel. Even there the water was so placid that we could hardly detect a current. Our efforts at synchronized paddling fell far short of Olympic perfection; in fact, it took a while before we stopped spinning down the river like a top turning counter-clockwise circles. I decided to try simply using the paddle as a rudder to steer and keep us in the channel, while Nancy paddled. It worked. Our canoe sliced smoothly through the mirror surface of the water, cutting a "V" that ultimately spread the width of the stream behind us.

Finally the river widened and we gained sufficient distance from the embracing willows that we could see our surroundings. It was a flawless fall day: probably 65 degrees and not a cloud in the sky, its blue brilliance rivaled and simultaneously complemented by the rich colors of early October. Amid blanketing stands of Douglas fir towered thick-trunked western larch trees, their needles burned gold by the season. Occasionally a breeze blew some loose and they drifted earthward, sparkling in the sun's rays like gold dust. Far to our east loomed the Swan Range, one of several mountain ranges contributing to a 1.5-million-acre wilderness complex that includes the Scapegoat, Bob Marshall, and Great Bear Wilderness Areas. Add to these the nearly one million acres of Glacier National Park, which is separated from the Great Bear only by a road corridor, and you've got a wildlands continuum larger than Yellowstone National Park.

The treeless tops of the Swan Range's highest peaks were dusted with white. We guessed that the snow had fallen the day before, while we were enduring hours of rain in the valley. To the west, and much closer than the Swans, hung the bulky peaks of the Mission Mountains Wilderness. I spotted an osprey high overhead in a dead snag some 50 feet off the river, apparently surveying all that was happening in her domain. Unfortunately, our intrusion spooked her; we could actually hear the large bird's wings cutting through the crisp fall air as she flapped into flight.

It seemed that each bend in the madly meandering stream was followed by a turn. We began wondering if there was a straight stretch on the entire river trail. A flock of coots scooted away, flying just above water level, as we rounded one bend. Then, there they were, waiting for us at the next, where they repeated their short flight to perceived safety. In some places the river twisted through willow thickets so high and tight that they blocked out the sun and surrounding mountains, causing us to lose all sense of direction. It didn't matter, though, because there was really no way to become truly lost. With the mountains obscured, the marsh environment made it easy to imagine that we were in Minnesota rather than Montana.

After about an hour on the water, we heard a strange "wobbly" noise. We rounded a left-hand bend and encountered the source of the sound: a common loon, bobbing along close to the starboard bank. (For you fellow landlubbers, that's the right side—as Nancy, who grew up in a Seattle seafaring family, informed me.) According to the canoe-trail brochure we'd obtained at the ranger station, the bird is anything but common here in the Northern Rockies. The brochure also informed us that in the spring, songbirds like thrushes, finches, and warblers are common along these waters. A host of other critters hang out in, on, and around the canoe trail, too: Part- and full-time residents include fish such as perch and landlocked kokanee salmon (whose fall spawning helps explain the presence of ospreys), painted turtles, muskrats, moose, and white-tailed deer. Even the occasional elk and mountain lion have been spotted by alert paddlers.

Shortly we pulled up to a clearing and stepped onto dry land. It was a heavenly spot for a picnic. Peanut-butter sandwiches, potato chips, and orange pop had never tasted so good. I lay down on the grass face-up, while Nancy tried her hand at tempting a trout by casting a fly. Ah, autumn in the Northern Rockies: intense sunshine, very few bugs, and the hearty scent of decaying leaves rich in the air. Absolute peace and quiet.

We pushed off again, and all too soon the Clearwater emptied into Seeley Lake, taking us along for the ride. In contrast to the intimacy enjoyed on the canoe trail, we suddenly felt overly exposed. Mellow waters yielded to a surface shattered by a gusty breeze. The final ½ mile to the take-out at the ranger station was our first real test at making forward progress. But we did get there, where we pulled the canoe up onto the sprawling lawn.

Underscoring just how wildly the 4-mile canoe trail twists and turns, we found the hiking trail that parallels the river and led us back to our car to be only 1 mile long. Though merely a few hundred feet from the river, it penetrated an altogether different world, a forest of old-growth spruce, larch, and pine, where the geese and ducks of the waterway were replaced by goshawks and owls. On that fall day the crackling forest seemed as desiccated as the canoe trail was waterlogged.

Exactly four hours after setting afloat we reclaimed our car. Our only wish was that the outing had taken twice that long.

—Adapted from *Montana Off the Beaten Path*
by Michael McCoy (Globe Pequot Press)

walls of both rooms, including elk, moose, mountain lion, bison, and beaver. Its specialty is beef, but it also serves chicken and seafood. If you're curious about trying Rocky Mountain oysters, here's your chance. Also known as "bull fries," they are on the list of appetizers. The restaurant serves breakfast, lunch, and dinner, stocks a full-service bar, and also has a club menu for kids.

LAUGHING HORSE LODGE $$–$$$$
P.O. Box 5082, 71284 Hwy. 83, Swan Lake 59911
(406) 886-2080
www.laughinghorselodge.com

Known by locals for its excellent Black Angus prime rib, Laughing Horse features traditional Montana cuisine with an international touch made to order, utilizing choice fresh ingredients from local farmers and ranchers. They unabashedly boast of the "best burger in the universe." Delicacies beyond beef include such lip-smackers as mango ahi steak, linguine ala pesto, and line-caught wild Alaskand salmon. From May 1 through Oct 31 the lodge serves dinner Thur through Sun from 5 to 9 p.m., and Sun brunch from 9 a.m. to 2 p.m.

SHOPPING

MISSION MOUNTAINS MERCANTILE
Highway 83, Milepost 45 to 46, Condon
(406) 754-2387

If you've forgotten something for your camping or fishing trip, you have a good chance of finding it here. On the site of an early trading post known as Buckhorn Camp, this store houses a mini-super market and deli with a full range of groceries, produce, beer, wine, household supplies, hardware, pet food, auto and picnic supplies, cosmetics, toys, greeting cards, and travel guides. They make baked goods on the premises and cut their own meat. They also carry horse feed, propane, diesel, and gasoline at 24-hour pumps. Mission Mountains Mercantile sells Montana hunting and fishing licenses.

i Swan Lake, which lies at the valley's north end, separates the "upper" and "lower" river sections. You may find these designations confusing, since "upper" refers to elevations at the headwaters, which lie at the valley's southernmost part.

MORLEY'S CANOES
P.O. Box 5149, Swan Lake 59911
(406) 886-2242

Greg Morley is a master craftsman who for years has been designing and constructing cedar-strip canoes by hand, using old-fashioned classic tools. Morley's canoes are owned by paddlers and crafts aficionados all over North America. At his shop in the village of Swan Lake, he and his son Steve meticulously craft the vessels from premium Northwest red cedar using wood-saving techniques to minimize waste. The beauty and performance of these canoes reflect the Morleys' years of experience building watercraft and even more experience plying North American lakes and whitewater. Stop in to see some examples of their customized canoes, skiffs, rowboats, and paddles.

SWAN LAKE TRADING POST AND CAMPGROUND
Highway 83, Milepost 71, Swan Lake
(406) 886-2303
www.swanlaketradingandcampground.com

Established in 1926, where the southbound road ended, this general store and post office originally ran the telephone switch-board for the area. Today it serves as a gathering place for summer and year-round residents who come to get their mail and chatter over a cup of coffee. It offers a full grocery, prepared sandwiches, local crafts, t-shirts, magazines, paperback books, household supplies, and stove fuel. They also have a small campground with tent sites, full RV hookups, showers, and laundry.

SWAN VALLEY CENTRE
Highway 83, Milepost 42, Condon
(406) 754-2397, (866) 754-2397

The words "Beer Beans Bacon," in woodblock letters on the outside wall of this general store, don't do justice to the variety of products and services offered inside. The original 1930s frame store has been enlarged over the years to accommodate many functions. Showers and a laundry await the tired and dirty backpacker just off the trail. While you're there, you can stock up on groceries, bulk natural foods, backpacker meals, and fishing supplies. The deli features home-cooked daily specials and freshly made pizzas. Year-round they offer 3 rustic rental cabins with full kitchens, water and electric hookups for campers (no septic), and monthly parking for RV campers.

Appendix

LIVING HERE

In this section we feature specific information for residents or those planning to relocate here. Topics include real estate, education, health care, and much more.

REAL ESTATE, RETIREMENT, HEALTH CARE, EDUCATION & CHILD CARE

The lure of Montana's mountains, rivers, and skies brings many people from throughout the country, and the world, to this "Last Best Place." Love of this land makes many want to stay—and perhaps you're one of them. It was only months ago that some residents were merely visitors or curious armchair travelers dreaming pioneer dreams. For others, it was generations ago that their families put down roots, giving children the chance to discover the beauty of wilderness in their own backyard. Living in Montana is like an adventure that starts anew each morning. No matter whether your day includes a routine of office, kids, and home, or whether it's full of the horizon—miles of driving, hours of wilderness, acres of farmland or ranch land—the life you can live here is a rarity in the 21st century. Imagine Glacier Country as home: glaciers, grizzlies, glistening streams. Then consider starting to make your dream come true.

Though the scenery may dominate this special place, you will not be moving to a cultural wasteland by any means. In fact, a standout feature of the area in general is its rich abundance of arts and entertainment. Local and regional theater companies, an excellent orchestra, smaller musical groups, resident artists and writers—they all contribute to an exciting mix uncommon for an area with such a small population base. The weekly entertainment section of the newspapers are chock-full of choices year-round, and most folks don't even try to keep up with the dizzying array of activities, especially around the holidays.

Sound like paradise? A note of caution: Consider what kind of environment this is for a long-term relationship and not just a summer romance. If you're moving from a warm, sunny place, talk to others who've come before you. Try to spend a few weeks here in the winter before making the permanent leap. Remember that the Flathead Valley records an average of just 71 sunny days per year (days when $^3/_{10}$ of the sky or less are covered by clouds) and that gray skies are often the norm in winter. Make sure you have a good job or enough retirement income to support you in a place where wages are generally low and the cost of living is above the national average. It's a magical place, but practical planning is needed to make your dreams come true. Visions of happily-ever-after aside, you probably can use guidance for some of the challenges you may face in the first weeks and months of your relocation. Let the sections of this chapter offer some "mile markers" to get you started down the right road.

Welcome to northwestern Montana!

REAL ESTATE

Location, Location, Location (Part I)

One of the hardest decisions you may face when planning a move to Glacier Country is deciding which view you'll wake up to each morning. Rural or in town? Mountain, river, or both? Forest or meadow? Lakeshore or golf fairway? With so many choices and each vista more beautiful than the previous, the home search can feel overwhelming. Try to stay patient and remember the things you need most to feel comfortable. A location in town can be much more convenient and more social—and sometimes more crowded and complicated. On the other hand, living miles from town might sound romantic— pristine, tranquil—and indeed be fine until your multiple trips to school, the sitter, and the supermarket make you feel like you spent the whole day in the car. If you're moving from a place where long commutes are common, but snow isn't, adjust your thinking to reflect local conditions. A half-hour drive over winding roads may seem like no big deal in the summer, but think about that drive twice a day during the winter, when the roads are icy and a deer could pop up in front of you on the road without warning. No matter how beautiful the view and peaceful the solitude are at the end of the day, they may not seem worth it after a few white-knuckle trips in snowstorms. Winter is a force to be reckoned with when making your plans.

Another practicality to consider is water and sewer. Many homes built outside of the city limits are on septic systems and pump their water from individual wells. If you're planning to build, this is a critical concern. Drilling wells can be expensive, and septic failure catastrophic, so do your homework.

Choices for heating and cooling your home also need to be considered. Natural gas is available in many areas of the valley, but other places—even some quite close to town—don't have gas. In that case, propane, wood, solar, geothermal heat exchange, or what? Extending utilities to new homes also can be expensive. Don't let the gorgeous view from a piece of mountaintop property blind you to the complications of building there. Some practical thinking now will save you a lot of headaches later.

Try to picture your new home in each of the four seasons. Think about that long, scenic quarter-mile driveway to your house. Then think about clearing heavy snowfalls from that long driveway. Who's responsible for plowing and maintaining the access roads? If you're not on a city or county road, you, the homeowner, must bear those costs. Some rural subdivision roads are pitted with potholes because residents won't agree to pay their share for repairs. Take a hard look at those mountaintop hideaways. The views may be breath-catching, but you've got to get up and down the mountain in the winter. Think about fire protection. If you want to settle in the country, where is the nearest volunteer fire department? Privacy may not seem so appealing in case of an emergency. Do you want room to expand on your property to keep stock and add outbuildings, or will you be content with the limitations of a standard city lot? If you're a social person, will you feel lonely or isolated with no neighbors in a 2-mile radius? Consider each option carefully and you'll avoid going too far in your quest to get away from it all.

Now add a buyer's market to the mix. New arrivals are often amazed at the number of homes for sale and their reasonable prices, compared to where they've come from.

Close-up

Native Plant Nurseries

As the population of the Glacier area continues to grow, maintaining its character—mountain views, open meadows, that special "feeling"—becomes more and more important and challenging. Landscaping with native plants is something almost anyone can do that is a real "win-win." Flowers, grasses, and trees are all part of the local ecosystem, obviously. They are the foundation of the food chain, whether its birds feeding on mountain ash berries or bears wolfing down huckleberries. Homeowners, especially those with rural acreages, need to control exotic and noxious plants that if left alone run wild, like thistle and knapweed, and can displace the native forage critters like elk and deer depend on. And native plants are already adapted to this area; they evolved here, after all, so they're used to our seasons. With over a thousand species of plants native to the Flathead and Glacier area, you can pick from many that will brighten the entrance or backyard of your home. If you're unfamiliar with such species, check out some local native plant nurseries to bring you up to speed. Graceful yellow columbine, purple wild asters, brilliant blanketflower . . . these and others will bring native color and beauty to your special place in Glacier Country.

Windflower Native Plant Nursery (406-387-5527; www.windflowernativeplants .com), headquartered near West Glacier, is a good place to start. The locally owned, small-scale nursery raises many varieties of native flowers and some native grasses, sedges, and shrubs. All are guaranteed to have been ethically collected Terry and Maria can offer suggestions on what grows best in sun or shade, or what combinations might work best in your unique situation. Call ahead (to arrange a time to visit and to get driving directions. Windflower also sells through local farmers' markets during the summer.

Planting your own native flower garden might be the beginning of something really big—the plants themselves are fascinating. If you find yourself wanting to know more, be sure to check out the Flathead chapter of the Montana Native Plant Society (www.mtnativeplants.org/Flathead_Chapter), which holds regular meetings and events open to the public. You'll find you're not alone by any means!

They get anxious, thinking of markets in Washington and California where homes sell in a matter of days, and buyers must move quickly to seal a deal. As elsewhere in the country—though not to the extent seen in certain markets—the economic downturn over the past couple of years has caused a drop in real estate prices in northwestern Montana. Kalispell and other towns have had their share of property foreclosures, as well. Combined with the current low lending rates, now looks like a good time to buy for those with the means to do so.

This area offers the presence of both nationally known and locally respected real estate offices whose agents can help you in your search. These agents are up-to-date on local trends and the latest developments in the market. Take your time and find one who specializes in what you're looking for (e.g., lakefront, small farm, etc.) and who picks up on your interests and style. Real estate is big business in Glacier Country. Personal recommendations are always a good way to find a Realtor. Ask your friends and acquaintances who they used when they bought or sold a home. Your search will be more enjoyable and more successful with an agent who can help match you with the right property. Then grab some of their publications, go online to scout out some possibilities, and you'll soon be home!

Real Estate Companies

The following is a short list representative of the many real-estate agencies in the region.

CENTURY 21 HOME & INVESTMENT CENTER
264 North Main St., Kalispell
(406) 755-2100, (800) 321-2401
www.century21flatheadvalley.com
Century 21 Home & Investment Center, in business for a quarter century, consists of at least a dozen brokers and agents. "We have the knowledge and integrity of experienced brokers and the power of Century 21," says owner/broker Edna Hellickson. The firm handles all types of transactions, with individual agents specializing in areas such as farms and ranches, commercial, and residential property.

CENTURY 21 WHITEFISH LAND OFFICE
110 East Second St., Whitefish
(406) 862-2579, (800) 933-9155
www.c21whitefish.com
Established in 1978, Century 21 Whitefish Land Office handles a variety of real estate, primarily in the Whitefish vicinity, but also serving outlying areas like Columbia Falls and Libby. They specialize in resort properties that are second homes for buyers. Whitefish Land Office, with around 10 real estate

agents, has been ranked one of the top Century 21 offices in Montana for closed sales. If it's a good time to invest in real estate, have a look at the web listing of a Whitefish Hills Drive property that's a little over 6,000 square feet in size . . . for a cool $5.25 million.

i To add a special focus to your visit to Glacier Country, try a field seminar with the Glacier Institute. Outdoor education classes cover many topics, ranging from outdoor photography to medicinal plants, to geology to predator-prey relations. Classes may last a single day or stretch over several days; some are tailored for children. Hike levels are rated for each course. The Glacier Institute is affiliated with Flathead Valley Community College and college credits can be arranged for many courses. For more information, visit www.glacierinstitute.org or write: The Glacier Institute, 137 Main St., P.O. Box 1887, Kalispell, MT 59903. The office phone is (406) 755-1211 year-round; the summer field camp at Glacier National Park is open from May through October, (406) 888-5215.

CHUCK OLSON REAL ESTATE INC.
241 Main St., Kalispell
(406) 752-1000, (800) 555-5376
www.chuckolsonrealestate.com
Chuck Olson Real Estate is a locally owned, independent firm established in 1972, and the largest office not affiliated with a national franchise. The agency has around 18 agents, including 6 owner/brokers. According to owner/broker Chuck Olson, the firm consistently ranks among the top agencies in overall sales.

COLDWELL BANKER WACHHOLZ & COMPANY REAL ESTATE
1205 South Main St., Kalispell
(406) 751-4300
www.beinmontana.com
This is the largest real estate firm in western Montana, with more than 100 agents in offices throughout the Flathead Valley and beyond. Paul Wachholz established his original office in Kalispell in 1981 and affiliated with Coldwell Banker in 1985. Since then the company has been a top-producing Coldwell Banker office and the recipient of numerous Coldwell Banker awards. The company handles all types of real estate, from commercial property to high-end homes, and from recreational properties to new communities.

EDGEWATER REALTY, INC.
1 Fifth Ave., Polson
(406) 883-5203
www.lakeshorestore.com
This company has been in business since 1965, with a name change or two along the way. As its name implies, Edgewater specializes in lake properties, mostly in the area between Polson and Rollins.

MONTANA BROKERS, INC. REALTORS
685 Sunset Blvd., Kalispell
(406) 758-4747, (800) 933-3177
www.montanabrokers.com
Owner Rick Doran is a self-described "local yokel" who grew up in the Flathead Valley and has been in the real estate business here since 1978. Montana Brokers was established in 1986 and currently has 14 agents, mostly brokers with an average of 15 years' experience, and one of the highest per-agent production in the valley. Although a number of the agents are natives, Doran says the firm

also welcomes people from other places, because "We all came here from somewhere, sometime." Montana Brokers handles numerous waterfront properties and has even sold an island in Flathead Lake.

NORTHWEST MONTANA ASSOCIATION OF REALTORS AND MULTIPLE LISTING SERVICE
110 Cooperative Way, Kalispell
(406) 752-4197
www.nmar.com
This organization can provide you with statistics on real estate transactions and general information about companies in the Flathead Valley. The association represents more than 100 real estate firms in Flathead and Lake Counties—a total of about 500 Realtors—and while it can't make recommendations or referrals to individual real estate firms, it can give the names, addresses, and phone numbers of its members.

Real Estate Publications

HOMES AND REAL ESTATE
The Daily Inter Lake
727 East Idaho, Kalispell
(406) 755-7000
Published periodically by the *Daily Inter Lake* newspaper, this is a comprehensive guide to current listings around the valley, with most prominent agencies represented.

THE MONTANA LAND MAGAZINE
Lee Enterprises
P.O. Box 1897, Billings 59103
(406) 657-1580
www.montanalandmagazine.com
This 6-times-a-year publication contains pages of statewide and Rocky Mountain listings, including the greater Glacier Country

region. It is sold both by subscription ($30 per year) and at newsstands and bookstores.

**POLSON AND LAKE COUNTY HOMES
 AND REAL ESTATE**
The Daily Inter Lake
727 East Idaho, Kalispell
(406) 755-7000
Published several times a year, this guide gives a comprehensive listing of property for sale in the southern part of the Flathead Valley.

In addition to these periodicals, some individual real estate firms publish booklets listing their properties. Some of these booklets appear as newspaper inserts, and others are available on the racks of free publications that are maintained at various locations outside grocery stories, motels, and shopping malls.

Building

New construction is not only an important marker of the region's economic well-being, it can also be the way for you to get exactly what you want in your home. Whether your dream is to build yourself, choose from the models in a new neighborhood community, or have a custom-built LEED-certified eco-friendly home, there are building contractors in the area prepared to deliver. The **Flathead Building Association,** 21 West Reserve Dr., Kalispell, (406) 752-2422, can refer you to a builder who specializes in the type of home you desire, or answer questions about the particular contractors bidding on your job. The association publishes the annual *Parade of Homes* consumer magazine, highlighting builders and other service providers in the region. You can visit the association's website at www.buildingflathead.com.

Once You've Unpacked the Boxes...

You're finally settled into your new home, and ready to get involved in the life of your new community. The Flathead Valley has the usual contingent of clubs, lodges, business associations, and groups for special interests. Whether you're interested in quilting, reading, photography, investments, Bible study, barbershop music, or duplicate bridge, a group of people of like interests probably exists here. If not, you can start a group of your own and ask your neighbors to join you. *The Daily Inter Lake* runs a comprehensive list of meetings every Sunday and once a year publishes a guide called *The Answer Book,* a compilation of various community resources that also can give you valuable information. Community bulletin boards and radio and newspaper announcements also let you know what's going on in your new home. You'll find that people are generally very friendly toward newcomers, and they're happy to share their love of this special place. Many of the people you'll meet were in your shoes not so long ago: A recent study classified one in six residents of Flathead and Lake Counties as newcomers. You'll find good friends and neighbors in the Flathead, as long as you're willing to be a good friend and neighbor yourself. So relax, take a deep breath of the fresh mountain air, have a look at the glories of nature that surround you, and enjoy your new home. You're going to love it here!

Home Rentals

Resist that urge to buy the first house you see, say locals, and rent for the first year—or at least through your first winter. Even if you've visited before, this advice makes good sense. Renting gives you the chance to test your instincts on neighborhoods, landscapes, and other practicalities of Montana life before committing to a particular property. You'll gain a sense of how much home you need to feel comfortable; a chance to prioritize, say, the fireplace versus the hot tub. Then when you're ready to buy, you'll have more information on what truly attracts you and what to avoid. Some rentals are beautiful homes languishing on the market or even vacation properties going unused during the off-season. Many owners prefer to have their homes lived in rather than sit vacant. It can be your chance to live in a great setting while you test the waters, without homeowner headaches like patching the roof or fixing the furnace.

Whether it's an apartment in a large complex, a privately owned home, or a professionally managed property, interview a prospective property manager or landlord carefully before signing any papers. Ask them to describe what their services to you will include. Some landlords can be very attentive to the needs of renters, especially dependable, long-term ones. Lovely places can often be found for a reasonable cost. Some agencies can even help you secure a temporary place to stay when you first arrive. But remember that an agent's primary customer is the property owner, not you. Overall, renting may not be the best option for people who like to feel "settled," but it works for a great many a newcomer to Glacier Country.

Rental Agencies

CORENTAL
435 South Main St., Kalispell
(406) 752-5600
http://coRental.net
CoRental, established in 1983, provides professional management for apartments, houses, and commercial property. Services offered are a full-time licensed real estate broker, free advertising, tenant screenings, and 24-hour telephone service. Their motto: "Setting the standard for professional property management in northwestern Montana."

EAGLE BEND FLATHEAD VACATION RENTALS
836 Holt Dr., Bigfork
(406) 837-4942, (800) 239-9933
www.mtvacationrentals.com
This firm specializes in vacation homes on Eagle Bend golf course and other areas, including Flathead Lake, Swan Lake, and Swan River. Owned and operated by Denise Grenier since 1990.

FIVE-STAR RENTALS
704 Baker Ave., Whitefish
(406) 862-5994
www.fivestarrentals.com
Five-Star Rentals manages a wide range of properties, from modestly priced condos to large homes, mostly in the north end of the Flathead Valley.

FLATHEAD PROPERTY MANAGEMENT
280 Fourth Ave. West North, Kalispell
(406) 752-5480
http://flatheadrentals.com
This licensed property management firm has been in business since 1981 and offers a variety of services to landlords. It also rents an array of storage units.

i No, you're not seeing cross-eyed . . . and no, that's not a typo. Kalispell does have addresses that read WN (West North) and EN (East North), and not the usual NW and NE. A few years ago, to accommodate the city's computer system, a proposal was made to change these addresses to the more usual configuration . . . but the residents rejected it soundly, preferring to keep their traditional "WN" and "EN" addresses. And they work just fine!

Location, Location, Location (Part II)

The great spots in Glacier Country are many. The rugged sportsman, the retired couple, and the growing family all find their places here in an eclectic and exciting mix. Neighborhoods may not be as clearly defined as they are in some cities, and exclusive parkside and waterside properties are located throughout northwestern Montana. But each major center enjoys a personality of its own. Other standard criteria for selecting a home will still apply, so ask a reputable agent for current information on the community resources, schools, and services in your area of interest.

Bigfork & Flathead Lake

Quiet and quaint, the village of Bigfork is home to delightful art galleries and fine shops and restaurants. In the summer the single main street is alive with visitors enjoying the ambience that sometimes can make Bigfork seem like a stage set rather than a real, living town. One of the best things that happened to Bigfork seemed like a disaster at the time— the highway bypassed the town. As a result, Bigfork has been spared the through traffic that can plague Kalispell and Lakeside, and its stoplight-less downtown retains a village

feeling. Parking is another matter, though, as summer visitors vie for a limited number of spots. Homes and cherry-orchard properties extend along the eastern shore of Flathead Lake down to Woods Bay, with summer cabins and year-round home retreats reaching along the Swan River out into Ferndale. You'll find newer homes on large wooded lots at the edge of the mountains along Foothill Road, near Echo Lake, and in the Many Lakes development, while west of the highway you can find older farm homes and estates with views of the Flathead River, fields of hay, mint, and dill, and marshes full of wildlife. If you must live where you golf and golf where you live, Eagle Bend golf community is just west of Bigfork Village. On the western shore of the lake, the community of Lakeside is booming with mid-priced homes boasting lake views and proximity to Blacktail Mountain Ski Area. And all along the lake, small summer cabins are being turned into year-round residences. Farther south is Polson, a pretty little town at the foot of Flathead Lake. The view of the lake coming over the hill on US 93 from Missoula is absolutely stunning. Polson is located in a relative banana belt, and residents boast they can play golf every month of the year (though not every day of every month!).

Kalispell

The commercial center and seat of Flathead County, Kalispell is the largest municipality in the valley and in northwest Montana, making it popular for those who like to be close to abundant services and community resources. Several years ago, *Mountain Sports and Living* magazine picked Kalispell as one of the best mountain towns in the nation based on quality of life criteria. Streets in the historic central part of town south of the railroad tracks continue to hold much of their charm from the town's early days. Stately maple and chestnut trees line the boulevards in the older sections of town, and the fall colors are striking. Many of the historic and larger homes are found on the east side near Woodland Avenue, while newer homes have developed north of the downtown near Lawrence Park and south of town near the city airport. Building lots within the city are rare, and many people opt for remodeling an existing home rather than building a new one. Living within the city limits provides many conveniences. Residents can walk to Woodland Park, to shops on Main Street, to the Kalispell Center Mall, and to movie theaters, museums, concerts, and art galleries. The downtown is experiencing an ongoing commercial revival, with development of several small shopping malls and restoration of the KM Building, a historic landmark that dates from more than a century ago. A special note about Woodland Park, which was donated to the city of Kalispell in 1903 by the widow of the town's founder, Charles E. Conrad. This 40-acre park is a treasure enjoyed by residents and visitors year-round. Flocks of ducks, geese, and swans delight park visitors and beg for handouts, and generations of children and their parents have kept generations of the birds well fed. You can purchase a healthy snack of cracked corn at the convenience store across the street from the park and delight the resident waterfowl population. The flower gardens here are a popular spot for summer weddings, a skating rink is open in the winter, and youngsters can splash in the municipal pool on hot summer days. Families wander across the wooden bridges and businesspeople take a lunch break in this beautiful spot, even on chilly winter days.

Whitefish

Popular as a ski-resort town for many years, Whitefish was a fur-trading, logging, and railroad town in its early days, and originally known as Stumptown. Not a great deal of its blue-collar roots remain now that Whitefish has gone upscale. Today it's a growing community that offers year-round outdoor attractions—first and foremost the Whitefish Mountain Resort and Whitefish Lake—as well as such community resources as new theater and public library buildings. With a downtown core full of restaurants and shops, and a slate of special events, Whitefish has developed an identity as a hip and lively scene to see and be seen in. Real estate in this area can be pricey, and you'll pay a real premium for lakeshore property on Whitefish Lake, if there's even any available.

Columbia Falls & Glacier National Park

The gateway communities to Glacier National Park have no trouble attracting new residents who want to live just a few minutes from the park's boundaries. Columbia Falls has long been a home for generations of employees of Plum Creek Timber and the Columbia Falls Aluminum Company (the latter shuttered its operations early in 2009, costing the community around 200 jobs). But like all areas of the Flathead, secluded wooded or riverside lots attract dream-house homeowners-builders. The communities of Hungry Horse, Martin City, and Coram lie beyond, and those who really want to get away from it all can travel up the North Fork Road into the remote Polebridge area near the boundaries of Canada and Glacier National Park.

Living in Grizzly Country

The forests and wilderness areas of northwest Montana comprise one of the largest expanses of grizzly habitat in the country. As greater numbers of homeowners settle in outlying areas of the Flathead, reports of contacts between humans and bears have increased. And in years when bears encounter food shortages (like a bad crop of huckleberries, their favorite food), the number of encounters is even greater. In just a week's time in Sept 2010, for example, Montana Fish, Wildlife and Parks trapped five grizzlies in the region, including one they euthanized due to its history of getting into trouble in the Swan Valley. Rangers advise special precautions for residents who live in grizzly country and along its edges. They discourage the feeding of birds, deer, or other animals and recommend that garbage and pet food be secured inside, not on porches or in sheds. Bears that sniff out and win these "food rewards," they advise, are essentially learning to return to human settlements for an easy meal. Once this behavior is learned, it is very difficult to train a bear to seek berries only in the forest. A bear that learns this lesson too well will probably wind up causing property damage and will end up being destroyed. Prevention rather than correction is advised so that sightings of animals might continue with few unfortunate consequences.

Living in Forest-Fire Country

Your home nestled amid the western larch and Douglas fir trees brings with it special concerns and responsibility—wildfire control. Large forest fires take on historic significance as they wipe out the trees that make up the livelihood of residents and support the local economy. Everyone takes the risk of fire seriously. For homeowners this means taking care of forested areas on your property and keeping underbrush—a source of fire fuel—controlled. Prevention of chimney fires through regular cleaning of stovepipes and flues is another important precaution. Make sure firefighters can find your hideaway. Efforts to quench fires at two remote homes near Kalispell were complicated by the fact that no house numbers were posted on access roads. Fire can quickly wipe out your dreams, so take all the precautions you can. To learn about firewise building, landscaping, and more, visit www.firewise.org.

A Note on Recycling

Moving to an area where you have to haul your own trash to the county landfill can take some getting used to. (Garbage pickup service is available most places in the Flathead Valley, but not all rural locations.) Recycling as much as possible—while it does take up some space in your garage, utility room, or basement—can dramatically reduce the amount of trash you and your family generate. This will ease pressure on the local landfill and make you feel good and "green" at the same time. For information on what can be recycled and where you can drop it off, visit **Valley Recycling**'s website at www.valleyrecycling.com.

RETIREMENT

Before retiring to the Flathead Valley or elsewhere in Glacier Country, it's important to know what facilities exist to care for you and/or other family members during the golden years. Retired "empty nesters" constitute a relatively large segment of newcomers to the valley, so housing options will be increasingly important to them in the future. Seniors make up a significant portion of the population and many activities and services are available for them, and lots of volunteer opportunities exist in the community as well. Flathead Valley Community College offers a popular "Senior Fridays" program in the winter, with classes ranging from computer training to gardening to foreign languages. Lunch and transportation from area senior centers are included in the reasonable fee.

AGENCY ON AGING
160 Kelly Rd., Kalispell
(406) 758-5730
http://flathead.mt.gov/aging
This county agency offers a variety of services to those 60 and over, including a meals-on-wheels program, transportation, information and assistance for a variety of concerns, legal and insurance counseling, a newsletter, reference library, homemaker program, and companion care.

EAGLE TRANSIT
723 Fifth Ave. East, Kalispell
(406) 758-5728
http://flathead.mt.gov/eagle
Adequate transportation is necessary for a comfortable life just about anywhere, and bus service can be a godsend for seniors who no longer can drive. County-run buses serve the general public in Flathead County with city routes in Kalispell, Whitefish, and Columbia Falls. The service offers special transportation for the elderly and passengers with disabilities. For information on routes and schedules, visit the website listed.

Senior-Citizen Centers

A number of senior centers offer a variety of activities. Here are some of the centers in the area:

- **Bigfork,** 639 Commerce St., (406) 837-4157
- **Columbia Falls,** 205 Nucleus Ave., (406) 892-4087
- **Kalispell,** 403 Second Ave. West, (406) 257-1598
- **Polson,** 504 Third Ave. East, (406) 883-4735
- **Whitefish,** 121 Second St., (406) 862-4923

THE SUMMIT MEDICAL FITNESS CENTER
205 Sunnyview Lane, Kalispell
(406) 751-4100
www.summithealthcenter.com
The Summit, a full-service health and fitness center, offers a variety of activities for members and nonmembers, including programs specially tailored for older folks. Call the center, or make either a virtual or actual visit, to learn more.

Nursing & Retirement Centers

BRENDAN HOUSE
350 Conway Dr., Kalispell
(406) 751-6500
www.nwhc.org/brendan_house
This is a skilled-nursing facility operated by Northwest Healthcare, which also owns Kalispell Regional Medical Center. A comprehensive team approach is used to deal with the individual needs of each resident, whether they are recovering from surgery or suffering from a terminal illness. "Comfort care rooms" are available to allow terminally ill patients and families a comfortable,

homey setting in which to spend time together. Adult day care is also available.

BUFFALO HILL TERRACE
40 Claremont St., Kalispell
(406) 752-9624

This retirement community, owned by the Immanuel Lutheran Corporation, is designed for seniors who can live independently. The 100-unit complex atop Buffalo Hill consists of studio and 1- and 2-bedroom apartments with kitchen facilities. Assisted-living services are available on one wing. Residents can eat in the dining room or cook their own meals. Basic services include 2 meals a day, weekly housekeeping, scheduled transportation, and a full-time activities and social director.

COLONIAL MANOR NURSING CENTER
1305 East Seventh St., Whitefish
(406) 862-3557

This is a 100-bed skilled-nursing facility that has both private and semiprivate rooms. A variety of programs and services are available, including Hospice/Respite care; physical, occupational, speech, and respiratory therapy; and an Alzheimer's/Aging Support Group.

EDGEWOOD VISTA
141 Interstate Lane, Kalispell
(406) 755-3240
www.edgewoodvista.com

This home specializing in Alzheimer's/dementia care opened in February 2001 and is one of 19 Edgewood Vista facilities in 5 states owned by a corporation based in Minot, North Dakota. The Kalispell home is one of four in Montana. The fully secured home features private and semiprivate rooms; organized, therapeutic, and social activities; 24-hour assistance; 3 meals a day; and transportation to appointments.

FRIENDSHIP HOUSE
606 Second Ave. West, Kalispell
(406) 257-8375

This is a state-licensed assisted-living facility for adults who can no longer live safely at home. It is located in a gracious historic home on Kalispell's west side and has a capacity of 18 residents. Adult day care on an hourly basis also is available; this was the first facility in the state to offer elderly day care, which it started doing in 1978.

GREENWOOD VILLAGE ASSISTED LIVING
1150 East Oregon St., Kalispell
(406) 752-4736

"Our Business Is Caring" is the slogan of this facility, which opened in June 2001. Greenwood Village has 47 studio and 1-bedroom apartments and a communal sunroom. Services include meals, laundry, housekeeping, medication assistance, activities, and bus service.

HERITAGE PLACE
171 Heritage Way, Kalispell
(406) 755-0800
www.heritagekalispell.com

Heritage Place is a skilled-nursing home and rehabilitation center that's part of Lantis Enterprises, a family-owned corporation based in Spearfish, South Dakota, that operates more than 40 assisted-living and nursing homes in 5 states. Heritage Place specializes in the needs of the elderly, both for long-term residency or short-term care after surgery, illness, or an injury. It has 31 semiprivate rooms, 6 private rooms, 5 "premier" rooms, 8 skilled-care rooms, and

28 special-care beds. Services include transportation, beauty and barber shop, a lounge, and dining room. An Alzheimer's unit has employees specially trained to care for the needs of residents with Alzheimer's and other dementia conditions.

i To learn more about the above and other assisted living facilities, nursing homes, and in-home care services, visit www.assistedseniorliving.net and search for "Kalispell," "Whitefish," or another community of your choice.

HEALTH CARE

The Flathead Valley boasts a load of top-notch physicians and surgeons, and its medical facilities are among the best in the state. With a medical staff of over 200 and a total of nearly 2,000 employees, Kalispell Regional Medical Center is the largest private employer in Flathead County. The beauty of the area and opportunities for outdoor recreation have been a major drawing card for medical professionals. Three full-service hospitals, Kalispell Regional Medical Center, North Valley Hospital, and St. Joseph Hospital, meet the regular needs of valley residents. Sports medicine is of course a specialty in an area that attends to the knees and backs of golfers, skiers, and hikers. Occasionally, for extensive or rare medical problems, residents are referred to larger cities such as Seattle, Missoula, or Spokane for further treatment or a second opinion. Naturopathic practitioners, acupuncturists, and chiropractors also enjoy the support of clients seeking nontraditional treatments.

KALISPELL REGIONAL MEDICAL CENTER
310 Sunnyview Lane, Kalispell
(406) 752-5111
www.krmc.org
Kalispell Regional Medical Center is a large acute-care hospital with a fully equipped intensive care unit, inpatient rehabilitation, free-standing birthing center, hemodialysis, home health, physical occupational therapies, the latest CAT scanners, MRI, diagnostic heart catheterization, and a cancer treatment center equipped with a Varian linear accelerator. The HealthCenter is located on Buffalo Hill, adjacent to many medical and professional offices and a pharmacy. Northwest Healthcare, the corporation that owns the hospital, also operates a number of other services, including Home Options/Hospice, the ALERT helicopter, and the Summit fitness center.

i In an emergency, call 911 in Glacier National Park and the surrounding area. The ALERT helicopter is in service, based out of Kalispell Regional Medical Center. ALERT has an outstanding reputation for providing the area with life-saving emergency medical services. Rescue and medical services may not always be immediately available, however. If you have an emergency, stay calm. Your best defense is to have a first-aid kit and be prepared for the unexpected.

NORTH VALLEY HOSPITAL
1600 Hospital Way, Whitefish
(406) 863-3500
www.nvhosp.org
North Valley's new health care facility is situated near the intersection of US 93 and

Highway 40 in Whitefish. The hospital provides care to a service area of approximately 30,000 people, including the communities of Whitefish, Columbia Falls, and Eureka. Services include obstetrics, emergency care, same-day surgery, geriatric services, and a number of wellness programs. It also supports urgent care clinics at Whitefish Mountain Resort and in Eureka, Montana. In 2010, the physicians and staff at the Professional Center in Columbia Falls joined forces with North Valley Hospital, and is now known as the North Valley Professional Center. It's located at 2165 Ninth St. West in Columbia Falls.

ST. JOSEPH HOSPITAL
6 Thirteenth Ave. East, P.O. Box 1010, Polson 59860
(406) 883-5377, (866) 344-2273
www.saintjoes.org
St. Joseph is a full-service hospital licensed for 24 beds that provides a full range of medical services, including home health care and an assisted-living center.

EDUCATION

Glacier Country continues to attract top educators, who come here for adventure and stay for the quality of life. The benefit of these highly skilled and enthusiastic teachers and administrators translates into the quality of education and care given to valley schoolchildren. In the public school system, you will find a good balance of basic skills with access to athletics, art and music, and computer resources. More than half of graduates continue on at 2- and 4-year colleges. Growth in the valley has put strain on the public school system, especially at the high-school level, and in 2007 the high school population was finally split between the remodeled Flathead High School and a new building, Glacier High School. Strong support for home schooling is also found in this region, a correlation to the independent streak possessed by many Montanans. Public schools in Flathead County are divided into many local districts. The smallest public elementary school in the county is Pleasant Valley, which has had as few as 4 students. By contrast the largest school in Kalispell's school district 5 is Edgerton Elementary (kindergarten through 5th grade), with more than 500 students. Enrollment in public schools in Flathead County totals more than 13,000 students. To the south, about 1,800 students are enrolled in Polson's 2 elementary schools, middle school, and high school.

FLATHEAD VALLEY COMMUNITY COLLEGE
777 Grandview Dr., Kalispell
(406) 756-3822
www.fvcc.edu
Established in 1967 and fully accredited by the Northwest Association of Schools and Colleges, FVCC offers more than 50 career and technical programs, including a respected entrepreneurship and business lineup. It also operates an extension campus in Lincoln County to the west. More than 10,000 credit and noncredit students enroll each year at the two campuses and nearby community sites. FVCC offers the Associate of Arts and Sciences and Associate of Applied Sciences Degrees as well as certificates in business management, office technology, medical assistant, criminal justice, computer applications, accounting, hospitality, human services, surveying, and natural resources. Montana State University and FVCC have a dual admission agreement that

admits qualifying students to both institutions at the same time. Through a number of partnerships with other institutions of higher learning, FVCC offers 4-year and advanced-degree opportunities.

GLACIER INSTITUTE
137 Main St., Kalispell
(406) 755-1211
www.glacierinstitute.org

Educational adventures in Glacier Country are offered through the Glacier Institute, an organization that provides high-quality, well-balanced outdoor experiences for children and adults of all ages. Courses emphasize a hands-on, field-oriented approach to learning, and highlight the diverse natural and cultural resources of the Northern Rockies Ecosystem. Many popular courses are offered each year, but still fill quickly. Facilities of the Glacier Institute include the Glacier Park Field Camp, a rustic facility located within the park that is the site of summer field courses for adults and children. Also used is the Big Creek Outdoor Education Center, a full-service residential facility that is situated along the Wild and Scenic North Fork of the Flathead River in the Flathead National Forest, home to youth field science programs, Elderhostels, and special workshops.

Private Schools

A number of private schools, both religious and secular, offer parents alternatives to the public education system. Enrollment in private schools, including home schooling, is on the increase in Flathead County at both elementary and secondary levels. You'll find a variety of choices of schools for your youngsters.

EDUCATION RECOVERY FOUNDATION INC.
655 West Reserve Dr., Kalispell
(406) 756-6645

Education Recovery is a free program for individuals from ages 16 to 20 who have dropped out of school, helping the individual establish educational goals and prepare for the GED.

FLATHEAD HOMESCHOOLERS ASSOCIATION
Kalispell
(406) 755-0168

This organization provides support to families who home school their children. Dave and Linda Creighton are the contact people for this group. A Home Learning Center offers curriculum support, and the association also coordinates support-group meetings for parents, along with sports and music programs.

KALISPELL MONTESSORI CENTER, INC.
349 Willow Glen Dr., Kalispell
(406) 755-3826
www.kalispellmontessori.com

The Kalispell Montessori Center "fosters the natural spirit of inquiry and thrill of discovery within each child by upholding the Montessori philosophy that learning is best achieved within a social atmosphere that supports each individual's unique academic, physical and emotional development." The school serves children ages 7 to 12 from 1st to 6th grade. Parental involvement is key to the Montessori philosophy and one of the program's goals is to create a partnership between home and school.

NORTH VALLEY MUSIC SCHOOL
432 Spokane Ave., Whitefish 59937
(406) 862-8074
www.northvalleymusicschool.org
The only nonprofit community music school in the Big Sky State, North Valley was started in 1998 by musicians and parents wanting to provide string training to students outside of the Kalispell School District. A faculty of 14 serves more than 700 students annually, offering instruction in instruments ranging from viola to electric guitar. Recent classes also included Celtic Music Group, Madrigals Group, and the Whitefish Xylophone Ensemble.

STILLWATER CHRISTIAN SCHOOL
255 FAA Dr., Kalispell
(406) 752-4400
www.stillwaterchristianschool.org
Founded in 1980 as Flathead Valley Christian School, the name of this school was changed in 2004 to establish a more distinct identity (the mascot was changed at the same time, from the Colt to the Cougar). This Christian school has an enrollment of around 300 in grades kindergarten through 12th grade. School facilities include a library, computer lab, cafeteria, and gymnasium. The school has accreditation from the Northwest Association of Accredited Schools and the Association of Christian Schools International. More than 50 churches of various denominations are represented in the school's enrollment. The school has 25 full- or part-time teachers, with a student-teacher ratio of 13 to 1. There is one class per grade. The school maintains a local chapter of the National Honor Society and is a member of the Montana Christian Athletic Association (MCAA). High-school teams compete in the MCAA as well as playing area public schools as schedules permit.

ST. MATTHEW'S CATHOLIC SCHOOL
602 South Main St., Kalispell
(406) 752-6303
www.stmattsaints.org
This Catholic school was established in 1917 and has an enrollment of 150 students from kindergarten through 6th grade. The program includes both academics and religious instruction. Preschool programs and after-school care are also provided.

TRINITY LUTHERAN ELEMENTARY SCHOOL
495 Fifth Ave. WN, Kalispell
(406) 257-6716
The school, founded in 1958 by the Trinity Lutheran Church, combines strong academic studies with religious education and has a good reputation for solid academics. Teachers—9 full-time and about an equal number of part-time—are state-certified and many hold advanced degrees. Music, fine arts, and sports programs are available. The school strives for excellence in education in a caring Christian environment. A chapel service is held weekly. Various classes, school staff, guest pastors, and Trinity's ministerial staff lead these services on a rotating basis. A hot lunch is available at noon for students and staff. Eligible students may receive a reduced rate. Enrollment is 245 students in preschool through 8th grade.

VALLEY ADVENTIST CHRISTIAN SCHOOL
1275 Helena Flats Rd., Kalispell
(406) 752-0830
This school for children in grades 1 through 8 is affiliated with the Seventh-day Adventist Church. The school provides a Seventh-day Adventist education for the youth of the church and any others who want a Christian

education and agree to abide by the school's standards. The educational program is based on the Bible. The curriculum includes weekly art classes, music classes, and physical education in addition to academic studies. Enrollment in grades kindergarten through 9th is about 25 students.

WHITEFISH CHRISTIAN ACADEMY
820 Ashar Ave., Whitefish
(406) 862-5875
www.whitefishacademy.org
Formerly known as Cross Currents Christian School, the vision here is to "assist parents in the spiritual, intellectual, social, and physical development of their children for the purpose of sending out Christian thinkers and doers of the Word to engage and transform our culture for Christ." The school promotes spiritual growth, academic excellence, sound family relationships, responsible citizenship, and moral and ethical values guided by biblical teaching. The evangelical, interdenominational school was established in 1978 and moved into its own building in 1989. Enrollment includes students in grades pre-K through 8th. The full-time faculty are all certified teachers. Areas of special emphasis include computer technology, art and drama, and creative writing in both poetry and fiction.

CHILD CARE

Finding high-quality child care is a top priority for working parents, and a variety of options are available, ranging from large day-care centers to stay-at-home moms who want to care for an extra child or two. Weekend and evening care, along with care for infants, are the hardest to find, but good choices do exist. Ask your friends and neighbors for recommendations, or take advantage of special help that's available for parents.

DISCOVERY DEVELOPMENTAL CENTER
75 Glenwood Dr., Kalispell
(406) 756-7295
www.ddckids.org
A nonprofit organization offering integrated child care since 1992 for children 18 months to 8 years, programs include Playgroup, preschool, pre-K (morning and afternoon), and kindergarten enrichment. Transportation is available. Specialists in speech and language therapy, physical therapy, and occupational therapy are available on-site for children with special needs. The center is licensed for 45 children. All staff members have degrees in elementary education or early-childhood development.

KALISPELL PARKS AND RECREATION DEPARTMENT
301 First Ave. East, Kalispell
(406) 758-7975
www.kalispell.com/parks
After-school sports camps are available throughout the school year through the parks department at a reasonable cost. These camps are for 1st through 6th grades and feature indoor activities such as indoor soccer, basketball, and floor hockey and new games and outdoor excursions for ice-skating, sledding, cross-country skiing, baseball, bike riding, and exploring city parks. A spring-break program offers another child-care option for parents of 6- to 11-year-olds, featuring indoor/outdoor activities, games, skits, arts and crafts, and field trips if the weather permits. "I'm bored" ranks high for most parents as a least-favorite phrase, and, let's face it, after the novelty of no school wears off, summers can be, well, boring. The

parks department also conducts a series of summer day camps at Woodland Park for children ages 3 to 12. The weeklong camp sessions run from mid-June to late Aug.

MOMS PROGRAM
Trinity Evangelical Lutheran Church
400 West California St., Kalispell
(406) 257-5683

Moms of young kids are welcome at this support group, which meets from 9:15 to 11:15 a.m. the first and third Wed of each month from Sept through May. Guest speakers, including doctors, lawyers, teachers, and nurses, are featured at each meeting, along with a craft project once a month. The program is free and child care is provided. MOMS stands for "Moms Offering Moms Support."

MONTESSORI CHILDREN'S HOUSE
1301 East Seventh St., Whitefish
(406) 863-4685

The Montessori Children's House and preschool provide before- and after-school care for children in grades 1 through 4 and Montessori education and child care for ages 2 through kindergarten age. Hours are from 7:15 a.m. to 6 p.m. Total enrollment is about 60 and maximum class size is 16 children per 2 adults. A summer camp program is offered for ages 2 through 9.

NURTURING CENTER
146 Third Ave. West, Kalispell
(406) 756-1414
www.nurturingcenter.org

Founded in 1978, this agency serves as a referral center for child care, matching parents with appropriate providers. A total of some 5 dozen child-care providers in Kalispell are registered with the Nurturing

Center, while several each are also listed in Bigfork, Columbia Falls, and Whitefish. The Nurturing Center also offers other support to families, including parenting classes, a reference lending library, and support groups.

SMITH MEMORIAL DAY CARE CENTER
329 Second Ave. East, Kalispell
(406) 755-9224

The Smith Memorial Day Care Center was the first child-care center in Kalispell, established in 1966 through a bequest from a member of the First United Methodist Church. The center, which is licensed for ages 2 through 12, has room for about 50 children and is generally at capacity. The center is located on the top floor of the Methodist Church. Activities include music, exercise, stories, outside play time, nap time, and snacks. Hours are 7:30 a.m. to 5:30 p.m. Mon through Fri.

THE SUMMIT
205 Sunnyview Lane, Kalispell
(406) 751-4100
www.summithealthcenter.com

A whole host of programs for kids are offered at The Summit. For details, visit the website and click on Programs, and then either on Child Care or Children/Youth. .

WHITEFISH MOUNTAIN RESORT KIDS CENTER
Whitefish Mountain Resort
(406) 862-2900
www.whitefishmountainresort.com

At its Kids Center, Whitefish Mountain Resort offers child care and ski lessons for youngsters throughout the ski season. Located in the new base lodge, the center includes day-care facilities, an indoor instruction area, storage units, and one-stop shopping for rentals, lift tickets, lessons, and more. The facility is open from 9 a.m. to 5 p.m. Hourly and full-day care is available. Call or check the website (under Families) for details and rates.

WHITEFISH MOUNTAIN RESORT SNOWSPORTS SCHOOL
Whitefish Mountain Resort
(406) 862-2900
www.whitefishmountainresort.com
The resort offers specially tailored ski and snowboard lessons for kids age 3 to 12. The emphasis for the younger kids is on having fun, and instructors are very child-friendly in their teaching methods. Both group and individual lessons are available at all levels. Reservations are recommended, but not required—just show up at 9 a.m. or noon at the ski-school meeting area. Check the website or call for information on half- and full-day programs. The ski school also offers a supervised lunch for kids.

MEDIA

Ever since circuit riders carried messages by horseback, stagecoaches clattered over our rough roads, and telegraph wires were first strung overhead cutting black lines across the big sky, residents of Glacier Country have been hungry for news and have devised clever ways of getting it. Residents here are wired into the Internet and cable and satellite television, and they're still avid readers of community newspapers (though, like everywhere, online readers are growing in relation to hard-copy readers). The following listings will give you an idea of the region's myriad communications opportunities and outlets.

NEWSPAPERS

Major Dailies from around the State

BILLINGS GAZETTE
Billings
(406) 657-1200, (800) 927-2345
www.billingsgazette.com
Available at newsstands throughout the state, this is Montana's largest daily newspaper. It is owned by Lee Enterprises, which owns papers in Helena, Missoula, and Butte, as well.

DAILY INTER LAKE
Kalispell
(406) 755-7000
www.dailyinterlake.com
This is the place to turn for daily information on the Flathead Valley. The paper has been in existence since 1889 and is a respected community business leader.

GREAT FALLS TRIBUNE
Great Falls
(406) 791-1444
www.greatfallstribune.com

Established in 1885 and still going strong, the *Great Falls Tribune* is owned by the Gannett newspaper chain and is available on newsstands throughout the state.

THE MISSOULIAN
Missoula
(406) 523-5200
www.missoulian.com
Part of the Lee newspaper chain, this daily has been in business since 1870 and is a fine source of information not only for Missoula, but for all of western Montana. It is available throughout the state.

The Local News

Each of these weeklies or semiweeklies is an essential part of the community it covers. Here you'll find quality reporting on local news events, coverage of the area's festivals and fairs, and information on local schools and clubs. You're not "in the know" unless you take the time to peruse these local papers. Don't think that just because they're small they're sub-par. Some of the finest writing and reporting in the state goes on at the local level—in part because in small towns, where "everybody knows everybody," reporters take special care to get their facts straight! (Though each started independently, today all of the following except for the *Seeley Swan Pathfinder* and the *Glacier Reporter* are owned by the Coeur d'Alene, Idaho-based Hagadone Corporation.)

BIGFORK EAGLE
Bigfork
(406) 837-5131
www.bigforkeagle.com

GLACIER REPORTER BROWNING
(406) 338-2090
http://cutbankpioneerpress.com

HUNGRY HORSE NEWS
Columbia Falls
(406) 892-2151
www.hungryhorsenews.com

LAKE COUNTY LEADER
Polson
(406) 883-4343
www.leaderadvertiser.com

SEELEY SWAN PATHFINDER
Swan Valley
(406) 677-2022
www.seeleyswanpathfinder.com

WHITEFISH PILOT
Whitefish
(406) 862-3505
www.whitefishpilot.com

RADIO STATIONS
Kalispell

KALS-FM, 97.1
Christian
(406) 752-5257

KBBZ-FM, 98.5
Classic Rock
(406) 755-8700

KOFI-AM, 1180
News Talk/Sports/Oldies
(406) 755-6690

KOFI-FM, 103.9
Country
(406) 755-6690

KUKL-FM, 89.9
Public Radio (University of Montana)
(406) 243-4931

KJJR-AM, 880
Fox News Radio
(406) 756-5557

Polson

KERR-AM, 750
Country
(406) 883-5255

Great Falls

KAAK-FM, 98.9
Top 40
(406) 727-7211

KEIN-AM, 1310
Adult Standards/MOR
(406) 761-1310

KGFC-FM, 88.9
Christian
(406) 265-5845

KLFM-FM, 92.9
Oldies
(406) 761-7600

KMON-AM, 560
Country
(406) 761-7600

KMON-FM, 94.5
Country
(406) 761-7600

KQDI-AM, 1450
News/Talk
(406) 761-2800

KQDI-FM, 106.1
Classic Rock
(406) 761-2800

KXGF-AM, 1400
ESPN Sports Radio
(406) 761-2800

Missoula

KGGL-FM, 93.3
Country
(406) 549-9393

KGRZ-AM, 1450
Sports
(406) 728-1450

KLCY-AM, 930
Classics/Entertainment/Information
(406) 728-9300

KMSO-FM, 102.5
Adult Contemporary
(406) 542-1025

KUFM-FM, 89.1
Public Radio (University of Montana)
(406) 243-4931

KXDR-FM, 92.7
'80s, '90s, Today
(406) 728-4100

KYLT-AM, 1340
Talk
(406) 728-5000

KYSS-FM, 94.9
Country
(406) 728-9300

KZOQ-FM, 100.1
Classic Rock
(406) 728-5000

TELEVISION STATIONS

Public television and all three major networks are available through local affiliates in Montana. Cable television supplements the local offerings through Bresnan Communications. The stations you'll get with or without cable depend on where you are in the state. Below are the closest local stations to the Flathead Valley.

ABC

KFBB-TV, CHANNEL 5
Great Falls

KTMF-TV, CHANNEL 23
Missoula

CBS

KAJ-TV, CHANNEL 18
Kalispell

KRTV-TV, CHANNEL 3
Great Falls

KPAX-TV, CHANNEL 8
Missoula

NBC

KCFW-TV, CHANNEL 9
Kalispell

KECI-TV, CHANNEL 13
Missoula

MEDIA

KBGF-TV, CHANNEL 50
Great Falls

FOX

KTMF-TV, CHANNEL 42
Kalispell

KFBB-TV, CHANNEL 5
Great Falls

BOOKS

The following books will help you appreciate and explore Glacier Country to the fullest.

BACKPACKING TIPS, TRAIL-TESTED WISDOM FROM FALCONGUIDE AUTHORS, 2ND EDITION,
by Bill and Russ Schneider

BEAR AWARE, 3RD EDITION,
by Bill Schneider

BEST EASY DAY HIKES GLACIER AND WATERTON, 2ND EDITION,
by Erik Molvar

THE BIG SKY,
A novel by A.B. Gurthrie

CENTRAL ROCKY MOUNTAIN WILDFLOWERS,
by Wayne Phillips

A CLIMBER'S GUIDE TO GLACIER NATIONAL PARK,
by J. Gordon Edwards

FISHING GLACIER NATIONAL PARK, 2ND EDITION,
by Russ Schneider

FISHING MONTANA,
by Mike Sample

GLACIER COUNTRY,
by R.C. Gildart

GLACIER'S GRANDEST, A PICTORIAL HISTORY OF THE HOTELS AND CHALETS OF GLACIER NATIONAL PARK,
by Bridget Moylan

GLACIER WILD & BEAUTIFUL,
by Chuck Haney and John Reddy

GOING-TO-THE-SUN: THE STORY OF THE HIGHWAY ACROSS GLACIER NATIONAL PARK,
by Rose Houk

HEART OF THE TRAIL: THE STORIES OF EIGHT WAGON TRAIN WOMEN,
by Mary Barmeyer O'Brien

HIKING GLACIER AND WATERTON LAKES NATIONAL PARKS, 3RD EDITION,
by Erik Molvar

HIKING MONTANA, 3RD EDITION,
by Bill and Russ Schneider

HIKING MONTANA'S BOB MARSHALL,
by Erik Molvar

IT HAPPENED IN MONTANA, 2ND EDITION,
by James A. Crutchfield

LION SENSE, 2ND EDITION,
by Steven Torres

LOGAN PASS: ALPINE SPLENDOR IN GLACIER NATIONAL PARK,
by Jerry DeSanto

LOOKING BACK: A PICTORIAL HISTORY OF THE FLATHEAD VALLEY, MONTANA,
by Kathryn McKay

MAN IN GLACIER,
by C. W. Buchholtz

MARK OF THE GRIZZLY,
by Scott McMillion

MONTANA BIRD DISTRIBUTION, 7TH EDITION,
by P. D. Skaar, published by the Montana Natural Heritage Program

MONTANA CAMPFIRE TALES,
by Dave Walter

MONTANA OFF THE BEATEN PATH, 8TH EDITION,
by Michael McCoy

MORE THAN PETTICOATS: REMARKABLE MONTANA WOMEN,
by Gayle Shirley

NIGHT OF THE GRIZZLIES,
by Jack Olsen

PADDLING MONTANA, 2ND EDITION,
by Hank and Carol Fischer

PLACE NAMES OF GLACIER NATIONAL PARK,
by Jack Holterman

ROCK CLIMBING MONTANA,
Randall Green, editor

SCENIC DRIVING MONTANA, 2ND EDITION,
by S. A. Snyder

STUMP TOWN TO SKI TOWN: THE STORY OF WHITEFISH, MONTANA,
by Betty Schafer and Mable Engelter

TRAIL RIDING WESTERN MONTANA,
by Carellen Barnett

WHEN YOU & I WERE YOUNG, WHITEFISH,
by Dorothy Marie Johnson

LIVING HERE

INDEX

INSIDERS' GUIDE®

The acclaimed travel series that has sold more than 2 million copies!

Discover: Your Travel Destination.
Your Home. Your Home-to-Be.

Albuquerque

Anchorage &
 Southcentral
 Alaska

Atlanta

Austin

Baltimore

Baton Rouge

Boulder & Rocky Mountain
 National Park

Branson & the Ozark
 Mountains

California's Wine Country

Cape Cod & the Islands

Charleston

Charlotte

Chicago

Cincinnati

Civil War Sites in
 the Eastern Theater

Civil War Sites in the South

Colorado's Mountains

Dallas & Fort Worth

Denver

El Paso

Florida Keys & Key West

Gettysburg

Glacier National Park

Great Smoky Mountains

Greater Fort Lauderdale

Greater Tampa Bay Area

Hampton Roads

Houston

Hudson River Valley

Indianapolis

Jacksonville

Kansas City

Long Island

Louisville

Madison

Maine Coast

Memphis

Myrtle Beach &
 the Grand Strand

Nashville

New Orleans

New York City

North Carolina's
 Mountains

North Carolina's
 Outer Banks

North Carolina's
 Piedmont Triad

Oklahoma City

Orange County, CA

Oregon Coast

Palm Beach County

Palm Springs

Philadelphia &
 Pennsylvania Dutch
 Country

Phoenix

Portland, Maine

Portland, Oregon

Raleigh, Durham &
 Chapel Hill

Richmond, VA

Reno and Lake Tahoe

St. Louis

San Antonio

Santa Fe

Savannah & Hilton Head

Seattle

Shreveport

South Dakota's
 Black Hills Badlands

Southwest Florida

Tucson

Tulsa

Twin Cities

Washington, D.C.

Williamsburg & Virginia's
 Historic Triangle

Yellowstone
 & Grand Teton

Yosemite

**To order call 800-243-0495
or visit www.Insiders.com**